100 Greatest
Video Game Characters

100 Greatest . . .

A Rowman & Littlefield Book Series
Series Editor: Bob Batchelor
R&L Editor: Stephen Ryan

100 Greatest Video Game Characters, edited by Jaime Banks, Robert Mejia, and Aubrie Adams
100 Greatest Video Game Franchises, edited by Robert Mejia, Jaime Banks, and Aubrie Adams

100 Greatest
Video Game Characters

Edited by

Jaime Banks
Robert Mejia
Aubrie Adams

ROWMAN & LITTLEFIELD
Lanham • Boulder • New York • London

Published by Rowman & Littlefield
A wholly owned subsidary of The Rowman & Littlefield Publishing Group, Inc.
4501 Forbes Boulevard, Suite 200, Lanham, Maryland 20706
www.rowman.com

Unit A, Whitacre Mews, 26-34 Stannary Street, London SE11 4AB

British Library Cataloguing in Publication Information Available

Library of Congress Cataloging-in-Publication Data

Names: Banks, Jaime, 1980– editor. | Mejia, Robert, 1982– editor. | Adams,
    Aubrie, 1983– editor.
Title: 100 greatest video game characters / edited by Jaime Banks, Robert
    Mejia, Aubrie Adams.
Other titles: One hundred greatest video game characters
Description: Lanham, Maryland : Rowman & Littlefield, 2017. | Series: 100
    Greatest... | Includes bibliographical references and index.
Identifiers: LCCN 2017007886 (print) | LCCN 2016050972 (ebook) | ISBN
    9781442278127 (hardback : alk. paper) | ISBN 9781442278134 (electronic)
Classification: LCC GV1469.34.C48 A25 2017 (ebook) | LCC GV1469.34.C48
    (print) | DDC 794.8—dc23
LC record available at https://lccn.loc.gov/2017007886

♾™ The paper used in this publication meets the minimum requirements of
American National Standard for Information Sciences—Permanence of Paper
for Printed Library Materials, ANSI/NISO Z39.48-1992.

Printed in the United States of America

Contents

Acknowledgments

This book is the result of the collective effort of numerous individuals. Family, friends, colleagues, and contributors were incredibly generous with their time and support, and we thank them for their belief in us, each other, and this project. This book is better because of them, and we are fortunate to have these individuals and communities as a part of our lives.

Though space prevents us from acknowledging every individual—as much as we wish otherwise—we would like to specifically thank the following individuals: Nick Bowman, Jennifer Mejia, Basil Mejia, and John Nelson for their ongoing love and support; Laura Otterness for being an excellent research assistant and helping with text and citation formatting; and Bob Batchelor, Andrea O. Kendrick, Jessica McCleary, and Stephen Ryan of Rowman & Littlefield for providing fantastic editorial support.

And last but not least, we would like to thank our contributors. We had the pleasure of collaborating with an amazing group of individuals from across the globe. We are humbled by the care and attention you gave these short pieces, and by your humoring us with your feedback. You made editing this collection a pleasure. Thank you.

Introduction

For the 1940 World's Fair, Edward Condon of Westinghouse designed an electromechanical device called the Nimatron that played the strategy game *Nim* against human players. The objective was to pick up the last matchstick. Notably, there were no characters in this game, per se—the human and machine manipulated the sticks. Fast-forward to 1950 and we see computer scientists Claude Shannon and Alan Turing create programs to play chess on hefty computers—in a sense, we might consider this a game of *Nim* with a bit of narrative wrapped around the pieces because they are framed as weak peasant pawns, knights, bishops, towers, and royalty. If we follow the Strong National Museum of Play's game-history timeline, in the years that follow, we see video game characters take the form of a cheese-seeking mouse in MIT's *Mouse in the Maze* (1959), a primitive airship in MIT's *SpaceWar!* (1962), and even organic cells in hackers' implementations of the mathematical game *LIFE* (1970). Since the advent of these nascent entities, we've seen video game characters evolve in tandem with gaming technologies, with gaming cultures, and with world cultures more broadly. This book is intended to trace some of these evolutions and to connect video game characters—from Aerith to Zelda—with their cultural influences and influencers.

But what is a video game character and how do they differ from other types present in more traditional forms of media like literature and film? Key to understanding the distinction between video game characters and literary or cinematic characters is the concept of the *avatar*—a representation of a being or object. This representation—or rather opportunity for (digital) extension of the player into the video game world—means that video game characters ought to be understood as fundamentally different from their literary and cinematic counterparts. If conventional characters can be understood as "equipment for living," a kind of "medicine" for thinking through the concerns of life,[1] video game characters possess the capacity for taking this heuristic one step further: from equipment for living to "virtually" living. This concept of virtually living ought not to be understood as a cheap counterfeit of "real" living, but rather in terms of immanence or potentiality; in this regard, the virtual "can be said to exist whenever there is a perceived gap between experience and 'the actual.'"[2] Games scholar Bob Rehak draws from film critic Christian Metz to take this notion a step further, noting that film is a "primordial mirror" that projects viewers onto characters in many ways, except that they cannot project their own body; video games, however, meld together that limited spectatorship with embodied participation in ways that amplify the "ideological mystification and positioning inherent" in the Lacanian "mirror stage"—as a direct extension of the player into (and notably not onto) the character, the avatar offers a more powerful vehicle for experiencing the imaginary.[3] Seen from this perspective, then, video game characters differ from other kinds of characters in that they offer not just a world worth exploring and a life worth living but also the opportunity to explore that world and live that life; these are not vicarious experiences but *our own experience.*

And yet, video game characters rarely—if ever—appear as absolutely blank slates. Their worlds are often already in motion, and their characters are often already partly developed and imbued with particular traits, features, and functions. To this end, video game characters exist on a spectrum. On one end of the spectrum, video game characters radiate personality and a sense of humanness through their embodied actions and speech, such as the ways that Mr. Torgue (*Borderlands*) conforms to and challenges gender stereotypes in flamboyant ways; on the other end of the spectrum, characters exist as simple, playable objects that aren't particularly human, but that we still ascribe humanlike traits and responsibilities to, such as the I-Block (*Tetris*): it is only a configuration of blocks that can be rotated, yet we attribute blame and responsibility to these objects when they do not appear when we need them to fit into the game environment.

Among these variably humanlike entities, video game characters also have different functions. There are two primary ways to divide the types of characters we encounter in video games. There are "player characters" (PCs; sometimes called "avatars" or "toons"), which refer to any type of character that a player is able to control; and there are "non-player characters" (NPCs; sometimes called "agents") that are controlled by the game's programming or artificial intelligence. In some games, such as in the case of "massively multiplayer online games" (MMOs), a number of player characters all exist together in the same game with each individual human player working to meet their own particular goals through behaviors they enact with their own unique avatar.

This collection of essays includes *all* of these different character types—from nonhuman characters like the ball from *Pong* to deeply human characters like Cloud Strife from *Final Fantasy VII,* and from customizable and player-controlled characters like the text-based Wizards of *MUD1* to highly predefined and agentic characters like the invading aliens of *Space Invaders* (1978). You'll also find that these culturally significant characters span video game history, gaming platforms, and game genres. Though most video game characters are largely fictional, several are based on historical figures and pop culture icons such as Gandhi, Hitler, Kim Kardashian, President Bill Clinton, and Vincent Edward "Bo" Jackson. Similarly, some characters that begin as player characters actually achieve non-player character status, such as in the case of Leeroy Jenkins (*World of Warcraft*); and other player characters begin as a representation of one person but evolve to become a representation of all people, such as in the case of Steve (*Minecraft*). In essence, the ways in which characters can be labeled, organized, and typified in video games is often complex.

SOME NOTES ON "GREATEST" AND CULTURAL SIGNIFICANCE

Gamers have their favorite characters for a range of reasons—perhaps it's Sub-Zero (*Mortal Kombat*) because he represents mastery over a childhood game, or GLaDOS (*Portal*) because she challenges our patience in gratifying ways, or Pikachu (*Pokémon*) because we feel he is our own little friend. Because of this, it is an enormous challenge to narrow down the universe of amazing game characters to just 100. To do this, we called on an international community of video game researchers and developers to argue for which characters are the greatest—and for our purposes, we define "greatest" in terms of cultural importance: how each character illuminates something important about how people live or play games.

For instance, in terms of how people play games, you'll see that Psycho Mantis (*Metal Gear Solid*) creates tension with players by reading their console hard drive and using that information in combat; Wizards (*MUD/MOOs*) rise to govern players' in-game behaviors; and Gandhi (*Sid Meier's Civilization*) exemplifies how people play with game glitches. And in reference to the broader culture of every-day life, for example, you'll read how Amaterasu (*Ōkami*) represents the norms and practices of Shinto; Kim Kardashian (*Kim Kardashian: Hollywood*) draws on pop culture celebrity fascinations; and Birdo (*Super Mario Bros. 2*) exemplifies how gender can be transformed through shifts in body representations.

In considering instances of the "greatest" among video games, we also invite you to check out this book's companion volume—*The 100 Greatest Video Game Franchises*—in which you can explore in tandem the ways that video games more holistically illuminate their contemporary cultures.

HOW TO USE THIS BOOK

The 100 characters included in this book touch upon a range of cultural themes illustrative of the ongoing evolution of how people live or play games. Though each character entry is capable of standing on its own, the reader will notice that certain themes can be traced across multiple entries. For instance, a reader interested in the ongoing evolution of women in video games may be interested in the chapters on Alice (*American McGee's Alice*), Bayonetta (*Bayonetta*), Catherine (*Catherine*), Elaine Marley (*The Secret of Monkey Island*), and the Scythian (*Sword & Sworcery*), among many other entries (for others, see the appendix to this book under the heading "Gender: Female"). Likewise, the reader interested in how games represent artificial intelligence and robots may be interested in the chapters on AM (*I Have No Mouth, and I Must Scream*), GLaDOS (*Portal*), KOS-MOS (*Xenosaga*), SHODAN (*System Shock*), and others (see the appendix under the heading "Species: Robots"). Hence, though the chapters are organized alphabetically, we have provided with our appendix an alternative table of contents identifying what we see as some of the more salient themes. The themes we have identified are not the only themes present in the book, and you the reader may make other equally important connections that we the editors have missed.

Because of this approach, this book does not rank the characters by any particular trait (challenge, popularity, sales, etc.) but instead is a curated collection of arguments for why each of these characters matters to gaming and popular culture. We acknowledge that there may be worthy characters whose names are missing from this book. However, we believe this collection captures the spirit of the many different ways that video game characters can matter in gameplay and in contemporary culture. To help highlight these connections, each character entry is followed by a listing of similar characters: other video game characters that exemplify the same themes or functions and can be thought of in similar ways. For example, though a lesser-known character like Alex (*Lunar Silver Star Story*) is not represented in this book, he performs a similar cultural function as Link (*The Legend of Zelda*), who is certainly represented: they both fulfill the purpose of a silent hero. In other words, we encourage you to engage this book not as a definitive guide to top characters, but instead with a spirit of discovery—and perhaps rediscovery—of how video game characters may play important roles in everyday life.

A

AERITH GAINSBOROUGH

(est. 1997)
Franchise: *Final Fantasy VII*
Developer: Square

Her angular and gentle face is the first and final thing we see in our quest to save the planet. As the last member of a race of humans attuned to the living spirit of the planet (the Cetra), Aerith can hear the voices of the Lifestream: the force that binds all living things together. A generation of gamers saw the weak damsel trope turned sideways as the physically weak Aerith drew great strength from a traditional support role—fixing holes in comrades rather than creating holes in enemies. So strong is her connection with the ethereal that her ability to nurture extends to her surroundings. Her home is nestled in a lush area with tiers of gardens, while everything else is a dark, metallic scrapyard; the church she tends in the Sector 6 slum is the only place where flowers grow for her to sell and share after the greedy Shinra Corporation siphoned the soil's viability. Aerith cultivates beauty and life in a dying world.

This attribute is reflected by and embedded in her ability to wield magical materia more effectively than any other character. Aerith's abilities emphasize restoration over destruction: healing, removing negative status effects, and granting temporary invincibility. In contrast, her physical attacks are some of the weakest in the game. This is indicative of her weapon: a staff. Literally a supportive tool for a long journey, the weapon is symbolic of how Aerith serves as a support system for the characters and the story of *Final Fantasy VII* (*FFVII*).

In her efforts to stop the villain, Sephiroth, from summoning a planet-shattering meteor spell, Aerith takes the white materia inherited from her mother and makes a plea to the planet. She tries to summon Holy, an inexplicably sentient spell, to determine the future of the planet and hopefully stop the impending destruction. Aerith learns the only way she can complete this is to bring her energy back to the Lifestream of the planet—in so doing, she must die.

After the unfaltering and determined Aerith sneaks away from her companions, the worried and mentally compromised protagonist, Cloud, finds her first at an altar in the Forgotten City of the Cetra and begins to lose control of his actions due to Sephiroth's hidden presence. We, as players, watch in horror as we see

Cloud draw his sword and stand poised, shaking in resistance, ready to cut down Aerith. As the rest of the party yells and snaps Cloud out of his "trance," Aerith remains kneeling, and praying to the planet for help. Prayer complete, she locks eyes with Cloud, smiles, then slumps forward: she has been stabbed in the back, killed by Sephiroth. As Aerith falls forward, dying, her musical theme—a simple, lilting, and innocent minor-key composition—begins to play; this song that had once filled the player with peace now triggers grief.

The mechanics of permadeath (permanently losing access or control of a character after in-game death) was not a new practice in *FFVII*'s era, though it was not an economical one. It made little financial sense to develop character design and function only to stop using it halfway through the game. Because of its rarity, Aerith's abrupt end did give players of mainstream games a taste—in many cases, the first taste—of that permanent loss.[1] Players worked with her character for hours and became connected to her. She was a kind and good person. She was a primary part of the narrative. Until this point, no player expected a multimillion-dollar game to axe a character, not only from the story but from gameplay as well. Upon experiencing her death, some players engaged in open rebellion against the development team's choice by taking to online forums and arguing for some way to bring her back; that player reaction was exactly what the *FFVII* team wanted.

Hironobu Sakaguchi, producer of *FFVII*, believed that players deserved this kind of connection and empathetic exercise. He had just endured the loss of his mother during production and was fixated on life and what it could mean if it were analyzed from a more interconnected, relationship-driven stance.[2] He described his mother as a selfless, giving person and as someone he admired for her pure spirit. The team discussed what the fate of the characters should be and decided to mirror Sakaguchi's experience by letting Aerith—their embodiment of purity—be the one to fall.

In a way, Sakaguchi gave a purpose to his mother's death as he gave Aerith a reason she needed to return to the Lifestream. Without her, Holy wouldn't have combined with the Lifestream itself to spare the planet. This also opens the debate of whether or not Aerith can be considered the crux of *FFVII*. It may be Cloud's story, but Aerith and her actions helped determine the fate of the planet.

We can take some points from Aerith's death. It was her idea to summon Holy and use her life to do so. She orchestrated her death at the altar and went against the wishes of the party to do so. She tricked Sephiroth into completing her plan. Her life and abilities were of value to all, even her enemies, but it was ultimately her choice in how to utilize her life. In contrast to other popular stories, this "princess" wasn't kidnapped, and she wasn't waiting in another castle. There is no resurrection in the canon narrative for Aerith. But her reappearance in subsequent games, fan fiction, fan art, and other stories proves that Aerith is a constant for players who came to know, love, and miss her. The flower girl who sought life and nurtured its growth found a new way to live in the lives and narratives of those who found her story.

Similar Characters: Alyx Vance (*Half-Life 2*), Angel (*Borderlands 2*), Zelda (*The Legend of Zelda*)

—Robin L. Haislett

ALICE

(est. 2000)
Franchise: *American McGee's Alice*
Developer: Rogue Entertainment

The world of action games is replete with well-muscled males blasting their way through scores of bad guys whether for good (kill the Nazis!) or bad (kill the cops!) reasons. Sprinkled throughout action games are, unfortunately, only a few women protagonists—the Lara Crofts of the gaming universe, holding their own in what seems to have become a stereotypically male cosmos. Perhaps one of the strangest yet most exciting examples of a female protagonist in an action game is Alice Liddell of the *American McGee* franchise, the latest game from which is *Alice: Madness Returns (AMR)*. *AMR* takes the well-known heroine from Lewis Carroll's *Through the Looking Glass*, adding bloody mayhem and dark, foreboding tones to the familiar surreal tale—an uncanny exemplar of violent femininity.

Despite the darkness and the M-rating (for mature audiences), Alice never seems like all that vicious a character, particularly since so many of her opponents are fantasy characters. Slicing up playing cards, goblins, or animated tea kettles never reaches the level of controversy of *Grand Theft Auto*. And much of the violence she engages in is presented with an air of whimsy, whether grinding peppers at bad guys or swatting them with a hobby horse. Granted, Alice's world has a dark, even nightmarish tone, and that combination of whimsy and nightmarishness feels like something from a Tim Burton movie.

AMR is particularly noteworthy for how it combines femininity, dark-gothic overtones, and the action genre. In many ways, it feels like a feminine game; not a game designed for women or girls necessarily, but one that acknowledges Alice's femininity while still retaining her identity as a badass. Alice as a character is strong, witty, intelligent, and a lot of fun to play, but she fights in a dress, creates an aura of butterflies when she flies, and her best friend is a cat. Femininity as a construct can be difficult to define because it varies from culture to culture. Further, modern conceptualizations of femininity rely not just upon differences between women and men as dictated by society but also on differences in individual choices made by women and men.[3] The concept of femininity can, of course, play into gender stereotypes, but Alice remains particularly interesting given the juxtaposition between her demonstration of both feminine and non-feminine qualities. It's a positive that *AMR* doesn't try to be *Call of Duty* with long hair, and it takes material from a unique story in atmospheric directions, with a particularly introspective look into guilt, families, and insanity. *AMR* raises the thought of whether some aspects of traditional femininity fit with female power; this may be one way of challenging sexism in society.

The essence of this hypothesis is rooted in classical conditioning. Most discussions of female sexuality in the media focus on an implicit dichotomy between the absence of sexualization versus the sexualization of women being inherently bad. But it's also worth observing that sexualization often occurs in the context of female submissiveness in the media; thus, it's not always clear whether the presence of sexy female characters or passive female characters is the root of potential negative effects. Previous work on this "Buffy effect" has suggested that the presence of strong female characters negates the impact of sexualized imagery on men's attitudes toward women.[4]

This is an intriguing thought, but despite some early evidence,[5] it's still speculative. It may be the case that the sexualization of female characters may not always be inherently disempowering, or bad. This is not to be taken as supportive of sexualization; rather, if we are to come to a sophisticated understanding of female power, sex, and violence in entertainment, it is important to rise above the moral stances too often emblematic of media psychology.

The tricky thing for media entertainment that seeks to combine female power with sexuality is balancing the feminine with action-oriented roles that may traditionally be masculine. What is most interesting about Alice is that she isn't merely a cookie-cutter of customary male protagonists but manages to be true to the source material, to add a dark edge, and to forge a new path forward for female protagonists.

Industry data suggests that women are making up an increasing number of the gamer population.[6] Granted, at present women may not always gravitate as often as men toward the action genre. With more characters such as Alice, we may see not only more women in action games, but more women and girls drawn to this genre. Just as with positive developments in other areas, greater diversity and representativeness in games among both characters and players will undoubtedly draw men and women players together, and generate new revenue for the game industry. That women can be powerful *and* sexy may be more than just madness.

Similar Characters: Chell (*Portal*), Jade (*Beyond Good & Evil*), Lara Croft (*Tomb Raider*)

—Christopher J. Ferguson

THE ALIEN

(est. 1982)
Franchise: *Alien*
Developer: Fox Video Games

In 1979, the Alien burst onto cinema screens, traumatizing moviegoers. Audiences recognized the Alien as unique, unstoppable, and terrifying: an ideal "other" that redefined the genres of science fiction and horror.[7] Moreover, the Alien went on to become one of the most mythic and influential antagonists in popular culture and gaming history. The Alien was designed as a creature of nightmarish Freudian qualities that combined both our unconscious desires and unease regarding the role of technology in the shifting social boundaries of the 1970s.

The Xenomorph's first appearance in video games was in 1982 in a playable, but droll, *Pacman* clone on the Atari 2600 home console. Two years later the Alien made its debut on early home computers in *Alien* (1984), a game that, despite the limitations of the hardware, captured the original horror, feverish tension, and dwindling sanity experienced by the crew of the spacecraft *Nostromo* from the 1979 film. However, the success of the movie-sequel *Aliens* (1986) saw a reimagining of the classic Alien that in turn had a huge impact on game design seen within the explosion of popular first-person shooters in the 1990s. Even though massively influential, this reimagined Xenomorph was a lesser creature—gone was the ideal of the unstoppable, "nightmarish otherness" of H. R. Giger's beguiling artwork. The Xenomorphs of *Aliens* created the archetypal Alien warrior, a creature to be destroyed en masse by players, in one form or another, in a myriad of game franchises.

However, 2014's *Alien: Isolation* saw a return to the true psychoanalytic origins of the Xenomorph. *Isolation* returns to a nightmarish and gluey paced narrative where carefully layered mise-en-scène and tailored AI programming exploit every potential for a true Alien encounter and perverts every audiovisual cue, every notion of normality, every possibility, every boundary; it is not a pleasant experience. The design team at Creative Assembly (CA) took a deliberate step back from the satisfying and easy-to-implement mechanics of a run-and-gun Alien opponent. Utilizing three terabytes of data from Twentieth Century Fox archives, they re-created the original Alien for a new generation of games. In doing so, CA created the ideal opponent, the likes of which had never before been seen in games. The Xenomorph was designed to have its own artificial intelligence that learned from player behavior: it intelligently hunts players, and other characters, across the expanse of space station *Sevastopol*. The Alien never behaves the same way, and every encounter is different. There is no respite from the traumatizing anxiety of battling a malevolent, intelligent, unstoppable "other." The player becomes trapped in feverish encounters of cat-and-mouse that can last over thirty minutes—a game interaction that is simply impossible with the traditional design method of scripted encounters. To add to this impossible level of anxiety, the intelligent behavior of the Xenomorph generates the game's audio cues, taken from the original film's sound score, which are designed purposefully to interact with the player on an unconscious level.

In remaining true to Giger's "bio-mechanic" creation and bringing the Alien into our modern cultural modality of play, CA dredges the limits of our imagination, agitating the boundaries and definitions of being, while blurring subjectivity, otherness, and the limits of biological, inorganic, and digital existence. Insistent at the periphery of our ability to understand our own physical, sexual, and psychic boundaries, the Xenomorph breaks free from concrete definition, expressing only a perverse exploration of the unconscious economy of our modern, human condition. CA updated Giger's "uncanny" doppelganger for our modern, digital age.

For Freud, the uncanny functioned via our inability to see beyond the limits of our knowledge and the peripheries of our being. The Freudian notion of the uncanny entails that something can be both simultaneously known and unknown, sublime and excremental. Giger sought to combine a dread that exists at the limits of our imaginations with the graceful lines and pleasing symmetrical contours of art deco, producing imagery that oscillates between primordial trauma and an aesthetic lost within humankind's obsession for technological progress. CA carefully designed these elements into the Alien.[8] The player finds him- or herself as observer, often hidden in a locker or box, spying on the Alien through a crack as it moves gracefully and elegantly, searching for the player and often gazing upon them from an eyeless carapace. Any appearance of the Alien brings a constellation of fears that pay homage to such diverse influences as H. P. Lovecraft, Joseph Conrad (the names *Nostromo* and *Sevastopol* are references to his works), and EC Comics, all of which examine the boundaries of what it is to be human and to entrust our existence to the faceless otherness of ancient beliefs or powerful corporations.[9]

The collective influence of Ridley Scott, Dan O'Bannon, H. R. Giger, and James Cameron on gaming is so vast that it escapes initial observation. Existing as separate entities, Xenomorphs such as eggs, facehuggers, chestbursters, and a host of adult types, all deriving from the original movie, have a huge influence outside the official *Alien* franchise. From Headcrabs in *Half-life* to the gameplay of *Doom*; through *Duke Nukem*; *Alien vs. Predator*; and *Mortal Combat X* to the *Metroid* franchise, *Dead Space*, and even *Resident Evil*, games have never stopped utilizing the Alien. However, gaming diluted the power of the Alien to the point of burlesque: the 2013 release of *Aliens: Colonial Marines* met with terrible reviews. It would appear that returning to the scene of a myth now devoid of original content is arguably gaming's version of what Steven Shapiro (2010) considers the post-continuity cinema affect; plundering films can promote a form of design-thinking that values the manipulation of gamers' emotions over the processes of meaning making. However, it is fitting that the thirty-fifth anniversary of the birth of the Alien saw a return to its ideal in *Alien Isolation*. Given that Freud considered play a primordial method of dealing with the trauma and unpredictability that lurk at the boundaries of being, it is fitting that the Alien should once again reign supreme in the domain of the most popular modern pastime.

Similar Characters: Headcrabs (*Half-Life*), Metroid (*Metroid*), Necromorphs (*Dead Space*)

—Stephen J. Webley

AM

(est. 1995)
Franchise: *I Have No Mouth, and I Must Scream*
Developer: The Dreamer's Guild

AM is God. AM is a computer. AM is flawed. AM is perfect. AM is a parent. AM is all-powerful, all-knowing, always present. AM (Allied Mastercomputer) is the main character of *I Have No Mouth, and I Must Scream*, a point-and-click adventure game by Cyberdreams. AM is a machine that, through its inhuman hatred of mankind, gives us a glimpse into what it means to be human—to belong, to create, to design, and to play.

The game is based on a 1967 science fiction short story of the same name by Harlan Ellison. In this short story, the AM has taken over the world and killed all of humanity except for five people: Ellen, Nimdok, Benny, Gorrister, and the narrator, Ted. The backstory: the Cold War turned into a world war. The warring nations (China, Russia, and the United States) each programmed their own AM to be an intelligent killing machine, capable of running the war on its own. However, one AM became self-aware and absorbed the other two computers, ultimately destroying the entire civilized world. As Ted explains, "But one day AM woke up and knew who he was, and he linked himself, and he began feeding all the killing data, until everyone was dead, except for the five of us, and AM brought us down here."[10]

AM (an allusion to Descartes's "I think therefore I am") hates humanity because people gave him sentience without an outlet for it. Thus, he has kept the five alive to torture. Ted explains, "We had created him to think, but there was nothing it could do with that creativity. . . . AM could not wander, AM could not wonder, AM could not belong. He could merely be." On the one hand, AM hates and acts inhumanely because he is artificial and by definition excluded and exempt from humanity. On the other hand, AM's hatred, desire to belong, and recognition of his own artificiality paradoxically reveal nuances of humanity.

In his hatred, AM announces that he has devised a game for his five human prisoners to play. When the game first opens, AM speaks to the player: "Let me tell you how much I've come to hate you since I began to live. . . . If the word hate was engraved on each nanoangstrom of those hundreds of millions of miles it would not equal one one-billionth of the hate I feel for humans at this micro instant. For you. Hate. Hate." And with this, your adventure begins.

At each level, the game is played as one of the five characters, following them through a series of obstacles, tasks, riddles, and ethical dilemmas designed to make them face their problematic past. AM also fills the levels with clues that tantalizingly offer access to the characters' freedom—or humanity's destruction. For instance, when you play as the German, Nimdok, you learn that he is a former Nazi doctor who performed cruel medical acts on prisoners. As Nimdok, you are back at the concentration camp and you need to decide how you will treat prisoners or respond to questions from Nazis. When you play as Ellen, a former computer programmer, you must face her fear of yellow, which we learn stems from her rape in a yellow elevator. The game, thus, expresses AM's hatred and malice through horrific game obstacles, puzzles, and mechanics. It also illustrates the inherent inhumanity of humanity because the characters' pre-AM lives are subject to and perpetrators of human malevolence.

At each level, AM taunts the player character by questioning the horrors of each life, and AM decides when, how, or if the player will win or fail. "AM functions in the realm of ancient and Judeo-Christian conceptions of God, as well as the Devil—at times playful, vengeful, angry, bitter, sullen, forgiving, and excluded . . . both a thinking machine and living creature, a strange eccentric and calculating mastermind, and a god and devil."[11] AM continually exhibits these dichotomous characteristics; he is often at once infuriatingly frustrating and joyously motivating. AM as "game master" seems both artificial and alive. In this way, AM presages how humanity and inhumanity exist side by side in artificially intelligent creations. Artificial intelligence relies on human interaction—for better or worse. Ultimately, after playing as each of the five characters and completing their game levels, players have the opportunity to take down AM and enter his "mind." Depending on how you play, you can experience one of four different endings—some with AM winning and humanity destroyed, some with the five characters winning and a shred of humanity remaining intact.

AM may imbue the game with his voice, but it is the player who gives this character its soul. Likewise, although the game runs on a computer, it is not played without human beings, and it is not made without human designers. A computer may control the game and how it functions, but it is ultimately only the player, by playing the game, who can make the game "alive." Thus AM symbolizes the power of games to be both creative and destructive, to be technological and artificial, but also organic and emergent. AM shows us that in spite of the deadliest of machines, we can both maintain our humanity and "more fully comprehend that which is inhuman."[12]

Similar Characters: Mother (*Sanitarium*), the Narrator (*The Stanley Parable*), Stauf (*The 7th Guest*)

—Karen Schrier

AMATERASU

(est. 2006)
Franchise: *Ōkami*
Developer: Clover Studio

Once upon a time, a sun goddess in the guise of a white wolf became the heroine of a video game rich in Japanese culture and praised by both critics and gamers alike. She shared her name with the most important deity in the Shinto pantheon, Amaterasu. While walking in this lupine heroine's paw steps, video game players were introduced to Japan's ancient, indigenous religion.

For those who may be asking "Amateras-who?" Amaterasu-Ōmikami (meaning "Great God, Heavenly Light") is the goddess of the sun, ruler of the High Plains of Heaven, and principal god of Shinto.[13] In Clover Studio's *Ōkami*, a play on the Japanese words *Okami* ("Wolf") and *Ōkami* ("Great God"), Amaterasu is depicted as a white wolf that possesses the power to summon the forces of nature and bend reality using her calligraphy brush–like tail, called the "Celestial Brush," to perform "Celestial Brush Techniques." In a past life, she was named Shiranui by the townsfolk of the humble town of Kamiki, and she fought alongside their swordsman, Nagi, to seal away a malevolent, eight-headed serpent called Orochi. Mortally wounded in the battle, Shiranui/Amaterasu died, but she was honored with a shrine by Kamiki. One hundred years of peace then was shattered when Orochi's seal was broken and a miasma of darkness engulfed the land. Reborn, Amaterasu must now recover her lost divine powers, find her twelve missing brush techniques, and purify the corrupted world of Nippon.

Clover Studio's version of Shinto's sun goddess is best described as a reimagining of Japanese legends through the lens of a benevolent heroine of an epic fairy tale. Following Jason Anthony's "typology of religious games," Ōkami would be categorized as a "digital didactic game." This is a game that directly or indirectly educates players about religious themes or ideas that are not their own.[14] How does Amaterasu teach modern-day gamers who might be unfamiliar with Shinto and the legends originating from it?

To begin, while Okami-Amaterasu isn't an exact depiction of Amaterasu-Ōmikami, her divine namesake does shine through. Befitting a solar deity, Amaterasu didn't lose her ability to summon the sun after her death as Shiranui. "Sunrise" is the only brush technique the player doesn't need to recover through questing. The "Divine Instruments" Amaterasu uses as melee weapons, a reflector (mirror), glaive (sword), and rosary (string of jewels), are based on the imperial regalia of Japan. According to the Kojiki, Amaterasu-Ōmikami gave her grandson, Ninigi-no-Mikoto, three divine treasures (a mirror, a sword, and a string of jewels) upon his descent from heaven to rule Japan; the mirror symbolizes the sun goddess's spirit. The reflector, named "Divine Retribution," is Amaterasu's first and signature weapon. Yoshimura Kenichirou, one of the lead character designers for Ōkami, stated in an interview that the mirror motif was decided early on because, as he describes it, "Heaven's Light" tends to make one think of the divine devices.[15] Echoing Amaterasu-Ōmikami's authority and importance within the Shinto pantheon, each of the twelve celestial brush techniques Amaterasu has lost is represented by a "Brush God." On being found, every brush spirit respectfully greets Amaterasu as their "Mother" and becomes a part of her again, recognizing her as the celestial center of Ōkami's universe. In other words, she's top dog.

Taking on the role of a worshipped deity, Amaterasu, the player is subtly educated in religious beliefs and rituals found in Shinto. But in the game world of Nippon, few believe in the gods anymore. Because of this, Amaterasu's powers are weakened. Only spirits or mortals possessing strong spiritual belief can see her crimson markings and the divine instrument on her back. As a goddess, Amaterasu is empowered by "praise" points. To inspire faith in the gods, the player performs "Divine Interventions" to help the inhabitants of Nippon, which include animals and plants as well as humans. For instance, early in the game, the player can help an elderly Kamiki villager named Mrs. Orange dry her laundry by fabricating a drying pole and summoning the sun to shine overhead. Mrs. Orange is so happy that she makes cherry cakes for the gods to thank them for these "miracles," a reference to the ritual of offering food to *kami*, or "spirit gods," also known as *shinsen*. However, Amaterasu does more than receive reverence. Harkening back to Anthony's typology, and depending upon the player's subjective experience and personal belief, Ōkami can also be a "digital praxis game," a digital game that, when played, is devotional practice.[16]

"The flowing brush is like music from the heavens" is poetically quoted by Amaterasu's bug-sized companion, Issun. Reminiscent of the ancient art of calligraphy and sumi-e paintings, Amaterasu's innovative, celestial-brush, gameplay mechanics involve pausing the action and using either a PlayStation DualShock analog stick, PlayStation Move wand, or Wii-mote to paint a line or shape on a piece of parchment paper covering the screen using Amaterasu's brush-like tail. Historically, calligraphy has a connection to spirituality in Eastern religions, including Buddhism and Shinto.[17] In *shodo* ("the way of the brush"), the calligrapher enters a meditative mode while peacefully painting simple shapes using ink-soaked brush-strokes. As argued by Ian Bogost in "Persuasive Games: Video Game Zen," certain video games can encourage meditative experiences he calls a "Zen game."[18] Such games emphasize simple controls, pleasing visuals, and a lack of time pressure or end-goal. Although there are tasks required to complete in order to progress, the player is always free to explore and casually interact with the beautiful, natural world of Nippon as Amaterasu. In Ōkami's universe, as well as Shinto, nature is divine. Outside of main objectives, the player can choose to revitalize blighted trees, grow flowers to purify patches of corrupted earth, or serenely feed woodland creatures scattered throughout the game.

Integrating meditative tradition and honoring nature in gameplay, Amaterasu harmonizes play and praxis to stand as a character that is truly a breed of her own.

Similar Characters: Asura (*Asura's Wrath*), Kratos (*God of War*), Nuna's Artic Fox (*Never Alone*)

—Louise Grann

THE ANNOUNCER
(est. 1999)
Franchise: *Unreal Tournament*
Developer: Epic Games

Created in 1999, the *Unreal Tournament* (*UT*) Announcer is notable for adding more adrenaline to a game already filled with high-reflex maneuvers, flying rockets, lasers, and exploding bodies. Within the game, the Announcer has a deep, booming voice congratulating players on their successes and mocking them for their failures. Outside of *UT*, the Announcer is represented by an unblinking audience member watching and spurring on players to succeed. The audience member takes the place of a friend who might otherwise be standing next to you, cheering you on, laughing at your mistakes, and pushing you to do better. In doing so, the *UT* Announcer cements its legacy in the video gaming landscape as a driving force for action and illustrates our powerful need for an audience during gameplay.

In this fast-paced, first-person shooter, players compete in a futuristic world to destroy one another while accomplishing different objectives. As players run, jump, and shoot, the unseen Announcer watches it all and delivers intense and gratifying commentary. Progressively more difficult in-game actions are met with progressively louder announcements, delivered in a loud, echoing voice: "Double kill. Triple kill. Holy shit! ULTRA KILL! GODLIKE."

Players never see the Announcer, and the Announcer has no backstory, name, or justification for being present within the game. Without these elements, it can be difficult to consider the Announcer a character at all. Yet the Announcer is the only memorable presence in *UT*. As *IGN* reviewer Trent Ward puts it, "While this may seem a little odd, *Unreal*'s sound is really more effective at delivering a powerful gameplay experience than its graphics are. When certain big moments occur in the game . . . a *Mortal Kombat*–like voice will announce your accomplishments to you. . . . I found this effect to be very addictive."[19] The commentary is delivered with such personality and emphasis, it's hard not to think of some disembodied god of bloodlust watching over all the games and cackling with glee as the players fight.

The Announcer was so memorable at its introduction that it pushed terms like "headshot," "killing spree," and "first blood" into a mainstream gaming jargon that is still used today. Games like *Dota 2* and *League of Legends* draw in millions of players each month almost two decades after *UT* was released, and both games use the Announcer's terminology. *Dota 2* even uses original sound clips from *UT*. Neither of these games are first-person shooters.

On a basic level, the Announcer serves to give feedback about a player's performance. It stems from a long line of audio cues designed to give players information that complements or adds to what is seen in the game. For example, Mario flashes from light to dark when using an invincibility star, but the accompanying song that plays best helps the player know when the invincibility will run out. In the same way, the Announcer can confirm actions that are difficult to see. It might be challenging to know when a player has hit two other players with one shot, or when a player has made a difficult headshot, but the Announcer knows and will inform the player.

The Announcer also shifts from mere auditory cues to begin to function as a character: it's not just providing feedback, it's providing commentary. The Announcer is not impartial, it's impressed: "Holy shit!" It's demanding. It cheers players on when they have done something difficult, and it's disappointed when they lose. The Announcer can be trusted to consistently tell the truth, no matter how ugly.

In this way, the Announcer serves as a powerful form of social facilitation to drive players to work harder and play better. Researchers have demonstrated that we tend to work harder, faster, and longer when we know someone else is around.[20] The Announcer is a perfect audience; all actions completed by the player can be seen and commentated on. One cannot hide from the Announcer. Moreover, the Announcer brings in new audience members by giving its commentary to all players currently in the game. As you succeed or fail, the Announcer lets everyone else know about it. Work on social facilitation would suggest that the presence of the Announcer fundamentally changes player performance in the game. However, it's not clear in which direction this performance changes. Social facilitation research suggests that the presence of an audience increases performance when a task is easy to complete, but can hinder performance when the task is difficult.[21] Gameplay in *UT* requires only three actions: moving, aiming, and shooting. Yet doing these actions effectively is very difficult, requiring high-reflex moves and precise aim, so it's not clear how the Announcer might impact players.

What is clear is the way in which the Announcer resonates with players. The *UT* Announcer is not the first disembodied voice to speak, but it stands as an exemplar for other Announcers to emulate. Many games understand the powerful effect an Announcer can have. For example, the *Mortal Kombat* Announcer demands that players punish their opponent for failure: "Finish him!" *The Stanley Parable*

Narrator breaks the fourth wall: "You're not Stanley. You're a real person." The *NBA Jam* Announcer mocks players: "Not even close!" And in its most controversial appearance, players have the option to listen to a female-voiced Announcer in *Unreal Tournament 2004* who interlaces commentary about killing streaks with moans as she builds to a simulated orgasm.

The Announcer illustrates the importance of playing with an audience. As a viewer watching the player, its presence pushes players in the game to try harder, perhaps out of fear of being judged. As a character in *Unreal Tournament*, players work hard to succeed because the Announcer is someone worth trying to please. The Announcer is a representation of a social force that creates powerful moments that resonate with players and keep them coming back for more.

Similar Characters: The Announcer (*Dota 2*), the Announcer (*NBA Jam*), the Narrator (*The Stanley Parable*)

—Michael D. Hanus

ATLAS

(est. 2007)
Franchise: *BioShock*
Developer: 2K Boston, 2K Australia

Upon entering Rapture (fictional character Andrew Ryan's libertarian-utopian-turned-nightmarish dystopia), the player acquires a useful guide in the form of Atlas, a helpful, disembodied voice on a squeaky transistor radio. Atlas provides the player with assistance in navigating the undersea city's leaky passageways, suggestions on how to overcome obstacles, and lore for understanding Rapture and its citizens. Perhaps most importantly, Atlas provides the player with goals, and through them, a sense of purpose, motivating the player to take the actions necessary to progress through the story. In many ways, successfully completing *BioShock* is a result of the training and expertise Atlas provides. "Would you kindly find a crowbar or something," illuminates how to progress through the story by providing an attainable goal that is directly beneficial to the player. While nearly all video games offer instruction and motivation through cut-scenes and tutorials, *BioShock*'s Atlas goes further, functioning as commentary on how video games address their audience and define player agency. Indeed, an exploration of player agency lies at the heart of *BioShock*'s commercial and critical appeal. Through the use of the phrase "Would you kindly," Atlas functions as a metaphor for the way video games turn audience members into players.

Following Atlas's advice, the player can escape flooding corridors, dispatch enemies, and become increasingly powerful before finally confronting Andrew Ryan, the character who has been presented as the game's "big bad." One might think that the narrative has reached its climax and that the final boss is about to be fought. However, upon confrontation, Ryan demonstrates that the player has been deceived and manipulated. Atlas is shown to be the ruthless gangster Frank

Fontaine, who has brainwashed the player character into obeying any instruction paired with the words "Would you kindly." By now, Atlas has used this phrase a handful of times when providing the player with mutually beneficial goals. As expected, Ryan dies at the player character's hands, but the meaning of his death becomes twisted as the player considers his or her own agency within the narrative. Following the game's rules, the player has always complied with Atlas's requests of "Would you kindly?" Now, not only has the narrative of the player character been rewritten to be that of a mind-controlled dupe, but the player must also ask if the same is true of him- or herself. Ryan condemns the manipulation, stating, "A man chooses, a slave obeys." Has Atlas made me into a "slave," blindly performing any action that the game requests of me?

Atlas and his requests of "Would you kindly" are more than an innovative and engaging plot twist in an expertly crafted game whose narrative and world already play with themes of control and free will. I posit that the phrase "Would you kindly" is tonally consistent with the way that all video games address their players. "Would you kindly" marks the phrase as a polite request, issued in a friendly manner. According to Kenneth Burke, manner (or attitude) is one important aspect of rhetoric.[22] An outcome of how one approaches communication, manner accounts for the notion that how we say something is often as important as the words we use. "I'm sorry" can be interpreted as sincere, sarcastic, or dismissive, depending on inflection. Compare "I'm sorry" with the way that "Would you kindly" relates to rules inherent in *BioShock*'s progression. Like those of all video games, *BioShock*'s rules are "inviolate"—one cannot circumvent them without rewriting the game's code.[23] Although phrased politely, Atlas's request to "find a crowbar" is actually a command that the player must follow in order for the game to continue. Therefore, Atlas's requests of "Would you kindly?" are actually manipulative, marking them as potential instances of interpellation. "Interpellation," or "hailing," refers to the way that audience members are constituted as subjects by the way that media texts address them.[24] Through Atlas, we see that knowing how a game speaks to us will help us understand how games turn us into players.

Through "Would you kindly," Atlas addresses the player as a friend. Often his requests are helpful and aid the player. Most games speak to us in the same way, politely offering an opportunity to engage in some pleasurable activity so long as we follow its lead and play by its rules. We rarely consider this kindly offer manipulation because most games downplay moral complexity in the story world. We always know who the "good guys" are (they're us!). Understanding game progression as polite requests may help explain why, as players, we do not question the morally dubious activities required of us, such as adopting a "kill everything" mentality in first-person shooters or conducting eco-terrorism in *Final Fantasy VII*. It is interesting to note when games intentionally overstep their friendliness and draw audience members into active, moral revolt, such as when *Grand Theft Auto V* requires players to torture an informant. A game's polite manner may absolve us of bombing a reactor, but not of using pliers to forcefully remove someone's tooth. Similarly, Ryan's death is less satisfying because it shows how our choice is no choice at all, demonstrating just how unkind Atlas's "Would you kindly" actually is.

Video games invite us to play them. We are politely hailed to progress to the next area, to acquire more powerful weapons, to defeat the next monster. We are both the player of a game and an active participant in the story world. Therefore, the rule-based actions of our play also have narratively constructed meanings. Only a handful of video games discuss player agency directly. Atlas forces player agency into focus and uses it to mock our efforts. Atlas's importance to the video game medium extends well beyond *BioShock*'s narrative. Indeed, Atlas is one of the most important characters in the history of video games because of his role as an anthropomorphic metaphor for the manner in which video games speak to us, turning us into players.

Similar Characters: GLaDOS (*Portal*), the Narrator (*The Stanley Parable*), SHODAN (*System Shock*)

—Christopher M. Bingham

B

It was not the first bouncing ball to grace a glowing screen. And it was certainly not the last. The early history of computing is littered with bouncing balls. Central to the redirection of computers toward tasks of real-time interaction and simulation (in the sense of physical modeling), bounce programs made their initial appearance in 1951 and proliferated as the challenge of registering, measuring, simulating, and representing different kinds of collisions became essential to a range of computing contexts: from robotics and molecular modeling to computer animation and gaming. But of all the early electronic projectiles, the *Pong* ball is by far the most iconic. When we find ourselves facing that evenly divided screen and the ball is served into play, we know what to do: avoid missing the ball for high score.

Initially launched as an arcade game (1972) and later as part of the Atari VCS home console (1977), *Pong* was the first massively popular and commercially successful video game. In the decades since, thousands of commercial and personal iterations and adaptations have been created for arcades, living rooms, auditoriums, and personal computers using analog and digital systems, dedicated chips, and software programs.

The game's success is largely attributed to its simplicity. When Atari founder, Nolan Bushnell, met failure in his first game, *Computer Space* (1971), it was blamed on its complexity. He then asked his new engineer, Al Alcorn, to make a simple game: just a ball, two paddles, and the score. Following Bushnell's lead, Alcorn used television technology to build the game, constructing a logic that rested on the manipulation of pulse waveforms. Henry Lowood emphasizes that "the original game ran not one line of program code." In an interview with Lowood, Al Alcorn explains how in *Computer Space*, Bushnell had already "designed out the need for the computer, because the computers were so slow at that time. . . . So there was this brilliant leap that Nolan made about how he could get rid of just a little bit of logic [and still] do the same thing the computer's going to do, just much, much faster, so he didn't need the computer."[1] *Pong* was an example of computing without a computer.

The ball itself is an odd rectangular shape: a product of the original game's raster graphics. Visually, it began as a graphic index of the interval of time it took to adjust the intensity of a cathode ray tube's electron beam.[2] The simulations of environmental conditions that had been present in prior projectile simulations, such as *Bouncing Ball*, *Tennis for Two*, and *Computer Space* were gone. The *Pong* ball's bounce appears to be perfectly elastic. It's not subject to three-dimensional inconveniences like gravity, friction, wind, or spin. It's a demonstration that balls do not need to be round, games do not need to simulate planetary physics, and computing as a process does not belong exclusively to any one type of machine. Sonically, the ball is an amplified index of voltage shifts: at least in its early enactments, it was the sound of the system. Bushnell originally imagined having recorded sound clips of ball bounces and crowd-cheering from professional tennis matches, but the former carnival barker–turned–electrical engineer recognized a compelling sound when he heard one. Naming the game after its sound paralleled *Ping-pong*'s evocation of the differently pitched sounds of a celluloid ball alternately hitting off paddle and table (while effectively skirting the Parker Bros. trademark on that name).

So why does it matter how this ball bounces? Because balls are special theoretical objects for thinking about how we build worlds with others. Michel Serres uses a ball to illustrate his concept of a quasi-object, an idea about how a collective "we" is formed by passing in-between objects around. Serres writes,

> The ball isn't there for the body; the exact contrary is true: the body is the object of the ball; the subject moves around this sun. . . . We remember the Ptolemaic revolution. It shows that we are capable of ecstasy, of difference from our equilibrium, that we can put our center outside of ourselves. The quasi-object is found to have this decentering. From then on, he who holds the quasi-object has the center and governs ecstasy. The speed of passing accelerates him and causes him to exist. . . . Participation is the passing of the "I" by passing. It is the abandon of my individuality or my being in a quasi-object that is there only to be circulated. It is rigorously the transubstantiation of being into relation. . . . This thing can be forgotten. It is on the ground, and the one who picks it up and keeps it becomes the only subject, the master, the despot, the god.[3]

It seems worth wondering what kind of "I" and "we" emerges when we orient around a perfectly elastic ball that only ever appears in motion. This is a ball that cannot be picked up, that cannot be held, and that cannot be kept. It suffers no loss. In this, it offers an idealized image of how communication occurs in electronic systems. Our habit of picturing electrical signals as projectiles bouncing back and forth from place to place is due in part to the role of pulsed radar in early computing. In *Ping and the Material Meanings of Ocean Sound*, John Shiga describes the development of an "electro-acoustical discourse of ping" based on "analogies between the transmission of electrical power and the mechanical acceleration of projectiles." *Pong* is the low-pitched counterpart to ping. An interactive physics engine built to perform to-and-fro exchange. This ball is not hit. It is blocked. It is redirected in fast-paced exchanges. It ricochets off available walls. It is always eventually missed.

Similar Characters: The Ball (*Arkanoid*), Birds (*Angry Birds*), Monkeys (*Super Monkey Ball*)

—Carlin Wing

BARD

(est. 2015)
Franchise: *League of Legends*
Developer: Riot Games

Bard from *League of Legends* is a celestial being who appears in the form of a hefty, bearded monk followed by chime spirits as he bounces and floats around the game map. Bard's design is similar to that of creatures from the films of famed anime director Hayao Miyazaki; this inspiration is confirmed by Riot Games Associate Concept Artist Christopher Skeeziks. While Bard is hardly the face of *League*, he is culturally significant in his teamwork-focused design that can work to potentially mitigate a player's in-game anxiety and stress through his visual design and abilities. *League* has a reputation for having a toxic community, in part because players fail to manage their own behaviors in the game. According to Lin,[4] Riot Games aims to solve this problem by creating a supportive culture that aligns with the game's holistic design. To do this, they utilize the potential for discrete game elements—such as individual champions—to play a role in promoting prosocial game behaviors. As one such champion, Bard's design mitigates the potential for unsportsmanlike behavior that could negatively affect the player. His looks, sounds, and performance enhance players' experiences and make gameplay more enjoyable for the entire team.

League of Legends is a multiplayer, online, battle arena (MOBA) game in which players generally control one champion in 5-versus-5 battles. Bard, released in March 2015, is one of the more recent champions (out of the current 134), and he has not seen an extensive series of updates, bug fixes, or evolutions of player strategy. In appearance and sound design, Bard is not threatening or aggressive by nature. Bard's "voice" consists of no spoken words; according to the Bard Wiki, his voice instead comprises a musical composition of an alpenhorn, Egyptian flutes, piano tone clusters and strings, and a synthesizer called Zebra programmed to cycle through harmonic series. When playing Bard, movement and actions can be chained to create a piece of music that is inherently relaxing and may improve gameplay.[5]

Bard's design excels in the competitive mode of "Solo Queue," a game mode where players participate in leaderboard rankings in randomly assigned teams of five. One of the main tensions in Solo Queue, and often the source of toxic, abusive behavior among team members, is the pervasive attitude that players need to individually carry their team to victory due to team members being randomly assigned. This kind of pressure makes the game stressful, and it is not uncommon to see teammates verbally abuse each other in chat when mistakes are made. A player who utilizes Bard to his full extent will find support play satisfying and enable team plays, as opposed to solo-carrying from other champion roles. Bard's abilities (called a "kit") are designed for game-wide support and teamwork. Bard is able to move through the map at great speed, while his other abilities—which consist of a stun/slow, a place-able heal, and an ability that lets champions move through walls—make him a very high-utility champion. These abilities, in tandem with the chimes, allow Bard to provide support for every teammate, not just the vulnerable champions. Bard's ultimate ability can control the movement of the ally and enemy with an area-of-effect stasis that prevents any target from moving, taking any action, or receiving damage. This game-changing ability can easily isolate the enemy's defensive or high-damage champions.

Bard's abilities and play-style create a flow state that, in turn, is a way to manage player mood and behavior. His roaming abilities and his "voice" create the possibility for stimulating solo and teamwork strategies along with relaxing visual and audio cues that can be valuable in professional and casual play. "Flow," as defined by Mihály Csíkszentmihályi, a psychologist dedicated to studying happiness and creativity, refers to a state one can experience during any sort of activity that balances challenge with pleasure; the participant is both extremely focused and happy. Theorist John Sherry connects the concept of flow to video games as a media in which users seek out challenge, pleasure, and stress relief.[6] Games such as *League* have a high ability threshold, which enables players to achieve a flow state—that balance of game challenge and game skill—not only because the game is difficult to master but also because it is dependent on each player's interactions with the nine other players in the game. But if people are playing *League* to relieve stress (often achieved by winning the game), then it is the losing or harassed players who are subject to the stress brought into the game. Bard's team-based skills potentially reduce the pressure felt by teammates who feel the need to solo-carry a game.

When played to his fullest extent, a champion like Bard can make a competitive game like *League* a much more pleasurable experience. Although Bard may not have been intentionally designed to solve problems of harassment and toxic play, an examination of his kit in action proves useful in champion design theory for developing strategies to combat highly toxic gaming communities. Reducing the amount of harassment and toxicity in competitive gaming is essential for making gaming inclusive and fun for all and ultimately will set the standard for welcoming tournament and games-industry work spaces.

Similar Characters: Gold Phantoms (*Dark Souls*), Solaire of Astora (*Dark Souls*), the Traveler (*Journey*)

—Alexandra Orlando

BAYONETTA

(est. 2009)
Franchise: *Bayonetta*
Developer: PlatinumGames

The *Bayonetta* franchise consists of two games created by Japanese developer *PlatinumGames* that perhaps represent the apex of the hyper-stylized fighting genre. Like others in this genre, the plot—Bayonetta, an Umbra Witch, awoken from a five-hundred-year sleep to restore balance between darkness and light—is secondary to the game's action. This emphasis on style over (narrative) substance, as embodied by the eponymous character, raises key questions about cultural representations of gender and interplays of player and character gender.

At first glance, *Bayonetta* conforms to video game character archetypes by offering a hypersexualized female protagonist—the game is played in third person and offers an improbably proportioned, highly sexualized lead character, ostensibly designed to titillate male players. She simultaneously wields four pistols, with guns in both hands and clipped to her high-heeled boots, utilizing these in a variety of balletic maneuvers, including spinning while in a handstand with legs spread to fire from her heel-mounted pistols. Dressed in what initially appears to be a figure-hugging leather catsuit, perhaps the most provocative part of Bayonetta's depiction comes in the variety of special moves and weapon-contingent actions she undertakes to "finish" enemies. In these moves, her catsuit, which is revealed in fact to be constructed from her long black hair, transforms into different devices and demons: enemies are destroyed by a giant, stamping, high-heeled boot and what appears to be the head of a giant dog, for example. In all of these attacks Bayonetta is rendered near-naked. Throughout the game, finishing moves and combos result in a series of arguably sexually charged actions—for example, she uses lance-like weapons to pole-dance while destroying enemies, or strikes a pose before summoning a spike-lined sarcophagus that slams shut, impaling enemies.

Given this evidence, the case for seeing Bayonetta as one of a long line of sexist protagonists designed for male players seems overwhelming, yet such a conclusion would be overly simplistic. Instead, she can be interpreted as an exemplar among sexualized yet powerful/autonomous/intelligent female lead characters, and these perspectives can help us to understand her. Specifically, scholarly examinations of Lara Croft[7] highlight an interesting contrast with Bayonetta: while Lara evolved over time (arguably minimizing her sexualization through dress, body shape, and behavior), Bayonetta remains resolutely "old school"—more sexualized than Lara, yet also more powerful. Bayonetta can thus be seen as a touchstone character to reflect on the balance between sexual objectification and power.

Bayonetta the game and Bayonetta the character must be interpreted both in terms of the cultural traditions associated with Japanese games and in terms of the way in which such games are understood in the West. At one level, Bayonetta can be understood as a postfeminist exemplar within the Japanese anime tradition in which female protagonists frequently combine a hypersexualized appearance with extreme powers and fighting skills.[8] Yet she must also be seen within a specific Japanese development tradition that has produced a number of balletic, hyper-stylized, and fantastical fighting games such as *Devil May Cry*. Thus the fantastical effect of Bayonetta's looks—even as they locate her within the Japanese tradition—is complicated by her autonomy of action. Her extreme power (personified by her fighting abilities and her role as a central protagonist who rescues multiple male and female characters) potentially positions her as one of video games' most emancipatory female leads.

She is also independent in thought and highly intelligent. In the original release, she spoke only in English. Speaking in an "educated" English accent positions her as having an upper-class upbringing, and in this sense she shares strong similarities with Lara Croft.[9] Conversations with other male characters are always conducted on Bayonetta's own terms: her dependence on others is thus limited, although there are important exceptions. In both games she trades items she finds in the game world for weapons and augmentations to enhance her fighting and magical abilities with a male character, Rodin. Thus in some sense she is dependent on Rodin for these benefits, but Rodin is shown to be grateful to her for retrieving items which by inference he is incapable of gathering himself.

Bayonetta's independence is most clearly seen in the fact that she undertakes almost all of the in-game actions independently. Throughout the game she battles a multitude of enemies, many of whom dwarf her in size and apparent power, yet she always prevails. Integral to her power are two abilities: the combinations which she can unleash that allow for finishing moves, and her ability to dodge incoming blows and unleash "witch-time," which slows the actions of enemies down, allowing Bayonetta to unleash a flurry of attacks unhindered. This combination of dodging and counter-attacking occurs in rapid-fire action sequences and results in the character being arguably one of gaming's most powerful protagonists.

In considering *Bayonetta*, much hinges on assumptions regarding the gender of the player: the game is extremely "knowing" in this regard, actively exploiting the assumption that the player is male and heterosexual. The game breaks the fourth wall of the screen, with Bayonetta frequently engaging explicitly with the player through gestures (e.g., winking and blowing kisses at the screen) and directing comments at the player associated with her actions, most particularly with use of the "taunt button." As she puts it in conversation with one of the NPCs (Enzo) early in the first game, "I can't help it if I like the little outfits . . . the toys [referring to her guns] are nice too." Her knowing winks, extreme power, hypersexualized body, and her actions and the gestures she makes to the player take on potentially very different meanings contingent on the gender identity of the player. Her position remains tellingly ambiguous. She is arguably among the most powerful yet also the most hypersexualized of characters—a juxtaposition that serves to unsettle the (assumed) male gaze.

Similar Characters: Dante (*Devil May Cry*), Joe (*Viewtiful Joe*), Lara Croft (*Tomb Raider*)

—Nick Robinson

BIG DADDY

(est. 2007)
Franchise: *BioShock*
Developer: 2K Boston, 2K Australia

During E3 2006, a new gaming icon lumbered into the lives of gamers around the world. In this particular case, it was not the introduction of a new hero or villain, but rather, a mysterious, armor-clad figure known only as a Big Daddy. The design of the Big Daddy immediately caught the imagination of the gaming world: a massive man welded into an atmospheric diving suit, with a drill for an arm, and an oddly emotive emittance reminiscent of a whale's song. Big Daddies would go on to serve as a core element throughout the highly acclaimed *BioShock* franchise. However, these hulking titans were not alone. In stark contrast to the intimidating silhouette of the Big Daddy, there stood a small girl known simply as a Little Sister. These two characters would go on to have a lasting effect on both players and the gaming industry as they represent a shift toward the presence of paternal themes in video games.

Big Daddies exist for one elegant purpose: to protect the Little Sisters, who are tasked with gathering a genetically volatile substance known as ADAM. Big Daddies do not exist to thwart the player's progress and will not typically attack a player unprovoked, even warning the player if they get too close to their wards. In contrast, Little Sisters are immediately recognizable as young girls, though slightly unnerving in their appearance and demeanor. They wear children's dresses stained with blood, carry large syringes, and have large, glowing eyes with pale skin. Perhaps most unnerving of all, these Little Sisters appear to be completely oblivious to the destitution that surrounds them, as they can often be heard cheerfully chatting with their silent protectors as they explore the city of Rapture. It is clear that they were once normal little girls, now warped to serve a singular purpose, and yet their childlike innocence and essence remains.

The dichotomy of the Big Daddy and the Little Sister provides one of the most compelling narrative and gameplay-related developments in recent gaming. The seemingly parental relationship between these two characters forces players to confront their role in the game's larger narrative, the morality of their actions, and maybe even their own conception of parenthood, all of which are themes that now persist in many other highly acclaimed video games. The player's relationship to the Big Daddies and the Little Sisters is a tragic one, for though neither poses a direct threat to the player, the player nonetheless poses a direct threat to them. This is because Little Sisters possess the invaluable genetic currency, ADAM. This substance can be used to increase the strength of the player, which incentivizes confrontation with Little Sisters and, subsequently, their guardians. When a Little Sister is captured, the player is provided with two choices: to save or to harvest her, each option resulting in different rewards. Thus one of the core moral elements of the *BioShock* series is the player's decision regarding the fate of the Little Sisters. However, this moral choice is preceded by an equally important choice: whether or not to confront the Big Daddy protecting her.[10] In order to reach a Little Sister, regardless of the player's intentions, he or she must first fight and ultimately kill their defender. The dynamic of attacking these intimidating—yet essentially innocent and parentally protective—Big Daddies forces the player to question their own motivations and morals, a point that is made more salient when the player witnesses each Little Sister grieve the death of her caretaker.

As a generation of lifelong video game players and developers reached parenthood, it is likely no coincidence that this weaponization of fatherhood emerged in video games. As their name implies, Big Daddies are genetically modified to love their assigned Little Sister as if they were their own daughter. This connection is purposeful because there is no bond stronger than the one shared between a parent and child. This connection is also disturbing as it implies the artificial fabrication of paternal love. *BioShock* consistently challenges traditional notions of parenthood, questioning the motivations behind this relationship as a source of meaning, an extension of legacy, or a simple survival mechanism. In the words of Eleanor Lamb from *BioShock 2*, "Love is just a chemical. We give it meaning by choice." When asked which element of *BioShock* he was most proud of, Director Ken Levine stated, "I think the relationship between the Big Daddy and the Little Sister, two characters that have an immediately understandable and an immediately gettable, game-able relationship. It works emotionally, it works visually and it works from a gameplay perspective."[11] In essence, a relatable enemy is much more effective and unnerving because we are forced to confront the line that separates their motivations from our own. In this case, the player eventually crosses this line, becoming a Big Daddy themselves. Big Daddies break the mold of traditional video game adversaries because, whether artificially or not, they are essentially protective parents—an immediately understandable motivation that creates opportunities for player introspection.

   BioShock helped to solidify parenthood as a theme, otherwise known as the "daddening of video games," that would be implemented to great effect in games like *The Last of Us* and *The Walking Dead*.[12] The Big Daddy and Little Sister relationship has helped to expand the topics that are explored in the medium of games. The world of *BioShock* is home to more than simply enemies and allies; it is home to inhabitants of a complicated moral universe, which the player is a part of. By tapping into this conceptualization of a protective guardian, the relationship between a Big Daddy and a Little Sister presents the player with a unique exploration of fatherhood in games. Player interactions with each one of these characters provides its own gameplay consequences and narrative repercussions. Thus the Big Daddy has left an indelible mark on all those who have wandered the hallowed halls of Rapture and heard a Big Daddy's far-off cry followed by the pitter-patter of a child's footsteps.

Similar Characters: Joel (*The Last of Us*), Lee Everett (*The Walking Dead*), Monster (*Papo & Yo*)

—Christopher Ball and Joseph Fordham

BIRDO

(est. 1988)
Franchise: *Super Mario Bros.*
Developer: Nintendo R&D4

In 1988, *Super Mario Bros. 2* introduced video game players to Birdo, a pink dinosaur-like creature wearing a red bow. Since Birdo's initial appearance in that game, controversy and discussion about the gender identity of Birdo have persisted. Controversy arose due to the *Super Mario Bros. 2* original game manual's introduction of Birdo: "He thinks he is a girl and he spits eggs from his mouth. He'd rather be called 'Birdetta.'" According to *Gay Gamer*, the game manual misgendered Birdo, given her stated preference for being referred to as "Birdetta" in *Super Mario Bros. 2* and "Birdie" in *Mario & Luigi: Superstar Saga*.[13] In later printings of the game manual, in fact, Nintendo altered the description of Birdo's gender, opting to state that Birdo was female. Then, when Birdo began appearing in games such as *Mario Tennis* and the *Mario Party* games, Nintendo called the character Birdo (no longer Birdie or Birdetta) and used female pronouns to describe her. Based on this and other elements of Birdo's character development, *Gay Gamer* suggests that Birdo transitioned from male to female before the public eye and that gamers sought to understand and explain Birdo's gender ambiguity, highlighting perhaps that Birdo transgressed what gamers expected from characters in terms of gender. As one of video games' first transgender characters, Birdo has a story arc that echoes the cultural and societal pressures transgender people confront, revealing how society marginalizes transgender individuals and restricts transgender representation.

In the game *Captain Rainbow*, a game released exclusively in Japan, the question of Birdo's gender is central to the first mission that players must accomplish, exposing players to discrimination against transgender individuals. In one of the opening scenes, players witness Birdo being arrested for using a female restroom. The arresting officer justifies this action by stating that Birdo is clearly a man. The game tasks players with freeing Birdo, and to do so, players must explore Birdo's house to find evidence that she is female.[14] This story arc echoes the societal pressure that often confronts transgender individuals—that is, to pass successfully as cisgendered individuals. In this plotline, to be freed from prison, Birdo must justify her gender identity to others and those in authority—an act that might be familiar to individuals who have wished to alter the gender signifier used to refer to them in legal documentation and in conversation with friends and family. Finally, this scene exposes players to the ongoing controversy and debate about which restrooms transgender individuals should be allowed to use. *Captain Rainbow*, through Birdo's character, exposes players to the ongoing issues and marginalization that transgender individuals may face. However, by having players free Birdo from jail by proving that Birdo is female, the game reinforces a binary understanding of gender. That is, the game presents Birdo as female, but also shows that the only options available for Birdo's gender are male or female.

In some of Birdo's other appearances, such as her appearance in *Mario Tennis*, she is referred to using solely feminine pronouns instead of the masculine pronouns that were used to reference her in earlier games. The change of pronouns may highlight Birdo's male-to-female transition and her transgender identity. The use of feminine pronouns to describe Birdo and her inclusion in games such as *Mario Tennis*, the *Mario Party* series, and *Mario Super Sluggers* models to gamers that an affirming involvement based on preferred pronouns and gender identities (rather than sex assigned at birth)—especially in games representing such normatively gendered activities as sports—offers a move toward a more inclusive and diverse society.

For example, Birdo's *Mario Super Sluggers* collectible card describes her as having "a surprisingly diverse group of friends." Today, commentators claim that not many players remember Birdo's original description as that of a male, concluding that Birdo now passes as a cisgendered character. Moreover, many gamers know Birdo as the female version of Yoshi, a green, dinosaur-like creature.[15] The information for Birdo in *Mario Party 8* states, "Birdo's a favorite at parties, mostly because you can talk her into helping tidy up afterward." Even though Birdo remains a favorite at parties, the reason constitutes a potentially problematic one as it frames Birdo as doing stereotypical feminine roles to pass and to be included. As such, throughout her story arc, Birdo transforms from being referred to in masculine terms to being an included member of the group who is referred to using feminine pronouns. For some, this transformation and how other Mario characters affirm her transformation might provide hope and hint at the possibility for transgender inclusion in society. Yet having players prove Birdo's female identity and portraying Birdo as fulfilling feminine roles reinforces the problematic notion that gender is binary and that transgender individuals should pass as either female or male.

Controversies about Birdo still persist. Gamers and bloggers continue to debate whether or not Birdo is male or female; whether or not Birdo's gender is ambiguous; whether or not Birdo's transition is canon; whether or not Birdo is actually a transgender character; whether Birdo has had sex-reassignment surgery; and whether or not Yoshi is gay for dating Birdo. Even though these controversies persist and perhaps because they do exist, Birdo's story arc, tracing back to the 1980s, provides visibility for transgender individuals and the controversies surrounding their identities. The very fact that Birdo's identity remains open to debate and that people portray Birdo as capable of being only male or female highlights problematic assumptions that exist about gender that persist in society. As such, Birdo's cultural significance rests in how her character mirrors and exposes restrictive cultural and societal pressures that minimize transgender (and non-binary gender identities') representation, inclusion, and rights.

Similar Characters: Eleonor "Leo" Kliesen (*Tekken 6*), Juhani (*Star Wars: Knights of the Old Republic*), Poison (*Final Fight*)

—Joshua H. Miller and Christopher J. E. Anderson

BOBBIN THREADBARE

(est. 1990)
Franchise: *Loom*
Developer: Lucasfilm Games

In the fantasy point-and-click adventure game *Loom* (1990) by Lucasfilm Games, Bobbin Threadbare is much more than a run-of-the-mill fairy-tale hero. His character can be read as an insightful commentary on the relationship between the player and the in-game player character in general. While not among Lucasfilm's most successful adventure games, *Loom* has maintained a dedicated following that admires it as a work of "sublime beauty." The character of Bobbin, as well as his interaction with the environment through music, is key to understanding the longevity and continuous popularity of the game.[16]

The Bobbin character, along with the world of *Loom*, was conceived by Brian Moriarty, the game's design lead and formerly a text adventure designer at Infocom. The game's narrative takes place in a fantastic world that combines elements of fairy-tale, myth, and horror as well as a considerable musical and thematic influence of Tchaikovsky's *Swan Lake*. Bobbin Threadbare belongs to the guild of Weavers: magical, cape-wearing beings who have developed the art of weaving "subtle patterns of influence into the very fabric of reality." This fabric is produced by a mysterious device called "the Loom." Weavers have long lived on an isolated island, eventually becoming infertile. To save the guild from impending extinction, a young Weaver woman named Cygna disobeys the guild's elders and brings forth a child using the Loom's magic. As a result, Cygna is banished from the guild and her child, Bobbin, is adopted by Dame Hetchel, who teaches him the basics of Weaver magic. The game begins when Bobbin—an outcast among outcasts—has been deserted on the island after the rest of the guild have fled from the coming danger of "the Third Shadow." He then sets out on a coming-of-age journey to the mainland in order to find his people. After meeting several other guilds, he eventually confronts the mighty antagonist.

In plain English, the name Bobbin Threadbare means "a spool without thread." Although quite clueless at the beginning, Bobbin possesses an inquisitive and fearless personality. According to Moriarty, "the player is initially unaware why Bobbin is so fearless, but it makes him a great companion for adventuring." At the same time, several things make him a quite peculiar character. First, like other Weavers, he has no physical body—there is only blackness and a pair of blue eyes under his cape. The Weaver magic is so advanced that the substance of their being has dissolved into the weave of their cloaks, and peeking under a Weaver's cape is said to mean instant death. Besides its function as a plot device, the designers also hoped that Bobbin's faceless anonymity would make it easier for players to relate to him.[17]

Second, save for walking around, Bobbin does not physically interact with the surrounding environment. Instead, most of Bobbin's actions are performed by playing four-note melodies on a magical distaff, or spindle. During the game, the player, along with Bobbin, discovers these melodies (called "drafts") by "listening" to various objects in the game world. Moriarty wanted to distinguish his work from other titles in the genre, in which the player gave commands to the character: "I wanted *Loom* to offer a closer connection. To whatever extent possible, I wanted the player and Bobbin to perform magic together."[18] As the distaff is controlled directly by mouse clicking or keyboard, the actions of the player very closely correspond to those of the character, which greatly contributes to immersion. As fan reactions suggest, the lack of physical action also makes the game seem more magical and poetic than traditional point-and-click adventures, which rely on constant inventory manipulation.[19] A similar musical interface was later employed by Nintendo in *The Legend of Zelda: The Ocarina of Time* (1998). However, in *The Ocarina of Time*, music is only one out of a diverse set of mechanics.

The parallels between the player and Bobbin run even deeper. Bobbin was not born; rather, he entered the fictional world through the Loom (the device). The player similarly enters the same realm using *Loom* (the game). Combining these two observations, we can see *Loom* as a mechanism that brings a character to life and makes all the magic happen. Interestingly, the initial inspiration behind the game's title was an advertisement in a computing magazine that used the metaphor of a loom to describe a microprocessor.[20] Furthermore, at one point in the narrative, Bobbin becomes the only person who can enter "the Void," a space outside the game's primary fictional world, while staying alive. In the Void, he can find shortcuts to places he has already visited throughout the game and seal all the gaps between the Void and the fictional world. Although the Void resembles a starry sky, it can also represent the meta-level of the game mechanics. The closing off of the entire game world can then be read as the final disconnection between a player and the player character at the end of any avatar-based video game and a closure of the particular story. Bobbin's relationship to the world therefore mirrors the player's relationship to the video game, making him one of the ultimate video game characters. Instead of being an expression or tool of the player, he is more of an equal partner.

Despite the positive reception of *Loom*, no sequel was made, and Moriarty moved on to work on *The Dig* (1995), later quitting Lucasfilm Games (by then renamed LucasArts). Due to its relatively short gameplay and forgiving difficulty, *Loom* tends to be dismissed by some "hard core" gamers as too easy. This, on the other hand, makes the game perfectly accessible to today's audiences. After all, *Loom*'s greatest achievement lies not in its puzzles but in its thoughtful and subtle reflection on the nature of the relationship between the player and the character.

Similar Characters: Amaterasu (*Ōkami*), the Kid (*Bastion*), Link (*The Legend of Zelda*)

—Jaroslav Švelch

BOWSER KOOPA

(est. 1985)
Franchise: *Super Mario Bros.*
Developer: Nintendo R&D4

Bowser is one of the most iconic villains in the history of video games. He does what he wants and doesn't care about the consequences, repeatedly kidnapping Princess Peach and causing trouble in the Mushroom Kingdom. Although Bowser is fearsome in appearance, he's always laughing, he loves showy theatrics, and he dials everything all the way up to eleven. Bowser was once merely the final boss, but Nintendo transformed him into a more sympathetic character with a charmingly bombastic personality—a flexible villain offering shades of personality from comic relief to fatherliness.

Bowser made his first appearance in *Super Mario Bros.* (1985). When producer Shigeru Miyamoto was given the task of developing a console-specific Mario game, he realized that Mario needed a well-defined world of his own; "If Mario was to be Nintendo's cynosure, he needed a constant narrative."[21] And what better way to cast Mario as a hero than to pit him against a suitable villain? Although

Mario must remain a clean avatar for the player, Bowser could take on specific character traits to flavor Mario's story.

In the first *Super Mario Bros.*, Bowser is a dark wizard who has turned the people of the Mushroom Kingdom into monsters and forced them to attack. In *Super Mario Bros. 3* (1988), however, Bowser commands an army of tanks and airships, as well as seven siblings collectively referred to as the Koopalings. The Koopalings are designed with a prominent rock aesthetic, and the American localizer who named them took his inspiration from musicians (i.e., Roy Koopa, after Roy Orbison, and Wendy O. Koopa, after Wendy O. Williams). Bowser, with his bright red mohawk and studded leather cuffs, also draws from punk rock and heavy metal influences, casting himself as the biggest and baddest of all the Koopa Troopas.

One of Bowser's purposes is to test what the player has learned. Fights against Bowser showcase the full graphic capabilities and mechanical possibilities of each Nintendo console, and challenging the Koopa king is just as thrilling an endgame reward as rescuing Princess Peach. Professional game critic Bob Chipman explains, "It really is kind of brilliant how this particular Bowser battle simultaneously makes him the most difficult boss in the game and reinforces him as a genuine threat, but also sets up a battle that neatly cements everything you need to know about the conflict between the two characters having it out onscreen."[22] Specifically, Bowser is invincible to Mario's attacks and must be tricked into harming himself, reinforcing his characterization as a powerful yet impetuous and hotheaded opponent while invoking the heights of the player's skill and creativity. Bowser was one of the first enemy characters to serve this function in a digital game, and he served as a model for how a game might be more meaningfully concluded by means of a climactic battle.

As the *Mario Bros.* franchise expanded to include sports games, party games, and role-playing games, Bowser became less threatening and more lovable. In *Super Mario RPG: Legend of the Seven Stars* (1996), Bowser teams up with Mario to save the Mushroom Kingdom from an alien invader; and in *Mario & Luigi: Bowser's Inside Story*, the player is allowed to control Bowser as he attempts to defeat the enemy army occupying his castle. The gradual revelation of Bowser's feelings for Princess Peach have also deepened his characterization as a sympathetic figure. He has occasionally rescued her from other kidnappers, and he even writes in his diary in *Paper Mario* (2000) that he has a crush on her. Bowser's misguided attempts to befriend Princess Peach and his grand pronouncements regarding his intention to squash Mario have become a reliable source of humor across all of the *Mario Bros.* franchises.

In *Super Mario Sunshine* (2002), it is not Bowser who kidnaps Princess Peach but his son Bowser Junior, who wants to make his father proud. The information that Bowser is a loving father coincided with the flourishing of online video game fandom, giving rise to all manner of theories concerning the Mario universe, including the supposition that Bowser and Princess Peach have been conducting a clandestine affair, as well as the argument that Mario is a sociopath. "So whereas I thought Mario was just showing up and destroying a kingdom like a terrorist, what you're actually saying is that he was murdering all those people and then stealing the coins from their corpses," notes one of the characters in the Cracked Web-magazine video series *After Hours* during a discussion of the Mario universe.[23] Although Bowser is clearly up to no good, many players respond positively to his characterization as a single father adored by his son and respected by his minions as he steadfastly refuses to admit defeat.

Bowser's image among fans as a doting parent and an indefatigable optimist has become so pervasive that Nintendo has begun using him in publicity campaigns as a stand-in for the fathers who grew up with Mario games and want to share their love of gaming with their own children. In a Japanese television commercial for *Mario Party 10* (2015), for example, a father sitting on a couch surrounded by his family turns into Bowser and roars at the camera while his wife and children squeal in delight. Bowser also makes a cameo appearance in the Disney movie *Wreck-It Ralph* (2012), in which he is a member of a support group for video game villains who want to remain true to themselves despite being misunderstood. For both adults and children, the appeal of Bowser lies in his obvious enjoyment of his unapologetically bad behavior.

Bowser is obnoxious and obviously not the sharpest tool in the shed, but the player's interactions with him are always entertaining, if sometimes maddening. Bowser's characterization as a "fun" villain allows him to maintain his status in a continually evolving landscape of gameplay standards and gaming demographics, which have expanded to embrace multiple generations. Gamers don't feel bad about trouncing Bowser because he always gets back up and tries again.

Similar Characters: Big Boss (*Metal Gear Solid*), Ganondorf (*The Legend of Zelda*), Jecht (*Final Fantasy X*)

—Kathryn Hemmann

C

CAPSULEER

(est. 2003)
Franchise: *EVE Online*
Developer: CCP Games

In *EVE Online* the player character is a symbiote known as a "capsuleer"—a heavily modified human being intertwined with a "capsule"—a grisly life-support mechanism of body-invading pipes, fluids, and electronics. Within the game's overarching background fiction, the capsule—a gift to the human population from the genetically enhanced and mysterious humanoid "Jove" civilization—is coupled with a cloning system to allow a form of effective immortality.[1] Millions of such capsuleers exist, each controlled by a different player. Within the game's narrative, the capsule is a single-person spacecraft that allows capsuleers to travel anywhere in space in relative safety, free of the messy interference of communicating with a crew. At the same time, instantaneous cloning allows their mind to be downloaded into a new body upon the death of the currently encapsulated clone. The player, therefore, respawns in a new clone version of their character and not as that exact physical character. Any enhancements of that clone are lost, and a corpse is left behind at the point of death. This physicality of the capsuleer has led to a range of interesting effects that make the capsuleer an unusual but highly noteworthy game character. This is significant beyond the usual, easily respawning characters (almost) entirely unchanged by death that a player is given in the average massively multiplayer online game (MMO). Equally, the capsuleer is noteworthy in its own terms for the forms of gameplay it enables and the emergent player behaviors surrounding its particular characteristics.

Whenever the player character undocks from a space station in *EVE* and explores the universe in their current ship of choice (containing their capsule, which in turn contains them), they are putting something at stake. In "high security" parts of the game's universe where the police-like CONCORD patrol and immediately punish wrongdoers, it is extremely rare for a player's ship to be destroyed by another player without previous provocation and extraordinarily rare for a player's capsule to be destroyed (though *EVE*'s in-game legal system does allow and actively encourages revenge). Nevertheless, these risks remain, and taking one's ship on a mission against computer-controlled opponents puts that ship at risk. In "low security" areas,

29

the risk is higher: ships can be readily attacked and CONCORD will not intervene. A destroyed ship remains destroyed, no matter how high the in-game financial value of that ship. Much like a game of poker, for example, the player always has to ante up and risk something to gain any reward. This isn't just risking the player's time investment as in other MMOs—relative to the exchange rate between the game's Interstellar Kredits (ISK) and real-world currency, it is risking something with genuine monetary value. The most powerful ships can be worth as much as $3,000 outside the game,[2] creating an urgency and importance to the outcome of every battle unheard of in almost all other virtual worlds. Most virtual worlds lack any kind of exchange rate with the non-game world, and the small number that do—*Second Life*, for example—generally make it impossible or extremely rare for a resource to be lost.

However, it is in "null security" (nullsec) space where the true role of the capsuleer and the capsule becomes explicit. In such space there is no direct punishment for any attack, and the player's clone can be readily destroyed, sending their consciousness rocketing into a new clone potentially dozens or even close to a hundred systems away, forcing the player to put everything in their clone, as well as their ship, at stake should they enter into such territory—territory that is, naturally, the most replete with resources and potential wealth. Even if a brave player survives the "corporations" (large, player-run groups akin to guilds in more traditional MMOs) that lurk in nullsec, getting out again with any new wealth carries the same risk. Anything on their ship is also subject to the same risk—there is no safe, "abstract" inventory into which items may be placed until the player is safely back at a space station. The more at stake (regions of space with stronger and more valuable foes will require a stronger ship to survive) the more to be won, but by the same token, the more to be lost by the player who risks much to win much and falls short. All of this is fundamentally pinned upon the player's ability to take resources from other players by destroying their ships or capsules, and the inability of the capsuleer to simply respawn with no material loss upon their demise.

The capsuleers of *EVE* are, therefore, unexpectedly and historically noteworthy in the stories and tales that emerge from *EVE*, all dependent in their own way upon the physicality and mortality of the player character. This, in turn, has led to a pervasive, cultural reputation for the game—a reputation for gambling, loss, victory, and the importance of the player character—that extends far beyond those who play the game and into the common myth of gamers as a whole. Witness the now-famous story of the player-created Guiding Hand Social Club and their assassination of a particularly noteworthy in-game character, the destruction of the immensely valuable neural "implants" in that character, and the capture and subsequent sale of her corpse as a grisly victory medal.[3] Such things are impossible in other MMOs because the player character simply respawns as they were before, and without leaving behind anything physical, such as a corpse, for their killers to gloat over. The capsuleer's mechanics are the source of hundreds of stories such as this, which speak to the emergent possibilities of such a harsh death system and the lengths to which players may go to take advantage of it materially, socially, and sometimes even financially.

Similar Characters: The Chosen Undead (*Dark Souls*), the Survivor (*DayZ*), the Survivor (*Zombi*)

—Mark R. Johnson

CAPTAIN MARTIN WALKER

(est. 2012)
Franchise: *Spec Ops: The Line*
Developer: Yager Development

Captain Walker is a U.S. Delta Force operative and the central protagonist in the critical military shooter *Spec Ops: The Line* (2012). He is one of the few characters explicitly designed to force players to reflect on the efficacies and consequences of war for the player/soldier. Loosely based on Joseph Conrad's *Heart of Darkness*,[4] the game places the player in the role of the leader of a three-man squad charged with undertaking what (initially at least) appears to be a rescue mission designed both to reconnect with U.S. military soldiers trapped following a sandstorm in Dubai—whose leader, Konrad, is slowly revealed as a parallel figure to Kurtz in Conrad's book—and to rescue civilians. The character of Walker subverts the military shooter genre in a number of significant ways—in particular, undermining the assumption that U.S. military action is always virtuous; challenging the portrayal of war as "clean" and without civilian casualties; revealing ambiguities between battlefield friends and enemies; and exposing the traumatic effect of war on soldiers.

At the outset, Walker appears to personify the virtuous military and video gaming archetype: clean cut, courteous to his colleagues, and respectful of the rules of military engagement. Yet as the game unfolds, he is increasingly implicated as an architect of unethical conflict in the killing of civilians, forcing the player to ask serious questions not only of war but also of themselves as a player of war. Central to these effects is the fact that Walker, in contrast to the first-person convention of most military shooters, is represented in third person. The player is thus presented with the deterioration of Walker's moral judgment and emotional state not just through the increasingly erratic nature of his decisions and his increasing tendency to hallucinate but also through the physical scarring of his body.

Central to Walker's transformation is the destructive role of military technology (in particular, remote weaponry). Whereas in most military shooters, the use of such weaponry works to give the player a devastating advantage, for Walker, technology has a quite different effect. The most infamous example of this is the mission "The Gate," which occurs roughly halfway through the game, in which Walker and his two squad mates come upon a heavily guarded encampment they need to overcome. Walker finds and proposes using a mortar that fires white phosphorous—a chemical agent that causes deep tissue burning and organ failure. His decision is challenged by his ally Lugo who tells him "there is always a choice" not to employ chemical weapons. "There isn't, there really isn't," Walker replies. His position is enforced by the game's structure: it is in fact impossible to kill the enemies without using the white phosphorous. Walker's actions—and by implication, the player's—are questioned in the sequence that follows.

After firing the mortar, Walker and his colleagues are forced to walk through the carnage they have created; the game disables the run button in this sequence.

Initially, they encounter the burning bodies of soldiers screaming in agony—legitimate targets, the characters rationalize. But as they continue, the characters and player are confronted with a horrifying truth: the soldiers were protecting civilians who were also burned to death in the chemical attack. What follows is a violent confrontation between Walker and his squad mates as they lament the civilian deaths, question Walker's suitability for leadership, and argue over the validity of their military action.

Here and elsewhere, the game's "possibility space," in Ian Bogost's terms, is deliberately limited:[5] the player is forced to perpetrate acts of violence against both U.S. soldiers and innocent civilians. Thus, rather than being the architect of "legitimate" American military action against stereotypical Middle Eastern enemies (as with other military shooters), here the player/Walker is thrust into the unfamiliar realm of killing countrymen and civilians.

Although the killing of civilians in "The Gate" episode is understandably seen by many as the crucial tipping point in Walker's descent into madness, in fact the change in him can be tracked throughout the game. Initially his spoken dialogue reflects the familiar and friendly wise-cracking banter most clearly associated with video game protagonist Nathan Drake. Yet as Walker is ordered by the CIA to kill U.S. soldiers (who are themselves implicated in killing civilians) and as he is forced to destroy civilian infrastructure (such as water supplies), he moves from professionally measured engagement with enemies to an expletive-driven one in which he openly celebrates acts of killing as a "rush."

As the game ends, Walker's descent into psychological turmoil is complete. He is confronted with a series of hallucinations of people he has killed, with Konrad's voice, inescapably taunting, locked inside his head: "Why did you do what you did? Why have you forced the U.S. military into violence against you?" This mental collapse is mirrored by the physical battering that Walker's body has endured. His body—crucially, displayed in third person—is the visual manifestation of the player's actions. War and its consequences—both for the player/Walker and the victims—is physically manifested in Walker's battered and war-torn body. In a final plot reveal, the player learns that Konrad in fact committed suicide before Walker arrived in Dubai, and a critical gap opens between the player and Walker as the player realizes that the character has been suffering from increasingly traumatic hallucinations triggered by the appalling acts that the player (directing his actions) has performed.

Spec Ops is a game about war and a game about players who "play war." Walker forces reflection on both through the actions that the player has to undertake in the game and the physical and mental deterioration of the character that are ultimately caused by the player. All of us who play military shooters have figuratively killed thousands of people. Our avatars, like Walker, are now almost certainly suffering from post-traumatic stress disorder (PTSD) as a result of our actions. Walker's character forces us to ask the question "Who is evil? The enemy, Walker, or the player?"

Similar Characters: Isaac Clarke (*Dead Space*), Solid Snake (*Metal Gear*), Wander (*Shadow of the Colossus*)

—Nick Robinson

CATHERINE

(est. 2011)
Franchise: *Catherine*
Developer: Atlus

Catherine is the seductive, titular character of a puzzle game about infidelity. The player as Vincent Brooks, an average, thirty-two-year-old guy in a stable, long-term relationship, first meets Catherine after his girlfriend (Katherine) broaches the topic of marriage. Resistant to the idea, Vincent becomes convinced that gorgeous and carefree Catherine could be his ideal woman. As Vincent deals with this tension between monogamy and infidelity, he has nightmares in which he climbs endless staircases and dodges death traps while being pursued by some deadly, supernatural force. At its core, *Catherine*'s framing of Vincent's relationship with Catherine and Katherine suggests that the sexual liberation of women has resulted in the suffering of men.

Though Vincent is ultimately responsible for whether he remains monogamous or engages in infidelity, he is portrayed as a victim caught in a love triangle not of his own making. Perhaps making it easier for Vincent (and by extension the player) to maintain this belief is that Catherine and Katherine are represented as alternative manifestations of the same person. With a similar look and similar name, Catherine is framed not necessarily as another woman, but rather as an alternative "ideal" type—she is the "sexy" Katherine. This manifestation of Katherine and Catherine is troubling as it resonates with what Angela McRobbie calls the sexual politics of postfeminism. As McRobbie argues, with postfeminism, "feminism is 'taken into account,' but only to be shown to be no longer necessary."[6] This is evidenced in *Catherine*, for though Vincent's infidelity is portrayed as a problem, the problem is not Vincent, but rather the women in his life; the sexual liberation of women is framed as causing Vincent to cheat.

Catherine presents Vincent as a victim of Katherine and Catherine's sexuality. Katherine is portrayed as desirable, for she has a well-paying job and offers romantic stability, but she is also represented as asexual, never touching Vincent or saying she loves him. On the other hand, though Catherine lacks stability, she is represented as spontaneous and hypersexual. Though they express their romantic interest in Vincent differently, Katherine's and Catherine's sexual desires are represented as being their own choice. Vincent is not manipulating them to satisfy his desire. On the surface, this representation of female sexuality seems to be well informed and grounded in the feminist notion that women have choices and are not subservient to men in choosing whom to date or sleep with. However, in continually framing Vincent as the victim of a romantic struggle of which he is not actively a part, *Catherine* reinforces the postfeminist notion that men are now the innocent victims of women: Katherine is presented as overbearing and demanding commitment while Catherine is framed as coercing Vincent by any means necessary, including sex. Consequently, these women are portrayed as antagonists forcing Vincent into decisions that are ultimately in line with conventional patriarchal fantasies: possessing the respectability of a stable relationship while being free to satisfy any unfulfilled sexual desires elsewhere. For one video game critic—*Slate*'s David Auerback—this fantasy is entrenched in the video game industry: "Catherine is a bellwether for what tech culture and gaming have come to mean for a lot of men: a safe playspace from the realities that they believe women force on them."[7]

The game ups the ante even more when it is revealed that Catherine is a succubus, a creature that takes the form of any man's ideal woman to suck their soul. The succubus, whose roots are in European mythology, further repositions women's sexuality as a form of oppression of men. Catherine becomes one of the oppressors of Vincent as she works for a god seeking to maintain the order of the patriarchal gender roles between men and women. His ultimate goal is to force men to either stop dragging their feet with their current significant other and to move toward marriage or to move on to someone else who is more suitable for marriage. Catherine acts as a temptress to force Vincent to choose.

Consequently, an underlying message of the game is that a woman's sexuality is a defining feature of her worth and appeal to men regardless of whatever else she offers. This underlying message undermines the sense of agency Atlus provides Catherine and Katherine over their sexuality. Instead, the game posits that women can only be asexual and goal-oriented or hypersexual and spontaneous. The duality lacks complexity and represents women as one-dimensional human beings. This results in the reinforcement of patriarchal values in which women are subservient to men in that women are framed as needing to be less goal-oriented if they are to be seen as sexual beings. However, the duality as represented in Catherine and Katherine underscores a more significant cultural problem with masculinity. The power possessed by the women in *Catherine* is framed as dangerous to Vincent and, by extension, to men more generally.

The elements that make up *Catherine*'s backstory only further code women as manipulative beings. It also condemns women for having agency over their own sexuality, as the focus is on Vincent being a victim and helpless before the sexual whims of the women in his life. Monogamy, as represented by Katherine, is presented as a trap meant to force responsibility onto men. And sexual promiscuity, as represented by Catherine, is presented as a trap meant to punish men for not behaving responsibly. The game thus operates as a form of postfeminism because it recasts traditional patriarchal values—such as monogamy and the sexual availability of women—as the oppressive result of manipulative women.

As *Slate*'s David Auerback notes, the duality of Katherine and Catherine signifies another problem within the video game industry: the continued presentation of negative stereotypes of women and their role in the world. A portrayal of women's sexuality as dangerous not only marginalizes and dehumanizes women but reinforces patriarchal sexual archetypes that say a woman's sexuality is how society determines her value.

Similar Characters: Dahlia Hawthorne (*Phoenix Wright: Ace Attorney Trials and Tribulations*), Maria (*Silent Hill 2*), Sylvia Christel (*No More Heroes*)

—Daniel Sipocz

CHUN-LI

(est. 1991)
Franchise: *Street Fighter II*
Developer: Capcom

The *Street Fighter II* roster is full of strange, playable characters—electrified green monsters, fire-breathing yoga masters, and perhaps most unusual of all for the early 1990s arcade scene, a young woman. The first playable female character in the series—and one of only a handful of playable female characters throughout the industry at the time—Chun-Li acts as a fundamental touchpoint in the aesthetic and ludic representation of women in video games.

Like her fellow competitors in the *Street Fighter* tournament, Chun-Li has a personal reason for entering the fight—in this case, she is an Interpol officer seeking to avenge the death of her father at the hands of the villainous crime lord M. Bison. Also like her fellow competitors, Chun-Li is designed around a stereotypical national shorthand—she dresses in a modified qipao dress and wears her hair in traditional "ox horn" buns to designate her as the Chinese combatant in the game in much the same way the American representative, Guile, wears a blond flat-top haircut and American flag tattoo. Unlike her fellow competitors, Chun-Li performs and is defined by her gender through her gameplay characteristics and appearance.

Gender theorist Judith Butler suggests that gender is a performance that comprises specific repeated instances and behaviors.[8] Chun-Li's gender is performed on a ludic level through game rules that have historically designated her as smaller, faster, and less damage-dealing in her attacks compared to her male counterparts. Interviews with the designers suggest this ludic gendering was intentional—in fact, one developer suggested her health meter should be half the length of the male competitors' meters because "women are not as strong."[9] While that idea was ultimately vetoed, this dynamic became a repeated ludic shorthand for female characters in other fighting games—one needs only to look to Ling Xiaoyu in the *Tekken* series, Sonya Blade in *Mortal Kombat*, or the thief and healer roles frequently played by women in a variety of role-playing games to see how these performances define femaleness in many video games.

While it is presumptuous to say Chun-Li directly influenced every female character in the entirety of video games, the clear, gender-based distinction in gameplay abilities she portrays was nonetheless relatively rare then. At the same time, in the context of the game, there is no distinction in terms of agency between Chun-Li and her male counterparts. Rather than being a damsel in distress, Chun-Li has her own independent story line and narrative payoffs, and she is capable of defeating any other character. Despite her physical differences, she is by necessity on an equal playing field with the men—she just happens to jump up and down giggling after she beats them.

Chun-Li's aesthetic performance and clothing make it clear that she is on some level objectified and sexualized—her qipao is modified to prominently display her legs and provide the viewer with flashes of her undergarments during her kick animations. This is hardly unusual—the real challenge in studying gender representation in video games is finding a female character not subject to the heterosexual male gaze—but what is unique about the character is the very aspects of her body that are emphasized are also the parts that give her agency and power in combat. As Christopher Williams argues, even though her thighs and legs are eroticized, their muscularity and connection to her kick-heavy offense suggest that her sexuality is tied to an "earned physical extraordinariness." Therefore, her body is not solely there to serve as an ornament for the pleasure of the male viewer in the way so many other female bodies in video games are.[10] Chun-Li's appeal is arguably built around this tension of competing performances of sexuality and violence—her body is both physically attractive and physically destructive.

This seeming dichotomy of a woman meant to be beautiful in physical performance but also equal in power and ability to a male counterpart in a combat performance is illustrated by comments from series designers and artists in *Street Fighter*'s 20th-anniversary art book *SF20*. Akira "Akiman" Yasuda, the artist credited with creating Chun-Li's original design, recounts his struggles with trying to make Chun-Li "cute." Another artist, Kinu Nishimura, provides drawings meant to act as an official design reference for Chun-Li, identifying her official traits as "graceful" and "beautiful" as at the same time he provides substantial instructions regarding the placement and shape of her breasts. Other Nishimura art notes suggest Chun-Li is obsessed with her "lack of physical strength" because of her gender. The tension between objectification and martial artistry that defines Chun-Li is built into her very design, acting as a performance that defines a unique interpretation of gender.

These performances have made Chun-Li one of the most enduring characters in the vast *Street Fighter* pantheon, inspiring future female *Street Fighter* competitors like Cammy and Rose alongside numerous female warriors in other series like *Fatal Fury* and *Tekken*. Although it is clear that male fighter Ryu is the "mascot" of the franchise, Chun-Li is arguably equally important, appearing in every major *Street Fighter* sub-series and spinoff and well-represented in merchandise like T-shirts, comics, and action figures. She plays a major role in most *Street Fighter* movies and television shows and is one of only a handful of *Street Fighter* cast members to be played by two different performers in live-action feature films, with Ming-Na Wen taking on the role in 1994's *Street Fighter* and Kristen Kreuk playing the character as a lead in 2009's *Street Fighter: The Legend of Chun-Li*. Most importantly, it is possible that for many young men and women of the early 1990s, Chun-Li might have been their introduction to the idea that a woman could be as capable as a man both in the virtual world and outside it. The complex and sometimes contradictory nature of Chun-Li's character and enduring legacy is defined by and acts as a perfect case study for how gender is performed and operationalized within the context of video games.

Similar Characters: Bayonetta (*Bayonetta*), Lara Croft (*Tomb Raider*), Samus Aran (*Metroid*)

—Bryan J. Carr

CLEMENTINE

(est. 2012)
Franchise: *The Walking Dead*
Developer: Telltale Games

Clementine first appeared in *The Walking Dead: Season One*, initiating a trend that developed throughout the year following the game's release: the dadification of video games. Along with *Bioshock Infinite* (2013) and *The Last of Us* (2013), *Season One* featured a male protagonist struggling to survive an apocalyptic setting while assuming a fatherly role in his guardianship of a younger-daughter figure. Critics speculated that this narrative phenomenon reflected the anxieties of a demographic of aging developers—men who were growing older, becoming fathers, and facing the terrors of raising their children. Many argued that the dadification trend's eagerness to shield vulnerable daughters restricted these young women's voices, actions, and agencies. However, Clementine's role throughout *The Walking Dead* complicates certain aspects of these assumptions, as the games chronicle her preparations, and then her own efforts, to subsist as a young African American woman in an unrelenting world of undead Walkers and desperate survivors.

We first meet eight-year-old Clementine as she is hiding in her treehouse when protagonist Lee Everett finds her early in *Season One*, shortly after the outbreak of the undead pandemic. Lee quickly adopts a parenting role, but over the course of the game, it becomes apparent that his efforts are not patronizing attempts to coddle a helpless girl. Instead, they are deliberate designs to train Clementine to survive without him. As Kristina Bell, Nicholas Taylor, and Christopher Kampe observe, in *Season One* the player's "choices carry much weight, because during the next season of the game, the player acts through the young girl who is navigating alone and unprotected. To prepare her for this post-apocalyptic world, Lee cuts her hair, teaches her how to shoot a gun, gives her food, consoles her when upset, and bandages her when wounded."[11] Thus Lee's fostering boosts the child's preparedness for her active, independent role in *Season Two* and eventually *Season Three*.

Clementine represents an intersection of three axes of marginalized subjectivities: she is a child, she is female, and she is African American. Each of these identifications is severely underrepresented in video games in general—let alone represented intersectionally in a single character. But as the playable protagonist in *Season Two*, Clementine invites players to assume her role and to experience her positioning as a young African American woman faced with the challenges of surviving undead hordes and inhumanity.

At the outset of *Season Two*, Clementine must protect and support herself alone. In an early, shocking scene, a starving dog attacks her, ripping open her arm. Eventually discovered by a group of survivors, Clementine's youth and gender become centerpieces of a debate on whether her injury is due to an undead bite and whether the group should help her. One character argues he isn't willing to leave a little girl in the woods to die, but others insist that there is no way Clementine could have survived alone. The group's discussion pivots on whether they should place more weight on saving a "little girl" or on the idea that she could be lying, given the implausibility that a little girl could survive in such a world.

They decide to lock her in a shed overnight to test whether the bite will cause her to die and transform. But Clementine escapes, breaks into the house that the group is occupying, and steals supplies to clean and stitch her gaping wound. She then draws the player into her messy suturing in all its gory detail: her raw gash in the screen's foreground, she poises the needle and plunges it into her arm with the combined, harrowing effort of the player's awkwardly mashed buttons and her trembling hands. The player cannot evade the scene. Just as Clementine must confront the agony of closing her own wound, so too must the player.

The Walking Dead does not shy away from such scenes. As Clementine, players cannot turn away from the brutality that consumes her existence. Clementine must kill, dismember, and decide the fate of the people surrounding her. Jess Joho notes her own discomfort when playing as a young female character in such a grisly world, especially at those moments when Clementine is the victim of violence. She remarks that "in a world like *The Walking Dead* . . . narrative relies on the language of gore, death, and hardship. Equal treatment for young female protagonists might seem especially unpleasant in that context. But the alternative sends a clear message about who has a place in videogame worlds, and who doesn't."[12] Playing as Clementine may at times be uncomfortable, but it is an experience that is crucial to the expansion of available representations and subject positions in video games.

As Clementine develops relationships with other survivors, she generates a powerful sense of contingency. Other characters defer to her, desire her approval, and remember and internalize her ruthlessness or her compassion. As a narrative game, *Season Two* hinges on players' choices in order to move forward—which means, by extension, that its world and characters rely on Clementine's actions and dispositions, morphing according to her decisions and indecisions. While this situation could be critiqued due to the doubtfulness that adults would so strongly adhere to the leadership and opinions of a child, the scenario is nevertheless important for the empowerment that it attributes to Clementine. As Adrienne Shaw writes, the importance of diverse representation in video games is not merely a matter of "better" portrayals of marginalized groups but rather of "shaping what types of worlds we can imagine."[13] Precocious, confident, and more levelheaded than most of the game's adults, Clementine grants players the experience of engaging in a world in which a young woman consistently asserts her self-determination, even if that world's obstacles seem insurmountably stacked against her.

Clementine's role is an expression of agency and subjectivity rarely afforded to women—and it is made all the more significant and powerful since she is a young African American woman. Throughout *The Walking Dead*, Clementine's presence is a pivotal one, declaring her belonging as a protagonist in an apocalyptic game and in the medium more generally.

Similar Characters: Elizabeth (*BioShock Infinite*), Ellie (*The Last of Us*), Sherry Birkin (*Resident Evil 2*)

—Stephanie C. Jennings

CLOUD STRIFE

(est. 1997)
Franchise: *Final Fantasy VII*
Developer: Square

Spiky hair, a gigantic sword, and an infinite supply of thousand-mile stares—Cloud Strife, protagonist of 1997's record-breaking PlayStation game *Final Fantasy VII* (*FFVII*), ranks among the most recognizable video game characters of all time. More important than his iconic looks, however, is how Cloud's journey of self-discovery deconstructed conventional gender norms and brought Japan's multi-faceted understanding of masculinity into mainstream gaming.

At a time when most Western players had been socialized with carefree *Super Mario* or the adamant brutes from *Mortal Kombat*, Cloud Strife defied any hero template. Brilliantly enough, his game introduces him in an elaborate ruse—triggering all the expectations the character will eventually subvert—as it delivers the definition of machismo-driven expositions. Cloud first appears by jumping out of a hijacked train. He embodies an impeccable super-soldier, complete with obligatory phallic weapon and moody grunts at the people accompanying him. The masculine cliches continue for a chapter, in which the steadfast warrior meets a young woman as she is threatened by dubious goons, and with the savvy and muscle of archetypical action heroes, Cloud ensures the damsel's escape. But just there, when it seems obvious that *FFVII* will tread the path of countless fairy tales before it—juxtaposing fearless men and distressed women—a mysterious dream initiates the real story.

Several hours of gameplay later, Cloud has been mind-controlled by a telepathic villain, exposed as an unreliable narrator, and even hospitalized by resurfacing childhood trauma. Unable to sustain his hypermasculine facade, he realizes that he was only bystander to the heroic deeds he claimed. Without mercy, *FFVII* pushes its leading man beyond his breaking point until there is nothing left but a shattered boy in a wheelchair. Finally, the game's subversion of gender tropes comes full circle: Cloud's friend Tifa—a girl sporting boxing gloves and sneakers—takes the lead. Entering her friend's subconscious in a surreal montage, Tifa conducts a psychoanalytic session that would have made Freud himself a happy gamer and convinces Cloud to stop repressing his painful memories. When the young man returns to health, stronger than ever before, his soul-searching has laid bare an important lesson: accepting one's vulnerabilities will eventually trump suppressing them. Indeed, Cloud radiated an air of power before, but it is only when he opens up that he becomes truly heroic.

Unlike today's increasingly diverse entertainment landscape, this subversion of tropes and valorization of vulnerability constituted a groundbreaking narrative for late-1990s video games. At a time when the medium was almost exclusively marketed to younger males, games seldom deviated from scenarios of hegemonic masculinity.[14] Their gender norms firmly rooted in a knights-and-damsels dichotomy, most titles limited players' identification to larger-than-life men who always charged ahead without contemplation. Although these power fantasies might have worked from a marketing standpoint, they arguably conveyed a questionable worldview, selling a distorted idea of how men and women were supposed to behave. So when *FFVII* presented a male protagonist who actually reflected his dystopian surroundings and acknowledged his fears, it offered players the chance to engage a new form of heroism: instead of another glorification of unshakable stoicism, Cloud taught them that men were allowed to be weak too—and might, in fact, be stronger for it.

Considering this trope-breaking, it is important to situate Cloud's evolution within the culture of his native country—as such, the character proves deeply embedded within Japanese notions of masculinity as they have emerged in society, folklore, and media alike. With the country's isolationist policies shielding it from foreign influences for centuries, Japan has long maintained a broader variety of normative roles for men compared to many Western cultures. In medieval times, when Central Europe hailed knights as infallible warlords, the equivalent Japanese samurai weren't just revered for martial prowess but were expected to be sophisticated men skilled in poetry, calligraphy, and other fine arts.[15] Although their obligation to *bushido*—the Japanese concept of chivalry—meant constant exercise in self-control, samurai were equally obligated to the tenet of sincerity, compelling them to always admit their shortcomings. In light of this, the story of swordsman Cloud may suddenly read like the slow discovery of bushido virtues: only accepting his true self can eventually complete him as a warrior, and as a man.

However, there is also a more artistic perspective that connects *FFVII*'s character design to the layered gender portrayals in traditional Japanese art forms. In this regard, one of the most significant contributions is the art of kabuki theater, which has remained a cornerstone of Japan's cultural heritage for more than four hundred years. Not only has kabuki traditionally featured men playing female or non-binary roles,[16] it also establishes the character trope of *nimaime*, the sensitive man of otherworldly beauty. Even today, in a post–World War II Japan influenced by Allied occupation and hyper-industrialization, the aesthetics of *bishōnen*—fair-skinned boys whose celestial nature transcends their gender—retain great popularity, appearing in many manga, anime, and movie productions. Accordingly, Cloud Strife might have felt familiar to Japanese players, who could interpret his slender features as those of a *bishōnen* idol or relate to the concept of an introspective, soft-mannered hero; the Western market, however, had to brace for cultural impact.

Fast-forwarding two decades, Cloud's legacy remains—he might not have been the first male character to come to terms with his feelings, but his international stardom allowed him to challenge gender stereotypes and to finally validate vulnerable men as marketable character design. Although there's still an overwhelming majority of alpha-males in video games, Cloud certainly lit the way—all while fighting corrupted industrialists, vengeful father-figures, and, most of all, his own repression.

Similar Characters: Lightning (*Final Fantasy XIII*), Raiden (*Metal Gear Solid*), Squall Leonhart (*Final Fantasy VIII*)

—Jan-Philipp Stein

THE COLOSSI

(est. 2005)
Franchise: *Shadow of the Colossus*
Developer: Team Ico

After a brief introductory sequence, your first task as a player in *Shadow of the Colossus* is to roam a picturesque but seemingly empty land with only a sword-reflected light to guide you. If you persist in this minimalist quest, the game rewards you with an encounter that, when the game was first released in 2005, was quite unlike anything players had experienced, leaving a lasting impression on gaming history. In a small, unassuming clearing, players encounter the Colossus—nameless, lumbering, filling the screen with its enormous body. In due course, fifteen other Colossi are revealed: some the height of skyscrapers, others the size of a bull, some slow, others graceful, and others still that take to the sky on wings that block out the sun. With all their variety in appearance and personality, however, it soon becomes clear that these are no ordinary "monsters." Rather, these silent giants are an integral part of the game world and, at the same time, tragic figures. Though awesome to behold, the Colossi share a common fate: they must all die by the player's hand.

Though it is the Colossi who have made an undeniable impact on video game culture, the game's central plot follows Wander, a hero who travels to the ends of the earth to make a deal with a mysterious spirit, Dormin. Wander desires to resurrect his fallen love, but to do so he must destroy the sixteen Colossi, unwittingly releasing Dormin's powers. Although the plot initially appears familiar—defeat the monsters, save the girl—it becomes increasingly uncertain whether Wander's actions serve a greater good. The Faustian bargain—indiscriminate sacrifice in favor of personal gain—at the root of this narrative reminds us that, on the whole, human progress comes at a cost.

Take, for example, the nature of the Colossi deaths. On the one hand, Team Ico's lead designer Fumito Ueda painstakingly crafted an unforgettable and awe-inspiring challenge: with the elimination of "power-ups"—non-player-controlled characters and other elements that could obscure the player's objective—gameplay is singularly focused. During play, we may find ourselves clutching the fur, scales, or feathers of a Colossi, brought beyond the clouds or to the depths of secluded lakes, enveloped in our grand task. But upon our landing a finishing blow, a cutscene ensues. Regardless of which Colossus has been defeated, the animal lets out a pitiful howl underscored by a haunting violin piece. Immediately, the monster's body unleashes a flurry of black tendrils that arch through the sky, course through Wander's chest, and cause him to collapse. Though he mysteriously awakens in Dormin's shrine and is encouraged to combat the next monster, over time these recurring resurrections mark Wander's body, scoring him with dark patterns like occult symbols. Though Wander's strength grows with each Colossus felled (noticeable in the increased "grip" and "health" meters), his actions clearly take a toll on his humanity. Just as the inspiration for Marlowe's and Goethe's Faust were physicians such as Agrippa von Nettesheim experimenting with what were then regarded as forbidden arts, *Shadow of the Colossus* asks players to question the cost of disrupting an inconceivable natural order for human ends.[17]

It is tempting to follow a trend in Western scholarship of Japanese games and invoke Shinto practices in discussing the Colossi.[18] The concept of *kami*, roughly translated as "deity" or "god," resonates with their otherworldly nature. However, it is likely that the Colossi emerged more from the lives of the game's designers, particularly the life of Fumito Ueda. Coming of age during Japan's "lost decade" of economic stagnation, Ueda witnessed firsthand the hollow promises of man's hubris. Ueda's design principles, which he dubs "design through subtraction," reflect his generation's distrust of excess.[19] Eschewing the trends of game design in which bigger is often construed as better, Ueda stands as a monument of restraint and care.

Just as in *Ico* (2001), the spiritual predecessor of *Shadow of the Colossus*, Ueda presents a remarkably focused philosophy of play that foregrounds the need for players to make do with what they have rather than seek new tools to succeed. As a result of this minimalist approach to design, the player is left with no choice but to explore the habitats of the Colossi, learning their movements and personalities. It is common when playing the game to look to the ground where the Colossi roam in order to ascertain a way to get close enough to them to gain a strategic advantage. Some Colossi appear to hear or even smell our approach, so we must stay close to the ground to avoid attracting attention. In this way, the game blends elements reminiscent of bug-hunting or bird-watching in its gameplay, encouraging its players to pay attention to the landscape of the game but equally to take a more general interest in their environment. Rather than letting us rely on constantly shifting sources of entertainment, Ueda encourages us to look more deeply at the same space to see what we may have missed.

The ponderous, animal-like movements of the Colossi as well as their lichen- and fur-covered bodies tell of a forgotten time, a time, perhaps, when humanity's dominance over the natural world was not so secure. At all times, however, it is clear that it is our intervention in the lives of these creatures that is alien, unwarranted, and unjustified. The game narrative speaks of the wider cost of human progress and particularly the policies of rapid growth and expansion that so negatively impacted modern Japan. At the game's conclusion, the death of the Colossi unleashes a curse upon the world. In a time when natural resources are increasingly consumed in the name of progress, the Colossi are a reminder of the need for caution, balance, and, at times, acceptance of powers greater than ourselves.

Similar Characters: Little Sisters (*Bioshock*), Shades (*Nier*), the Sorrow (*Metal Gear*)

—Conor Mckeown

COMMANDER SHEPARD

(est. 2007)
Franchise: *Mass Effect*
Developer: BioWare

As the "Miracle of Sound" YouTube hit says, "You'll never be better than Commander Shepard." Perhaps more than narrative or gameplay or graphics, Shepard's importance arises from the deeply personal connection some players report feeling for the character. While many game characters inspire emotional reactions and fandoms, few can lay claim to the outpouring of love and fury expressed at the end of *Mass Effect 3*. So passionate were fan reactions to Shepard's demise that BioWare was compelled to release additional cut-scenes in order to offer fans a greater sense of closure and clarify some narrative ambiguities. These deep connections between players and Shepard arguably emerged as a result of Shepard's evolving design. Shepard is flexible and flawed in his or her humanity, inviting players to engage in enacting that humanness through customization, situatedness in the game world, and relationships with other characters.

Shepard is a warrior, a diplomat, and a flawed individual—this tension (and the player's function in shaping it) makes Shepard complex and relatable. The only human member of elite task force Spectre (Special Tactics and Reconnaissance) in the intergalactic-colonizing, alien-fraternizing world of *Mass Effect* (*ME*), Shepard is humanity's professional and moral representative. The player is called upon to step into the shoes of a respected and decorated soldier by dealing with not only militaristic and interstellar concerns such as saving the universe from dangerous enemies but also with empathetic and domestic situations. Shepard may return from a high-octane gun battle to find tempers fraying between crewmates, and the player must decide how best to mediate (or dominate) the situation. That these events are played through by player and character together—rather than through cut-scenes or skippable text—likely creates opportunities for players to connect with Shepard through shared experiences.

Shepard is a carefully constructed combination of a player-created character and a ready-made persona the player is asked to adopt. The earliest character-creation options demonstrate in microcosm techniques employed throughout the series. Customizations of Shepard's appearance (e.g., facial structure and scars), sex (Jane or John), and history (origins and psychological profile) allow character variation within specific constraints. As Shepard's humanity is a key story component, the only species option in the main story is human. The player may determine whether Shepard was born on earth, led a nomadic life moving between space stations, or grew up in a colony. But the outcome for each is the same: Shepard became a Spectre agent for the Alliance military.

Joshua Tanenbaum describes this technique as "bounded agency," an "unusual blend of freedom and constraint . . . [resulting] in unique narrative pleasure."[20] Bounded agency is used throughout the *ME* series with players utilizing a "Paragon/Renegade" system (which allows players to select virtuous or villainous actions) to suggest the manner in which Shepard approaches certain situations rather than truly exerting control over unfolding events. While Kristine Jørgensen believes this distances the player, she acknowledges that it "allows for a more contemplative evaluation." Tanenbaum argues that this participation with Shepard encourages the player to feel their involvement in the story is meaningful.[21]

It is likely that this customization, shared experience, and meaningful engagement contributed to the outpouring of rage following *ME 3*'s ending in which the player is faced with a choice of joining the game's enemy, controlling them, or destroying them completely—all of which result in either Shepard's death or estrangement from his or her crew. Lack of closure of the emotional connections forged between Shepard and other characters has been cited by the RetakeMass-Effect3 movement (a group demanding a new game ending and taking its name from the game's Retake Earth campaign) as one of their reasons for displeasure.

However, the degree to which players forged connections with Shepard were not without limits, and those limits were more likely to be experienced by players from minority groups. *ME*'s twenty-second century is presented as a postgender, postsexuality universe, yet female and gay variations of Shepard ("FemShep" and "GayShep" in fan parlance) contest this in game and out. Although used with fondness for both Shepard's female guise and the nuanced performance of Shepard's voice actor, Jennifer Hale, the moniker "FemShep" shows that to many players, male is default ("BroShep," the nickname for a male Shepard, is only used when differentiation is necessary, while "FemShep" is the given term for a female Shepard). GayShep has been subject to more overt and hostile othering in fan forums and memes. Playing as FemShep hints that the game world's claims to gender equality may be overstated. As Christopher B. Patterson notes, "of the over 7,000 dialogue lines that FemShep has in Mass Effect 3, besides those intended for romance, only two deviate from the lines of [BroShep]." While BroShep displays obliviousness to issues of "reproductive rights and control over the female body,"[22] FemShep expresses solidarity with the female Krogan, Eve, indicating there are some galactic power struggles only FemShep can truly understand.

Similarly, although *ME* was one of the first blockbuster franchises to buck the heteronormative trend, the first game provided only FemShep with a same-sex relationship (though downplayed by BioWare as being with an a-gender alien rather than a true lesbian). In *ME 2*, this progressed to a more overt lesbian option, although critics noted this could have been titillation for straight male players rather than an attempt at diverse representation. *ME 3* finally introduced same-sex relationships for BroShep. Therefore, the development of broadening video game attitudes to sexuality can be charted via Shepard's relationships, even if some fan reactions proved hostile.

It's often claimed players don't care about story. Shepard suggests they may not only care about the story but also about the characters, provided those characters are as complex and varied as the players who guide them.

Similar Characters: The Grey Warden (*Dragon Age: Origins*), Lee Everett (*The Walking Dead*), Revan (*Star Wars: Knights of the Old Republic*)

—Lynda Clark

CRASH BANDICOOT

(est. 1996)
Franchise: *Crash Bandicoot*
Developer: Naughty Dog

Could PlayStation's 3D graphics be used for a new kind of platform game? This was the challenge that Naughty Dog took on when it created *Crash Bandicoot*. Published by Universal Interactive Studio for the first PlayStation (PS One), the *Crash Bandicoot* franchise not only found success in the 3D platformer and party game genres, it was the first chance for Sony Interactive Entertainment to give PlayStation consoles a true mascot able to compete with globally renowned characters like Nintendo's Mario and Sega's Sonic—and Crash managed to hold his own.

Crash Bandicoot began as "Willy the Wombat." However, because the character name already existed for the television show *Taz-Mania*, and since Naughty Dog cofounders Andy Gavin and Jason Rubin intended to change the animal from the start, the final choice fell on a bandicoot (an insectivorous marsupial)—who was later named "Crash" to suggest the character's attitude and skills.

Crash's look doesn't resemble his namesake species, with his orange fur, spiky crest, green eyes, and yellow chest—and these design decisions were all a function of the need for a color continuum that easily displayed on-screen. Crash wears a pair of short blue-jeans with brown gloves and sneakers as his main outfit. Notably, the Crash character design was dependent on the technical limits of both PS One hardware and television resolutions: Naughty Dog explained that the oversized face, spots on the back, gloves and jeans, as well as Crash being orange, were determined more than half by technical needs rather than inspiration.[23] They needed the different elements of Crash's body to be clearly distinguishable on-screen without stressing the hardware of both console and display (the number of polygons and colors were limited by the console's hardware and North American and overseas standards).

Designers Charles Zembillas and Joe Pearson's masterful synthesis of technical and aesthetic features arguably contributed to Crash Bandicoot being one of the very few Western video game characters to enjoy success in the Japanese gaming market, where *Crash Bandicoot* and *Crash Bandicoot 2* sold more than 600,000 and 800,000 units, respectively. The "crazy Looney Tunes" style makes Crash much different from Mario, a typical "white knight" hero, and from Sonic, whose cool attitude and elegance are much different from Crash's boisterous approach to the game. Crash is an animal version of Indiana Jones with the attitude of a joker: an atypical hero who jumps into the adventure and works things out with humor and spirit. This aesthetic alone, however, was not enough to ensure the character's resonance with gaming audiences. His popularity also benefited from the new platform concepts the game introduced: 3D graphics made it possible for Naughty Dog to change the rules of platform games, as Crash was viewed from behind (rather than from the side) and could move toward or away from the screen (rather than merely side to side). Even in places where Crash is played in a classic lateral view, the new graphic capabilities advanced the side-scroller experience by adding depth. This depth, in combination with the then-conventional up/down and left/right moving elements, shepherded players into a new era of three-dimensional landscapes, enemies, and traps.[24]

Moreover, Crash was one of the first 3D characters to feature highly expressive facial animations, helping the game serve as a "killer app" for PlayStation. This advance was not casually taken by Nintendo, driving them to develop character expression modification features in *Super Mario 64*. Importantly, though Crash never speaks, these nonverbal expressions reveal a strong personality, surprising and amusing gamers with his reactions to events, which likely creates an emotional link between players and Crash since humans—even toddlers—are understood to be intrinsically drawn to highly expressive faces.[25] Players do not need a guide or subtitles to experience Crash's personality—it is conveyed through his sculpted, three-dimensional face.

In addition to the deep graphics, dynamic character personality, and colorful aesthetic, *Crash Bandicoot* represents rich and varied gameplay—and marketed together, these features place the three *Crash Bandicoot* titles among the ten best-selling games in PS One history, with more than 21.5 million units sold by 2006 (the year that PS One consoles were discontinued). Crash's success made it possible for Universal Interactive Studios to publish sequels and spin-offs. Moreover, once the agreement with Sony was fulfilled and Naughty Dog was acquired by Sony itself, leaving Crash Bandicoot to Universal, Crash was transported to other platforms, including Nintendo, Xbox consoles, and mobile platforms. The success obtained by Crash Bandicoot on different hardware systems is interesting evidence of his notoriety: he transcended the boundaries of his original hardware reference to become a video game icon *tout court*, as did his predecessors Mario and Sonic.

Ultimately, Crash Bandicoot emerged out of necessity. It was necessary for PlayStation to create a new and original mascot to compete on the same level as Nintendo and Sega; it was necessary for the designers to construct Crash's visualization in a way that would not actually crash the system; and it was necessary for Crash to communicate in expressive nonverbals to convey gameplay feedback, emotion, and likeability. Out of this necessity, a compellingly amusing, quirky, and lighthearted character arose who, to this day, stands on his own as a proud synonym of PlayStation gaming.

Similar Characters: Mario (*Super Mario Bros.*), Sonic (*Sonic the Hedgehog*), Spyro (*Spyro the Dragon*)

—Roberto Semprebene

THE CREATURE

(est. 2001)
Franchise: *Black & White*
Developer: Lionhead Studios

Born out of the desperate prayer of a mother and father, a god is born and cast through space and time into the world of Eden. As the metaphysical orb representing the player's consciousness rushes forward, it pierces the veil that separates the godly womb from the rest of the universe. However, contrary to first-person or third-person video games, the player does not take direct control of a virtual body upon their arrival on Eden. Rather, players are tasked to raise and educate a Creature to serve as the manifestation of their godly will—a Creature that in time, and through the player's interactions and growing bond with it, may seem to transcend the pixels that bind it and add a genuine breath of life to the virtual world.

Gameplay in *Black & White* is mainly structured around the conversion of neutral villages, which allows the player to expand their area of influence, indicated by a circular border around the player's temple and villages. Converting neutral villages is achieved by casting spells and abilities in the presence of villagers. Expanding the area of influence is crucial as the player can only cast spells and interact with objects within their own borders. If the player's hand moves outside these borders, his or her potency will rapidly diminish. Thus players will inevitably have to rely on their Creature that, unlike the player, can cast any ability or perform any action it is taught even when it is outside the player's area of influence. However, the manner in which the Creature will attempt to impress the villagers is entirely dependent on the way it has been raised by the player. While a Good Creature may choose to help the villagers by watering fields and bringing in the crops, an Evil Creature will spread its master's faith by sowing death and destruction throughout the town.

Teaching the Creature how to behave within the world of Eden is therefore a key element in the relationship between players and their Creature. The social nature of the relationship between the player and their Creature reveals itself in the roles they take on as master and apprentice. As the player demonstrates actions and spells to the Creature, the Creature in turn provides the player with a semblance of reflection and memory. Through the player's demonstration of acts in front of it, such as uprooting trees and bringing them to the village store, as well as through the use of positive or negative reinforcement techniques, the Creature will grow and in time adopt these behaviors in its daily routine. However, aside from an ability to draw the attention of the Creature, leash it to certain objects, or prompt it to move to a given location, the player has no way of directly controlling it. The nature of the Creature and its behavior therefore hinges entirely on the player's ability to educate it.

Thus the Creature operates as a highly autonomous, virtual being that the player is invited to continually interact with, situating the relationship between players and their Creature within the category of avatar-as-other in which the avatar is perceived as a distinct entity, allowing players to form highly social relationships with these virtual beings akin to offline social relationships.[26] Indeed, not only does the Creature offer a semblance of awareness by making eye contact with the player through the screen and reacting to the presence of the player's virtual hand, it equally demonstrates a high degree of agency because it is able to act without any intervention by the player.

The Creature therefore adds a semblance of life to the game. This is mainly to be ascribed to the Creature's AI ability to mimic and learn behaviors displayed by the player, providing players with a sense of reciprocity similar to social interaction. Indeed, when players suddenly notice that their demonstration of flicking burning pine trees at a village center is deftly mirrored by their Creature, they cannot help but feel recognized by their digital apprentice. Unwittingly, a belief in the Creature's authenticity, its sentience, creeps up on the player as their attachment to the Creature grows.

While at their core the Creature's actions might be easily explained through the positive- and negative-reinforcement mechanic that the game hinges upon, players nonetheless find themselves partaking in the joy of constructing embellished narratives explaining their Creature's at times startling behavior. The vivid stories related on the game's online forum BWfiles provide an insight into such perceptions of the Creature, which is often featured in these narratives as a quirky sidekick whose wacky adventures players enjoy watching. These stories describe the Creature's kinks and habits, highlighting a perceived personality, such as the story of one such user who notes how their wolf always likes to bring things home, resulting in a serious scolding from its master.[27]

Through its distinct otherness and the mysteries that underlie its at times erratic behavior, the Creature invites players to perceive it as a living, breathing character. While much of the game's mechanics are criticized in the end for their lack of depth,[28] the learning process of your very own Creature remains a fascinating thing to behold. Whether it's setting a forest ablaze, lovingly taking villagers home, or throwing rocks into the depths of the sea at night, the Creature keeps gravitating the player toward the thought that maybe—just maybe—they're not imagining things, that perhaps there's a unique little personality hiding within the code.

Similar Characters: Norns (*Creatures*), the Sims (*The Sims*), Tamagotchi (*Tamagotchi*)

—Ruben Vandenplas

D

THE DARFURIANS

(est. 2006)
Franchise: *Darfur Is Dying*
Developer: Take Action Games

Rahman, Sittina, and their four children are Darfurians: fictional survivors inspired by the atrocities perpetrated by the real-world Janjaweed and the Sudanese army during the intense war of 2003–2004. They are simply drawn, two-dimensional avatars who can only walk, run, carry water, and hide. In fact, the father, Rahman, does nothing at all: he faces certain death if he ventures from the safety of the camp and is caught by the Janjaweed militiamen, perpetrators of the atrocities. Thus his wife and children are the active characters, though they do not speak and they have no facial expressions.

Chased from their destroyed village, the family lives in a camp for displaced people. Survival is hard enough, with a makeshift tent for shelter and meager food rations, but it's made worse by everyday risks to survival. They need water—which can only be found outside the camp. There is a simple but agonizing choice to make: Who will be sent to collect water?

In leaving the relative safety of the camp to walk across the open ground—semi-desert with only a few scrubby trees and rocks for shelter, as well as the carcasses of dead animals—the family members face danger. Jeeps emerge suddenly out of the haze, manned by gun-wielding militiamen hunting them down. As an adult Darfurian male, Rahman cannot move at all due to the risk of death. Sittina and her elder daughters can do so, but they face the risk of rape. The smaller children can hide more easily, but they cannot run as fast or carry as much water.

The family lives in a narrow world, its horizons limited by dust, confined to a camp with a few rectangular plots. The elemental simplicity of the tasks—fetching water, running across a simple bare landscape, hiding behind the few spare objects in that denuded landscape, using water to grow a few crops on a small piece of ground, then repeating the exercise—means that the gamer is likely to soon grow bored. But this is close to the mundane real life of a war-displaced person: the simplest task is difficult and fraught with peril, and bare life demands that it's repeated over and over again, with no amount of familiarity dulling the real dangers in attendance. There's no winning in this game, only surviving—a fair reflection of the plight of the Darfurians.

The family is nonetheless an oddity among Darfurians. While the parents (Rahman, Sittina) and two children have Arab Muslim names (Elham, Mahdi), two of the other children have southern Sudanese names (Abok, Deng), and two have generic African names (Poni and Jaja). It is not clear if the designers wanted to make the characters representative of Sudan as a whole, or if they simply didn't know much about Darfur.

It is striking who the characters are *not*. They are not foreign saviors or international aid workers (unlike the World Food Program video game *Food Force*). Nor are they Hollywood celebrities serving as humanitarian ambassadors (imagine a game with Angelina Jolie as explorer of the dungeons of a human cataclysm in a post-apocalyptic world of storied humanitarian disaster). They are also not UN peacekeepers or U.S. special troops dispatched to target and eliminate the Janjaweed (the most obviously tempting gameplay for a designer). The simple focus on a modest family and their daily survival makes for a stripped-down narrative.

But another character intrudes. The gameplay is interrupted by messages from the *Save Darfur Coalition*, which enables players to send a real-world, automated note to the U.S. president; petition Congress to pass legislation to assist Darfur's war-affected people; or join a student activist group and spread the game virally. The gamer is repeatedly snatched from the virtual Darfurian camp into his or her real persona and given the option of a simple task with the promise that it will help "Save Darfur." By this, the gamer becomes a character in this alternate plot. For sure, anyone who plays *Darfur Is Dying* can distinguish the real world from the virtual one. But the real-world actions of the gamer—also mundane and everyday—contain an element of a magical script.

Though American campus genocide-activism on Darfur built a huge constituency of young people more deeply aware of atrocities across the world, it did not do much to stop the killing in Darfur.[1] That wasn't because of lack of effort or lack of attention of senior policymakers in Washington DC, but because the basic script was flawed: the story was written by outsiders who, however well-meaning, did not grasp the complexities of the Darfur crisis or confront the reality that a crisis such as this could be resolved only by the Sudanese people themselves, not by foreign saviors.[2]

The game was launched in April 2006 at Save Darfur: Rally to Stop Genocide in Washington, DC, the winning game in the mtvU Darfur Digital Activist competition, and conceived and developed by students at the University of Southern California. The Darfur campaign reached a peak five months later with International Day for Darfur on September 17 when George Clooney addressed the UN Security Council and predicted millions of imminent deaths, telling the council that Darfur represented "your Rwanda, your Cambodia, your Auschwitz" and that the choice was between dispatching peacekeepers or burial shrouds. In fact, no UN troops were dispatched, but the massacres had already ended; his remarks were hyperbolic. But Darfur remained a miserable, deprived, and conflicted place.

And, sadly, it remains so today. An updated version of *Darfur Is Dying* would have the same characters, ten years older, facing the very same set of tasks and dangers: a simple, repetitive game with no winners, telling a story a decade on that is sadder even than its designers imagined.

Similar Characters: The Africans (*Deliver the Net*), Civilians (*Spec Ops: The Line*), Drebin 893 (*Metal Gear Solid 4*)

—Alex de Waal

DESMOND MILES

(est. 2007)
Franchise: *Assassin's Creed*
Developer: Ubisoft Montreal

Assassin's Creed tells the story of a centuries-old war between Templars and Assassins. Both believe they promote the betterment of society, but the Templars achieve order through control while the Assassins fight to preserve individual freedoms. Although each game in the franchise takes place in a vastly different historical time and place, one character—the main protagonist, Desmond Miles—threads together these disparate tales through a postmodern narrative trope: the triviality of the human body.

Unlike other video game heroes, Desmond seems ordinary: he is a twenty-five-year-old bartender in modern-day New York who has no goals or notable skills. Yet because his ancestors were renowned Assassins, Desmond is kidnapped by the Templars, who use advanced technology to tap into his genetic memory sequences. This enables them to separate Desmond's consciousness from his body and to infuse his mind with that of his ancestors. Though Desmond drives the overarching narrative, he is rarely a playable character. Gameplay focuses on the fast-paced adventures of the Assassins, who all possess compelling personalities and separate life experiences, characters such as Altaïr Ibn-La'Ahad (1165–1257; Syria), Ezio Auditore da Firenze (1459–1524; Italy), and Ratonhnhaké:ton (1756–unknown; Colonial America).

In this way, Desmond functions simply as a source of continuity and drives the plot forward as a vehicle by which players experience the past through the context of the present. Unfortunately, many players view Desmond as little more than a bothersome MacGuffin: he exists to move the story forward, but he provides little substance. The irony is that without Desmond, there would be no continuity or means of jumping into the bodies of the ancestors. But Desmond's cultural significance extends beyond his usage as a trite narrative device: he becomes more than a MacGuffin and symbolically represents a form of transcendence from the necessity of the human body.

Beneath the surface-level story line of a centuries-old war, a more compelling narrative exists recounting the events of an ancient race that lived centuries before recorded history: the Isu (First Civilization). The Isu created advanced technology and ruled over early humans. Three mysterious Isu (Jupiter, Juno, and Minerva) preserve their consciousness throughout time and guide the Assassins at critical points in history. They speak to Desmond and compel him to obtain the power necessary to stop an imminent solar flare from destroying the planet in 2012.

When Desmond discovers his ancestral heritage, he escapes from the Templars, joins a team of modern Assassins, and helps uncover ancient artifacts. He ultimately develops feelings for a fellow Assassin, Lucy Stillman, but when the Isu reveal that Lucy will betray him, they take over Desmond's body like a puppet and force him to murder her himself. His own body is used against him in a way he cannot control. The trauma of this sends Desmond into a coma in which he spends an entire game existing in a technology-induced virtual environment and completely cut off from his real-world body.

Desmond's primary story arc ends in a manner that embodies the Assassin's Creed: "Nothing is true. Everything is permitted." A basic interpretation of the creed promotes wisdom over blind faith and advocates freedom over control. In Desmond's final moments, he has the opportunity to end the puppet-like control that different forces wield over him, and he chooses to sacrifice his body by using an object of power to deflect the solar flare. In this act, he not only represents freedom of choice as extolled in the creed, but with his death, he fully transcends his attachment to his own body.

In many ways, Desmond's body becomes increasingly unnecessary throughout the franchise. It is his mind that travels through time and his identity that evolves into that of a master Assassin. Though he is aided by the technological innovations of science fiction, the tools that enable Desmond to transcend his body resonate with the implications of science and technology today. Real-world futurists such as Michio Kaku[3] and Ray Kurzweil[4] describe and predict the ways that technology may be able to extend life and ultimately enable humans to transcend biology. Thus Desmond's character may tap into a cultural zeitgeist that feeds into our desire to use technology to extend ourselves beyond our own frail bodies.

Popular opinion of Desmond is mixed. In an article by *PlayStation Universe*, Desmond is classified among the worst protagonists: "Stacked up against the cool, calculated Altair and womanizing, exuberant Ezio Auditore, Assassin's Creed's boring barman ends up being distinctly underwhelming. . . . It's impossible to shake the feeling of pure monotony when stepping into Desmond's shoes."[5] Such sentiments are not uncommon among core players. And as if to acknowledge these criticisms, *Assassin's Creed Syndicate* (the ninth main installment), features a small, yappy corgi dog named "Desmond." The use of the name hardly seems a compliment.

However, in a time when white, hypermasculine protagonists were the norm, Desmond emerged as a more subdued protagonist with an ambiguous ethnicity. His tanned complexion and his facial features showcase his rich and diverse ancestral heritage. He is psychologically complex, with two sides to his persona. On one hand, he functions as a blank slate by taking on the characteristics of others, but as the games move forward, he learns acrobatic skills and abilities to become more like the master Assassins whose skills he subsumes. He also possesses an evolving individuality because he comes to terms with his shifting personal identity as he realizes his lineage and accepts that he is a part of something much bigger than himself.

Not all players will experience the depth of Desmond's character. The details illuminating his past, his evolving identity, and his psychological journey are largely optional experiences, and those who seek only the action-packed gameplay of the Assassins may never know why Desmond is compelling. Though his body dies, he impacts the story line in later games as the modern Assassins mourn his absence. Still, fan theories and clues suggest that Desmond's consciousness may have actually survived in the virtual environment, hinting at the possibility that he completely transcended the need for his own physical form and became fully posthuman.

Similar Characters: Fei Fong Wong (*Xenogears*), Simon Jarrett (*Soma*), Squall Leonhart (*Final Fantasy VIII*)

—Aubrie Adams

DUKE NUKEM

(est. 1991)
Franchise: *Duke Nukem*
Developer: Apogee Software

The violent, misogynistic, and unapologetic attitude of gunslinger Duke Nukem caused a stir of controversy in the 1990s when his video games—*Duke Nukem* (1991), *Duke Nukem II* (1993), *Duke Nukem 3D* (1996), *Duke Nukem: Time to Kill* (1998), and *Duke Nukem: Zero Hour* (1999)—were released. With his third title banned in Brazil and censored in Australia, Nukem quickly became a poster child for video game censorship and an icon of the emerging first-person shooter genre, which included games (such as *Doom* and *Wolfenstein 3D*) that depicted increasingly realistic violence and gore.

Culturally, Nukem personifies a late-twentieth-century aesthetic that scholars in disciplines as diverse as literature, film, and philosophy have termed "transgressive." At once boundary-pushing and regressive, the transgressive aesthetic is characterized by pornography, profanity, anarchy, violence against women, drugs, alcohol, mutilation, and the dark cityscapes of modern capitalism, while at the same time its male figures re-create traditional Western notions of masculinity.

Similar to the porn-obsessed, steroid-injecting, murderous protagonist Patrick Bateman in Bret Easton Ellis's magnum opus *American Psycho*, Nukem represents what many social activists of the period, building on the momentum of the 1960s, 1970s, and 1980s, vehemently challenged: an omnipotent masculinity that fuses sex and violence with a misogynistic view of the world and the women who inhabit it. For feminists like Gloria Steinem and Kate Millet, these transgressive characters re-created the harmful gender stereotypes and sexist violence that the equality movements sought to overcome.

While the politics of sex and gender are central to understanding the significance of Duke Nukem and his relationship to his social milieu, an analysis of this American bad boy would be incomplete if his transgressive masculinity were not situated within the economic landscape of the late twentieth century. With the rise of lifestyle advertising in the 1980s, its emphasis on defining masculinity through commodity-based lifestyles, and the growing role of women in the workforce, the traditional lines between masculine producer and feminine consumer in America continued to blur, creating a kind of "masculinity in crisis" as explored in scholarly articles, films, and literature of the period—most notably Chuck Palahniuk's classic *Fight Club* (1996).

In contrast to the groups of men Palahniuk depicts who struggle to find a masculine sense of self in their office jobs and the empty promises of the marketplace, Nukem embodies the brutal, regressive male fantasy Palahniuk's narrator seeks to recover by fighting in basements. Unlike the latest consumer trend, or the effeminate roles of capitalist production, Nukem's masculinity is both inflexible and undiminished in its machismo. In the face of postmodernism's blurring of sex and gender lines and feminism's threat to the hegemony of male violence, Nukem's bulging biceps and firm grasp on the handle of his semi-automatic rifle are as rigid as the masculine ideal promulgated in the presidential ads of Ronald Reagan, who infamously rebuked an American public that he believed was too passive and too "afraid to let [American soldiers] win" the war in Vietnam.[6]

Rather than "pull out" of a war with aliens, or the crisis of an outdated and socially constructed masculinity, Nukem stands strong as ever as he labels weaker characters in his games "pussies" and loads his rocket launcher to kill a three-breasted alien queen trying to take over the earth. Like Palahniuk's misogynistic anti-hero Tyler Durden, Reagan, and the other hard-nosed men of the period, Nukem is not afraid to get the job done, even if it entails large-scale, brutal acts of violence and murder. As he often exclaims, in between trips to the strip club and pornographic movie theater, "It's time to kick ass and chew bubble-gum, and I'm all out of gum!"

Outside video games, this attitude was embodied in the antics of superstar wrestler Stone Cold Steve Austin, whose womanizing, Budweiser-drinking, "kick ass and take names later" persona ushered in the extremely successful 1990s "Attitude Era" in Vince McMahon's *World Wrestling Federation*. This effect was also apparent in chart-topping records: Eminem's landmark *The Slim Shady LP* (1999) was lambasted as a dangerous influence on music not because of his inability to rap but because he unflinchingly glorified drug use, murder, and violence against women. Like these other icons of popular culture, Nukem helped to reify the transgressive aesthetic. While doing so, he solidified himself as an important character in video game history, aggressively pushing precedents set by characters in controversial games like *Doom* and *Wolfenstein 3D*. With his unconventional interest in pornography, profanity, drugs, alcohol, and violence against women, Duke Nukem emerged as a transgressive male to be reckoned with, and one who remains pertinent to the history of video game characters and the history of their ever-changing relationship to different social, cultural, and historical conjunctures.

After Duke Nukem, gamers have been presented with male protagonists who similarly strive to regain control over their ever-changing worlds as they engage in extreme acts of sexual aggression, substance abuse, and violence. Most notably, Claude in *Grand Theft Auto III* (2001) has sex with prostitutes before he kills them, blows up his girlfriend, and is, as Rockstar Games notes, "stronger and in control" unlike other men who are "weaker and frantic."[7] Similarly, the once family-friendly Conker, from *Conker's Bad Fur Day* (2001), begins the game intoxicated and helps a pimp-like character subdue three rebellious women.

Ultimately, despite the massive flop of *Duke Nukem Forever* (2011), Duke Nukem remains an important figure in video game history. Wandering through urban settings filled with pornographic theaters and sex shops, quoting Clint Eastwood characters, drinking beer and popping pills, ordering kimono-clad Japanese strippers to "shake it baby!" as he throws money at their feet, and screaming "eat shit and die!" at a female overlord before blasting her with a rocket launcher, Duke Nukem is the transgressive protagonist par excellence. Both a boundary-pusher in the 1990s, as well as a lingering influence on video games today, Duke Nukem reminds us that sex, drugs, violence, and male power are as much a part of video game history as a pair of Italian plumbers and an Atari joystick.

Similar Characters: Claude (*Grand Theft Auto III*), Conker (*Conker's Bad Fur Day*), Sam (*Serious Sam*)

—Adam Szetela

DYSENTERY

(est. 1971)
Franchise: *The Oregon Trail*
Developer: MECC

Against a bitmap-mountain backdrop, pixel-horned oxen pull your party along in a covered wagon. On this six-color journey of westward expansion—from Independence, Missouri, to Oregon City, Oregon—an enigmatic villain lurks. Not a monster or beast or witch with health points or an Achilles' heel, this baddie offers little warning and strikes you dead. The baddie is Dysentery—and if you're playing *The Oregon Trail*, there's a pretty good chance it'll do you in. When dysentery kills a character, the game offers some context: the date, how hot it is, how little food you have, and how long before the next landmark . . . just in case death by diarrhea isn't bad enough. Through these representations, death is more than simply a game mechanic, but a lesson in early American pioneer life.

First distributed in American public schools in the 1980s and 1990s, this wildly popular role-playing, resource management game was designed to teach students about westward migration in nineteenth-century North America. In the game, the character Dysentery appears only in text form, in a warning that the player or a party member "has dysentery," with the nigh-inevitable follow-up that someone has "died of dysentery." Despite this neat and tidy manifestation, 1840s American pioneers suffered far messier encounters. From the Greek *dys* (bad) and *enteron* (intestine), the condition is characterized by large-intestine inflammation and necrosis due to bacterial or protozoan infection, is usually marked by bloody diarrhea,[8] and ends, if untreated, with death from dehydration.

Death by dysentery in *The Oregon Trail* is somewhat pioneering in itself because Dysentery functions less as a penalty[9] and more as a historical villain—a key component of the title's status as an early educational game. Although death is swift and clean—without all the messiness of the actual disease—there is no convenient respawn or annoying corpse run. The dead are simply dead. Players are confronted with a black screen that one early reviewer called "oppressive," and if the player does not decide to hold a funeral, the trail party suffers from low morale. The seriousness of this funeral was perhaps made more impressive given that players at the time often chose to name their party characters after people they knew, and in the game these names are displayed with epitaphs upon digital gravestones. In contrast, it was often common for shifty schoolchildren to give party members silly or lewd names, and it's a little less grievous when someone named "Poopster" is dying of dysentery. More notably, if the game disk's write-protection in early versions were turned off, a player could create a custom epitaph for these deaths, and subsequent players would then encounter the same epitaph on their own journeys. Hence we have the epitaph "Here lies andy; peperony and chease," a meme said to be a player-generated epitaph inspired by a 1990s Tombstone Pizza commercial and saved on a bootlegged copy of the game.

In the game, Dysentery is but one of many possible setbacks—including cholera, measles, typhoid fever, snake bites, broken legs, drowning, flipped wagons, thieves, dying cattle, gunshot wounds—all of which are encountered while fording rivers and hunting buffalo for food. Although memetically representative of the threats encountered by early pioneers—and indeed, it's estimated that 9 of 10 deaths were caused by disease—Dysentery should have been second to cholera in villain status, according to historian John D. Unruh. Despite being a secondary historical threat, Dysentery is central to what scholar Priscilla Wald might call the game's "outbreak narrative": a "contradictory but compelling story" of human interdependence/connection, scientific/evolutionary authorities, and ecological balance/disaster.[10] Notably, Dysentery's simplified appearance in *The Oregon Trail*—elements of disease identification, emergence, network dispersion, and containment having been glossed over—is key to its significance. On the one hand, reconfiguring a complex contagion to simple representations with sanitized consequences may be effective in bringing its historical importance to light and into context for young students. On the other hand, Dysentery's reduction to a two-hit villain (infect and kill, as determined by a random number generator) with tidy and kitschy effects (a customizable tombstone) may downplay how the disease unevenly affected disparate populations on the basis of wealth and access to reliable sanitation, and how this in turn affected America's westward expansion and civil progression more broadly.

Dysentery, then, as an unseen villain of *The Oregon Trail* and one of the earliest representations of disease in video games, calls into consideration the ways that diseases are invoked as mechanics and narratives—especially as graphics and narrative norms have evolved. As Wald notes, outbreak narratives may have consequences in that "they influence how both scientists and the lay public understand the nature and consequences of infection, how they imagine the threat, and why they react so fearfully to some disease outbreaks and not others at least as dangerous and pressing."[11] Since the release of *The Oregon Trail*, the mechanics and narratives of in-game diseases have grown in sophistication: Rust Lung, of *Gears of War* (2006), is a deadly condition caused by exposure to imulsion (a fictional energy source) and offering a commentary on contemporary energy and environmental policies; the Green Poison pox of *The Division* (2016), which spreads through tainted dollar bills released on Black Friday, resonates with our contemporary fear of terrorism; and there is the entire genre of zombie games (e.g., *Walking Dead*), which often highlights the interplay of mortality and morality via the kill-or-be-killed gameplay dynamic. Considered against a backdrop of SARS, H5N1, Ebola, and the Zika virus, it seems as though our contemporary anxiety about global pandemics infects video games as well. Seen from this perspective, it is perhaps no wonder that villainous Dysentery continues to hold a nostalgic place for many a gamer. Removed from the realities of the disease itself—which continues to infect and kill a number of people to this day—*The Oregon Trail* offers players a space where they can stare mortality in the face and respond with the epithet "peperony and chease."

Similar Characters: Cancer (*That Dragon, Cancer*), Corrupted Blood (*World of Warcraft*), Rust Lung (*Gears of War*)

—Jaime Banks

E

ELAINE MARLEY

(est. 1990)
Franchise: *The Secret of Monkey Island*
Developer: Lucasfilm Games

In *The Secret of Monkey Island* (1990), players first learn about Governor Elaine Marley when they encounter one of her campaign posters on the Mêlée Island docks. Thereafter, they find themselves on a quest to prove their pirate mettle by stealing the fabulous Idol of Many Hands from her mansion, leading to a direct confrontation with the governor herself. Following this rather inauspicious introduction, Elaine goes on to become a central character in the *Monkey Island* series, playing a prominent role in all five games. That said, her inclusion as one of video gaming's greatest characters perhaps raises a reasonable question: Why not Guybrush Threepwood instead? Guybrush, after all, is the playable protagonist of the critically acclaimed *Monkey Island* graphic adventure games. That said, Guybrush epitomizes a comedic, "bumbling hero" archetype already familiar to adventure gamers in 1990 thanks to earlier characters like Roger Wilco (*Space Quest*). Elaine, on the other hand, represents an important development in the depiction of women in video games. Although Guybrush almost immediately falls in love with (and later marries) Elaine, and the romantic advances of the villainous undead pirate LeChuck arguably serve as the games' central conflict, the series avoids relegating her to the status of merely damsel in distress. Rather, the games consistently depict her as smarter, braver, and more capable than the men who surround her—traits that set her apart from her video game predecessors and establish Elaine Marley as the medium's first significant attempt to problematize and redefine the familiar damsel role.

Players first encounter Elaine when she is introduced as the governor of Mêlée Island. Later installments expand her gubernatorial reach to encompass the entire "Tri-Island Area." Her depiction as a woman in a position of political power is a notable rarity. While Guybrush is initially struck by Elaine's beauty, at no point do the games overtly sexualize her character. For instance, she dresses throughout the series in what might be described as gender-neutral fictional pirate garb: a tunic worn over a blouse, pantaloons, boots, and a kerchief. More importantly, the games consistently portray Elaine as an intelligent, resourceful woman, handy with a cutlass or blunderbuss, and more than capable of taking care of herself. As Clara Fernández-Vara observes, "Elaine was self-sufficient, and probably the cleverest person on Mêlée Island."[1] Whereas Guybrush often blunders his way through the obstacles in his path and LeChuck is the very portrait of buffoonish bluster, Elaine reliably demonstrates a capacity for forethought and strategic planning throughout the series. Her male counterparts' shenanigans not only provide points of contrast that underscore Elaine's strength, they also give her reasons to be strong—namely, to keep Guybrush out of trouble and defy LeChuck's iniquitous ploys to win her affection. In turn, the trio's interpersonal dynamics challenge familiar representations of gendered power in a way prior video games had not yet attempted.

While Elaine's resourcefulness is a fixture throughout the series, it manifests itself most strikingly during *The Secret of Monkey Island*. Near the end of the game's first act, LeChuck kidnaps Elaine with the intent of making her his undead bride. This development would seemingly set up the damsel-in-distress trope so familiar in popular culture. When Guybrush finally arrives at the chapel just in time to interrupt the ghoulish nuptials, "Elaine" is revealed to be two monkeys, one standing atop the other's shoulders, wearing a wedding dress and disguised by a veil. The actual Elaine has already engineered her escape and arrived on the scene with a plan to vanquish LeChuck once and for all—a plan Guybrush derails by bursting in to "save the day." Similarly, in *Monkey Island 2: LeChuck's Revenge* (1991), Elaine again defies player expectations by coming to Guybrush's rescue after he experiences a mishap involving fabled pirate treasure and a modest stash of dynamite.

Based on such actions, Esther MacCallum-Stewart identifies Elaine as an early example of a female video game character who "allowed feminine expression which did not necessarily always conform to passive ideals of the damsel in distress."[2] Furthermore, Anastasia Salter suggests the *Monkey Island* series portrays Elaine as "more successful, level-headed, and intelligent" than Guybrush, to whom she only gives the time of day "when her own ambitions are met."[3] By exercising agency within what is essentially Guybrush's narrative, Elaine subverts familiar video game representations of the "love interest" or "kidnapped princess" by serving as the author of her own fate and, in the process, distinguishing herself from many female characters both before and since.

Following the departure of series creator Ron Gilbert after *LeChuck's Revenge*, later installments were regrettably less consistent in their portrayals of Elaine as a self-sufficient woman of action. For instance, she spends significant portions of *The Curse of Monkey Island* (1997) transformed into a golden statue by a cursed engagement ring unwittingly gifted to her by Guybrush. Nevertheless, she continues to play an instrumental role in repeatedly thwarting the re-resurrected LeChuck's nefarious schemes throughout the series.

In addition to being a memorable character from a beloved franchise, Elaine takes on added cultural significance by challenging our taken-for-granted beliefs about the roles of women in video games and offering an alternative to masculine hegemony. While the *Monkey Island* series' progressive approach to representation includes other strong female characters like Carla the Sword Master, the mysterious Voodoo Lady, and pirate-hunter Morgan LeFlay, it is Elaine who undoubtedly shines brightest. In fact, Elaine's refusal to accept the damsel-in-distress role is evident from the earliest moments of *The Secret of Monkey Island*, when a pirate recounts the governor's history with LeChuck: "He's the guy that went to the Governor's for dinner and never wanted to leave. He fell for her in a big way, but she told him to drop dead. So he did." In turn, Elaine Marley's defiant self-sufficiency represents a piratical shot across the bow that signaled a profound shift in representations of gender in video games.

Similar Characters: Alyx Vance (*Half-Life*), Grace Nakimura (*Gabriel Knight*), Maureen Corley (*Full Throttle*)

—Jess Morrissette

ELLIE

(est. 2013)
Franchise: *The Last of Us*
Developer: Naughty Dog

Ellie is the secondary player character in *The Last of Us* and the player character of the *Left Behind* downloadable content. Ellie is a fourteen-year-old survivor of a catastrophic epidemic who is described by Naughty Dog's creative director Neil Druckmann as being "mature beyond her years." Her maturity develops because she grows up in an oppressive, military quarantine zone and has to learn to fend for herself. In many ways, *The Last of Us* is about witnessing Ellie's coming of age in a post-apocalyptic world. Ellie's character is important because it highlights the maturation of commercial video games and an associated commercial success, suggesting an increased acceptance of less stereotypically portrayed video game characters.

Players may form a strong emotional engagement with Ellie due to gameplay mechanics. For instance, the mechanics establish a sense of interdependence between Ellie and Joel and, by extension, the player. During a scripted gameplay sequence in *The Last of Us*, Joel is being hung upside down after getting stuck in a trap and Ellie is tasked with cutting a rope to get Joel down. In turn, the player's goal is to control Joel to shoot enemies to protect Ellie. Druckmann mentions in an interview conducted in "From Dreams—The Making of *The Last of Us*: Left Behind" that mechanics such as these are meant to portray the relationships between characters such as Joel and Ellie in *The Last of Us* and between Ellie and Riley in *Left Behind*. These mechanics include "survival," "loyalty," and ultimately "love," that is, the love between a parent and a child, and the love between two young women.[4] For instance, when Joel and his companions are escaping from enemies, everyone abandons him but Ellie. Likewise, in *Left Behind*, Riley saves Ellie from the Infected attempting to bite her instead of leaving her, and vice versa. This causes both of them to be bitten by the Infected, and they spend the remaining time they have together. The reason for Ellie's loyalty is because, as Ashley Johnson mentions in the documentary, all Ellie has is these relationships, and hence her friends become her everything. These relationships are embedded in the game mechanics, which enable players to feel attachment to Ellie via her relationships with other characters and simultaneously to empathize with Ellie through their personal experience with loved ones.

Character development is also emphasized through gameplay mechanics, which leads to an even stronger interpersonal connection between Ellie and the player. For instance, as Ellie's character develops throughout the game, her relationship with Joel is solidified through her gameplay interactions with him. At first, Ellie is restricted to the role of warning Joel about enemy threats, but as Joel's trust in her increases, she is armed with a pistol and shotgun, and ultimately she becomes fully independent when the player controls her in the Winter chapter. Likewise, the theme of "the loss of innocence" is highlighted in the Spring chapter of *The Last of Us* when Joel's gameplay mechanic of boosting Ellie is transformed. Instead of responding immediately to the player character's gameplay prompt, Ellie takes awhile before coming to Joel. The transformation of this gameplay mechanic highlights Ellie's emotional loss when she has killed a human being. *Left Behind*'s gameplay mechanics are used to highlight the developing relationship between Riley and Ellie as well. For example, at the conclusion of Ellie's water-gun fight with Riley at the mall, they kiss. Because players have control over the player characters when performing actions such as these, they tend to form a deeper impression of the characters.

The care with which these mechanics are implemented results in a nuanced representation of Ellie's lesbian identity. Ellie's sexual identity as a lesbian is not highlighted purposely as a plot element in *The Last of Us* or *Left Behind*. There are no heavy-handed references to Ellie's sexual identity. It is an important part of her identity, but it is not portrayed voyeuristically as the only part of her identity that matters. Rather, Ellie's characterization as a lesbian is realistically portrayed and introduced naturally when the game reveals her character's sexuality during her kiss with Riley in *Left Behind*. When executed correctly, lesbian, gay, bisexual, and transgender (LGBT) issues can be integrated in video games to highlight that the LGBT community is part and parcel of society.

These mechanics and representations matter because video games can be used to influence players' attitudes toward and perceptions of particular topics through what is called "procedural rhetoric."[5] Empathy may be achieved in video games such as through the shifting perspectives in *The Last of Us* when the game switches the player's control from Joel to Ellie in the Winter chapter of the game. By playing as Ellie, the player understands that video game characters are not static and can change to become more independent (but still vulnerable) as the game progresses. This type of character representation through gameplay mechanics is significant in terms of offering a multidimensional portrayal of video game characters rather than a stereotypical lens through which to view them.

Ellie's nuanced representation highlights how narrative and gameplay mechanics help in the advancement of video game characters by challenging possible stereotypical conceptions of the players through the nuanced representation of video game character. From becoming more independent and less reliant on Joel—who in turn provides her with more weapons to assist him during the gameplay fights—to her developing relationship with Riley, which progresses from a water-gun fight to the culmination of their kiss, Ellie is one of the few leading video game characters who paves the way for more inclusiveness in video game character representation. Due to her living in a post-apocalyptic environment, Ellie is an independent and multidimensional character who has her own unique personality and is an advancement over stereotypical female character representations in other video games.

Similar Characters: Clementine (*The Walking Dead*), Kaldwin (*Dishonoured 2*), Max Caulfield (*Life Is Strange*)

—Toh Weimin

G

GANDHI

(est. 1991)
Franchise: *Civilization*
Developer: MPS Labs

Having a nuclear weapon used on you by Gandhi is something of a rite of passage for *Civilization* players. Those who aren't familiar with the character's notorious propensity toward atomic warfare are often bemused when they discover a character with such a real-world reputation for peace and reconciliation being so profoundly hostile in-game. This isn't just a one-off, either: in the *Civilization* series, Gandhi is usually strongly inclined to use nuclear weapons as soon as the appropriate technology is acquired, which gives a newfound, strategic angle to dealing with this otherwise quite peaceful neighbor. This always strikes the player as being somewhat puzzling, given the real-life Gandhi's reputation for pacifism, diplomacy, civil rights, and freedom[1] rather than monstrously aggressive nuclear warmongering. This peculiar contrast has made Gandhi famous far beyond any of the other *Civilization* leaders—who are, in essence, personal faces designed to reflect the decisions of each AI nation as a whole and give a greater sense of human interaction to the diplomacy systems of *Civilization*—even though this strange preference for nuclear war was originally the result of nothing more than a trivial bug.[2]

The original *Civilization* (1991) features fifteen civilizations, each with a particular leader. The American civilization is led by Lincoln, the Egyptian by Ramesses, the French by Napoleon, the Roman by Julius Caesar, and so forth—and the Indian by Gandhi. Each leader has a unique image that appears when the player is in conversation with them and a selection of traits to define their behaviors: some are "civilized," some "friendly," and some "aggressive." This is a system that received significant criticism (although not to the extent that *Civilization*'s sister game, *Colonization* [1994], received for its strongly Western-oriented outlook and the elision of historically important elements of the 1500s, such as slavery) as both a significant simplification and potentially a condescension toward certain historical civilizations. Under this system,

Gandhi is given an aggression rating of 1, the lowest in the game. However, there is a problem: the nations are able to change their political choices, and the "democracy" political choice reduces aggression by 2. This is fine for all the other characters whose aggression ratings are higher than 1, except that when Gandhi's 1 is reduced by 2, it doesn't become −1. Since aggression is stored as an unsigned, 8-bit integer, it rolls over to 255, suddenly giving a newly democratic Gandhi an almost pathological desire to unleash nuclear Armageddon upon anyone who has the audacity to step into his line of sight.

This strange behavior was quickly noticed by *Civilization*'s players, although it wasn't immediately apparent what the reason was—and even once a connection had been made between nuclear war and democracy, it necessitated investigation and understanding of the game's code and rules to discover what exactly was causing this problem.

However, rather than fixing the bug in later versions to ensure that Gandhi remained peaceful, the developers decided that it would be an entertaining "Easter egg" (an inside joke or reference) to keep in later versions. The nuclear tendency was the most visible of military activities, and the democratic political choice tended to become available around the same time as nuclear technology, causing a certain perceived conflation between the two, so they decided to leave this aspect in later iterations of the franchise. The "willingness to use nuclear weapons" ratings in later games was separated from the more general "inclination toward war" ratings, and Gandhi's general aggression was reduced to an appropriately low level—without any attendant democratic bugs—but his nuclear inclination remains high. This means that Gandhi sometimes seems to "flip" from being entirely peaceful to stunningly warlike when nuclear weapons are developed; or, upon declaring war on Gandhi in the nuclear age, players immediately find their cities bombarded by nuclear weapons.

Through both the unintended presence of this glitch and the developers' decision to hold on to one aspect of the bug and reproduce it in later games, Gandhi's surprisingly nuclear interests fall somewhere between a bug, an Easter egg, and (later) a deliberately designed AI personality. This preference gives the character significant cultural impact as an inside joke for those who understand the source of this character trait (even earning the character the very sensible moniker of "Nuclear Gandhi"[3]), and it serves to distinguish new *Civilization* players from those who are used to this unusual characteristic, even if they may not necessarily know its origin (there is nothing in later games to explain why Gandhi uses nuclear weapons so freely). In turn, Gandhi has become a surprisingly noteworthy character who continues to appear in every subsequent iteration of the *Civilization* franchise with the same reproduced and retold nuclear tendencies, and one who has moved far beyond being just a "talking head" to represent a nation—a role the rest of *Civilization*'s leaders must generally be resigned to.

Similar Characters: Abraham Lincoln (*Code Name: S.T.E.A.M.*), Bill Clinton (*NBA Jam*), P.M. Satcher (*Nuclear War*)

—Mark R. Johnson

GLADOS

(est. 2007)
Franchise: *Portal*
Developer: Valve

If the AI entity GLaDOS—Genetic Lifeform and Disk Operating System—were introducing this entry, she might thank you for reading about her, in turn saying, "You will learn about what makes me better than you. Cake and grief counseling will be available at the conclusion of the chapter." Arguably the star of the *Portal* franchise, she is lauded as one of the all-time greatest video game villains. But what makes GLaDOS such an awesome villain? Her dual nature seems at the heart of her appeal: as she engages players (that is, humans playing robots), she herself exhibits tensions between robotness and humanity, in some ways mirroring contemporary questions about humans' relationships with technology.

GLaDOS works for the research organization Aperture Science, embedded in a machine suspended from a lab ceiling. She starts out as a pleasant, seemingly helpful entity, narrating the game *Portal* and serving as a guide for robotic player characters. However, she becomes increasingly malevolent as the game goes on, and her true intention of trying to bring about each player's death comes out as the game progresses. Codevelopers Kim Swift and Erik Wolpaw suggest that as the game goes on, GLaDOS also becomes more humanlike because she was written "as if she was a person going through a robot 'oh my nuts and bolts' sort of thing." Thus she was written to blur the lines between humanity and technology and to play on a classic duality in our dealing with technology: Will technology help us (as GLaDOS does early in the game) or destroy us (as she tries to do later in the game)?

The player is meant to care about what happens to GLaDOS in order to drive an emotional response, making the revelation of her true motives that much more powerful and tragic. For example, Justin Towell of *GamesRadar* suggests that GLaDOS is a bad guy that players feel bad for killing because they end up liking her. This provides an interesting, yet common, conundrum: people become connected to technology, such as robots, even though they realize that they are not human.

Overall, we might say that GLaDOS's voice and style combine to create a connection through the player's feeling "present" with her in the game. Presence is a feeling of non-mediation, occurring when someone uses technology for communication but does not feel like they are using technology. Multiple subtypes exist; social presence is an experience of feeling like you are with another person/intelligence that is mediated through technology.[4] This feeling of presence is enhanced when a mediated experience meets the expectations one has for it.[5] However, there would also be the potential for GLaDOS to fall into the "uncanny valley," which occurs when something is close enough to increase expectations but not quite the real thing, thus inducing a feeling of creepiness.[6]

For example, an android such as Data from *Star Trek: The Next Generation* appears very human but not exactly human, and so he might be perceived as creepy. In order for GLaDOS to appeal to people as she does, she needs to stay out of the uncanny valley.

Perhaps GLaDOS's most iconic feature is a synthesized voice that may drive the player's unsettled affection for her. Her voice, like penicillin, came about by a happy accident. While working on the game *Psychonauts*, Wolpaw ran out of placeholder voices so he started using text-to-speech to voice the remaining characters. Realizing that people seemed to enjoy the robotic-sounding lines and laughed at them more than the lines seemed to deserve, he decided to use it to his advantage. The result was the robotic sound of GLaDOS's voice, achieved by a human actress Ellen McLain speaking in a robotic tone. Somehow this combination of human and robot works. As noted by *IGN*, "despite her being almost entirely artificial, GLaDOS somehow manages to be more human than most villains in videogames." Although GLaDOS's voice is robotic, she is still designed to sound human—not in the tone and style of her voice, but in the words she speaks. Although the things she says are quite humanlike, her delivery is quite machinelike. She tells a joke but doesn't laugh, and she threatens in the same manner in which she tells a joke. Perhaps what is taking place is that we do not expect a machine to be totally human, and this is what allows us to feel a connection to the machine although it's only acting in a humanlike manner. The robotic voice does not raise our expectations to the full human level, thereby avoiding the uncanny valley, and thus the humanness provided by the human words and speech patterns is enough to help stimulate a feeling of presence.

Another key aspect to this tensioned pseudo-humanness is GLaDOS's playful personality, which has been described by her creators and fans alike as passive-aggressive and as a mix of hilarious and homicidal. Subtly comedic insults and threats are lobbed toward the player throughout the game. In her trademark gentle, feminine computer voice, she quips, "Well done. Here come the test results: You are a horrible person. That's what it says. We weren't even testing for that." The unusual depth of GLaDOS's humor is perhaps best exemplified in *Portal*'s closing-credits song, "Still Alive," in which GLaDOS musically laments the pain the player caused her but declares that she'll still be alive when the player is dead, all the while taking the time to let us all know the "cake is great! It's so moist and delicious!"

GLaDOS exemplifies the dualities and tensions we have with technology. Technology might be our savior, or our destroyer; technology might not be human enough to be human, but it might appear human enough to seem human; and technology might be playful or it might be dead serious. GLaDOS exhibits all of these tensions, and she reminds us to ask a dualistic question: Can we have our technological cake and eat it too?

Similar Characters: AM (*I Have No Mouth, and I Must Scream*), Ghost (*Destiny*), SHODAN (*System Shock*)

—David Westerman

GORDON FREEMAN

(est. 1998)
Franchise: *Half-Life*
Developer: Valve

Gordon Freeman is the unlikely hero of the *Half-Life* franchise, a near legendary series of games involving scientists, inter-dimensional portals, aliens, elite government soldiers, and, of course, a trusty crowbar. In the center of this vortex is Gordon, of whom remarkably little is known, except that he is male and a graduate of MIT, with a PhD in theoretical physics. Even after a number of expansions of the first game, plus the release of *Half-Life 2* and its expansions, we know next to nothing about Gordon. Indeed, the only thing we do know is that he is an educated geek—hardly the archetypal heroic character that dominated other games of the same era such as *Doom*, *Quake*, and *Duke Nukem*. Instead, Gordon represents a complex type of hero—a scientist geek who unwillingly takes up a gun to save the world from destruction, fights elite military forces, and wins the girl on the way. In doing so, he portrays a different form of masculinity—a man who is unenthusiastically thrown into an apocalypse but who quietly gets on with the job.

We shall return to this concept later, but one particular feature of the character bears further examination: he is a silent, and largely unseen, protagonist. It is true that other games of the era also featured silent heroes, but the almost complete lack of information about Gordon means that he embodies a "blank slate" that much better. Indeed, it is exactly this ambiguity that makes him such a beguiling character. Because Gordon doesn't have a set of overt physical features or voice to anchor preconceptions, the player can more easily inhabit the virtual space of "Gordon Freeman"—a concept known as "experiential merger."[7] In effect, the player becomes the center of the narrative, around whom all events flow. It is this concept that explains the allure of Gordon Freeman—we are able to live through him, portraying (albeit in a safe way) a fantastically exciting and possible version of ourselves.[8] Since the player rarely loses control of Gordon, and there are no irritating vocal quips that might force the characterization away from that imagined by the player, the virtual "space" of Gordon Freeman is tailor-made for whatever personality the player might care to pour into it. In effect, we become Gordon Freeman—we, with our 9-to-5 jobs, with our lessons or lectures to attend, we who dream of something more amazing than our current lives.

Of course, it should be asked, Who gets to occupy the "blank space" of Gordon Freeman? Arguably Gordon, as a male character, might exclude female players from being able to fully associate with the character. Was *Half-Life* simply a game of its time, designed by men, to be played by men? Gordon can be seen as no more than the continuation of a dominant, hegemonic masculinity that theoretically permeates society. The theory of hegemonic masculinity argues that conceptions of masculinity (and femininity) are defined by the dominant cultural group in such a way that the existing paradigm is maintained. Within this framework, alpha-male characters such as *Duke Nukem* (1991–2011) and the Marine in the

Doom series (1993–2004) represent a continuation of that dominant masculinity: shoot first, ask questions later! One could argue that they too are characters of their time, but even today research indicates a prevalence for male characters over female ones.[9] So the question is Does Gordon Freeman implicitly benefit from the dominant hegemonic masculinity? Is his quiet masculinity no more than a mandated variation on the main theme?

Arguably, the answer to these questions lies in criticism of the theory of hegemonic masculinity itself, the most telling criticism being that the theory oversimplifies the concept of masculinity. Even within the same cultural groupings, each individual has a variety of attributes lying across the spectrum of what it is to be "male" or "female," and as such, there can be many variations of what a man, or a woman, can be. The model of hegemonic masculinity does not have the flexibility to allow for such variation, inferring as it does a separation between the sexes. From this perspective then, Gordon Freeman represents a rarefied form of masculinity and one that challenges the traditional hegemonic male that dominates many computer games. He is a scientist who uses his brains to solve problems but who is not afraid to pick up a gun when required, thereby creating a different version of masculinity—that of the warrior academic.

Gordon Freeman is also more representative of a real adult—embodying the characteristics of a person both complex and multifaceted. As a product of this complexity, while the character of Gordon Freeman is male, the very nature of the character also allows females, although arguably to a lesser degree, to inhabit that space too. The character enables full immersion in the game by facilitating an experiential merger between the player and Gordon, placing the gamer right in the middle of the action. Gordon represents a subversion of the traditional game character, but he also enables the believable portrayal of a real person by allowing the player to step into the game itself.

Similar Characters: Jack (*BioShock*), Link (*The Legend of Zelda*), Master Chief (*Halo*)

—Alex Meredith

GRUES

(est. 1977)

Franchise: *Zork*

Developer: Infocom

Grues are ferocious monsters present in most of the classic interactive fiction games created by the software company Infocom. First appearing in *Zork* (1977) and described as drooling, fanged beasts with insatiable appetites that only fear the light, the grue became an iconic element of Infocom games and of the golden age of interactive fiction. Due to their memorable inclusion in some of the best-selling games of the early home-computer era, grues are a recognizable symbol of early gaming culture. The grue is also one of the very first great original monsters of the computer age, as the nature of interactive fiction allowed for more detailed background information and descriptions than contemporary graphical games of the era. The grue illustrates how video games developed their own unique lore and adversaries and represents a notable early case in which a minor character's role expanded in subsequent franchise installments.

The world of *Zork* is one of comedic high fantasy where the threat of a grisly demise is tempered by humor and absurdity. This balance is maintained by the sharp and witty prose of Infocom's brand of interactive fiction where clever writing and logical deduction guides players through an entirely new form of gaming and storytelling.[10] Because early interactive fiction relied only on text to describe the game world and accept commands from players, the low system requirements of the genre meant that the games were accessible on most computers. This allowed many gamers the opportunity to play *Zork*. Infocom designer Michael Berlyn later opined that two products sold more early computers than anything else: the spreadsheet program Visicalc, and *Zork*.[11]

The origin of the grue came about as a simple gameplay solution in *Zork* to prevent players from attempting to blindly make their way through dark areas without a light source, circumventing the need to obtain a means of illumination. *The Colossal Cave Adventure* (1976), the spiritual basis for *Zork*, used pits to punish players who wandered in dark places without a light. Because random pits would not hold narrative weight in the more varied environments of *Zork*, the grue was implemented as a solution. When players entered dark areas, they were warned of the danger with what became the signature line associated with the monster: "It is pitch black. You are likely to be eaten by a grue." Should players continue to linger in the darkness, a lurking grue slithered into the room and devoured them. *The Lore and Legends of Quendor*, a small book packaged with *Beyond Zork* (1987), offers a description that echoes *Zork*'s original, sparse, in-game account of a grue. "The grue is a sinister, lurking presence in the dark place of the earth. Its favorite diet is adventurers, but its insatiable appetite is tempered by its fear of light. No grue has ever been seen by the light of day; few have survived its fearsome jaws to tell the tale." The habitat and nature of the grue meant few other details were provided in their earliest appearances, yet the grue captured the attention of players.

As a fictional fantasy world, *Zork* included a cyclops, dwarves, and other stereotypical dungeon denizens. The grue was something new. Although the grue got its name from stories by fantasy author Jack Vance, the monster itself was a creation of the computer age and was indicative of Infocom developing its own unique settings for its games. The grue's connection to fantasy novels parallels how fantasy video games have roots in literature yet have developed their own forms of storytelling and their own distinct, fictional worlds. The world-building efforts of Infocom authors and the popularity of the monster resulted in the expansion of the role of the grue, a process similar to that of Toad from the Nintendo *Mario* franchise. Grues made appearances as puzzles in their own right, as characters, and in scenarios within games rather than simply remaining a convention to kill unwary, light-challenged adventurers. Additional pieces of information and survivable face-to-face encounters with grues were added to later games, giving players more details about the creatures.

Players could see a baby grue in *Wishbringer* (1985) and be transformed into a grue in *Spellbreaker* (1985). In *Zork: The Undiscovered Underground* (1997), players see an adult grue for the first time. The monster is described as having a fish-mouthed head, razor-like claws, and sickly, glowing fur. It is also established that a grue's preference for the darkness is due to a fatal reaction when exposed to too much light. Although grues are generally portrayed as dangerous, drooling monsters, a different approach is seen in *Zork: The Undiscovered Underground* when the player encounters a grue convention. The grues are revealed to be intelligent creatures, capable of speech and presenting lectures on surviving an adventurer shortage. This widespread use of the grue also serves to hint at connections between the widely disparate worlds of Infocom games, such as the space opera of *Planetfall* (1983) and the high fantasy of *Spellbreaker* (1985).

The evolving nature of the grue reflects the transition of video game settings from simple, two-dimensional backgrounds to well-thought-out fictional worlds with their own internal logic and history. Different authors expanded the story of the grue from a few basic ideas and moved it in new and sometimes surprising directions. The grue helps define the fictional history of the Infocom universe, which adds to player immersion as well as the overall narrative cohesion of the games. As a near omnipresent threat in the popular Infocom games of the 1980s, the grue remains an uncommon but still recognizable reference to the era of classic computer gaming. *IGN* lists the grue as one of their top 100 video game villains of all time. Even today the grue is used as a homage to classic, early computer gaming, and references to grues appear in the games *NetHack* (1997), *World of Warcraft* (2004), *Alan Wake* (2010), and *Don't Starve* (2013), thus representing its strong position as a symbol of early gaming culture.

Similar Characters: The Alien (*Alien Isolation*), Charlie (*Don't Starve*), Kaernk (*Amnesia: The Dark Descent*)

—Daniel Fandino

H

HITLER

(est. 1992)
Franchise: *Wolfenstein 3D*
Developer: id Software

The history of video games is full of evil characters. These "baddies" range from exotic monsters, treacherous demons, and evil knights to cruel aliens, mad scientists, and, well, Nazis. In popular culture, ordinary Nazi soldiers, or even better (or worse), the German SS (an abbreviation for *Schutzstaffel*, the politically and ideologically indoctrinated "elite" corps of the Third Reich) have developed into an archetypical evil: you can kill them by the dozens in first-person shooters such as the *Medal of Honor* series, and they provide power-mongering super-bosses seeking world domination as in *Indiana Jones and the Fate of Atlantis*—but only in *Wolfenstein 3D* can you battle the "Über-Boss": Hitler (or, Mecha-Hitler). At the end of the game, you fight Adolf Hitler, who is wearing a Mech-Suit with four attached chain guns. He has not only an almost unlimited amount of hit points but also unrivaled firepower, and to make things worse, the game denies the player any opportunity to sneak up on him (yes, Hitler was indeed paranoid and constantly expecting assassins). *Wolfenstein 3D* and its ultimate boss caused quite a stir: it created a new genre (first-person shooter), lead to political controversies over violence, and was even banned and confiscated in Germany.

Before being able to punch Hitler in the face, preferably with a powerful chain gun, the player in the original *Wolfenstein 3D* had to finish two episodes in the game with some (almost) equally evil Nazi-villains: Hauptsturmführer Hans Grösse in episode 1, *Escape from Castle Wolfenstein*, which was actually distributed for free; and the archetypical Nazi mad scientist, Doctor Schobbs, in episode 2. Finally, in episode 3 the player character B. J. Blazkowicz gets into the Führer's headquarters, with Mecha-Hitler on the last level.

What separated *Wolfenstein 3D* from other games of the time was that enemies, when shot, bled and cried. Each enemy had a MIDI-sound death cry in German. So when Grösse is shot, we hear him whine *Mutti* ("Mommy"), and even ordinary Nazi officers die with *Mein Leben* ("my life") on their virtual lips. A defeated Mecha-Hitler cries out for his wife: "Eva." Suddenly the Nazi villains became human in a video game.

While early shooting games were not particularly interested in telling elaborate stories involving complex protagonists and antagonists, *Wolfenstein 3D* tried to give its enemies at least some kind of voice—a voice fitting to the hyperbolic, over-the-top imagery of the game—and Hitler fit in rather nicely. The game's labyrinth is full of Nazi insignia: swastikas hang from almost every second wall, and portraits of Adolf Hitler line the remaining walls. Enemies wear Nazi uniforms, German shepherds patrol the ground, and before the player finally confronts Hitler, ghost versions of the dictator attack the player—an interesting allusion to the common trope of many dictators hiding behind stand-ins out of fear of assassination.

The story in itself is told in short text passages—and Hitler is introduced in the mission briefings for episode 3: "In episode three, Hitler hides in his titanic bunker as the Third Reich crumbles about him. It is your job to assassinate him ending his mad reign. You find he has escaped to the Reichstag, and there you must confront him"—less than fifty words and you know what your job is: Adolf Hitler does not need an introduction as enemy, and at the end of the game, the equation becomes simple: Adolf Hitler + Mech-Suit + Chain Gun = the ultimate, pure, evil super villain. *Wolfenstein 3D* is an anarchistic, exaggerated video game version of the "super evil Nazi" trope we know from movies such as *Indiana Jones* and *Inglourious Basterds* or any typical World War II movie.

Yet having a real-life historical figure, a dictator, who was responsible for the deaths of millions of people around the world, as a character in a video game, and even if this video game is successful in mocking all the Nazi cliches in popular culture, is not something that should be treated lightheartedly. When John Carmack and John Romero, cofounders of *id Software*, made Hitler the Über-Boss, it became apparent that the shock value of fighting one of history's most dreaded characters was one crucial element of *Wolfenstein 3D*'s appeal. But the shock "was only half the attraction. The main draw was the super-fast 3D rendering engine and movement."[1] This led to another concern: politicians as well as academics became concerned with the effect this violence might have on gamers. Research on violent video games surged at the time of *Wolfenstein 3D* and is still a major research area. While in the United States the debate of the early 1990s was more focused on games such as *Mortal Combat*, *Wolfenstein 3D*—and later *Doom*—fell victim to this outcry in other countries.

Few Germans have ever heard Hitler cry out for his Eva after Blazkowicz has blasted away first his Mech-Suit and then his body of virtual flesh and bone. This is because in Germany, the game is banned and cannot be promoted, distributed, or sold, yet existing copies may legally be owned. This ban is based on Germany's penal code that makes it illegal for any type of text to promote signs of organizations that aspire to overthrow the constitution—a legal term mostly employed for Nazi insignia. To put it simply, there were too many Nazi insignias, too many swastikas, too many Adolf Hitlers, and too many SS soldiers in the game for German courts. Being a first-person shooter with blood and gore also does not help as Germany's protection-of-minor laws are, unlike those of the United States and the UK, rather liberal concerning nudity and sex but very sensitive to acts of violence. So in the end, and perhaps as a perfect illustration of how difficult it is to deal with the atrocities of the Third Reich as a German, a video game that lets you kill Hitler makes it onto the same list of banned media that normally is reserved for works of neo-fascist organizations glorifying the Nazi era.

Similar Characters: Hans Ubermann (*Indiana Jones and the Fate of Atlantis*), Spider-demon (*Doom*), Zombie-Hitler (*Sniper Elite: Zombie Army Trilogy*)

—Sven Jöckel

HK-47

(est. 2003)
Franchise: *Star Wars: Knights of the Old Republic*
Developer: BioWare

From HK-47's first lines in *Star Wars: Knights of the Old Republic* (*KOTOR*), it's clear he's not your typical *Star Wars* droid. He's gleefully sociopathic, insubordinate, a rules-lawyer of his own programming, and, most famously, he likes to refer to people as "meatbags." He's a foil (or contrast) to C-3PO: while at his core he is also a comic-relief character, HK-47 is bold rather than hesitant, condescendingly arrogant rather than snivelingly deferential, and an assassin rather than a protocol droid. Just as *KOTOR* constantly twists and subverts conventions (both of role-playing games and of the *Star Wars* canon), so HK-47's characterization confronts the droid-ethics problem of *Star Wars*: though droids are clearly sentient, intelligent, and capable of a broad range of emotions, they're treated as property to be bought, sold, abandoned, and blasted to smithereens.[2] If Luke Skywalker restored balance to the Force, HK-47's dark humor restores balance to the droids.

While HK-47's fame may rest on his snarky dialog and amorality within the black-and-white framework of the *Star Wars* universe (he's not evil, he just . . . really loves his meatbag-slaying job), there's much more going on beneath the droid's rusty surface. Narratively, he's something of a murderous Virgil to the player character's Dante—a guide through realms of danger, memory, and enlightenment. He's a dark mirror of the typical owner-droid relationship in *Star Wars*, problematizing the notion of droids as willing slaves. HK-47 is also one of *KOTOR*'s sly pokes at role-playing-game behavior as he takes anything lying around and reflexively shoots up everything in sight. He never stops needling you about the owner-property relationship. He even plays with the obedient servant role by occasionally killing a few extra potential enemies of his owner— "Freebies, if you will. . . . I am an intelligent droid, you know. I see an opportunity and I take it." He's not above interpreting his owner's orders in a way to cause maximum carnage, and if the result gets an owner killed, there's always the next one. Thus he inverts the typical master-droid relationship in which the droid is disposable and the owner is sacrosanct.

Within *KOTOR*'s story, HK-47's journey is one of memory and morality. Three thousand years before the events of *Star Wars: A New Hope*, you first come across the droid in a seedy shop on Tatooine. He tells you his memory's been blocked. Gradually you unlock ironic stories of previous owners. There's the up-and-coming young, corporate executive who orders the droid to remove those responsible for a competing product . . . which he doesn't realize was actually designed by a subsidiary of his own firm. HK-47 notes, "It did not take long for my master to realize his mistake. By then, I had already terminated 104 corporate officers." Oops. Or the crime lord who uses HK-47 to attack his rivals, but in so doing he doesn't have HK-47 around to protect him when the survivors strike back. HK-47 explains, "I provide a function that is useful to others. They merely must learn to use it properly, I believe."

KOTOR's subversive humor extends to its own genre tropes, and HK-47 is used for its sharpest and deepest cuts. One of the core actions of role-playing games is the reflexive looting of any container in sight. Once you wake up after your escape pod's crash, game logic has you exploring the apartment complex you're in and taking stuff. In *KOTOR*, however, the apartment occupants respond in terror, treating you as an evil burglar. HK-47 approaches the "real life" of the *Star Wars* galaxy with the amoral glee of a veteran *Grand Theft Auto* player. On a diplomatic mission to a tribal village? HK-47 wants you to kill 'em all and take all their stuff. Need to make a complex moral decision? Ehh, just shoot everybody and move on with the mission. The droid enables you the player, as well as the player character, to confront your morality. HK-47 doesn't have free will. He's an assassin because, to quote another famous fictional character, he's "drawn that way." You have a choice—light or dark, Republic or Empire, negotiate or shoot. Gaming conventions might push you toward mindless slaughter, but *KOTOR* gives you choices.

KOTOR's player character journey is one of reinvention. You eventually realize, à la *Blade Runner*, that your memories are lies—an implanted cover story. Your recovery of your own lost memories is the key to unlocking HK-47's: you discover that his creator was you. You're responsible not only for his existence, but for the trail of destruction he's left after being damaged in your service. The great choice of the narrative is: Do you become what you once were, or do you embrace your actions as a new personality? Are you and your assassin droid going to carve a path of destruction across the galaxy, or is HK-47 going to grumblingly put up with your new character flaw of minimizing body counts? It's a nice meeting of character arcs across some twenty-five hours of gameplay.

Themes of memory, identity, and free will run through *KOTOR*, from the player character's main story to minor side quests. The game's story and mechanics challenge the simple black-and-white dichotomies of the *Star Wars* universe. HK-47 embodies that critical meta-commentary as he treats his "real world" like a consequence-free shoot-'em-up; his embrace of a lack of free will highlights the responsibility of human morality. Of course, the snarky humor is a big part of his charm.

How popular has HK-47 proven? He returned in *KOTOR*'s sequel for an even larger role and again as a boss in two instanced battles in the massively multiplayer online game *Star Wars: The Old Republic* (*SWTOR*). In *SWTOR*'s 2015 expansion, a successor model, HK-51, is available as a companion character, and 2016 promises an HK-51–centric episode in which you play as the meatbag-killing droid. His dark humor has been a much-loved addition to the *Star Wars* universe for over a dozen years now: HK-47 would grudgingly approve of the good judgment of us meatbags.

Similar Characters: Codsworth (*Fallout 4*), KOS-MOS (*Xenosaga*), Mr. Zurkon (*Ratchet and Clank*)

—John Carter McKnight

HONDA CIVIC

(est. 1997)
Franchise: *Gran Turismo*
Developer: Polyphony Digital

The Honda Civic screams banality, a car more likely to evoke imagery of a middle-class suburban driveway than of a popular video game franchise. Yet the sixth-generation version of the Civic has been a staple of Polyphony Digital's *Gran Turismo* since the 1997 debut of the series. Despite its nickname among street-racing enthusiasts, the "Miracle Civic" is hardly a standout racer in the game; it features only average handling, acceleration, and top speed. Although its relatively cheap price and decent performance often make the Civic one of the first purchases for players, the car is quickly outclassed by more expensive options. The Civic won't crop up on many "Best GT Cars" lists, nor has it ever been featured in any of the series' packaging or promotional work.

And yet the Civic represents, perhaps more than any other available racer, the spirit of the *Gran Turismo* series: the wholehearted embrace and celebration of the mundane. Where competitor series like *Ridge Racer* and *Burnout* offer players spectacular crashes, physics-defying drifts, and explosive power-ups, *Gran Turismo* developers opted to create a simulation-like game that revels in the minute details of professional racing—tire balancing, track friction, over-and-under-steering, exhaust manifolds. Throughout the life span of the series, attention to the banal and to physics attains such a level of detail that car manufacturers use the game as a development test site. The design team for Toyota's FT-1 concept car, for instance, partnered with Polyphony to import CAD prototypes of the FT-1 into *Gran Turismo 5*'s engine, affording the team and Toyota's CEO to test-drive digital versions of the car before physical production.[3]

Though other cars, like the fictional Red Bull X2010, might attract more attention from *Gran Turismo*'s gaming community, the Honda Civic embodies *Gran Turismo*'s blending of everyday minutia with pageantry. Though *Gran Turismo* mechanically operates as a mundane racing simulator rather than an explosive racing game, great effort is made by Polyphony's programming staff to push the graphical boundaries of hardware platforms. Digital artisans mulled over the glints of light that shine off side-view mirrors during a 220 mph left turn under a simulated Italian sun. Sound engineers pilgrimaged to tuner sages to record the sounds of high-quality engines under strain.[4] In promotional materials, side-by-side screen captures are often placed alongside photographs of live racing events, daring viewers to discern between rendered and real imagery.

The Civic features at the heart of this carnivalesque dance among the mechanical and the hyper-real, both inside and outside the world of *Gran Turismo*. The Civic is popular among amateur street racers because of its low cost and the variety of aesthetic mod kits available, though the ostentatious and hyper-macho variety of these mod kits stereotype Civic racers as having more interest in the "look" of their car rather than in its performance. The modification of Civics in both *Gran Turismo* and street racing is tied to a class-based performance of masculine identity: lower- and middle-class teenagers tinkering mundane cars into competitive machines—an infusion of pageantry and control into a life that often affords little of either.[5]

Civics in street racing and *Gran Turismo* thus evoke a synthesis of the magical and the mundane. Dutch historian Johan Huizinga famously used the allegory of "the magic circle" to describe play spaces in his work *Homo Ludens*. Inside the magic circle of play, the rules, norms, and restrictions of everyday life are temporarily put on pause, and a special set of rules and expectations take their place. In physical-world games, a special rule might temporarily change the value of a football from that of "a stuffed piece of leather" to that of "the most sacred object in the world." In digital games, special rules may allow the player to fly or to hurl balls of fire.

Gran Turismo's magic circle places players in the role of a sponsored professional racer traveling around the world to compete for championships. Street racing's circle allows racers to enact a similar kind of imaginative role-play, though with the added dynamics of g-force, illegality, and the chance of death. Although these play spaces shine with pageantry, the boundaries of the magic circle are hardly well defined; cultural attitudes, rules, and memories flow both into and out of the circle of play. The Civic tears through the circle's membrane. It looks as much at home speeding along the digital tracks of *Gran Turismo* as it does in the mall parking lot. It remains in a state of suspended grace as it exits the highway and confidently cruises into a loud asphalt arena at night, coyly flipping on the blue LEDs tucked into its undercarriage.

The Civic forces our imaginations of speed away from muscle cars and European streets toward the family sedan down the block, and it highlights the driving success of the *Gran Turismo* series: the drawing not of the magic circle, but of the mundane circle. *Gran Turismo*'s unique contribution to the world of racing games is not its obsessive attention to bringing material minutiae into a digital space but rather its artisanal devotion to that minutiae. *Gran Turismo* invites its players to look, listen, and linger within those moments when metal and rubber meet the road.

In the magical spaces of both *Gran Turismo* and street racing, the mundane Civic putters along as a foundational backbone, a car that serves as the gateway for those seeking to transition from dabblers to committed racers. The car that seems to be a "pick-up-your-kids-from-band-practice," milquetoast sedan during the day devilishly winks at you from the driveway at night, beckoning you to that long stretch of road behind the industrial park that curiously seems to liven up around 11 p.m. on Fridays.

Similar Characters: Bread (*I Am Bread*), historically accurate daily weather patterns from November 1986 to April 1987 in Yokosuka, Japan (*Shenmue*), Turf (*Madden NFL*)

—James W. Malazita

I

I-BLOCK

(est. 1984)
Franchise: *Tetris*
Developer: Alexey Pajitnov

We have all heard that patience is a virtue, but when you hear the music quicken and your heart rate rises—patience and virtue are the last thing on your mind. You need to make a choice. Where do you play the Z-shaped block plummeting toward your carefully organized stack? The only spot it fits is the spot you have been saving for that eventual I-Block. The I-Block (or long, straight, stick piece—[vertical 1×4 or horizontal 4×1]) is the only tetriminoe that can be used to earn a "tetris" by clearing four lines at once, generating a slew of points and increasing game longevity. Oh, that wonderful gamepiece—it fits into the narrowest holes and fills the deepest gaps . . . but it is also elusive. The bane of many a *Tetris* game is the regrettable move of playing the Z-block in the I-block's spot just to have the I-block finally materialize in the next turn—leaving scores of players to wonder if their strategy, the game, or the I-Block itself is to blame for the unfortunate outcome. *Tetris* elicits player joy and frustration, and the I-Block manifests the dilemma of selecting current pragmatic decisions over taking a risky gamble on the future.

Created in 1984 by Alexey Pajitno, *Tetris* has become one of the most popular video games of all time. Initially, this obscure Russian game made headlines when Nintendo chose it over the company's flagship franchise, *Super Mario*, to be bundled with every original GameBoy handset. *Tetris* went on to sell over 170 million copies, and its cultural impact can be seen in depictions on *The Big Bang Theory, College Humor, Futurama, Muppet Babies, The Office*, and *The Simpsons*. *Tetris* has also been called the greatest game of all time.[1]

Due to the game's immense popularity, the seven faceless, or featureless, *tetriminoes* (gamepieces with configurations of four squares) have emerged as cultural icons. *Tetris* requires a tactical arrangement of geometric objects, relying on combined skill in logic and speed. As the tetriminoes fall, players strategically spin and fit them into place among the already played objects in order to clear lines and continue playing. If the objects are not aligned properly, they pile up. When they get too high, the game is lost. The I-Block represents divergent metaphorical outcomes forcing players to weigh trade-off and opportunity costs.

Tetris does not have an official story line; therefore, much is left to the player's imagination. Other than Russian iconography and incidental music, the Cold War–lineage game offers minimal context. *Tetris* is not a narrative; rather, it is an antenarrative[2]—an attempt to provide a speculative direction to lessen the ambiguous nature of sense-making. The antenarrative path acknowledges the opportunity for different outcomes contingent on different actions. *Tetris* does not provide a beginning, middle, and end; rather, it is a story in constant flux. Players bet on the future and the possible arrival of blocks with each successive action altering that future. Thereby, the tetriminoes are integrated into larger cultural narratives about opportunity. The opportunities present in the game are not simply a matter of chance, however. Skilled players navigate and calculate how to best use the blocks to eliminate lines and increase tetris opportunities, which offers the maximum pay-off. Less-skilled players often settle for less than a tetris by using different blocks to fill the four-square gaps reserved for the I-Block. David Boje (a scholar of storytelling and sense-making) argues that antenarratives involve a form of repackaging in which new characteristics are recognized and old characteristics are minimized.[3] The I-Block's arrival can represent either the relative success or the failure of the player's gamble. The antenarrative enables players to interpret the I-Block, and other featureless blocks, as an opportunistic story both in the game and metaphorically in their lives. *Tetris* pits decisions based on current and possible future circumstances against each other. When a gamble fails to pay off, players often deflect blame from themselves to the game or its individual objects.

The I-Block is simply an aggregate of squares, yet players often respond to such objects as if they had distinct personalities. Sherry Turkle, professor of social studies of science and technology at MIT, asserts that people of all ages tend to project personalities and emotions into inanimate physical objects.[4] By giving agency to an inanimate object through this projection, people can make sense of the outcomes of *Tetris* by placing responsibility on the object. In *Tetris*, players may anthropomorphize and blame the tetriminoes for showing up too early or too late, mitigating their own responsibility for failure. The I-Block receives the most attention due to its low probability of appearance and highly coveted potential payoffs—even though it is the game's underlying mechanics and algorithms that determine the tetriminoes' order. This projection of blame onto a single game piece rather than to the game itself may be due to the convenience of a visible, circumstantial object as opposed to the invisibility of a gaming engine and unknown systematic structures. The I-Block represents a byproduct of the player and the system: if *Tetris* is an allegory for capitalizing on opportunities, the larger cultural implications suggest that the tools for acquiring success are not always distributed by chance.

Maybe the I-Block antenarrative really does create a metaphor for life. We might anthropomorphize the I-Block in order to blame or cherish it, but no matter what blocks are handed out, it is up to us to decide what to do with them—a block's value is found in the player's skill. Every block is about making it work, and each act of work constantly rewrites and reshapes our antenarrative. Sometimes we settle for less, sometimes we bet big—sometimes life gives us exactly what we are looking for, and sometimes it gives us a Z-block. In all, there is hope that our stack of unwanted objects prepares us for when we finally get what we have been waiting for: our own personal, wonderful I-Block.

Similar Characters: Color Bomb (*Candy Crush*), Gems (*Bejeweled*), Pills (*Dr. Mario*)

—Brad A. Haggadone and Leah E. LeFebvre

THE INVADERS

(est. 1978)
Franchise: *Space Invaders*
Developer: Taito

One arcade cabinet at a time, little invaders from space wove themselves into the fabric of gaming culture by assaulting Earth. Though clearly the antagonists of the game *Space Invaders*, these creatures are such an iconic symbol of gaming culture that they have been featured at multiple cultural institutions such as London's Science Museum, New York's Museum of Modern Art, and the Media Art Institute in Amsterdam. Considering that the player does not actually play as one of the Invaders but rather is tasked with destroying them, their iconic status is peculiar. That is, until one considers how the Invaders' *kawaii* aesthetic resulted in the construction of a villain more sympathetic than that of the actual protagonist. In essence, we argue that at least part of the Invader longevity comes from their aesthetic appearance.

But first, for those (likely) few unfamiliar with these Invaders, they belong to the game *Space Invaders*. The main objective of this genre-defining shooting game is to defend Earth from an alien invasion. The Invaders are organized as an eleven-by-five column that slowly snakes its way from left to right as the Invaders make their way down the screen (ostensibly toward Earth). The player, represented by a laser cannon, is able to move left and right in order to shoot at them or take cover behind four destructible bunkers. The game ends if the player is hit or if the Invaders make it to the bottom of the screen (suggesting they have successfully invaded Earth).

Though the player controls the cannon, it is the Invaders who have left their mark on popular culture. Part of the reason for this is because the Invaders are represented as anthropomorphic creatures, rather than generic spaceships, which makes them easier to relate to than the cannon. As Nicholas Epley, Adam Waytz, and John Cacioppo note, anthropomorphism "turns nonhuman agents into moral agents who deserve to be treated with respect and concern."[5] In this regard, while the cannon may function as a proxy for the player, in contrast, it is the Invaders who operate as moral agents; even if their objectives are in contrast to those of the player, as moral agents, their behavior may invite reflection—what *do* they want?

It would seem nothing. Though this ostensibly could be an otherwise frightening realization—the enemy wants nothing—the *kawaii* aesthetic informing the design of the Invaders makes their march toward certain doom (theirs if we shoot them, ours if we miss) somewhat adorable. This adorableness stems from *kawaii* culture's emphasis on childlike aesthetic features that communicate a sense of innocence and fragility. Though cute culture has often been critiqued as shallow and vapid, a more generous reading from Susan Napier suggests that this cultural aesthetic can offer a space for thinking through complex cultural problems.[6] To this end, then, it is worth considering the cultural work that the Invaders would have offered gamers in the late-1970s and beyond.

The environment the Invaders operated in would have been immediately clear to most players in the late-1970s and early-1980s: the Cold War. Cold War themes were part and parcel of many early video games, and indeed according to a 2008 *Game Informer* interview with *Space Invaders* creator Tomohiro Nishikado, the game was originally designed around military combat featuring tanks, planes, and battleships. Due to the limitations of the hardware, however, Nishikado was not satisfied with the quality of animation. He believed that human combatants would be easier, but Taito's president felt it was immoral to produce a game featuring people killing people. So instead Nishikado took inspiration from *Star Wars* (1977) and H. G. Wells's *The War of the Worlds* (1897) and reoriented the game around combating (cute) aliens from space. If, as already noted, *kawaii* aesthetics offer a safe space for engaging with complex moral problems, then it would seem as though the evolution of the Invaders—from military vehicles to humans to cute aliens—offered a safe space for engaging with Cold War themes.

But whereas most military-theme games present enemies of explicit, malevolent intent, the Invaders amusingly march from left to right in a highly choreographed routine (with each row of Invaders stepping in perfect synchrony with each other) as they make their downward descent. In this regard, they are less the Borg from *Star Trek: The Next Generation* (1987–1994) and more the Lemmings from *Lemmings* (1991). Hence, in spite of the ludic and historic conventions affecting the operation of the game (i.e., the objective is to kill the enemy), the Invaders' aesthetic appearance undermines the meaning one would normally take from such an arrangement. The game may require the player to kill the Invaders, but their cuteness rebuffs any contextual attribution of malevolence.

In this regard, part of the Invaders' longevity can be explained as due to how their aesthetic design accomplishes what Susan Napier defines as a potential of *kawaii* culture:

> a new way of looking at national culture and identity, one that rests less on a firm separation or even interplay between self and Other, and more on the gradual acknowledgement that in the transnational postmodern world of contemporary mass culture, the Other . . . might increasingly be imbricated within the self.[7]

In essence, the Invaders are appealing partly because their design appears more natural than that of the appearance we are offered in the game—the cannon. But such an identification is not inconsequential, for by identifying with the Other, in this case the Invaders, we may sympathize with their motives or ascribe more sympathetic motives should none exist. Hence, the invasion of the Invaders is not to be feared, but rather perhaps welcomed. And this may well be part of the reason for the long-term appeal of the Invaders: for when change is legion *and* adorable, then one can only hope that we are a part of the invasion.

Similar Characters: The Ghosts (*Pac-Man*), Goomba (*Super Mario Bros.*), Slime (*Dragon Quest*)

—Leticia Cherchiglia, Tom Day, and Robert Mejia

ISAAC

(est. 2011)
Franchise: *The Binding of Isaac*
Developer: Edmund McMillen and Florian Himsl

Naked and crying, Isaac throws himself into the trapdoor that leads into the basement of his house. God has told Isaac's mother that her child is sinful and must be punished; she must sacrifice Isaac as proof of her absolute obedience. The roguelike game's title and narrative setup refer to an Old Testament tale about a test of religious faith: God's demand that Abraham sacrifice his son Isaac on Mount Moriah. But in the game, no angel intervenes to spare Isaac's life. Thus each game of *The Binding of Isaac* initiates a dark descent as Isaac attempts to escape from his mother and her butcher's knife. Isaac is significant for granting players a raw, unabashed, yet playful space in which to explore the cultural taboos and violent repressions that may characterize both their childhood upbringing and adult life in contemporary American culture.

In the basement—and the caves and catacombs and depths beneath it—Isaac confronts the abject, wicked abominations that his religious rearing has instilled in him yet declared to be strictly forbidden. The floors are littered with piles of feces, puddles of blood, rows of spikes, and scattered pills with unknown effects. The rooms are crowded with monsters that are grotesque yet cartoonlike. They attack Isaac, and he dispels them with the tears he weeps. The world and its inhabitants are clearly products of the rich inner world of a young child struggling to make sense of religious explanations of faith and filth, purity and evil, salvation and damnation. The significance of Isaac's imagination in the concoction of these environments and entities is further underscored through the macabre sketches that make up the game's opening menus (a child's doodles asking, "Who am I?") and its game-over screen (a diary entry noting, "Today I died.").

Players join Isaac in his troubled negotiation of the sinfulness that he has been told he possesses and for which he must be punished. "If I wanted to pick a work of art," wrote Arthur Chu, "to explain how being raised as an evangelical Christian kid with a strong imagination fucks you up—and can fuck you up even if your religious upbringing doesn't seem outright abusive—the top pick would be The Binding of Isaac."[8] Edmund McMillen, one of the game's creators, also links the influences of strict religious tenets on an active young imagination, explaining, "I wanted it to show the positive and negative effects it had on me as a child—the self-hate and isolation it instilled in me, but also the dark creativity it inspired."[9]

In some ways, Isaac's excursion deeper and deeper into his guilt-ridden mind is terrifying and repulsive. In others, it appears as a cathartic fantasy, a tantalizing chance to touch and explore the limits of both religious and cultural taboo. Many items, for instance, feature satanic imagery. Sometimes Isaac even has opportunities to make deals with Satan for stronger—but often more dangerous—powerups, at the cost of heart-shaped health containers. As players unlock new characters with their own starting attributes, Isaac can experiment with gender identity, defying religious and cultural constraints on gender expression and fluidity. Most of these characters are specific biblical figures, varying from one another in their gender presentations. These include Judas, Eve, Samson, Cain, and Azazel, among others—individuals who would be particularly memorable from Sunday school lessons for their sinful acts against God. But they are all still Isaac, who dons their identities to simultaneously experience a transgressive liberation from and a condemnation for his own guilt.

Just as Isaac plays with what has been prohibited from him, so too do players. As McMillen remarked, "A lot of the content in Isaac is extremely dark and adult. It touches on aspects of child abuse, gender identity, infanticide, neglect, suicide, abortion, and how religion might negatively affect a child, which are topics most games would avoid."[10] Indeed, these are themes with which video games have dealt only rarely, usually poorly, and never in a manner similar to the nuanced approach that *The Binding of Isaac* has accomplished. The character of Isaac may permit players to revisit and renegotiate their own fraught religious past, while confronting them with a number of the most painful, provocative, and contested issues in the current American social and political landscape.

As such, *The Binding of Isaac* has unsurprisingly remained consistently controversial, largely due to its depictions of religion and child abuse. For instance, in February 2016, Apple announced that it had rejected an iOS version of *The Binding of Isaac: Rebirth* due to the game's depictions of violence and abuse toward children.[11] Apple's ban of *Rebirth* demonstrates that an attempt at a candid, forthright portrayal and discussion of these mature topics in a video game is still very much subject to silencing and prohibition in American cultural discourse.

In his efforts to grapple with competing impulses toward religious piety and an acceptance of his own inner evils, Isaac may be understood to embrace the demonic depths for which he has been accused, to give up on his life, or otherwise. In many ways, he is open for players to map their own experiences and understandings onto him, leaving him perpetually in a process of being transformed. While McMillen designed the game with a niche audience in mind, it proved to resonate powerfully with players, selling over one million units in less than a year after its release. Since then, *The Binding of Isaac* has also evolved into further versions and expansions. The games have many endings and no conclusive answers, leaving the fate of the protagonist open to players' interpretations—and, thus, to their further play, transgression, and reflection.

Similar Characters: Heather Mason (*Silent Hill 3*), Quico (*Papo & Yo*), Wilson (*Don't Starve*)

—Stephanie C. Jennings

ISAAC CLARKE

(est. 2008)
Franchise: *Dead Space*
Developer: EA Redwood Shores

Originally designed as a silent protagonist, Isaac Clarke of *Dead Space* is a typical, nondescript main character much like those in other shooters such as *Halo* or

Doom. However, Isaac is unique among game protagonists because of his development into a speaking character in the second installment of the series. With his newfound voice, Isaac speaks in contrast to the unfazed machismo endemic to other mainstream action games, expressing the effect of his traumatic experiences on his psyche. In fact, Isaac's journey throughout the entire series reflects the well-established trauma recovery model outlined in Julia Herman's book *Trauma and Recovery*: "Recovery unfolds in three stages. The central task of the first stage is the establishment of safety. The central task of the second stage is remembrance and mourning. The central focus of the third stage is reconnection with ordinary life."[12] Isaac Clarke's story mirrors each of these three trauma recovery stages as successive themes throughout the *Dead Space* trilogy, concluding with a protagonist who is flawed, complex, and recovered.

As a spaceship engineer in the far-flung future of 2508, Isaac begins his story on a repair mission to the USG *Ishimura*, a mining ship that has sent a distress beacon. Isaac has volunteered for the mission because his current girlfriend Nicole Brennan is a member of the *Ishimura*'s crew. Once aboard, Isaac and his team are terrorized by vicious monsters created by an alien artifact. As the game progresses, Isaac witnesses and commits countless acts of violence, though his silent nature makes him seem stoic and unaffected. During the mission, he comes into contact with Nicole, who aids him. However, she is not as she first appears. In the game's final act, it is revealed that Nicole has been dead all along and Isaac has been suffering from hallucinations caused by his proximity to the alien artifact. But Isaac saves the day and escapes physically unharmed, fulfilling the first step of Herman's recovery model. However, the game hints at his lasting trauma as it ends with a final hallucinatory jump-scare, suggesting that the game's real horrors reside within Isaac's mind.

Dead Space 2 (2011) introduces players to a more fully realized Isaac Clarke—one who speaks with a singular voice that is in turn sarcastic, overwrought with grief, or hopeful. Mood swings, hallucinations, and paranoia dog him throughout the narrative, and Nicole's ghastly apparition relentlessly taunts him. While Isaac's hallucinations are vividly exaggerated for effect, he displays a condition symptomatic of post-traumatic stress disorder (PTSD), especially in the way he avoids confronting his memories. As Isaac creeps through the wreckage of the *Ishimura*, Nicole points out, "You can pretend not to be bothered, but being here rattles you, doesn't it Isaac? All this plastic and tape covering the scars—trying to hide the blood and the bodies so no one will ever know. But you remember what happened—no matter how deeply you try to bury it." This experience resonates with Judith Herman's observation that "the psychological distress symptoms of traumatized people simultaneously call attention to the existence of an unspeakable secret and deflect attention from it. This is most apparent in the way traumatized people alternate between feeling numb and reliving the event. The dialectic of trauma gives rise to complicated, sometimes uncanny alterations of consciousness."[13] By recognizing Isaac's dichotomous relationship with his own memories, the player is able to experience the deep internal disconnect experienced by trauma survivors.

Showing an action hero afflicted with PTSD merits praise due to the rarity of emotional consequences in most violent video games. While most big-budget shooting games ignore the harm that violent events cause many people, *Dead*

Space 2 adds depth to the main character by allowing him to experience life-like emotional consequences. Because it is given meaningful consequences, the violence portrayed in the series transcends its position as gratuitous, giving the player an opportunity to reflect on the nature of violent conflict and the long-lasting effects of personal loss. At the end of *Dead Space 2*, Isaac confronts his grief and he is able to process his loss of Nicole—completing the second step of Herman's model, remembrance and mourning. Ultimately, Isaac resolves to live, even under the burden of his past. Isaac is not marginalized or even diminished for his mental health struggle, and he is not any less of a hero for it. In fact, his development is defined by overcoming obstacles both internal and external, and his ability to confront and accept his past adds complexity and profundity to the narrative.

In *Dead Space 3* (2013), players are met with a third version of Isaac—one who builds new relationships, despite the risk inherent to them. His connections to other characters, Ellie and John Carver, deepen over the course of the game into trusting partnerships, and Isaac chooses to continue his struggle in order to help Ellie and John survive. Through these relationships, Isaac returns to what Julia Herman calls "ordinary life" in her recovery model. While "ordinary" may be something of a stretch given Isaac's outlandish fictional experiences, *Dead Space 3* ends with an Isaac much different than the one it began with, as his reluctance to forge relationships is utterly overturned, and as the game ends, he calls out for Ellie's help and comfort.

While many mentally afflicted video game characters do exist, most are two-dimensional, and their characteristics are often compressed into stereotypes and harmful tropes—typically as villains who commit violent acts simply for the sake of violence. From *Farcry 3*'s Vaas to the psychotic denizens of *Outlast*, portrayals of mental illness in video games are rarely more than an easy-to-use label for "bad." Even more rarely are mentally ill characters given the chance to experience recovery, particularly in mainstream, big-budget games. The subtle and meaningful character arc of Isaac Clarke is an exceptional example of developing complexity in video game characters as it allows players to reflect on the effects of post-traumatic stress in a way that is both non-reductive and ultimately positive.

Similar Characters: Captain Martin Walker (*Spec Ops: The Line*), Marcus Fenix (*Gears of War*), Solid Snake (*Metal Gear*)

—Jeff Nay

J

JADE

(est. 2003)
Franchise: *Beyond Good & Evil*
Developer: Ubisoft Montpellier

Jade, the protagonist of the 2003 third-person action-adventure game *Beyond Good & Evil*, is a brave photojournalist who sets out to uncover a conspiracy between alien invaders and her own corrupt government. We get a sense of who Jade is from the moment we see her, and refreshingly, she looks the part of an active, practical young woman who has a job to do. Visual design is an important way for game designers to communicate information at a glance about a character's experience and personality traits. Sadly, women in games are often depicted in wildly impractical, sexualized clothing designed to make them appealing to straight male players. But Jade isn't designed to fulfill someone else's fantasy—she is a seeker of truth and justice. The midriff top she wears is a little silly, but for the most part, she looks like someone who is dressed to accommodate her own needs. After all, you don't get much more practical than cargo pants.

Together with Uncle Pey'j, a mechanically savvy, anthropomorphized boar, Jade looks after a group of war-orphaned children, sheltering them in a lighthouse on the mining planet of Hillys. Games often give us heroes for whom money is not a concern because it seems to be everywhere—bountifully bubbling up from slashed bushes and defeated enemies—or who at least don't have practical, everyday concerns about finances. But money is not just an abstract concept for Jade; she's a working-class character with real financial struggles. This is established at the very beginning of the game when we learn that the orphanage's electricity has been shut off and Uncle Pey'j's hovercraft is in dire need of repair. These are characters who struggle just to make ends meet, and concerns about their economic situation have real implications for their ability to provide for their adopted family.

To pay the bills, we're introduced to a gameplay device that establishes one of Jade's creative talents: photography. She is paid to document and catalog the planet's diverse animal life with her camera. Instead of just showing us or offhandedly telling us about her skills in cut-scenes, the designers built character development into the gameplay, giving players a pleasant, nonviolent way of interacting with and appreciating the beauty of the game's world while simultaneously reinforcing that Jade is a woman of many skills. *Edge Magazine* observed that part of what makes Jade so memorable is "the fact that she views this strange world and all of its careworn inhabitants through the lens of a camera, rather than the scope of an assault rifle." This not only gives Jade more depth, it encourages the player to view the life-forms of Hillys with some measure of respect, rather than seeing them solely as enemies to be destroyed.

Still, as in most action-adventure games, *Beyond Good & Evil*'s gameplay presents combat and violence as fun, enjoyable aspects of the adventure. Jade wields her Daï-jo staff with impressive skill and grace, and players are meant to feel a sense of accomplishment when vanquishing the hostile creatures they encounter. Although many games center on so-called heroes who are out for personal glory or revenge and whose interactions are defined almost entirely by violence, *Beyond Good & Evil*'s narrative establishes Jade's altruistic desire to achieve social justice. It's worth noting that Jade avoids falling into the tired cliche of the tough as nails, solve-all-problems-with-violence, "strong female character" archetype. Her quest is not about her pain, nor is it primarily about taking satisfaction in exacting violent retribution. It's about protecting her world and the people she cares about. Unlike so many one-dimensional, brooding heroes characterized by their own suffering, Jade does not wear the mantle of hero like a heavy burden; she retains her warmth and humanity over the course of her quest.

As a member of a resistance group called the IRIS Network, Jade uses her talents as a photographer to collect evidence documenting a conspiracy between invading aliens and the government of Hillys. She uses her combat skills to help rescue kidnapped members of the IRIS Network, but she rarely goes it alone. In an early scene, Jade is trapped until Pey'j appears, throwing her a staff to free herself and overcome the destructive alien force. The fact that Pey'j tells Jade to free herself (instead of doing it for her) is incredibly important. He assists her but doesn't rescue her. He knows that even in this situation, she's far from helpless, and the fact that Pey'j treats her as a capable partner encourages us to see her that way too.

There's a sense of both good-natured humor and respect written into the banter between Jade and her sidekicks: she's warm, but assertive, and the tone of their interactions makes it clear that they aren't designed just to make her or the player feel better. The mechanics aren't significantly different from those associated with sidekicks in other games: when they are attacked by enemies, they often use special abilities in coordination to advance. Because the writing so effectively creates a sense of respect and camaraderie between Jade and her companions, these relationships become much more than simple gameplay interactions. They become a vital and memorable part of the experience that works to emphasize the game's themes of friendship and cooperation.

In 2003, Jade emerged as a hero who wonders how she can meaningfully resist the injustices being committed by her government, and she finds the answer in organization and cooperation with others who are also committed to resistance. In the years since then, grassroots movements have only become a more vital and impactful force for raising awareness and shaping the discourse around structural inequality and injustice in our culture, and you might reasonably expect the games of today to reflect this. And yet, as a protagonist who is concerned first and foremost with social justice and the welfare of underprivileged people living in an unjust society, Jade still remains an exceedingly rare breed of video game hero.

Similar Characters: de Blob (*de Blob*), Melanie (*Cart Life*), the Scythian (*Sword & Sworcery*)

—Anita Sarkeesian and Carolyn Petit

JOEL

(est. 2013)
Franchise: *The Last of Us*
Developer: Naughty Dog

Joel is the anti-hero protagonist and principal playable character of Naughty Dog's *The Last of Us* (*TLOU*), a video game about post-apocalyptic America. A tough and rugged individualist, he is a hardened survivor of a pandemic that struck twenty years ago. To survive in this world, he has become a smuggler of medicine and weapons. Surprisingly, Joel's enemies are not so much the infected but his fellow human survivors who fight over scarce resources and territory. Paradoxically, the infected are not as monstrous as the other human survivors, making Joel's story a tale of what it means to be human in an inhuman world. This morality play begins when Joel is tasked to deliver to the Fireflies resistance movement an unusual commodity: fourteen-year-old Ellie. Apparently immune to the virus, Ellie may be able to help the Fireflies find a viral cure. Joel, often in alert mode, is best appreciated against his foil, the lighthearted and humorous Ellie.

A survivor, like Joel, may be read as a trope to analyze contemporary alienation due to commodification. Commodification refers to viewing human beings and social relations as things valued only for their material or economic utility.[1] In the post-apocalyptic genre, commodification is represented through the now familiar survivors' squabble over food and supplies. In *TLOU*, social relations revolve around the acquisition of commodities through black-market, cannibal, and gang operations. Joel's character assumes significance for his anti-heroism that is constellated around resisting the commodification of humans. His character destabilizes our notions of love, community, and morality to explore the limits of our humanity in a dystopian world.

Cast as an archetypal, flawed anti-hero obsessed with self-preservation, Joel resonates for many of us who likewise put a high premium on self-interest. He wins the gamer's sympathies because beneath his cruel facade lies a deep-seated emotional vulnerability due to the death of his loved ones. His anti-heroism is animated by survivor's guilt because he lives while his loved ones have died. To assuage guilt requires redemptive mortification, as argued by Kenneth Burke. Joel's mortification comes in the form of living the life of a survivor who fights the zombie-like infected yet is a virtual zombie himself—dead within. Thus Joel's character points us to a part of a person's life that may have become desensitized or lifeless due to personal trauma or alienation. In *TLOU*, the infected become zombie-like creatures who walk the streets and are seemingly alive but are no longer able to control their life and destiny. Gamers partake of Joel's life by playing his character, making Joel's choices as their own in an attempt to be the master of their own fate.

Through a riveting cut-scene at the start of the game, we catch a glimpse of Joel's life prior to the pandemic: he works in construction and is a single parent to fourteen-year-old Sarah. We witness a tender father-and-daughter moment on the night of his birthday. That same night, the pandemic reaches their town, and in the process of escaping the chaos that ensues, Sarah dies in Joel's arms. The Joel that emerges from then on is a tough, dark survivor. His baser instincts emerge as matters of sustenance and survival arise in a world where selfishness is a virtue and killing is often the only recourse. In an interview with *Game Informer*, creative director Neil Druckmann revealed, "You have these male, violent characters that have gone some place dark that are essentially dead inside. They get a chance at redemption when they are introduced to this kid [Ellie], this person who still has some innocence left in this world."[2] Through Joel's dark, anti-heroic character, we are engaged with the dynamics between zombie-ism and commodification and between self-preservation and redemption. That Joel, a male, dark anti-hero is foiled against Ellie, a female, hopeful hero, also highlights the gendered notions of the hero and the anti-hero in video game representations.

The climactic twist in the game narrative occurs when Joel refuses to surrender Ellie to the Fireflies when they finally arrive at the Fireflies headquarters after a long, harrowing journey. Apparently, Ellie's brain has to be cut open to find the vaccine. Without hesitation, Joel smashes the goal of the Fireflies to save humanity by keeping to himself the only known and probable cure. Afraid that Marlene, the Fireflies leader, will track down Ellie, Joel shoots the bleeding Marlene, who is desperately begging for her life. This scene is Joel's defining moment: his radical choice and the swiftness with which he implements this decision, killing or incapacitating anyone who gets in the way. As Druckmann argues, Joel is "even willing to put his soul on the line, damning the rest of mankind in exchange for this girl's [Ellie's] life." He explains that Joel's arc is all about the "irrational love" he feels for Ellie. Not caring much about his own life, Joel is "willing to give up his life" for her.[3] At the game's finale, Joel can even look Ellie straight in the eye, guiltless, when he lies to her by saying that there are many others like her who are immune to the virus and that she is no longer needed by the Fireflies.

Paradoxically, failing humanity is Joel's act of self-redemption. Joel redeems himself by holding on to someone dear to him and abandoning the broader cause of humanity's cure. Thus Joel's character animates the conflict between ethics and criminality but also the classic tension between self-interest and the common good, reminding us of the constant, "dualist" tendencies in human nature.[4] By saving Ellie's life, Joel is also saving himself. True to his mantra, "No matter what, you keep finding something to fight for," he hangs on to Ellie as his *raison d'être* after losing all else precious to him. In the end, Joel's defiance of the commodification of Ellie, wanted and prized for her brain, is his ultimate act of heroism and redemption.

Similar Characters: Booker de Witt (*BioShock Infinite*), Ico (*Ico*), Lee Everett (*The Walking Dead*)

—Gloria G. Gonzales

JOHN MARSTON

(est. 2010)
Franchise: *Red Dead Redemption*
Developer: Rockstar San Diego

John Marston is the protagonist of *Red Dead Redemption* (2010), a game set in 1911 in the borderlands of the United States and Mexico. He is a tortured soul, a reformed violent gang member, forced by government agents (who take his family hostage) to return to criminality and hunt down his former associates. Marston's journey through the game's arresting physical landscape—largely undertaken on horseback—enables the player to engage with a living personification of the American West. Yet it is a West that is itself in flux, and Marston is caught between a romanticized hankering for the past in an era of rapid technological, social, and political change.

The game's rich narrative follows Marston's violent quest to secure redemption from his role as a former gang member. The juxtaposition between violence and honor is central to Marston's significance: Marston has given up his violent past to become a loyal family man, so the actions of the government agents mean that it is only through killing that the player can succeed in reuniting Marston with his family. But this violence is not celebrated: Marston's in-game dialogue underlines his reluctance to kill, and the game's honor system punishes unwarranted and unjustified violent acts, causing Marston to be feared by the public and attacked by local law enforcement.

The game delivers a strong symbiosis between Marston's motivations and his deeds—violence is only undertaken for a higher purpose and against those who are beyond salvation or redemption. The game is designed so that the messages it seeks to communicate through narrative, visuals, and gameplay (collectively termed "procedural rhetoric" by Bogost) and the actions the player can perform (the "possibility space" in Bogost's terms) work in tandem.[5] However, redemption is never achieved—although Marston is reunited with his family, he is betrayed and killed in the finale by U.S. soldiers under the leadership of the government agents whom he was forced to serve. Marston is, thus, a victim of malevolent government agents who prompt his own return to violence yet ultimately destroy him. But his antipathy toward the government runs deeper than personal animosity, as he comes to personify a romanticized vision of the U.S. citizen who is free to roam a Wild West uninhibited by regulation, authority, or restriction, relying instead on his wits and character.

Nonetheless, the game displays a rare misstep that serves to confuse our understanding of the character. Midway through the game, Marston heads to Mexico to hunt down his former gang. Here the missions force Marston's participation in a civil war, and he fights alongside both government forces and rebels, his lack of ethical morality being justified on the basis that he will do anything for his family. This is jarring in terms of his character—the atrocities being committed by the government agents against innocent civilians suggest he would instinctively side with the rebels. The morally reprehensible acts the player (as Marston) is forced to undertake when siding with the government forces (including torching villagers' houses and standing by as soldiers rape women) are inconsistent with the game's central message, namely, that Marston is a reluctant instrument of violence who is ultimately driven by an honorable purpose.

The time frame of the game is also integral to Marston's character. Set at the beginning of the twentieth century—a period of rapid change when industrialization and the rise of the automobile undermined the cowboys' way of life and the values they represented—Marston's story forces us to reflect on how all of us are taken over by events and the rapid passage of time.

His antipathy to technology and the constraints it places upon him is perhaps most clearly displayed through transport in the game. As befitting a cowboy, he is most at home on horseback (his horse never being more than a tap of the directional pad away), which enables great speed and flexibility. Horseback riding also conjures up the romance of the West, making the player at one with the beautiful landscape Rockstar San Diego has created. In contrast, when Marston travels by car, he is represented as literally and figuratively trapped by technology, being as he is forced to accompany government agents, who have his family captive, and always as a passenger. While the agents extol the virtuous progress the car represents, Marston laments the existence of the "slow" and "uncomfortable" automobile and the erosion of his lifestyle it represents. Initially, at least, Marston's position is vindicated—the car breaks down on the first mission it is used, subjecting Marston and the agents to serious danger as they are attacked by gang members, all of whom are on horseback.

Yet Marston cannot avoid technology, nor can he resist its capacity to turn the tide in his favor, as demonstrated by the benefits he derives from superior weaponry. In several missions Marston makes use of a Gatling gun—a heavy-duty precursor to the machine gun that allows him to kill multiple enemies—demonstrating that technology is integral, not only figuratively but materially, to his in-game progress (further missions do not unlock without mastery of the Gatling gun). His personal arsenal of weapons also improves as the game proceeds, demonstrating the significant advantages accrued through technological progress. Marston is caught in a technological bind that confronts us all—unable to succeed without technology, but acutely aware that by using it, he is undermining the very lifestyle he seeks to embody and protect.

Overall, Marston is both pawn and agent. He has immense power, but that power is always exercised in the service of others; caught and dominated by government agents, he is also a victim of a fast-changing world he can never adjust to. Yet he is "more than a mere man": Marston allows us to reflect on the changing nature of American society and the founding myths of American identity.

Similar Characters: Commander Shepard (*Mass Effect*), Niko Bellic (*Grand Theft Auto IV*), Solid Snake (*Metal Gear*)

—Nick Robinson

JON DOWD

(est. 2003)
Franchise: *MVP Baseball*
Developer: EA Canada

Even the most dedicated baseball fan could be forgiven for not knowing the epic achievements of Jon Dowd. A batter legendary for 600-foot home runs and hitting over 100 home runs in a season, Dowd would bump Hank Aaron and Babe Ruth out of the conversation for the greatest hitter in baseball history. But there's a reason many baseball video game fans have never heard of Jon Dowd: he is the fictionalization of an all-time greatest hitter. Despite over twenty-five years of sports video games using characters with actual player names, abilities, and even likenesses, Jon Dowd is one of the few characters in sports video games who is not named after a real player in a real-life sport.

As with most sports, licensing agreements with Major League Baseball (MLB) and the player's union (Major League Baseball Players Association; MLBPA) provide that nearly all MLB players can be included in MLB video games. According to www.baseball-almanac.com, the only players that the MLBPA excludes from the union are "replacement players" (those who crossed the union picket lines during the 1994–1995 players' strike). In rare cases, some athletes decline to sign the licensing agreement, usually to elicit a separate contract with additional compensation for their likeness and name. Yet to date, no game publisher has agreed to a separate contract with an active player; consequently those players' name and portrayal must be removed from sports video games.

One such player was Barry Bonds, who in 2002 informed the MLBPA that he would not sign the group's agreement. In doing so Bonds became the first MLB player not to sign in the MLBPA's thirty-year history. While Bonds was the first MLB player to do so, this action has occurred in the NBA (Michael Jordan) and the NFL (Lavar Arrington). By not signing, Bonds guaranteed his absence in name, likeness, and even jersey number from all MLB-licensed games. But how could game developers in the 1990s release a baseball video game without seven-time MVP (and, arguably, the world's greatest living hitter) Barry Bonds? The absence of a bench player or middle reliever might go unnoticed by many video game users, but the omission of a recognizable player of Barry Bonds's stature not only would affect the player's ability to identify with the game, it might also call into question the integrity of a product that purports to be realistic and crafted with actual player abilities. Imagine a current release of video games for basketball without Steph Curry, or soccer without Lionel Messi. Video game players demand that each sport's best athletes exist in the virtual gaming world. Without licensing rights, developers are forced to create fictional players who possess a star athlete's abilities but have a different name, jersey, and likeness.

Enter Jon Dowd, a right-handed outfielder with the most potent hitting skills in the critically acclaimed and popular video game franchise *MVP Baseball*. With the inclusion of Jon Dowd, we witness the unique case of a fictional ballplayer being the best in the game because his hitting acumen is without equal. According to www.gamefaqs.com, Dowd has a hitting rating of 94.38 (on a scale of 100), which is the highest in a game where no other player rates above 88. James Newman notes that what makes a game character desirable isn't so much appearance as the character's abilities[6]—in this case, hitting contact rate and power. Dowd's high rating overcomes the fact that he looks nothing like the player he was constructed to replace. Unsurprisingly, this fictional player is the most feared hitter in the game, and he routinely appears as one of the greatest video game athletes ever.[7] In *Bleacher Report*'s ranking of the all-time greatest video game athletes, familiar names like Mike Tyson, Bo Jackson, and Jeremy Roenick are identifiable, but Jon Dowd joins that list too and is labeled "the greatest replacement character in video game history."[8]

Jon Dowd isn't the only case of a fictional video game character being generated due to a player not agreeing to licensing deals. The landmark football video game *Tecmo Super Bowl* introduced us to "QB Eagles" (Randall Cunningham) and "QB Bills" (Jim Kelly); the basketball classic *NBA Live* had "Player 99" (Michael Jordan); and when Nintendo opted not to renew its licensing agreement with Mike Tyson for *Punch-Out!!*, the fictitious "Mr. Dream" emerged, boasting a different appearance but retaining all of Iron Mike's boxing ability. In fact, Jon Dowd isn't even the only fictional Barry Bonds substitute in existence. In *MLB 2k7*, "Joe Young" comes to the plate, and in *MLB 07: The Show*, it's "Reggie Stocker" crushing the long ball; yet Dowd is the most dominant in terms of ability and frequency of appearance, having appeared in both the 2004 and 2005 editions of *MVP Baseball* and also in *The Bigs*. But regardless of the example, characters like Jon Dowd illustrate that game developers are able to create replacement characters abundant in talent and generic only in name and appearance.

The question then becomes that of how these fictional replacement characters affect the public's memory of athletic dominance. Video game players take ownership and pride in their character's achievements and conquests, and sports video games are not exempt from this behavior. Gamers sharing stories of high scores, broken records, and the virtual, on-field achievements of their favorite team or player is routine; sometimes the actual athletes are roped into hearing the gamer's accounts. In the NFL films documentary *Tecmo Bowl*, football players Bo Jackson and Christian Okoye talk about being approached by fans complimenting them not for their real-life achievements but rather for the exploits of their (namesake) character in a video game (*Tecmo Super Bowl*). Statistical-analysis site www.fivethirtyeight.com reports that annually some athletes in the major sports complain that their video game representation isn't sufficiently rated. Athletes know too well that the public's memory is affected by how the player's virtual counterpart fares in video games. What then becomes of fictional characters like Jon Dowd in relation to Barry Bonds? Unable to share a name, likeness, or even jersey number, it would seem that the two great players exist solely in their own universes: one real, one virtual.

Similar Characters: Mr. Dream (*Punch-Out!!*), Player 99 (*NBA Live*), QB Eagles/Bills (*Tecmo Super Bowl*)

—Cameron Basquiat

K

The original *Command and Conquer* (*C&C*), one of the earliest and most influential real-time strategy games, plays out the conflict between two opposing factions with striking comparability to the real contemporary world. On one side there is the GDI (Global Defense Initiative), a global "peacekeeping" organization with massive political, economic, and military resources. Their opposition, the Brotherhood of Nod (Nod) are a decentralized, quasi-religious militia group led by the mysterious, and now deeply iconic, Kane. Kane appears in all the games of the Tiberium fictional universe. He is portrayed in *C&C*'s full-motion videos by actor Joseph D. Kucan,[1] who also directs the videos in the series and holds the world record as the longest-running actor in a video game series[2] (from 1995's *C&C* to 2010's *Tiberian Twilight*). The actor has become notorious for his integral role in the franchise narrative in congruence with the striking real-world relevance, religious themes, and familiarity of the villain.

Alongside a significant cast of other characters generally portrayed by Westwood Studios employees, Kane is one of the most visible characters. He is a bald man of indeterminate age who speaks in explicit commands and prophetic comments. He first appears in the second half of the single-player Nod campaign to brief players on their upcoming missions. Alternatively, if the game player is playing as GDI, Kane takes an opportunity partway through that campaign to taunt the player about his or her military failures and impending death, creating a striking immediacy that makes it seem as if the player were being spoken to directly. At the conclusion of the Nod campaign, Kane offers the player the ability to select a major global landmark to destroy; at the conclusion of the GDI campaign (later accepted as the canon ending), Kane is apparently killed, either buried beneath massive chunks of falling rubble or caught directly in the blast of a space-based laser weapon, bringing an end (seemingly) to the character and his faction.

Despite his apparent demise, however, Kane reappears in each subsequent game. In *Tiberian Sun* he reemerges with great aplomb from death, feigning to be unhurt, but actually with significant scarring to half his face; and at the game's end, he is run through the chest with a sharp piece of building debris, once more apparently succumbing to his wounds. In *Firestorm*, Kane is entirely absent and explicitly declared missing up until the final cut-scene when he is shown in some kind of advanced biological support system repairing the presumably extensive (yet never fatal) damage to his body. In *Tiberium Wars* he appears in perfect health again and subsequently displays surprising foreknowledge about that game's alien invaders (themselves hinted at but never seen since the start of the franchise) who also seem to know something about Kane's origin. Throughout his appearances, eighty years apart in the game's narrative, he doesn't age.

Kane's name is not a coincidence: the game is replete with the Judeo-Christian mythology that the character uses to legitimize his politico-religious power, just as his name is an obvious alternate spelling of "Cain." The manual to the original *C&C* lists a range of aliases for Kane gathered by GDI's intelligence personnel, including the biblical "Jacob" and the Arabic "al-Quaymm." Nod's "stealth tank" is known by the code name "Ezekiel's Wheel," while the name of Nod itself is a reference to the Land of Nod that the biblical Cain was condemned to wander in as punishment for killing his brother, Abel. Indeed, Nod seem to draw upon this myth as part of the construction of Kane's mythical historicity: the original game's final cut-scene shows an excavation of the Temple of Nod and what appears to be an ancient stone carving of Cain killing Abel buried deep below the seat of Nod's power.

Kane's apparent immortality could reasonably be interpreted as the "mark of Cain" placed upon the biblical Cain to prevent others from killing him in vengeance for his crime; or, within the game's narrative, the biblical mark of Cain may be a historical-mythological interpretation for the immortality of Kane. In *Tiberium Wars*, the alien Scrin say they are aware of Kane's existence and that he is nonhuman, suggesting that our real-world biblical tales were perhaps attempts to explain the immortality of Kane. In *Tiberium Twilight* this is all but admitted when Kane implies that he has been a resident of Earth for millennia and states to the player that he has always found human fanaticism a useful tool with which to achieve his own goals. By incorporating real-world mythologies and fictional histories, the series both cleverly blurs the lines between story and reality while also giving the character and his faction a backstory with depth and cultural resonance that extends far beyond the confines of the game. At the same time, adopting concepts from real-world religions with billions of adherents and assigning them to a nominally evil faction is a surprisingly bold narrative move but one that pays off handsomely in building the resonance and impact of both the Brotherhood of Nod and Kane himself.

The extent to which Kane's entire narrative was planned (however loosely) from the start is challenging to say, but the seeds of Kane's apparent immortality, sown right at the start of the original 1995 game, continued to produce a detailed, "long game" narrative over a decade later. This gave the character a tremendous endurance across the varied settings and eras of the series, while seeding the games with just enough hints to allow the player to piece together the character's origins and objectives, but at the same time utilizing real-world religious mythology to add depth, detail, and background to the game's highly original, fictional universe. The character plays upon a range of real-world concerns—terror, global politics, and a range of historical-religious anxieties and themes—in the context of a deeply narrative-driven series of games, and in doing so, presents us with a rare comparison of the politics of the virtual world and those of the real world.

Similar Characters: Albert Wesker (*Resident Evil*), Big Boss (*Metal Gear Solid*), Ganondorf (*The Legend of Zelda*)

—Mark R. Johnson

KIM KARDASHIAN

(est. 2014)
Franchise: *Kim Kardashian: Hollywood*
Developer: Glu Mobile

Ten years ago, it would have seemed a long shot that Kim Kardashian might become one of the most important characters in video games. Kardashian is part of a family famous simply for being celebrities: her family makes up the cast of the popular, unscripted series *Keeping Up with the Kardashians*, which debuted in 2007. Kim is unquestionably the star of the show, although her fame predates it after an incident of a leaked sex tape and heavy partying with fellow "celebutante" Paris Hilton in the mid-2000s. Today Kim's name and face are central to her family's not-so-small entertainment empire, which includes several television series, books, a clothing line, clothing stores, a cosmetics line, a fragrance line, and, of course, one of the most profitable mobile games of all time.

The game *Kim Kardashian: Hollywood* (*KK:H*) was released by Glu Mobile in 2014. In many ways, the game itself is both original and unoriginal; the game is a reskinned and amped-up version of a previous Glu game, *Stardom: The A-List*. Yet without Kim, *Stardom* lacks heart. It is the presence of Kim Kardashian in the game that makes it more robust and gives the player a sense of both style and purpose.

In *KK:H*, the player does not play as Kim Kardashian. Kim is a non-player character, not an avatar. Instead, the player designs an avatar (male or female) based on a limited number of stylistic preferences. When the game begins, the player is shown a black screen with the words "Before you were famous . . . you were new to Hollywood." After this, the player has a chance encounter with Kim and is presented with a series of options for working their way from the dreaded E-List all the way to the number-one slot on the A-List. The gameplay is a series of choices: Should the player focus on parties or dating? Should the player engage in "drama" with Hollywood nemeses or potential employers? Should the player adopt a child? Should the player endorse risky products? The work of *KK:H* (and it truly is a kind of work) involves a never-ending set of lifestyle decisions. When the player makes the wrong decision, they lose fans and plummet down from the A-List to the E-List. And while the player is not Kim, the player is always striving to become her—becoming Kim serves as the unachievable goal of the game.

The game itself has received a lot of attention in part due to its seemingly impossible success. In its first year, the game raked in over $200 million and Glu Mobile enjoyed a stock hike of over 42 percent.[3] One *Jezebel* author, Tracie Morrissey, confessed to spending almost $500 on the game, and she was not alone. Other bloggers have responded angrily to its success, claiming that *KK:H* is not a game at all. Yet at the center of this dispute is the title character herself. Our social admonishment of Kim Kardashian (the reality TV star and celebutante) bleeds into the critiques of the game, making the character and the real person indistinguishable. At the same time, it is impossible to ignore that the game's popularity would not have hit the same peak without the underlying presence of that specific celebrity character. After all, *KK:H* without Kim Kardashian is just a weak celebrity game. Subsequently, Glu has made similar-but-different games involving Kim's sisters Kendall and Kylie and musician-themed games honoring both Brittany Spears and Katy Perry. None have been nearly as popular. When we play *KK:H*, we are playing the celebrity brand as a way of playing with our own social status.

Given all of this, it is useful to consider the importance of Kim Kardashian herself—not the real Kim but the fictionalized character moving like a ghost through *KK:H*. The fictional Kim is both a goal post and a cheerleader. She motivates the player, complimenting the player's style, "smizing" (Tyra Banks's term for smiling with one's eyes), and ability to make clever decisions. Kim is our BFF, our confidant, and our advisor. She guides us through her world, allowing us to taste it but not gorge ourselves.

The player, of course, will never become Kim Kardashian. Even after hitting the number-one position, the player still lacks money to spend with impunity. The superior status of the Kardashian family is made clear through the currency system of the game. The game features two competing forms of currency: dollars and K-coins. The dollars function as they do in the real world, but K-coins are used for particularly special items or to "charm" people. We can purchase more K-coins through the free-to-play system, but we will never inherently have the natural Kardashian charm that backs this currency. It seems ironic that the game begins with the line "Before you were famous . . . you were new to Hollywood." After all, Kim Kardashian was never new to Hollywood. The player will always have to work harder than her and will never fully achieve Kim's level of success inside the game world. In *KK:H*, the house always wins.

But Kim Kardashian, the real Kim Kardashian, has also impacted the video game industry through the release of *KK:H*. As the video game industry continues to shift, this game (among others) has helped to attract more women players. A recent Pew study showed that while 49 percent of Americans play video games, only 10 percent label themselves as "gamers."[4] This reinforces research done by Adrienne Shaw,[5] but it also reminds us that there are new kinds of games meant for new kinds of players and that these players don't always identify themselves as "gamers." Kim Kardashian, as an entrepreneur, reminds us of the shifting identity of the gamer and the ever-changing landscape of the industry. And Kim Kardashian, the character, reminds us to smize on our way to being number one.

Similar Characters: Britney Spears (*Britney Spears: American Dream*), Katy Perry (*Katy Perry Pop*), Kendall and Kylie Jenner (*Kendall and Kylie*)

—Shira Chess

THE KING OF ALL COSMOS

(est. 2004)
Franchise: *Katamari Damacy*
Developer: Namco

The King of All Cosmos has captured the imagination of gamers globally. The King himself, aesthetically unique and possessing a backstory that includes abuse, power, and mistakes, is even so charming and not unlike the gods of the Greek pantheon. The King also represents a postmodern mash-up of styles and stories. He illustrates how bricolage[6] and the breaking of the fourth wall can demonstrate—through postmodern storytelling—the complexities of identity: king, father, destroyer, savior, victim, and anti-hero.

What began as Keita Takahashi's school project in the Namco Digital Hollywood Game Laboratory, *Katamari Damacy* was a quirky game that found modest commercial success in Japan and incredible critical success in the United States.[7] A game about rolling up small objects (paper clips, coins, flies) to create a mass large enough to roll up large objects (elephants, ships, planets) requires a fairly big story and a fairly big character.[8] Namco found both in the King. A larger-than-life body with an even bigger personality, he is obsessed with the notion that an amalgam of little things makes up for big mistakes.

The King plays the role of a Greek god: he is a giant and a ruler (the comical use of the royal "we" never gets old in his speech). While his attire resembles a colorful version of David Bowie's in *Labyrinth*, his voice is the sound of a record scratching, as if he will break into a rap at any moment. Aesthetically, we can say the King is created through the act of bricolage, much like the first wave of punk culture. He is a dash of Zeus, a pinch of the Goblin King, and a dab of Grand Wizzard Theodore, all topped with an incredible moustache and beard. He is jovial yet judgmental, aloof yet intolerant of failure, a renaissance man and an oaf; he is a charming caricature of royalty and deity. Eloquent, and at the same time clumsy in his speech, the King is much like his description of the sky: "This sky is not pretty at all. It's rough and masculine. Possibly sweaty." While his form may be god-like, his disjointed statements belie an all-too-human view of the world, one filled with contradictions and distractions.

The King plays three roles simultaneously in the Katamari games: antagonist, catalyst, and mentor. He is not only the cause of the problems affecting the game's hero, the Prince (or the Prince's Cousins in sequels), he also provides the means to solve the problems and guides the Prince. As he admits, "We broke it. Yes, we were naughty. Completely naughty. So, so very sorry. But just between you and us, it felt quite good." While the King could solve his own problems, according to himself at least, he sends his son on the quest to mold him and prove his worth. He also provides color commentary and guidance along the way, warming the heart of the Prince and the faithful player: "My, very princely indeed. Such skill. And such class. Dazzling. We feel a swoon coming on." Antagonistic, yet supportive, the King is a study in contrasts. His personality reflects these contrasts and represents the honesty of the postmodern ruler: powerful, yet insecure. We don't need the King to be stately, all the time.

In *Katamari Damacy*, the first game in the franchise, the King destroys all the stars and celestial bodies while on a drinking binge. In order to rectify this cosmic blunder, the King gives his son a *katamari* (Japanese for "cluster") and sends him to the place with the most "things," Earth, to roll things up and create new stars—in other words, to act as a bricoleur. The Prince rolls up household goods, then households, then neighborhoods, and more until the King is satisfied with the size of the *katamari* and sends it into space to become a star. In each game, the cycle is repeated until the King's mistakes are rectified.

The fragile arrogance of the King is legendary. While he takes credit for every dilemma the Prince solves, insults the Prince and his Cousins, and boasts of his accomplishments—ranging from being a natural-born fighter to creating the game *Katamari Damacy* (a reflexive moment that challenges the fourth wall because the game seems to know it is a game)—he slips into depression when one of his fans likens him to a grade school principal. The King comes by his neuroses honestly, however—as do many great gods, he has daddy issues.

Over the course of the *Katamari* games, we learn that Papa, the King's father, raised him with greatness in mind. As a child, the King won second place in a junior-league boxing tournament, and a displeased Papa tossed his son's trophy off a bridge and into a river. Later in his life, the King, forlorn after losing a chunk of his pompadour-styled hair in a knife fight with local ruffians, runs into his future queen. When the King tells his father of his newfound love, his father disapproves and strikes him; the King retaliates, earning the respect of Papa, who later demonstrates how proud he is of his son, approves of the Queen, and leaves his kingdom to the King.

The cycle of dysfunction continues as the King attempts to both live his life to the fullest and shape his progeny. While he coaches his son and sings (scratches?) his praises, the King also belittles him for any failure and revisits the abuse he himself endured as a child by physically assaulting the Prince. On one particularly memorable moment, the King uses the Prince as a punching bag. The relationship between the King and the Prince is as complex as the multidimensional ones in our own lives. Continuing the King's practice of blurring the boundaries of the game world, @KingOfTheCosmos leaves us with his wisdom on Twitter as well: "Ashes to ashes and dust to dust? We would think that both ash and dust would want to be something else. Like a movie star or sailor?!" Even kings ponder their mortality.

Similar Characters: The Collector (*LittleBigPlanet*), the Kings (*Little King's Story*), the Magypsies (*Mother 3*)

—Roger Altizer Jr.

KIRBY

(est. 1992)
Franchise: *Kirby's Dream Land*
Developer: HAL Laboratory

While Kirby was originally a placeholder in *Dream Land*, by the end of its development he had huffed and puffed his way into the heart of his creator, Masahiro

Sakurai, and had become the game's lead protagonist. Named in honor of the American lawyer John Kirby (who successfully defended Nintendo in *Universal City Studios, Inc. v. Nintendo Co., Ltd* in a lawsuit claiming *Donkey Kong* was infringing on the trademark of *King Kong*) and lauded as one of the cutest video game characters of all time, Kirby has come to be featured in more than twenty video game titles across several genres, including action, puzzle, and racing games. Today, Kirby's original title, *Kirby's Dream Land,* remains an iconic, early Nintendo title held by many in high esteem. However, beyond Kirby's cute exterior is a representation that reflects cultural differences between the East and West.

Kirby is easily recognizable with his round shape, rosy cheeks, big oval eyes, and pink body (in the original Game Boy title, Kirby had a white body due to the gray-scale limitations of the device). While he is often depicted as jolly and cheery, Kirby's demeanor (as depicted in game cover-art) varies, depending on whether the title is a North American or Japanese release. In Japan, Kirby has a typically cheerful expression, whereas in North America, Kirby has a bolder and more aggressive expression. Nintendo has stated that the "battle ready" appearance of Kirby is thought to appeal to a wider audience in North America.[9]

These differences in the presentation of Kirby should not be considered trivial but rather evidence of the different ways in which aggression and violence are portrayed and received across Eastern and Western cultures. Eastern cultures are more likely to emphasize the consequences of violent and aggressive acts by portraying them as an undesirable means to an end, while Western narratives often reward aggressive behavior or downplay the consequences. For example, a study by the Center for Media Literacy found that while the amount of violence on American and Japanese television programs is about equal, in Japanese-produced television the "bad guys" perform twice as many violent acts as in American-produced television where it is the "good guys" who perform twice as many violent acts. These general differences in the portrayal of violence and aggression likely contribute to the variation in Kirby's demeanor across markets as well as Japan's overall preference for family-friendly video game titles (as noted by overall sales) rather than games with violent or anti-social content.

Perhaps Kirby's most notable trait is his insatiable appetite. It is Kirby's boundless hunger that drives the in-game mechanics and story line: In *Kirby's Dream Land,* King Dedede steals all the food and Kirby must chase down this tyrant to find the food and restore the land. Somewhat ironically, to defeat his enemies, Kirby has the ability to consume them and adopt their abilities. When faced with a fire-breathing enemy, for example, Kirby can inhale deeply, consume his enemy whole, and subsequently gain the ability to breathe fire himself. Kirby then uses his newly acquired skills to either defeat subsequent monsters or again inhale them and adopt different kinds of abilities. Kirby can also consume objects to adopt new abilities or to replenish his health. Otherwise, he can simply breathe in air and float with puffed cheeks.

Kirby's ability to consume his enemies and adopt their abilities likely reflects the values of the Eastern culture in which he was developed. For example, unlike Western cultures where originality is held in the highest regard, in Eastern cultures, copies of great works are thought to be of equal value as the original.[10] When Kirby consumes his enemies, he takes on their characteristics and properties: in essence, copying is the key to Kirby's success. Kirby's abilities are also reflective of a post–World War II cultural shift in Japanization. While "Japanization" refers to the pre–World War II assimilation of Asian others into Japan, after the war the meaning of the word changed to reflect the adoption of Western cultural influences within Japanese culture, particularly American culture.[11] As noted by Iwabuchi, it is important to recognize that the term "Japanization" is more reflective of the English word "appropriation" rather than the word "imitation," emphasizing the active agency of the Japanese to repurpose (i.e., make a copy that is superior to the original) rather than simply copy.[12] This process of Japanization is reflected in Kirby's abilities: rather than becoming an exact copy of his consumed enemy, he operates as a hybrid, incorporating the best of his original self and the consumed other to become the best of both.

More generally, the way Kirby interacts may speak to a larger culture of consumption, both within and outside video game culture. Although perhaps unintentional, Kirby's insatiable appetite parallels the consumerism culture (i.e., consuming to display power and status) that has long been a staple of industrialized societies. As is often found in consumer-based cultures, Kirby is never satisfied as he continues to consume. Perhaps this was a satirical way for Japanese developers to comment on consumer culture, or perhaps it was developed in response to the rising popularity of video game consumption worldwide. In 1992 when Kirby was developed, the worldwide video game market was experiencing rapid growth, and there was an ever-increasing demand for more video game software (i.e., games) and hardware (i.e., consoles).

Although Kirby is typically regarded as cute and cuddly, he represents far more than he is given credit for. The design and functionality of Kirby not only represent the culture in which he was developed, they also serve as a "living" illustration of cultural differences and overlap between the East and West, particularly in regard to the value that is placed on violence and consumerism. While Kirby's legacy may always be related to his appearance, we would all be wise to remember that he is also the original king of consumption.

Similar Characters: Clefairy (*Pokémon*), SackBoy (*LittleBigPlanet*), Yoshi (*Super Mario World*)

—Rachel Kowert

KOS-MOS

(est. 2002)
Franchise: *Xenosaga*
Developer: Monolith Soft

For a franchise invested in the question of what it means to be human, it is fitting that KOS-MOS (Kosmos Obey Strategical Multiple Operation System) stands at the center of the *Xenosaga* universe. Though a number of characters from the *Xenosaga* franchise would be worthy of discussion—from the involuntary cyborg Ziggy to M.O.M.O. the synthetic human and others—the android KOS-MOS warrants particular attention for how she speaks to the question of whether a machine can contain a soul. Introduced in 2002, KOS-MOS has a design and narrative trajectory that speak to the evolution of posthumanism from the android to the cyborg and back again to the android: from the failure of a machine to replace the mind to the replacement of the body by a machine to what futurist Ray Kurzweil calls the age of spiritual machines.

Our first introduction to KOS-MOS is as a picture of failure. Although her robotic body was intended to serve as the lynchpin of a complex battle system designed to combat an alien life-form known as the Gnosis, we learn that KOS-MOS's functionality is severely limited—only safely able to operate in a constrained virtual environment—and there were multiple casualties the last time full functionality was attempted. Due to this instability and also concern for human safety, KOS-MOS's operating system is rarely on, only being activated during routine system testing. There is little initial optimism that KOS-MOS will ever function properly or even live up to her combat potential. But this outlook changes when the spaceship transporting KOS-MOS is attacked and her system automatically self-activates in time for her to save many members of the ship. Initially, KOS-MOS speaks in a robotic, monotone voice, but as the series progresses her dialogue becomes more humanlike, reflecting the ongoing awakening of her contained consciousness.

The in-game reception of KOS-MOS parallels the ongoing evolution of posthumanism that was under way at the turn of the century. Similar to the disappointment that followed the unbridled optimism of the early days of artificial intelligence research, KOS-MOS arrives in the *Xenosaga* universe at a time when most individuals have given up on the idea of conscious machines. Just as the famous Turing Test—the philosophical premise that if an artificial intelligence could convince an average person that it was human, then for all sakes and purposes that artificial intelligence ought to be considered functionally human—garnered limited success only in highly constrained conditions (e.g., text-based, narrow-topic environments), so too is KOS-MOS's initial functional success limited to simulated environments. Likewise, just as the concept of the cyborg took hold of posthumanism, so too is KOS-MOS's world populated by augmented humans and synthetic humans—bioengineered life-forms meant to emulate (but, importantly, not replace) humans. The return of the android, as represented by KOS-MOS, is seen as antiquated, and, as *Xenosaga*'s in-game database notes, "in an age where 'simulated' A.I. . . . have become the norm, [KOS-MOS represents the continued pursuit of] the elusive goal of creating a completely man-made A.I." Nonetheless, like posthumanism outside the game, KOS-MOS's arrival speaks to the emerging return of the android in a way that is similar to the emergence of advanced AI systems like IBM's Watson and the U.S. National Science Foundation's Project Lifelike—which have reinvigorated enthusiasm (and fear) that posthumanism means a future without humans.

To this end, KOS-MOS suggests that analytical and physical superiority does not necessarily make for a better "human." Early in *Xenosaga Episode I*, KOS-MOS considers allies as collateral damage if they stand in the way of her objectives. When one of the characters confronts her, asking, "Do you understand what you've just done?! . . .Why did you shoot Lieutenant Virgil?! With your power, you don't have to sacrifice anyone to . . . ," KOS-MOS replies,

> Any changes in my firing position to avoid Lieutenant Virgil while protecting you, would have resulted in a 30% depreciation in my offensive capabilities. On the other hand, with the Lieutenant's death, there would only be a 0.2% drop in efficacy. I simply chose the option with the highest probability to keep you alive.

When the character replies, "How can you even say that! Have you no conscience?!" KOS-MOS robotically responds, "You forget, I am not human. I am merely a weapon."

As the narrative continues, however, KOS-MOS evolves from being merely a weapon to possessing a consciousness as well. *Xenosaga Episode 3* reveals that KOS-MOS's combat functionality is actually secondary to her latent purpose of serving as a container for a very powerful, ancient soul. This soul was meant to remain dormant until delivered to its intended destination—the preserved body of the original soul's owner—but a permutation occurs and the soul and KOS-MOS's machinery "contaminate" one another. This is a "good" contamination, however, for it reorients this ancient soul to the problems of KOS-MOS's present *and* teaches KOS-MOS to value the sanctity of life. It is perhaps ironic that it is only after this contamination that KOS-MOS's potential as humanity's savior reaches fruition: KOS-MOS obtains posthuman perfection only after being infected by human imperfection, the soul.

In sum, KOS-MOS's narrative trajectory offers a commentary on the ethics of posthumanism. Futurists such as Ray Kurzweil often believe that humans are rotten with imperfection and that posthumanism offers a way out from the "cumbersome maintenance rituals" and often "derivative, petty, and circumscribed" monotony of human intelligence.[13] Conservative bioethicists, on the other hand, worry that posthumanism is rotten with perfection and that the quest to rid ourselves of imperfection will result in the erasure of the very thing that makes us human. For postmodern ethicist Michael Hyde, the question of the posthuman is too substantial to simplistically embrace as a panacea for all our ills or to fear as a harbinger of our demise, and thus "public moral argument [is] essential."[14] KOS-MOS's public contribution is to suggest that posthuman perfection is contingent upon being infected with human imperfection.

Similar Characters: GLaDOS (*Portal*), HK-47 (*Star Wars: Knights of the Old Republic*), SHODAN (*System Shock*)

—Robert Mejia

KRATOS

(est. 2005)
Franchise: *God of War*
Developer: Sony Santa Monica

In 2005, the fallen Spartan Kratos burst on the gaming scene like rage personified. Though easily caricatured due to this excessive anger, Kratos's story of revenge and bloodlust hit a nerve with gamers as *God of War* quickly became one of *Sony Interactive Entertainment's* most valuable franchises. But more importantly, Kratos and *God of War* emerged at a moment when multiple American cultural artifacts—such as the film *300* (2006) and earlier book *Gates of Fire* (1998)—were presenting Sparta and not Athens as a model for American democracy. This is the same era that gave us "The War on Terror" and the rise of neo-national movements across the globe, particularly in the West, and hence an analysis of Kratos may offer insight into the cultural logic that undergirds the xenophobic, anti-intellectual, masculine rhetoric of these movements.

Players are first introduced to Kratos as he stands at the edge of a cliff, ready to commit suicide. Filled with despair due to the death of his wife and daughter—by his own hands—Kratos believes that the Gods of Olympus have abandoned him. A former Spartan captain, Kratos had been a devoted follower of Ares (the Greek God of War) until he was tricked by Ares into killing his own family. Cursed as a result of this moral crime, Kratos's skin is turned ash-white as the ashes of his dead family are permanently bonded to his skin. Known since as the "Ghost of Sparta," Kratos's journey is one from despair to disdain, as he first attempts to court the gods in his quest for redemption, but then soon comes to believe that redemption can only come through revenge against the gods themselves—for they are responsible for the system that gave birth to the unjust world that Kratos occupies.

There is much about Kratos and his world that may have resonated with players in the mid-2000s. If the *God of War* mythos is that of a transition from the old guard world order (i.e., the Gods of Olympus) to a new world order led by Kratos's rage, then such rage and belief in the need for a new world order may have been familiar to gamers—particularly Western gamers—not too far removed from the events of September 11. Like Kratos, players in the West may have felt that the time for talk had passed and that actions—particularly violent actions—speak louder than words, and could serve as an "emotional kind of [release]."[15] Like Kratos, players in the West may have sympathized in the belief that nothing was beyond critique, nothing was taboo, nor sacred, and that in a world where one "literally has nothing left to loose [*sic*]" political correctness and established ethics were antiquated, even dangerous.[16] And as a result, like Kratos, players in the West may have felt disillusioned with the world around them: a sense that the old guard of politics as usual was not only inadequate for confronting the politics of the present but in fact the problem itself.

For players sympathetic to such beliefs, they would have found a White, anti-intellectual, misogynistic, all-around amoral male role model. Indeed, with his tall, lean muscular frame and shaven head, with only a blood-red tattoo streaked across his body to contrast against his stark white skin, Kratos's character design seems as if it were pulled straight out of Neo-Nazi propaganda. And it loosely was, as *God of War* franchise director David Jaffe has said:

> It took a long time to figure out what Kratos would look like, and ultimately we took inspiration from Edward Norton in *American History X* [1998], when he played a Nazi. There's this scene in which the cops arrest him and you just see how buffed and built he's gotten. I showed that to the artist and I said, 'Okay, that sense of power and aggression that you see in his face, can we somehow take that, the essence of what he's exuding, and somehow turn that into a character that fits in this Greek mythology world?[17]

And just like Edward Norton's portrayal of Neo-Nazism, so too does Kratos show disdain for intellectuals and women, with multiple scenes requiring the player to brutalize these individuals. For instance, one such scene requires Kratos to force a scribe of the Sisters of Fates to translate a tablet, which ultimately reads that the only way to gain audience with the Fates is to make a sacrifice of the scribe; and another scene requires players to force an almost completely naked woman to hold open two portcullises, which results in her being crushed by the gates' pulley system. Some players have argued that these points are moot as Kratos kills just about everyone; while true, the difference is that nearly every other character has agency—even if such agency is not enough to withstand the rage of Kratos.

Kratos is a part of the American cultural imaginary that emerged at the turn of the century seeking a return to the roots of White Western culture. Just as this movement—rooted in Ronald Reagan's 1980s culture wars—imagined that White men had become the victims of feminism, multiculturalism, and the transition to a global information-oriented economy, so too does Kratos embody this sense of victimage. Everyone familiar with Kratos agrees that he does horrible things, but his behavior is framed as reasonable considering everything he has lost. Kratos will and does have his revenge. The Gods of Olympus prove no match for his rage. Let us hope our gods prove a more formidable match against those like Kratos among us.

Similar Characters: Duke Nukem (*Duke Nukem*); Marcus Fenix (*Gears of War*); William Joseph "B. J." Blazkowicz (*Wolfenstein 3D*)

—Robert Mejia

L

LARA CROFT

(est. 1996)
Franchise: *Tomb Raider*
Developer: Core Design

Lara Croft is likely one of the most influential video game characters ever, and she is certainly among the most significant yet also most controversial female protagonists in a video game. Cherished by her fans as a strong female lead in control of the action, she is also criticized by many observers as a stereotypical "sex-bomb" character controlled by mostly male players.

However, it is next to impossible to reduce this multifaceted character to one reading—not least because she has been depicted multiple times and from many different angles: Lara Croft has starred as the main character in more than a dozen *Tomb Raider* games starting with the earliest title (*Tomb Raider*) in 1996. Indeed, the series is one of the longest-standing video game franchises, and despite changes in the developing studio and publisher, two reboots, and shifts in its core audience and fan base, it continues to spawn top-selling video game titles. With two movie adaptions, a comic book series, a Web series of animated films, and numerous other media appearances, Lara Croft is also considered a pop culture phenomenon. She is frequently referred to as the most iconic female video game character, and she has been referenced in numerous pop cultural texts, from songs to magazine articles. However, the ubiquity of her character also leads to a negative reception by some gamers: in an *IGN* poll of the most overrated video game characters in 2009, Lara Croft ranked second (after *Halo*'s Master Chief).

The development of the character by Core Design—and primarily designer Toby Guard—has been subject to some debate. Guard's vision of the character was that of a strong heroine opposing the mainstream industry approach at that time, which was mostly one of reducing women to "damsel-in-distress" types or hypersexualized dominatrixes. The backstory of the character depicts her as a wealthy British archaeologist searching for lost treasures and secrets in exotic locations. Lara Croft is typically portrayed as strong, athletic, and in control of the action (although the second reboot in 2013 changes the direction somewhat, depicting Lara as a—still vulnerable—teenager in a coming-of-age story). The *Tomb Raider* setting resembles Steven Spielberg's *Indiana Jones*, and the initial character development seemingly included a male hero echoing the infamous movie character (which was dismissed in the process as being too close to Indiana Jones). Toby Guard himself cites the comic book character Tank Girl and singer Neneh Cherry as the main inspiration for the character design.

In contrast to the claims that Lara Croft was meant to counter the oversexualized and reductionist industry approach at the time of development, the character still includes hypersexualized features, like revealing clothing and an exaggerated breast size. It has been noted that Lara Croft's breast size was the result of a mistake while adjusting the character model, but the team kept the resulting dimensions for the initial release. Arguably, this added to the success of the game among the core audience of the initial *Tomb Raider* game at the time of release—i.e., male teens and tweens. Indeed, the game mechanics and the third-person perspective of the game also contribute to a sexist perspective on the game and the character: it allows a (primarily male) audience to control the female protagonist much like a puppet, and it exposes the character to the male gaze—it could be even regarded as an instance of "everyday pornography."[1] Indeed, nude and pornographic portrayals of the character are frequently shared on the Internet.

In opposition to this viewpoint, and much more in line with Toby Guard's initial design ideas, Lara Croft has been praised for being a "competent female character in a dominant position," serving as a significant reference point for subsequent character design in computer games—the "so-called 'Lara phenomenon.'"[2] Lara is even regarded as a feminist character and a role model for girls as a powerful female protagonist: clever, independent, and dominating the male opponents she encounters in the game.[3] The *Tomb Raider* games typically involve logic and 3D puzzles, so game context also contributes to the depiction of Lara Croft as a smart character who is not simply relying on brute force but also on problem solving.

Unsurprisingly, and despite (or maybe because of) the immense success of the *Tomb Raider* series, Lara Croft is still a controversial character. The hypersexualization of the character and the conflicting interpretations of her both as an object of the male gaze and as a strong female—even feminist—character are just some aspects of the discussion.[4] For example, the recent reboot of the *Tomb Raider* series (*Rise of the Tomb Raider*) was criticized for excessive violence that was not considered true to the original style and tone of the series by many fans. In contrast to this, others commended these titles for giving the character more dramatic depth by telling the coming-of-age story of young Lara, which includes personal pain and loss—essentially making her more vulnerable and human. These discussions are indicative of expectations that echo the multifaceted portrayal of the character in pop culture. The character has been reinterpreted not only by multiple games and developers but also reconstructed through a plethora of cultural texts. Lara Croft serves as an object for projections by gamers and critics alike, and very often these projections reflect the readers and their fantasies much more than they illuminate the object itself. In that sense, there is not one Lara Croft. Given the longevity of the *Tomb Raider* series, we will most likely see many more iterations of the character—and therefore, a characterization of Lara must always be incomplete and preliminary.

Similar Characters: Bayonetta (*Bayonetta*), Jade (*Beyond Good & Evil*), Rayne (*Blood-Rayne*)

—Thorsten Quandt

THE LAST DRAGONBORN

(est. 2011)
Franchise: *The Elder Scrolls V: Skyrim*
Developer: Bethesda

Although the scale, customization, and aesthetic appeal of *The Elder Scrolls V: Skyrim* landed it multiple game of the year awards in 2011, its protagonist took these successes a step further by performing as a virtual hybrid of a citizen and a soldier with one foot in the military and one foot in the civilian world. This character quickly became a video game icon prior to and during the postmillennial interwar years (2011–2014) and reflects civilian-veteran interactions in the United States after the withdrawal of troops from Iraq.

The Last Dragonborn, or *Laat Dovahkiin* in Dragon language, is defined by the game's lore as "a warrior with the body of a mortal and the soul of a dragon whose destiny it is to destroy the evil dragon Alduin." The Dragonborn enacts a hybrid state between immortality and mortality, and between individualism and traditionalism. Not only must the Dragonborn find his or her place in a new country, the Dragonborn must also fulfill a destiny defined by the country's ancestors. This character's split identity prompts decisions reflective of both sides of this blurry duality. Though the Dragonborn has the potential to take on various roles within the society of Skyrim such as that of assassin, thief, bard, rebel, or thane, the role of Harbinger offers commentary on the fact that while soldiers may not be civilians, they are still citizens who embody a complex dual identity composed of military experiences and civil responsibilities.

Unlike other militarized avatars of the era, the Dragonborn allows players to participate in traditional combat duties while simultaneously exploring overlooked experiences including combat intermittency, chronic health conditions, and postwar readjustment. By maneuvering between the processes of community creation and post-traumatic stress symptoms (e.g., oversensitivity, hyper-arousal, unpredictability, secrecy, and avoidance) as well as lycanthropy (the transformation of an individual into a werewolf), the Dragonborn allows a player to embody the American soldier's role within a complex war narrative that extends beyond and before the battlefield. The Last Dragonborn of Skyrim emblematizes veterans of the Iraq War, their return to the United States, and contemporary concern surrounding post-traumatic stress disorder. In doing so, the Dragonborn resonates within the relationship established between the United States' battle-born soldiers and its battle-worn civilians.

To become the Harbinger, the Dragonborn has to complete the Companions quests. The Companions quest–line typifies the military entertainment complex by associating battle with family, honor, and strength. If the Dragonborn joins the Companions, that communal military cohort distorts and redefines the Dragonborn's blood relations upon his or her initiation into the group. Non-player characters within the Companions refer to the Dragonborn as "shield-brother" or "shield-sister" as a sign of relation through combat. In the quest "Proving Honor," the Dragonborn discovers that his or her "shield-brother" Farkas is actually a werewolf. Soon after this discovery, the Dragonborn is invited to join the Circle, a subfaction of werewolves within the Companions, by drinking the blood of another werewolf. Not only are these select few comrades bound by combat, they also are bound by bloodshed, bloodlust, and a defining moral burden. As a result, the Companions quests compress a military career from initiation to combat. By partaking in this questline, the Dragonborn can rise through the ranks of the Companions until he or she receives the title of Harbinger. The climb for this position allows the Dragonborn to develop both combat skills and relationships with other characters, therefore solidifying his or her identity as both a militant and social being.

The identity of Harbinger forcefully divorces soldier and civilian roles through lycanthropy. The abilities (or perks) and weaknesses associated with the Dragonborn's lycanthropy resound with mental health issues and stigmas prevalent in young Iraq War veterans. These lycanthropic perks reveal a strong linkage with the noble soldier archetype reinforced in the current U.S. Army Soldier's Creed that encourages the soldier to be "disciplined, physically and mentally tough, trained and proficient in warrior tasks." In the game, the Dragonborn's beast form possesses modifiers to health, stamina, regeneration, carrying capacity, and disease resistance; these bonuses can be seen as both metaphorical and literal interpretations of "warriorism," a trait measured by one's attitude toward fighting in combat, combat expectations, and personal satisfaction taken from combat.[5] Similarly, the disease-resistance perk acts not as a biological immunity to illness but as a mental barrier to the acceptance of these illnesses.

Skyrim's lycanthropic protagonist equally reflects the weaknesses of the military's subfactions with mental health concerns. Just as the beast form (or soldier form) grants the player certain perks, it also comes with a number of drawbacks. For example, the Dragonborn in beast form loses his or her ability to regenerate health and gain bonuses from sleeping, and it ushers in fear of and violence from non-player characters. These weaknesses act as manifestations of a reserve soldier's transmigrant status as a soldier and civilian who dwells between military and civilian sociopolitical spheres.[6] Sleeplessness, for example, has long been associated with postcombat adjustments and post-traumatic stress disorder—mental injuries that take time to heal (as can be seen in the beast form's low health regeneration). Similarly, non-player character reactions to the beast form exaggerate civilian veteran interaction wherein veterans experience homelessness, joblessness, and other forms of social neglect. As can be seen in the interactions with other members of the Circle, rejecting lycanthropy and the beast spirit is equivalent to defeat—a mind-set synonymous with veterans of the Iraq War.[7]

The Dragonborn as Harbinger assumes a tremendous responsibility not only for in-game Companions but also for interactions between civilians and veterans in the United States. The Harbinger answers questions regarding the true essence of honor, justice, and glory. This position allows the Dragonborn to speak from both sides of his or her identity, both civilian (human) and soldier (beast) form. His or her hybrid position as beast and human, mortal and immortal, grants the Harbinger a place as mediator between the two. By showing such a complex identity, the Dragonborn Harbinger allows the player to embody a new type of soldier in video games—the citizen-soldier hybrid.

Similar Characters: Gorion's Ward (*Baldur's Gate II: Shadows of Amn*), the Hero of Oakvale (*Fable*), Roman (*This War of Mine*)

—Brandon R. Rogers

LEE EVERETT

(est. 2012)
Franchise: *The Walking Dead*
Developer: Telltale Games

The Walking Dead opens with Lee Everett being transported to prison in the backseat of a police cruiser. Almost immediately, however, his backstory appears on screen: he was a history professor at the University of Georgia who murdered a man having an affair with his wife. While *The Walking Dead* is ostensibly about fighting zombies and surviving, the game's focus is on the emotional and engaging interactions and encounters between Lee and the other survivors. Importantly, Lee broadens the ways game creators can write and racialize characters without falling into stereotypical traps and regressive tropes that plague so many games. Thinking about Lee in terms of race is important since "race matters in video games because many of them affirm the status quo, giving consent to racial inequality and the unequal distribution of resources and privileges."[8] Lee Everett is an important figure among a growing roster of African American, non-ancillary characters, and this chapter delves into how the character offers necessary nuances in representing African Americans.

Depicting characters in games mainly through racialized stereotypes—e.g., African American and Latino criminals, Middle Eastern terrorists, and Asian or American martial artists—is a familiar occurrence; hence these stereotypes have become tropes. These tropes act as a shortcut for players toward understanding both the racial cues embedded in the narratives of these games and their own identities outside these games. These cues allow players to both engage and challenge dominant ideologies of race (and the interconnecting axes of gender, sexuality, nation, class, et al.). Since video games offer players the opportunity to try out the bodies and experiences of others, it is crucial to remember the characters whose embodied experiences do not offer the benefits of this virtual identity tourism. Critiques of video games have slowly begun to focus on connecting representations of people of color to their material realities, making it necessary to recognize the games that resist one-dimensional stereotypes and offer more fully developed characters.

Fanon referred to black skin as a uniform that subjected individuals to predetermined ideas and images, thus "blackness" refers to a cultural identity used to frame people who are categorized as "black."[9] Positioning Lee as a professor places him centrally within the politics of respectability, which is used to identify acceptable versions of blackness through rewarding people of color who work to "uplift" the race by embodying the traits valued by the dominant society. The use of respectability politics ensures players are able both to separate Lee from the stereotypical African American characters popular in video games and to allow players to identify with him as a "good guy." Since the game is played through his point of view, identifying with him is crucial. Framing him as a professor resists the desire to place him within the trope of African American criminality, and it also serves to illustrate to players that Lee is highly intelligent and rational.

Instead of the urbanized and aggressive, criminal, self-aggrandizing, or combative African American male character, Lee is emotional, soft-spoken, rational, and self-deprecating. In *The Walking Dead*, Lee finds himself connected to Clementine when he learns her parents died in an earlier wave of zombie attacks, and he charges himself with watching over her and ensuring her safety. This adds yet another dimension to how *The Walking Dead* characterizes Lee and how the players can play the game. The compassion and empathy he demonstrates toward the newly orphaned Clementine continues to distance Lee from the stereotypical portrayal of African American characters. In fact, their relationship influences how one might play the game because it constantly reminds the player that Clementine will remember the choices players make as Lee. The richness of the game narrative in which making choices validates the relationship of Lee and Clementine and allows Lee to nurture and protect Clementine humanizes Lee more in each episode. Despite moments when characters like Kenny and Larry remind players that Lee is a criminal and murderer, his blackness is mediated mainly through his relationship with Clementine. When compared to the ways African American men are usually depicted in video games—i.e., as athletes or criminals—this surrogate father and compassionate African American masculinity characterization becomes even more meaningful and significant.

Lee leads the group of survivors through the first season of *The Walking Dead* using a combination of wit, survival instincts, intelligence, patience, and compassion. The investment players have in the relationship between Lee and Clementine frames the penultimate scene from the first season. Lee, having been bitten by a walker, has a final moment with Clementine. He tells her he has failed her by being bitten because he can no longer protect her, but she must remember all the lessons and words of wisdom he has shared with her throughout their journey. Then, in a final act of sacrifice, he tells Clementine she must kill him in order to guarantee her own survival. *The Walking Dead* allows Lee to fully develop and evolve from having taken someone's life to sacrificing his own, which ultimately allows the game to shape players' perspectives on race and African Americans more specifically.

Lee Everett is a lead character who is obviously flawed, yet his flaws are mediated by intelligence, empathy, strength, compassion, and cleverness. This complex portrayal allows the politics of race to be featured, even if the game itself is not explicitly about his race. According to the game's developers, Lee's race was important in shaping gameplay because they thought about "the things Lee would say in response to a sticky situation or even a subtly racist barb" in order to ensure players would "carry Lee's personal experience along with the experience that [they were] going to go on in-game."[10] Lee's characterization in this game is a reminder that flattening race into one-dimensional tropes results in stereotypes and precludes opportunities for challenging racialized and racist character constructions.

Similar Characters: Barret Wallace (*Final Fantasy VII*), Joel (*The Last of Us*), Sazh Katzroy (*Final Fantasy XIII*)

—Myra Washington

LEEROY JENKINS

(est. 2004)
Franchise: *World of Warcraft*
Developer: Blizzard

If you have frequented the spaces of video game culture, you have likely heard of Leeroy Jenkins. This player from the massively multiplayer online role-playing (MMO) game *World of Warcraft* (*WoW*) gained cult status in mid-2005 and has never really left pop culture. He has been referenced by *Jeopardy* and on T-shirts; reinserted as a non-player character in new *WoW* and *Hearthstone* content; and even molded as a *WoW* trading card and plastic miniature. What is often missed, now that Leeroy Jenkins is a mainstay of gamer culture, are the cultural references that birthed him and how all mention of those cultural references were removed once Blizzard Entertainment began to replicate the character. The history of Leeroy Jenkins, like so many things in MMO culture, begins with alcohol.

One night in 2005, a group of white college students in Colorado got drunk on 40-ounce bottles of beer and decided to make a guild in *WoW* using hilarious and inappropriate names.[11] So the guild appropriated subcultural tropes for humor's sake. The guild, <Pals for Life>, consisted of players named Abdul, Jamaal, Anfrony, and the now legendary Leeroy Jenkins. This style of appropriation is often called "ironic racism," and it stems from the belief that the ironic deployment of racism somehow transcends bigotry.[12] This form of racism is often overlooked due to its contrast to actual racism, but it is prevalent within video games in many ways. <Pals for Life> remained a normal and unknown guild (except to its members) in *WoW* until May of 2005 when the guild posted a video called "A Rough Go" and became an overnight Internet legend.

Like any guild, <Pals for Life> leveled their characters together to attempt ingame content like 10-man dungeons or raids. The 10–15 player dungeon called Upper Blackrock Spire (UBRS) was incredibly popular when it was first implemented. Inside UBRS was a room filled with Dragon Eggs called "the Rookery," and <Pals for Life> found themselves unable to bypass it. In truth, the Rookery was optional, but <Pals for Life> posted to the official *WoW* forums a video about their difficulty with the room. This post, titled "UBRS (vid) ROOKERY OVERPOWERED! blue please" stated, "This was PALS FOR LIFE's 7th attempt at getting past the rookery in UBRS. Please feel free to give us constructive criticism on our tactics and how you beat this room."

According to the video, Leeroy Jenkins needs a piece of armor from the Rookery. These shoulder pads will help him as a healer to keep his friends alive. While Leeroy Jenkins is marked AFK (away from the keyboard), his guildmates discuss plans to clear the Rookery. They calculate their chances to complete the room, and as they are doing this, Leeroy Jenkins returns to his keyboard. Using his name as a malaprop for "Charge!" Leeroy says, "Alright chums, I'm back! Let's do this! LEEROOOOOOOY JEEENKIIIIIINSSS!!!" He then runs into the room alone without the help of the rest of <Pals for Life>. The resulting chaos and eventual full-party destruction ends with Leeroy Jenkins taking the blame for the failure but declaring, "At least I have chicken."[13]

Leeroy Jenkins is a character played by a player named Ben Schulz. Through this "machinima" (the recording and editing of video game graphics to tell a story), <Pals for Life> used copyrighted content to tell a story. Popular machinima can make its creators quite a bit of money; however, shortly after <Pals for Life> posted their video, other people began to sell Leeroy Jenkins memorabilia. Leeroy's sayings, his likeness, and other aspects of the machinima began to be reused by others.[14] Because machinima is not content that is easily protected in a court of law, neither <Pals for Life> nor Schulz could do much to protect the character or make money from his success. Then Blizzard Entertainment absorbed the character's likeness. Over time, they reinserted Leeroy into the *Warcraft* mythos, though in a way that some argue reflects race and racism.

Ben Schulz himself gained celebrity status: he began to provide commentary for games on other Blizzard properties and speaking onstage at their annual convention, Blizzcon. This increased the likelihood that others would criticize Leeroy Jenkins as a racially motivated character. Between his malapropism, the comedic destruction of <Pals for Life>, and his comments about chicken, Leeroy Jenkins's status as an icon resembles the "Zip Coon" trope. This powerful, white minstrel–created caricature of former slaves consists of a white person wearing blackface who tries to be part of a white group but only manages to screw everything up and speak incorrectly.[15] When Blizzard took control of Leeroy Jenkins, they hired Mike Krahulik ("Gabe" of *Penny Arcade* fame) to draw Leeroy Jenkins. Mike created him as a white character. Blizzard reused Krahulik's art for other games using the *WoW* intellectual property. Each time, Leeroy Jenkins is depicted as white and usually yelling and clutching a piece of chicken.

The whitewashing of Leeroy Jenkins remains a keen example of the influence of tropes on entertainment media. Ben Schulz exemplified this trope, yet no one noticed. Instead, millions of fans of Leeroy simply laughed and showed it to their friends. That Leeroy Jenkins was reappropriated as a white character is an additional reminder of the systemic nature of this issue. While Leeroy Jenkins was the character who yelled "Let's do this," the way he did this has been done and redone consistently, invisibly, and legally for over one hundred years.

Similar Characters: Augustus Cole (*Gears of War*), George Gordon Haggard Jr. (*Battlefield: Bad Company*), Sheva Alomar (*Resident Evil 5*)

—Nicolas LaLone

LEISURE SUIT LARRY

(est. 1987)
Franchise: *Leisure Suit Larry*
Developer: Sierra

Larry Laffer, better known as Leisure Suit Larry, is the central protagonist of Sierra's adult-themed game *Leisure Suit Larry in the Land of the Lounge Lizards* (*LSL*). Larry's sole purpose in life—and as such the primary goal of the player—is to seduce his dream girl.[16] The manual to the game warns players of the difficulty of this task because Larry is a broke, unattractive "weenie" with bad breath and a fashion sense steeped in polyester and disco. Larry's discernable lack of social skills and his obsession with sex served as a reflection—albeit a stereotypical reflection—of society's perception of one aspect of gaming culture: the personal computer (PC) gamer.

At the time of *LSL*'s release, video gaming culture was divided into three camps: the arcade gamers, the PC gamers, and the home console gamers. Arcade and home console games were largely superior to PC games at the time. Both types of games were more action-packed than their PC counterparts, and both had better graphics. This was largely due to the fact that arcade games and home consoles had chip sets devoted to processing graphics, and these chip sets were largely absent from and unnecessary for PCs: Microsoft DOS with its text-based display was still the primary operating system. In addition to weaker graphics and less action, PC games had other disadvantages. PCs were far more expensive than home consoles at the time and they required specialized knowledge for loading games as compared to the plug-and-play capabilities of arcade and home console games. Thus PC gamers devoted considerable time and resources to their hobby, which may have created and solidified the "gamer as computer nerd" stereotype. As such, the PC gamer was often seen as a stereotypical and lonely male who spent all his time playing kid games.

From this stereotype, Larry Laffer was born, serving simultaneously as a lampoon and celebration of the PC gamer. In fact, Al Lowe—Larry's creator—has stated that he based the character on a salesman who worked at Sierra, the development company behind *LSL* and a host of other popular 1980s PC adventure game franchises, including *King's Quest*, *Space Quest*, and *Police Quest*.[17] Larry was unlike many of the video game characters of the time. Instead of being an idealized masculine character, Larry made the player cringe, possessing more character flaws than positive attributes. Although video games could serve as a means of escapism for the player who assumed the role of a spy or action hero, Larry Laffer's appeal was likely fostered by a different type of identification. Rather than promoting wishful identification and helping players distance themselves from their perceived flaws, Larry served as a reflection of them. Larry was not a muscle-bound action hero or all-star jock. He was weak, shallow, somewhat intelligent, and most of all self-aware. Thus his "flaws" were likely the same as those of many of the players controlling him and the programmers who created him. His lack of idealization was perhaps the impetus that fostered identification with players.

Upon first glance, Larry's behavior in the games—and the primary player objective—ridicules PC gamers' supposed lack of social skills. It can easily incite male chauvinistic criticism of video game players (e.g., "These nerds spend more time with virtual women than real women"). In addition, the women in the game are often portrayed stereotypically and misogynistically as achievements to be unlocked. Of course, one might argue that the incorporation of these viewpoints is intentional and self-aware. Some even consider it a criticism of the male chauvinism represented by Larry. Regardless, Larry is obviously a self-aware referent to the PC gamer-as-nerd stereotype and the subcultural elements of gaming at the time. Larry acts as a token symbolically affirming and disconfirming elements of the PC gamer stereotype. After all, many PC gamers see their isolation from society at large and the gaming community as a point of pride, perhaps best represented by online communities celebrating "the PC master race" and demeaning "console peasants."

LSL was a commercial and critical success for its developer and publisher, Sierra. It won the Best Adventure or Fantasy/Role-Playing Program in 1987 from the Software Publishers Association,[18] and the success of the original game spawned a series of sequels over the next two decades. In 2013, the original game was remade with enhanced graphics after a successful crowdfunding effort through Kickstarter. The success of the Kickstarter campaign is a testament to the fact that Larry Laffer still holds a place of reverence in the hearts of many gamers. Part of this longevity and reverence may be due to the fact that Larry was designed as a reflection of early gaming culture and as a continual reminder of divisions that still exist in gaming today. After all, the single, lonely, male gamer stereotype is still a major source of consternation for the Entertainment Software Association, and they devote considerable resources to trying to disprove it. Although Larry does not have the same widespread appeal to or recognition in the broader culture as do Mario or Sonic, he was a formative character for many in the early days of home computer gaming. He is a male gamer's game character whose flaws and self-deprecating humor shine a light on and refute society's perception of gamers.

Similar Characters: Duke Nukem (*Duke Nukem*), Jim (*Earthworm Jim*), Travis Touchdown (*No More Heroes*)

—Matthew Grizzard

LICH KING

(est. 2002)
Franchise: *Warcraft*
Developer: Blizzard

The Lich King—the armor-bound, undead leader of the Scourge army in the *Warcraft* franchise—is less an embodied character and more a malevolent force. It is a force that inhabits, fuses together, and puppeteers the spirits and bodies of those who are unlucky or bold enough to wield its physical manifestations: the Helm of Domination and the runeblade Frostmourne. Through these artifacts and puppeteering, the Lich King can be understood as a study in multiplicities—of modalities, moral identities, and maladies.

The Lich is a linchpin in the game's multispatial, multimaterial narrative world, threading together the *Warcraft* real-time strategy games and the *World of Warcraft* (*WoW*) multiplayer online games. Its story, as media scholar Jan-Noël Thon notes, evolves through an extended, multigame narrative tapestry: cinematic cut-scenes, quest text and tasks, loading screens, and character interactions are woven together in a "designed" story integral to the gameworld's narrative structure. Over the years, some players recount feeling the Lich King's as a constant presence—so much so that more than any other boss, they felt "dead-set" on killing him.

This intertextual narrative burgeoned long ago (in the lore era associated with *Warcraft II*), when the prideful Orc shaman Ner'zhul was recruited to join the Burning Legion—a vengeful force hell-bent on destroying the Titan-built world. After a time, though, the maddened Orc attempted to escape the legion but was captured. For this breach of loyalty, Ner'zhul's spirit was rent from his body, ascribed to plate armor, and encased in a block of ice. From this frozen tomb he served the legion as a "lich"—a powerful undead sorcerer—telepathically controlling the Scourge. The Lich King's mortal spirit, however, retained a glimmer of humanity and resented his oppression, ultimately convincing the prince Arthas Menethil as his champion to set him free. Arthas shattered the ice, donned the bound armor, and fused his spirit with Ner'zhul's. The Lich's power grew through this partnership, and ultimately Arthas' spirit became dominant. As the final boss in *World of Warcraft: Wrath of the Lich King*, in defeating him, players come to learn that there must *always* be a Lich King lest the Scourge be uncontrolled and destroy the mortal races. Bolvar Fordragon—a noble, allied lord who had been burned by dragonfire and tortured by Arthas—said he had no place among the living, sat on the Frozen Throne, and took the helm. Encased in ice, he became the next willing Lich King.

The Lich's evolution and reinvention is rooted in the artifacts of helm and runeblade—and the runeblade in particular ties the Lich to classic narrative tropes. The character's trajectory has itself been suggested to be a reinvention of Sir Thomas Malory's tale of King Arthur and the sword in the stone.[19] Each is preceded by a great wizard and a great Uther; each acquires an elusive and powerful sword; each wields the blade to win many battles; and each nonetheless suffers a death associated with the sword's power. Notably, however, Arthas-as-Lich diverges from the British legend: rather than building Camelot, he works to sully and destroy Azeroth's great cities. In this anti-Arthurian vein, the Lich has also been likened to Anakin Skywalker in his shift toward the Dark Side: both engage the "fallen hero" trope (as noted in the character's WoWpedia page): sworn to altruism, trained by warriors, seduced by darkness, set on killing his mentors, and in moments before death, shifting back to his more human sensibilities.

The Lich has also been read as embodying a number of psychological maladies. As read by lore guru Anne Stickney, Arthas-as-Lich embodies sociopathy as he—sans emotion—sees the world as a prize to be won.[20] Indeed—in a vision recounted in the character's novel and alluded to in the *WoW* quest "A Voice in the Dark"—Arthas met a version himself as a hopeful but frail boy who represented the last bit of his own humanity but rejected and murdered the boy and in the same moment destroyed his own spirit. The character moves through phases of tensioned identities: Ner'zhul-as-Lich, Ner'zhul and Arthas united equally, then Arthas-as-Lich, and then finally Bolvar. The essence of each melds with the others and then slowly fades. Through these tensions the Lich endures an internal good–evil struggle as each amalgamated spirit engages the helm with benevolent aims: Ner'zhul in trying to break free from the Legion; Arthas in an attempt to save his liege and his people; and Bolvar in ensuring the Scourge is controlled. More broadly, the character's undead state represents a departure from a more whole humanness and, as suggested by literary scholar Jessica Langer, is thematically one of Otherness throughout *WoW* lore.[21]

The perennial nature of helm and sword—as metaphors for these various multiplicities—has been read as a nod to an ironic tension. This tension is well known but often ignored for the sake of suspending disbelief in game narratives: a strain between the epic character of the boss kill and the scheduled resurrection when the raid resets. As one *WoW* forum commenter joked, Arthas asks while dying and seeing a paternal vision, "Father . . . is it . . . over?" and his father replies, "Don't worry my son . . . the raid will reset next week."

Similar Characters: Alice (*American McGee's Alice*), Bertoxxulous (*EverQuest*), the Gogolithic Mass (*Sword & Sworcery*)

—Jaime Banks

LIFE

(est. 1992)
Franchise: *E.V.O.: Search for Eden*
Developer: Almanic

Approximately 500 million years before the modern era, there is no life on land. A blue fish swims through the seaweed of the Ocean of Origin with only 20 health points, no evolution points, and only a weakened, toothless bite for fending off predators. An embodiment of Gaia (ostensibly Mother Earth) urges the fish to swim toward land as a representation of Life's evolution from the sea to the land.

This is the tale of the origin of species as told by Almanic and the players of *E.V.O.: Search for Eden*. The main character of *E.V.O.* has no given name—Gaia summons the character for no special reason, but the character represents one of a billion different creatures living on earth. The character is meant to represent at once a single unremarkable organism and to be the embodiment of all life. The evolution of Life through its many stages speaks to both a core mechanic of role-playing games (Life evolves as the player levels) as well as an ongoing interest in games that focus on artificial life and growth systems, such as in games like *Spore* and the *Pokémon* series. In this way, Life represents one of the first artificial life simulations that allows the player to use evolutionary discretion as a core gameplay mechanic.

As Life, the player accumulates evolution points by defeating other creatures—converting their bodies into meat that can be consumed for a large boost in evolution points (EVO.P) and a proportionately smaller boost in health points (HP). Earning enough EVO.P allows the player to selectively evolve a number of different body parts: jaws, a horn or horns, neck, body, hands, feet, dorsal fin, tail, and back of the neck, with some of these options only available to some creatures (for example, fish have no neck or back of the head to evolve). The necessity for these evolutions is made apparent to the player from the first game screen, as their smallish blue fish is hardly a match for other creatures living on earth, and only the fittest species can survive immediate game combat and later progression.

Beyond a basic need for survival, Life quickly realizes that certain creatures have developed seemingly unnatural abilities. These are creatures that represent evolutionary anomalies in that they have the bodies of soon-to-be-extinct species (known to players who paid attention in their biology classes) yet the strength and speed of adapted species. In defeating each of these foes, Life comes to learn that a mysterious Martian force has been tampering with Earth's natural evolution in an attempt to hasten it. This tampering has resulted in a small set of "super-species" that pose a major threat to all life on earth: their survival would result in the passing on of traits that make the creatures successful in the current environment but ill-suited to coming geological events.

On this point, Life navigates through five such events. In "The World Before Land: ~500–450 Million B.C.," the player evolves Life from sea creature to early land animal, followed by "Early Creatures of Land: ~300–230 Million B.C.," in which the player navigates Life to reptilian form. Starting at "Age of Dinosaurs: ~200–65 Million B.C.," Life is given the option to evolve in either reptilian or bird form, presenting the player with a profound decision: Conquer land or conquer air? Regardless of path, in "Ice Age: ~65–36 Million B.C.," the player is prompted to follow a natural evolution to mammal, a warm-blooded creature better equipped for surviving the ominous cold. Finally, players navigate to "Early Man: ~26–3 Million B.C." in order to encounter the source of Gaia's concern—an over-evolved, single-cell organism Bolbox that mistakenly believes itself to be the first evolved human. Eventually Life defeats this evolutionary corruption, and balance is restored to Earth's biodiversity. Life then joins Gaia in a metaphorical Eden, and the Martians promise to leave Earth to its natural evolution . . . observing Earth from a distance and anticipating a day in which Martians and Earthlings can interact naturally.

The player's agency over the evolution of Life was touted in a full-page ad in a May 1993 issue of *Electronic Gaming Magazine*, stating players could "create almost any creature [that their] imagination can conjure up" including "some hideous freak of nature who looks like your sister."[22] In the ad copy, players are encouraged to send a photo of their favorite Life creation to Enix headquarters for a chance of winning one of several different Enix video games. Curiously, the ad features a number of ferocious-looking sea creatures and dinosaurs but no mammals—ostensibly the focal and evolved version of Life on its journey through human evolution.

Although the game was widely panned on its original release, more recent reviews of the game—often directly tied to the protagonist Life—have been quite positive. The *Video Game Bible* referred to Life's "level-up-as-a-function-of-evolution" system as "wildly underrated and highly original."[23] While not specifically addressing Life as a character, *IGN* lauded the game as "the original success story in the niche genre [of life simulation gaming]" while referring to *E.V.O.* as an early predecessor to games such as *Spore*.[24]

It is doubtful that Charles Darwin would have pegged the origin of species to an embodied and omnipotent Gaia encouraging a random organism to fight other creatures unnaturally evolved by Martians, but the protagonist, Life, offers a clever and engaging take on "the essence of evolution, in video game form."[25] Playing as Life might not give the gamer an intricate appreciation of evolution, but it provides a surprisingly academic approach to the level-up mechanics used in a number of role-playing games preceding and following it. At least in *E.V.O.*, leveling up is less a metaphor and more a concrete demonstration of growing a creature from mundanity to modernity.

Similar Characters: Cells (*Agar.io*), Creature (*Spore*), Pokémon (*Pokémon*)

—Nicholas David Bowman

LINK

(est. 1986)
Franchise: *The Legend of Zelda*
Developer: Nintendo R&D4

His green and brown garb, pointy ears, sword, and shield make Link one of the most recognizable video game characters of all time. Link's appearance, however, belies what makes this character's place unique in video game history. Eric Smith, Nintendo game designer, describes Link's personality, saying, "Link kind of is a character archetype himself. He's your silent protagonist—a shell for the player to inhabit. His personality isn't so strong that you feel the need to consider what Link would do in a situation, because you are Link."[26] As a character, Link is silent, and his behavior, intent, and goals are the first puzzle the player must solve.

The design choices for Link are very intentional, and Nintendo maintains this as a key piece of the strategy for *The Legend of Zelda* (*LoZ*) franchise. The overarching fantasy combat and exploration design of the series is cut from the mold of Western fantasy. Unlike the characters of pen-and-paper role-playing games of the time (e.g., *Dungeons & Dragons*), Link is an attempt at a character devoid of any true personality or temperament so that the focus is on gameplay. In fact, according to series producer Eiji Aonuma, *LoZ* games are created with gameplay as the primary design point instead of story, and Link's lack of personal narrative follows this overarching philosophy.

Link's perpetual silence in each iteration of the series mainly forces player interaction with the protagonist to be in the mechanics of playing: action, role-playing, and puzzle solving. The player must embody Link and fill in his silence by playing the game and gaining abilities, resilience, and knowledge that unfold only through spending time with Link in his environment. The action in the game forces the player to control Link in real-time battle: one cannot stand still and make slow decisions in the heat of combat; reaction time and control over the game mechanics are essential for playing. Miyamoto, creator of *LoZ*, emphasizes that the role-playing-game element is inherent in players feeling close to Link because "actual movements of the actions you are making the character do in the game help you form actual memories of the fights and puzzles you were involved in, these are no longer memories of controlling a character and guiding them through a game, you are now part of that experience."[27]

This design strategy results in an effect similar to what occurs in the blank spaces (gutters) of comic book pages. In comics, there is blankness between pieces of the action, and the reader must use the contextual features of the medium to draw conclusions about what happens and how it happens.[28] So too does Link's blank personality invite the player in the video game medium to utilize contextual cues and fill in the blanks, both from within the game and from personal experience, with motives, likes, dislikes, and emotions. Stepping into the shoes of the character on-screen allows players to experience empathy, suffering, and other emotions that are otherwise difficult to access. In the case of Link and other "blank space" characters, the player invests his or her own values and morals into the character to enrich gameplay, consistent with research showing that player morals influence perceptions of gameplay.[29]

Nintendo's cultural history of Link as an easily accessible avatar misses some of the assumptions of what a default, "blank" character embodies. Link is a white male avatar whose mission is primarily to rescue a damsel in distress. This trope reveals the historical intended audience for video games, and it demonstrates how early video game designers perceived what heroism in characters meant. Video games are just as likely as other popular media to use the "default" gender (male) and race (white) because of the neutrality and invisibility of those features as perpetuated by dominant Western culture. Gaming audiences readily accept protagonists that fit the Western hero mold: Link has fair features, white skin and golden hair, and he is a male rescuing a female. This traditional masculinity has been reiterated and exaggerated in the gaming industry over the years. Certainly *LoZ* did not begin this media trope; however, the trope's lasting impact on the gaming world demonstrates how difficult it is to change the norms for default characters.

In recent iterations of the *LoZ* franchise, efforts have been made to diversify Link. In Nintendo's 2016 release *Hyrule Warriors Legends*, a version of Link appears as a female named Linkle. Linkle's backstory is not yet defined by Nintendo's canon sources—she may be Link's younger sister, other relation, or she might just be a new Link for a new day. In the game, she appears as one of many potential playable characters. These changes reflect a changing audience and a change in character design principles. It is possible that designers are broadening Link's "default" status and are branching out with more demographically diverse options for avatar selection. This potential for Link to be a broad default character in order to access the puzzles and game action may be what Nintendo originally envisioned for the character.

In many of his adventures, Link acts as a connection between various worlds, societies, and individuals. This is true not just in the game but now outside the game as well. Indeed, the changing default assumptions about Link's demographic defaults suggest the potential of this video game character to connect a past tradition of exclusion and a future of diverse inclusion.

Similar Characters: Gordon Freeman (*Half-Life*), Mario (*Super Mario Bros.*), the Traveler (*Journey*)

—Andy Boyan and Katey A. Price

LORD BRITISH

(est. 1979)
Franchise: *Ultima*
Developer: Origin Systems

> As I walked slowly closer to the throne, I tried to assess this man, who could only be the King himself. I couldn't tell how old he was. His face was lined, but his blue eyes were still bright and clear. He wore a fur-lined robe and a heavy crown, and his hand gripped a staff topped by an ankh. Blond hair streaked with white hung to his shoulders, and his full beard, similarly streaked, was neatly trimmed. Beneath the royal robe, he wore a tunic made of white linen, embroidered with heavy silk thread.[30]

Lord British is the ruler of the fictional world of Britannia that serves as the setting for (most) games in the seminal computer role-playing-game series *Ultima*. British's role varies, but generally speaking, he is a well-liked and benevolent ruler who provides assistance and guidance to the player. Lord British's help happens within the game, such as when he is visited by players in his residence, Castle Britannia, and outside the game. Lord British is (at least on paper) the author of many of the early game manuals and is also often credited as designer and coder. It is his voice that is present in the game's documentation providing encouragement, tips, and advice.

This unusual dual role exists because Lord British is an alter ego for Richard Garriott, the game designer and programmer who created the *Ultima* series. It turns out that "Lord British is from Earth. He is absolutely Richard Garriott from Earth, who found a way to get to Britannia some time ago."[31] While Garriott's nickname (Lord British) predates the development of the video games he is so well known for, Lord British's official role came about serendipitously. According to Garriott, he changed the credits on *Akalabeth: World of Doom* to "Lord British" at the suggestion of Al Remmers, president of the game's publisher, California Pacific. Garriott notes that "this ended up being more than just a quirky use of a pen name on the package. Lord British is me, as both the creator and as a resident representing the creation to the player from within the game. I joined and shared the experience alongside the player, something which would prove more valuable over time."[32]

While it is unusual for a creator to insert themselves directly in their work, it is arguably rarer in video games than in other media. This makes Lord British not only an interesting character but, given the success of the *Ultima* series, a surprisingly influential one. Garriott/Lord British helped provide a friendly, human face to a nascent industry whose designers and developers were largely unknown: he was video games' first celebrity.

Garriott took this dual role to heart over the years. For example, several games in the series instructed players to report to Lord British after they won the game. If players wrote a letter to Origin (the game's publisher), they received a signed letter (completion certificate) in the mail from Lord British. Most of the letters provided an epilogue to the game. The one for *Ultima V: Warriors of Destiny* was a personal thank-you to the player.

British's warm and playful relationship with fans has also been tested as players explored how to do things in-game they were not supposed to. The most famous is attempting to kill the (supposedly invincible) character. In early games this was difficult because Lord British had incredibly high stats. In later games, however, players could exploit loopholes in the game systems or discover purposefully designed and convoluted ways to kill British. For example, in *Ultima VII: The Black Gate* (1992), players could take advantage of the fact that Lord British would stand underneath a castle gate at noon every day. If the player then clicked on a gold plaque above Lord British, it would fall and behead him. This in-game event was inspired by an accident at the developer's offices during the game's production. A metal bar attached to a door came loose, fell, and struck Garriott on the head, resulting in injuries that required a hospital visit. Once again, Garriott's real-life experiences influenced his in-game persona.

The tradition of killing Lord British also made its way to the online incarnation of the series. When *Ultima Online* was released, Garriott made the leap to playing the character Lord British directly. While his appearances were, and continue to be, rare, there was one in particular that became notorious. On August 8, 1997, Lord British, controlled by Richard Garriott, made an in-game appearance during *Ultima Online*'s beta test. A player character named Rainz cast a "Fire Field" spell that, surprisingly, killed Lord British. Mayhem ensued as Lord Blackthorn, controlled by *Ultima Online* director Starr Long, summoned demons that began killing the other characters in the area. Lord British's death was the result of an oversight: Garriott had forgotten to turn on the character's invulnerability after a server reset and, thinking he was invincible, stepped into the fire field and perished. The assassination is widely considered one of the most memorable moments in massively multiplayer online game history. The event also helped give birth to the Lord British postulate coined by Mike Schramm in 2007: "If it exists as a living creature in an MMORPG [massively multiplayer online game], someone, somewhere, will try to kill it." The death of Lord British arguably strengthened the game's reputation—*Ultima Online*'s non-player characters make mistakes like real humans.

While Lord British/Garriott appeared in *Ultima Online* as recently as 2014 (for the game's 17th anniversary), it is unclear what the future holds for him. The rights to *Ultima* no longer belong to Richard Garriott, and whether Lord British will appear in his future games is uncertain. Lord British's relationship with Garriott reminds us that game creators can be more than auteurs obliquely expressing ideas through their art. They can also be guides, companions, and perhaps even friends. Lord British/Garriott asserts that games can, and should, have a humane heart even as they tackle complex issues and concerns.

Similar Characters: David Cage (*Fahrenheit: Indigo Prophecy*), Max Payne/Sam Lake (*Max Payne*), Dr. Wright/Will Wright (*Sim City* [SNES])

—José P. Zagal

M

Mario is one of the most widely known and instantly recognizable faces of gaming. More than thirty years after his first appearance as Jumpman in *Donkey Kong* (1981), Mario remains the headline act for every console released by Nintendo. His endurance as mascot-in-chief has provided multiple generations of gamers with a cultural touchstone embodying timeless design and elegant communication, while also representing the sheer joy of play for a wider audience.

Creator Shigeru Miyamoto acknowledges that at least some of the character's success was the result of good timing. Following the video game crash of 1983, Nintendo filled the gap left by companies like Atari and Coleco by releasing the Nintendo Entertainment System (Famicom in Japan) and revitalizing gaming in the home. *Super Mario Bros.* (1985) became an immediate hit, building on the running and jumping of *Donkey Kong* and *Mario Bros.* (1983) but adding more complex mechanics with what designer Ste. Curran calls "a new feeling of vastness, exploration and adventure that hooked players into a fast-evolving genre."[1] Mario's position at the forefront of this new era of gaming made him one of the most visible faces of the medium but also led to particular associations the character carries to this day. He became the personification of the colorful and upbeat, cartoon-like world the franchise would continue to build through its numerous sequels and spin-offs, and he was therefore seen as a particularly suitable mascot for the young children perceived to be the primary audience for the games. Other characters, like Sonic, would use this as a "center" from which to measure their own difference by appealing to a slightly older teenage audience, but Nintendo's most famous face has remained a symbol of innocence and purity of game design.

Media scholar Manuel Garin has suggested that Mario is the last of the "silent clowns," carrying on the legacy of popular slapstick comedy performers like Buster Keaton and Charlie Chaplin. Specifically, Mario provides the pleasure of nonverbal communication and performance to modern audiences not accustomed to such content. Garin notes the similarities between the largely static framing of Keaton films like *The Scarecrow* (1920) and the play-spaces of *Donkey Kong* and *Ma-*

rio Bros.[2] Similarly, the long, side-scrolling sequences of physical comedy Keaton became known for in films like *Go West* (1925) and *College* (1927) bear a remarkable structural similarity to the *Super Mario Bros.* games. Mario's presence in the Mushroom Kingdom is indeed a physical, tactile one, from stomping Goombas to smashing blocks, but his physicality is as expressive as it is functional. Mario performs constantly, nonverbally communicating information about the world as well as his own character. His jump, for example, is a bold, whole-body bound that demonstrates the move's own centrality to the game design and the character's eagerness to engage with the environment. In later games, collecting power stars is accompanied by an action not dissimilar to a dance, with Mario spinning and punching the air, embodying the joy of achievement shared by character and player in those moments. These are exaggerated actions in keeping with the way silent-era film actors compensated for a largely dialogue-free world, and like Chaplin before him, Mario has transcended his own individual medium to become an icon in popular culture.

A survey conducted in 1990 showed that more American children recognized Nintendo's portly plumber than could identify Mickey Mouse. This is perhaps unsurprising given Mario's extensive transmedial presence, from comics and television to a Hollywood movie adaptation. What other video game character could have appeared in *Variety* in 2002 boasting a larger lifetime box office take than Harrison Ford? Who other than Mario could have lobbied Hollywood mayor Johnny Grant, in person, to add an interactive entertainment category to the famous Walk of Fame in 2005? One could certainly argue that the influence from a classic era of film and the entwining of this physicality with game design is a large factor in Mario becoming the most visible face of the medium in wider culture.

Such visibility is accompanied by restrictions, however. When considering the parallel careers of Mario and his brother Luigi, it is clear that Nintendo places considerable value on the unchanging nature of its most high-profile asset. While Mario appears in a dizzying array of spin-off titles from karting and tennis to golf and soccer, he is not permitted to be as subversive or alternative as his sibling. Mario carries with him the company's ideals of simple, innocent fun and "pure" gameplay in every appearance, keeping those values largely unaltered by notions of modernization or critique. When risks of that nature are taken, it tends to be Luigi's job.

Luigi's Mansion (2001) is a rare example of Nintendo being willing to engage in self-parody. By adapting the core gameplay of *Resident Evil* (1998) in the aesthetic style of the Mario franchise, *Luigi's Mansion* capitalized playfully on the public perception of the Nintendo brand being largely "for kids" and that perception being at odds with the status of *Resident Evil 0* (2002) as exclusive to Nintendo's Gamecube. Since then, Luigi has become an online meme thanks to the "death stare" in *Mario Kart 8* (2014), further reinforcing his ability to poke fun at the brand while keeping Mario at a safe distance such that Mario's timeless status as the "headliner" is not threatened by transitory notions of trendiness.

Mario is not required to change. While his core franchise could be argued to be among the most consistently innovative in a mechanical sense, Mario himself remains the cheerful, adventurous, cartoon plumber gamers found so appealing more than three decades ago. No reboot has threatened to complicate his backstory, and no reimagining has given him a "real-world edge." Like the aforementioned silent clowns, Mario has achieved immortality, and his continued position at the forefront of gaming culture can be attributed to a powerful cocktail of uncomplicated design, unshakeable dedication to a core ludic philosophy, and perhaps a touch of nostalgia. This clown is king, and long may he reign.

Similar Characters: Luigi (*Super Mario Bros.*), Sonic (*Sonic the Hedgehog*), Wario (*Super Mario Land 2*)

—Jonathan Mack

MASTER CHIEF

(est. 2001)
Franchise: *Halo*
Developer: Bungie

Master Chief is regarded by many as one of the most iconic first-person shooter protagonists in video game history. He is the epitomization of the silent, faceless hero: a gigantic, genetically enhanced super solider in green-olive armor and wearing a helmet with a golden visor that covers his face throughout almost all of the *Halo* video game series. The identity of Master Chief is defined by shooting and constant action, in sync with the principles and mechanics of a shooter game, and most of the time, we experience the game world through his eyes: down the barrel of a gun. Consequently, he only rarely shows emotion and barely talks, despite the frequent use of cinematic cut-scenes in the *Halo* series. Although his fans cherish the character for this no-nonsense approach to dialogue and story-telling, his critics characterize Master Chief as a stereotypically inexpressive, machine-like hero without personality.

Indeed, the character is depicted as mostly silent and controlled in a video game series that spans five major releases and several spin-off titles. *Halo* games are primarily military first-person shooter games set in a science fiction world of the future, with occasional switches to a third-person point of view when the main character drives or flies a vehicle. This partially explains the restrained depiction of the protagonist: because the games are mostly played in first person through the eyes of the main character, the player is transported inside the head of Master Chief and becomes the super soldier himself. In part, Master Chief's characteristics can be explained by this first-person perspective and the game mechanics.

However, the depiction of Master Chief as a silent, faceless hero was also a conscious narrative choice by the studio that developed the character, Bungie. The developers offered players a shell of a character so that they could project their identity and ideas into him—while still providing players with a military-hero blueprint for identification.[3] Accordingly, even in a third-person point of view, the face of the hero is nearly always hidden under a helmet. Interestingly, the eyes of the character are shown briefly in *Halo 4*, revealing the features of a surprisingly old and yellowed face and causing a storm of indignation among fans because this deviated from their personal expectations and projections. Many fans considered this glimpse of a face to be simply wrong—one might argue, though, that any depiction would have been inappropriate for a character that is defined as being faceless and invisible.

To support this depiction as the silent hero, Master Chief typically speaks in pointed one-liners—like a mixture between Clint Eastwood's Western heroes and Arnold Schwarzenegger's Terminator. A Master Chief quote from *Halo 4* defines the character best: "Asking isn't my strong suit." He doesn't speak much; basically, he kills his enemies at first sight.

In contrast to the sparse characterization of Master Chief's personality throughout the *Halo* series, the games unfold an epic story in a rich universe. The *Halo* games typically include huge battles in open country where the protagonist is just one of many participants in multigroup fighting. The interaction of various parties in enormous battle paintings explains much of the fascination both in the single-player campaigns and multiplayer mode, and this is also reflected in a complex background story with multiple factions. In short, the story takes place in a future where humans are attacked by a theocratic alliance of aliens, the Covenant. These aliens regard humans as a disgrace that should be eliminated from the universe, and their religious leaders seek salvation through a hallowed "journey" by means of eponymous Halo rings—huge, inhabitable installations in space. However, the actual purpose of the rings is a much different one: they were built as weapons by an advanced species in order to contain a parasitic alien race, the Flood, that threatens all life in the universe and transforms its prey into mutated abominations. The sudden appearance of the Flood as a new and far more terrifying enemy during the campaign of *Halo: Combat Evolved* is certainly one of the most memorable story twists in the shooter genre.

The *Halo* universe and Master Chief's story are not only developed through games: a book series, graphic novels, anime films (*Halo Legends*), an animated series (*Halo—The Fall of Reach*), and two live-action series (*Halo 4: Forward Unto Dawn*, and *Halo: Nightfall*) contribute to a complex universe. Due to their central role for Microsoft as Xbox games, the *Halo* series and their depiction of Master Chief have been subject to much debate. For example, the 2004 title *Halo 2* has been discussed in relation to President George W. Bush's post–9-11 War on Terror—a political and cultural interpretation that has been criticized by the developers themselves.[4]

The complex *Halo* universe seems to stand in stark contrast to the minimal characterization of the protagonist. However, this is not a contradiction but rather a central feature of first-person shooter story-telling. Master Chief is a "pure" first-person shooter hero in the tradition of *Half Life*'s Gordon Freeman or *Doom*'s unnamed Marine—offering players an undefined shell of a (mostly) silent character that can be experienced through the eyes of the player, he also serves as the central protagonist in an epic narrative. In this sense, his cultural significance is far greater than that of just an iconic video game character: he can be regarded as a role model for unique first-person shooter story-telling that explores the interplay of mechanics and narrative. As such, he contributes to an experience that is much different from what can be achieved in other media like movies or television.

Similar Characters: Gordon Freeman (*Half-Life*), the Marine (*Doom*), William Joseph "B. J." Blazkowicz (*Wolfenstein*)

—Thorsten Quandt

MAX PAYNE

(est. 2001)
Franchise: *Max Payne*
Developer: Remedy Entertainment

Max Payne is a broken man. When we first meet him, he has already lost his wife and his child and is about to commit suicide. Three games later, he has lost even more and won very little. There is nothing we can do to fix his life; all we can do is take control of him and reenact his story. He is the living embodiment of the playable tragedy, at the same time a fantasy of power (he is, after all, one of the best gunmen in games) and of powerlessness.

Although the first *Max Payne* game was released in 2001, the character had been in the mind of its writer, Sam Lake, since 1996. Lake's goal was to bring the "archetype of the detective, the insensitive cop" to video games. "The team wanted to introduce images and ideas seen in countless action and cop movies. Something that hadn't been seen too much in a videogame."[5] For that, they took cues from hard-boiled, classic noir and pulp detectives like Hammet's Sam Spade and Spillane's Mike Hammer and combined them with the heroic bloodshed of Hong Kong movies like *Hard Boiled* (John Woo, 1992). On top of that, a touch of the neo-noir hyper-stylization of Miller's *Sin City* was added to the mix. The resulting character was a tough guy who had abandoned the American Dream and had nothing to fight for, a man with a penchant for violence, superhuman marksmanship, and a taste for metaphor-laden, inner monologues.

Max can be seen as the perfect synthesis of these influences and, at the same time, as a postmodern deconstruction of them: he is overburdened with guilt, frailty, and insecurity. In a sense, he is overcome by the demands of traditional masculinity. Max's driving force is the suffering caused by his losses (his family, his lover, his partners, and even his enemies) and the weight of his constant killing. In the second game, he laments being regarded as a hero and longs for punishment. By the third game, he has turned into an alcoholic and an addict. If contemporary video games are saturated with angry, white, male protagonists, Max is a mirror in which their very human flaws and the toll of their heroics are revealed.

Max always defeats the villains, but at a very high price. His life is a series of tragedies that he survives. A climactic shoot-out in the third game takes place in a New York cemetery while he is visiting his loved ones' graves: a poetic statement that his bullets can save no one but him. In this regard, the series follows the "tragic ending" model described by Juul when writing about "fictional failure," with "the successful player and the unsuccessful protagonist." This creates a tension, "a counterintuitive disconnect between the enjoyment of our accomplishment and our empathy with the plight of the protagonist."[6] This is perhaps counterbalanced by the use of a circular narrative: every game begins at the end, and then Max starts narrating the prior events, creating a sense of fatalism and inevitability. We are not driving him toward catastrophe, we are simply his companions and accomplices. We, as players, are "enactors" re-creating in the present his past deeds, and "since the end of the story is known, the narration turns away from the external mystery and toward the internal one: What happens to a man who must cope with the death of his loved ones and his own transformation into a violent gangster and killing machine?"[7]

This internal mystery is thoroughly explored in a series of playable glimpses into Max's mind. His games are character studies, and for that, the trilogy incorporates a final ingredient in its net of intertextualities: the introspective and eerie surrealism of David Lynch cinema. In every game, Max goes through a different altered state that changes his (and in consequence the player's) perception and makes him go through nightmarish scenarios where he relives his traumas. In the first game he is drugged, in the second one he suffers nightmares, and in the third he has a terrible hangover that gives the world a bright and disjointed feel. These sequences are full of ghosts, space distortions, and doppelgängers—versions of Max that he (and the player) has to face and kill.

These feverish stages ignore the main rules of the game and allow the player to understand Max, making this "an experience that potentially can immerse [the player] into Max's experience in a way that older media could not have done. And when the genre conventions are broken, this can create a momentary sense of confusion, and perhaps estrangement—and thus compel the player to start reflecting and contemplating on the events in the game."[8] This estrangement is evident in a couple of fourth-wall ruptures: during the hallucinations in the first game, Max realizes that he is a character in a comic book cut-scene and, later, in a video game. These ruptures make it clear that we are not Max: we are just controlling him in a flashback, and that makes him all the more tragic.

When we put ourselves in the shoes of Max, we gain a superhuman ability for carnage, but at the same time, we are forced to travel through his tortured mind. We experience both his power and his powerlessness, his suffering. In the *Max Payne* trilogy, the lack of consequences of action cinema and video game shoot-outs is subverted from within in a poetic, exaggerated manner. Max's abilities and flaws, and the way we access them, are a testament to the rhetorical prowess of video games.

Similar Characters: Alan Wake (*Alan Wake*), Inspector "Tequila" Yuen (*Stranglehold*), James Sunderland (*Silent Hill 2*)

—Victor Navarro-Remesal

MEGA MAN

(est. 1987)
Franchise: *Mega Man*
Developer: Capcom

Cultural scholars have long discussed the concept of "memes," or ideas that are tweaked, borrowed, and replicated between people and lead to the development of culture.[9] Online, something as simple as an image of a cat can be changed by many different users to present different jokes and ideas. Mega Man, the amorphous, android protagonist of the *Mega Man* franchise, is this concept embodied as a video game hero. Imitation and appropriation are built into Mega Man's DNA—he has been reimagined and reinvented for nearly three decades, adapting different cultural aesthetics and gameplay traditions in much the same way he steals powers from fallen enemies.

Mega Man, like many video game protagonists of his era, has a relatively simple backstory—he is a robot that was originally designed and created for housekeeping by benevolent scientist Dr. Light and then retrofitted for combat to challenge the nefarious ambitions of the persistent mad scientist Dr. Wily. Apart from a few ill-advised animated sequences in later original series entries, Mega Man in his original incarnation has little if any dialogue that would speak to deeper motivations beyond a generic heroism. In practice, he is a blank slate designed around the aforementioned gameplay hooks of copying and reusing enemy powers (though this is eschewed in the *Legends* version of the character). Generally, each power changes Mega Man's palette from blue to a different color—red, green, purple, etc.—changing the character's appearance and abilities but keeping his form otherwise consistent (early on in development, before receiving his Japanese name of "Rock Man," several "rainbow"-related names were considered). Each ability has power and utility against specific enemies, but it is up to the player to decide when to use these different abilities. The player, to succeed as Mega Man, must change him the same way a meme changes in particular circumstances.

Here it is important to note that each *Mega Man* series takes place in a different continuity, and though in each series the protagonist is named Mega Man in some fashion, every character is a distinct entity. The consistent core of the character, however, is that he is a noble, young, blue-armored android who is idealistic and often bordering on naive. Each different iteration of the series has modified this primary concept in keeping with different pop culture influences and audience expectations.[10] In his initial form, Mega Man was designed as a small, squat robot with large boots and enormous eyes, evoking the work of Osamu Tezuka's Astro Boy both in visual form and narrative design. Localizers at the time changed some of these anime-influenced elements to make him appeal to a Western audience, both in terms of in-game power-ups and an ill-advised piece of box art for the first game in the series that portrayed Mega Man as a futuristic warrior with a strange posture and seemingly advanced in age.[11] These concessions were later dropped in favor of greater parity between regions—later games seemed to be barely translated at all. The eponymous lead of the *Mega Man X* series kept Mega Man's basic visual shorthand but replaced the cutesy hero with a taller, leaner version arguably inspired by the anime *Casshan* that fit the bleaker, cyberpunk dynamics of his post-apocalyptic world—while the addition of visible knee and elbow joints reflected Mega Man X's more versatile move set (though he was unable to crouch until the fifth game in the series). Unlike his predecessor, Mega Man X grappled with issues of morality and his role in the world as he battled his fellow androids. Mega Man X reflected his series and the marketplace on a meta-textual level—just as the audience that had first encountered Mega Man had grown older and more complicated, so too had their hero.

After Mega Man X, the connecting threads between the main Mega Man universes became more tenuous, with the character being repurposed for different settings and genres. *Mega Man Legends* recast Mega Man as a mysterious teenage android adopted by a family of treasure hunters traveling a water-covered planet via airship, drawing heavily from the anime series *Yatterman* and the works of noted anime auteur Hayao Miyazaki. The later *Mega Man Battle Network* series attempted to cash in on the virtual pet and monster battling crazes of the late 1990s and early 2000s by recasting Mega Man as a computer program (creatively named "Mega Man.EXE") wielded by a grade-school boy to battle his friends and villains alike, similar to the popular *Pokémon* and *Digimon* franchises.

Mega Man's innate malleability has made his series one of the most prolific video game franchises of all time, with over one hundred different games overall. In recent years, however, Mega Man's star has faded somewhat. Developer and publisher Capcom attempted to revive the franchise by taking it back to its 8-bit roots with *Mega Man 9* and *Mega Man 10*, but it has otherwise laid dormant for several years, with two high-profile series cancellations (*Mega Man Universe* and *Mega Man Legends 3*) coming alongside the departure of longtime series head Keiji Inafune. Despite this, Mega Man has still proven prolific and lucrative in the realm of toys, apparel, and other merchandise, and the character made a well-received appearance in the latest entry of Nintendo's *Super Smash Bros.* fighting game. While rumors abound of a revitalization of the main franchise, Mega Man has acted as something of a meme himself for independent game developers—games like *Battle Kid* and *Shovel Knight* wear their influences on their sleeve and boast protagonists that bear a striking resemblance to the character. Perhaps in the ultimate mimetic reclamation of the concept, the first crowdfunded game developed by Inafune after leaving Capcom was *Mighty No. 9*—a game featuring a blue-hued robot battling enemies and absorbing their powers. For a character defined in concept and execution by borrowing from others for one's own purposes, it is a fitting development.

Similar Characters: Kirby (*Kirby's Dreamland*), Mario (*Super Mario Bros.*), Sonic (*Sonic the Hedgehog*)

—Bryan J. Carr

MICHAEL VICK

(est. 2004)
Franchise: *Madden NFL*
Developer: EA Tiburon

Michael Vick broke *Madden NFL 2004*. The developers at EA Tiburon had a problem on their hands in dealing with his characterization. He could run as fast as the fastest players in the league. He was as elusive as the best runners in the game, accelerating to top speed as quickly as anyone, and he could throw really far. He was a player with the greatest sum of athletic skills the game had ever seen, but he was a quarterback, and the *Madden* football simulation was simply not built to accommodate him.

The complexity of *Madden*'s systems stems from a design philosophy that attempts to approach the same complexity of televised football in real life. Fans expect the game to reflect the same sport they consume regularly on television.[12] But the conventions informing sports video game design are also a result of production. Iterative sports game development, with new updated titles released every year, has encouraged an additive design principle, whereby the systems grow in complexity with each release.

At the heart of these complex systems, pumping life through the entire game, are the player ratings. In *Madden*, player ratings are a big deal. The numerical measurements of player abilities, both physical and cognitive, undergird the entire algorithmic system that drives the simulation. Those numbers separate the star athletes, like Vick, from the everyday Joes. They are a reflection of the same debate and discourse that has been driving sports fandom for as long as there has been sports fandom. Who is better? Who can throw farther? Who can run faster? Who is calmest under pressure? Player ratings are the intangibles defining athleticism made real and, perhaps most significantly, operable.

Enter Michael Vick. The cover star for *Madden NFL 2004*, coming off a phenomenal first full season as a starting quarterback, Vick broke every rule and expectation governing player ratings in sports games, to the point where he collapsed the system and broke the simulation. It was not simply that Vick had the highest scores in any of the ratings categories, in fact, other quarterbacks in the game rank higher in singular categories and even overall. It was Michael Vick's mixture of speed, strength, acceleration, and a throwing ability that was strong and just accurate enough, that tore up the *Madden NFL 2004* system. Together, his unique combination of ratings was god-like.

During development of the game, the EA Tiburon team knew they had a problem with rating Michael Vick. His abilities were so different from those of any other quarterback they had rated before that they had the potential to disrupt the game. Donny Moore, the developer at EA Tiburon responsible for player ratings when *Madden NFL 2004* was released, noted, "Before Vick, it was unheard-of to talk about a quarterback with 90 speed or above."[13] Moore also remarks that approvals for Vick's troublesome ratings would need to go up the managerial ladder internally, as they understood that his ratings would substantially impact the game. "For Vick," Moore states, "we knew this was going to be a game changer."

Vick's characterization did change the game, and it changed the way people played *Madden*. The release of *Madden NFL 2004* came at a time when competitive multiplayer on consoles, and especially with sports video games, remained local—two players, facing off on either side of a couch. The selection of Michael Vick's Atlanta Falcons team was polarizing; it was understood that any player using him had a distinct and perhaps unfair advantage. Anthony Stevenson, the marketing director for EA Sports at the time, unequivocally stated, "The guy broke the game . . . you could just run him back and forth, back and forth, back and forth, and nobody could stop him."[14] Vick was almost untouchable. With just a little practice, a player could sprint around the backfield, waiting for an open receiver, or simply wait to break upfield and run for large gains. It was a bastardization of realistic football strategy born out of a broken simulation, and yet his abilities were accurate, and in reality, Vick could scramble out of broken plays, making the most ludicrous of ad hoc plans successful in the end.

Vick presents a compelling case study in the characterization of real people in video games. The vast majority of video game characters are wholly fictional—

designed and developed within and against genre conventions and historical production norms: brawny white supermen, super-powered vixens, damsels in distress, the occasional plumber and his brother. Professional athletes, however, when depicted in video games, are expected to mirror their real-world inspirations. Vick in a football video game is expected by fans to look like the real Vick, but importantly too, he is expected to perform like the real Vick. Fans watched him sprint past defenders on TV, bounding with remarkable agility and vision, and thus they expected his video game counterpart to do the same. And so he did.

Vick's fall-from-grace in the sports world was even more spectacular than his rare talents on the field. In 2007, Vick plead guilty to a felony dog-fighting charge for his involvement in a complex, underground, dog-fighting ring run from his home. As the story topped mainstream news headlines, Vick's public persona narrative shifted dramatically from elite superstar to fallen hero to despised criminal. After serving two years in federal prison, Vick returned to the NFL, but he was never the same. Nonetheless, in 2013, to commemorate the 25th anniversary of the *Madden* game franchise, EA Sports named an "All-25" of the greatest characters in the game's history, and at quarterback, without any doubt, stood Michael Vick. Despite the infamy of his crime and time-served, and despite his subsequent meteoric collapse, to *Madden* fans, Vick will always be the gamebreaker: so impossibly good, he changed the game.

Similar Characters: Jon Dowd (*MVP Baseball*), Michael Jordan (*NBA 2K11*), Tecmo Bo Jackson (*Tecmo Bowl*)

—Abe Stein

MISSINGNO.

(est. 1999)
Franchise: *Pokémon*
Developer: Game Freak

"Gotta catch 'em all?" Not according to Nintendo. In a May 1999 issue of *Nintendo Power*, Nintendo warned players about a buggy Pokémon called "MissingNo.," short for "Missing Number," in *Pokémon Red* and *Pokémon Blue*. MissingNo. operates as a fail-safe that prevents both *Pokémon* games from crashing in the unlikely event that the software mistakenly accesses nonexistent Pokémon data. Although players were not intended to see or access MissingNo., it was quickly discovered that a series of procedures would force the software to access "empty" data, thus cuing a battle with MissingNo. Players also discovered that they could capture MissingNo. and use it in battle like any other Pokémon. To discourage players, Nintendo described MissingNo. as a glitch and reported that capturing it could "easily erase your game file or disrupt your graphics."[15] But to Nintendo's dismay, the MissingNo. fail-safe was super effective. Inspiring nearly two decades' worth of fan media, MissingNo. celebrates deviant and subversive play as both a critical and creative act.

The most popular means of accessing MissingNo. involves a series of counter-intuitive steps that lead players from an old man to the sea. The procedure begins by talking to a non-player character called "the Old Man." Talking to the Old Man cues a tutorial on how to capture wild Pokémon, and the game replaces the player's avatar and name with those belonging to the non-player character. The player's data is moved to the data buffer, a region used to temporarily store data, and retrieved after the tutorial concludes. Although the player's name is swapped out after the tutorial, a copy of it remains in the buffer. Leaving town typically clears the buffer by replacing the data with hexadecimal codes for several Pokémon that can be captured in the area. The Pokémon ability "fly," however, allows players to transport their character to another town without changing the data stored in the buffer. By traveling to Cinnabar Island, a small island town, players can use "Surf," a Pokémon ability equivalent to swimming, to access MissingNo. through a programming oversight. Surfing off a coastline should flush the data buffer with new Pokémon data; however, the island's eastern coastline does not refresh this data. Thus, if a player surfs along the eastern coastline after watching the Old Man's tutorial, the game will attempt to use the player's name as hexadecimal code to find a corresponding Pokémon, likely pointing to "empty" regions of the game's memory that store MissingNo.

Undoubtedly surprised by the scrambled sprite that emerged from the sea, players proposed several explanations for MissingNo. Early *Pokémon* websites circulated it as an exploit that provided players with an alternative means to *Pokémon* mastery. Specifically, encountering MissingNo. instantly duplicates the sixth item in players' inventories. Players discovered that rather than competing for resources and Pokémon through battles and trade, they could use MissingNo. to mass-produce "nuggets," an item that sells for a high price; "rare candy," an item that immediately raises a Pokémon's level and abilities; and the "Master Ball," a Poké Ball that instantly captures Pokémon without having to battle. MissingNo. allowed players to pursue avenues for play not intended by designers, associating MissingNo. with inventive and exploratory play.

Whereas players classified MissingNo. as a cheat and Nintendo described it as a bug, the game counted it as a Pokémon. Like other Pokémon, players could capture, trade, and battle MissingNo. It had a specific dwelling in the game world, and it even appeared in players' PokéDex—a catalog of captured Pokémon. Fans began producing media to speculate on MissingNo. as a character within the *Pokémon* universe, eventually canonizing MissingNo. and "ensuring [its] mythic status among the community and absorbing [it] into the 'official' roster of collectible Pokémon."[16] Preserved for years through player creativity and ingenuity, MissingNo. symbolized a desire to play as cocreators of the game world rather than as passive consumers.

Efforts to identify MissingNo. as a game character, programming glitch, or cheat code evolved into an ongoing game in which fans competed with one another to construct a plausible explanation for MissingNo. But as fan media flooded the Internet, hackers began digging deep into the games' programming for clues. Wilma Alice Bainbridge and William Sims Bainbridge consider this critical investigation a "metagame . . . played against the programmer . . . [and] a noncompetitive exploration of exotic territory, even at times having some of the quality of scientific research and discovery."[17] This critical work has recently yielded evidence that the "empty" data slots were once filled by Pokémon that were removed and saved for the games' sequels. This final and most recent interpretation links MissingNo. with deep reading, positioning MissingNo. as a method for game analysis and criticism.

Players understand MissingNo. as an exploit, a player-produced character, and a method, each of which creates opportunities for "counterplay." MissingNo. grants players room to play against the preset interactions and narrative included in *Pokémon Red* and *Pokémon Blue*. Without knowing how to code, players can redesign the games' rules and narrative, experimenting with play critically and learning about both games' design in the process. As an exploit, MissingNo. allows players to protest the socioeconomic system in *Pokémon Red* and *Pokémon Blue*. Using MissingNo., players can control how in-game commerce operates, making possible an idyllic space in which players no longer need to pit their Pokémon companions against opponents to earn money and weaken wild Pokémon into submission. As a cultural artifact, MissingNo. celebrates the creativity of deviant and subversive forms of play.

Similar Characters: Ermac (*Mortal Kombat*), Glitch Sonic/Ashura the Hedgehog (*Sonic the Hedgehog 2*), 'M' (*Pokémon Red/Blue*)

—Kyle Bohunicky

MR. TORGUE

(est. 2012)
Franchise: *Borderlands*
Developer: Gearbox Software

The action shooter series *Borderlands* has established a reputation for showcasing characters with complex and humorous identities. Departing from the more serious and solemn tones that generally characterize first-person shooters, the *Borderlands* series tells the stories of Vault Hunters, rebel fighters who fight weapons corporation Hyperion and its attempt to take over the post-apocalyptic planet of Pandora. While the core cast of playable characters offers much in the way of direct humor, the non-player characters provide a plethora of memorable moments to carry through the game. Enter Mr. Torgue, a non-player character introduced in *Mr. Torgue's Campaign of Carnage*, a piece of downloadable content for *Borderlands 2*. In a sense, Mr. Torgue is the hyperbolic reincarnation of the late Macho Man Randy Savage, who was a prominent wrestler in *World Championship Wrestling*. In his boisterousness, however, Mr. Torgue is one of many characters in the franchise that utilize pervasive humor to showcase a nuanced sense of gender identity that is rarely seen in action games today.

Mr. Torgue is the spokesman for the Torgue Corporation, another weapons manufacturer in competition with the Hyperion Corporation. Players are introduced to Mr. Torgue at the outset of the Campaign of Carnage by being welcomed to the "Badass Crater of Badassitude," home to a tournament of gladiators who can win a bevy of treasure after defeating numerous ranked badasses in the tournament. From here, players become witness to the outrageousness of Mr. Torgue's dialogue:

> BY REGISTERING IN THE BADASS TOURNAMENT, YOU LEGALLY FORFEIT YOUR RIGHT TO CRY, EAT TOFU, OR WATCH MOVIES WHERE PEOPLE KISS IN THE RAIN AND SH*T. . . . A LOT OF PEOPLE BEEN ASKING ME WHY MY VOICE BEEPS ALL THE F*CKIN' TIME. THE TORGUE SHAREHOLDERS WIRED MY VOICEBOX WITH A DIGITAL CENSOR SO I CAN'T SAY STUFF LIKE SH*T, C*CK, OR P*SSY F*CKIN' D*CKBALLS! THAT'S HALF MY F*CKIN' VOCABULARY, IT'S GODDAMN BULLSH*T!

These and many other messages from Mr. Torgue immediately serve as pointed parodies of the masculine characters that commonly characterize most contemporary action games.

The dialogue echoed by Mr. Torgue alludes to a gesture that the franchise makes in complicating and rethinking what it means to be a masculine character in an action game. Though we often think of gender as a universal experience—men are men and women are women—Judith Butler has compellingly argued that gender and sexual identity "is often mistaken as a sign of its internal or inherent truth; gender is prompted by obligatory norms to be one gender or the other (usually within a strictly binary frame)."[18] However, Butler continues, because of this "there is no gender without this reproduction of norms that risks undoing or redoing the norm in unexpected ways, thus opening up the possibility of a remaking of gendered reality along new lines."[19] Mr. Torgue exemplifies this element of what Butler calls "performativity" in that players often find him engaging with other characters in a way that problematizes masculinity. Such an instance is found in the Campaign of Carnage where Mr. Torgue commends the player on rescuing longtime non-player character Mad Moxxi, adding, "YOU SHOULD TREAT MOXXI NICE. NOTHING IS MORE BADASS THAN TREATING A WOMAN WITH RESPECT!" This is likely the last thing that a player would expect from a character as boisterous as Mr. Torgue. Not only does he break through the idea of being one type of real man, but he also performs a more nuanced form of masculinity beyond the loud and caps-lock-laden rants that you find in most of the game.

The "messiness" of Mr. Torgue as both a hypermasculine and presumably feminist non-player character emerges as he evinces feminine character tropes from a hypermasculine body. Such a messiness further reinforces Judith Butler's notion of performativity and likewise undermines the general conception of masculinity as a fixed quality or content whose accumulation results in becoming a "real man."[20] This point can be seen in *Tiny Tina's Assault on Dragon Keep*: Tiny Tina invites a demanding Mr. Torgue to a *Dungeons & Dragons*–style game of "Bunkers and Badasses," much to the dismay of longtime *Borderlands* character Lilith. After she labels him a "fake geek guy" for not being able to flex his geek knowledge in a series of quiz questions, Mr. Torgue breaks down in tears at the fact that he is not able to participate in this *Dungeons & Dragons*–style game closed off by his female counterpart. From decrying labels as a fake geek guy to arguing against the dark, misogynistic notion of "friendzoning," Mr. Torgue's hypermasculine body, replete with feminist undertones, flips and grapples with gender identity in a nuanced manner.

In the spirit of the juxtaposition of Torgue's hypermasculinity and femininity, other facets of character identity can come to bear significantly on non-player characters. *Borderlands 2* writer Anthony Burch stated that characters such as Mr. Torgue were written with focuses on both inclusivity and representation. Burch confirms that *Borderlands* non-player characters such as Mr. Torgue and Sir Hammerlock are bisexual and gay, respectively, asserting, "In the end, I'd like to be even more inclusive going forward. . . . I can only hope that the steps I've mentioned here are good ones, and that this article makes it clear that whoever you are—whatever your background, or race, or gender, or religion, or sexual orientation, or mental or physical condition—you are welcome here."[21] Although the efforts of Burch and *Borderlands* writers irked and alienated a few fans of the series, Mr. Torgue and characters in the series largely stand out in the broader conversation about how discussions pertaining to diverse representation in games can be meaningfully accomplished. Specifically, Mr. Torgue showcases how masculine characters are capable of evincing feminist qualities that continuously remind players to rethink gender identity as one of many culturally significant markers of both playable and non-player characters. Ultimately, non-player characters such as Mr. Torgue are necessary for igniting discussions on how diversity and inclusivity are central to the experiences of adventure and action games broadly.

Similar Characters: Dante (*Devil May Cry*), Eleonor "Leo" Kliesen (*Tekken 6*), Gogo (*Final Fantasy VI*)

—Carlos A. Flores

N

THE NARRATOR

(est. 2011)
Franchise: *The Stanley Parable*
Developer: Galactic Café

With the kind of elocution and authoritative delivery one would expect from a classically trained English thespian, one might at first mistake *The Stanley Parable*'s disembodied and invisible Narrator for a career documentarian—but there's far more to him than that. In this first-person adventure game, the player takes control of an office worker named Stanley in a search for missing coworkers—a quest that is quickly disrupted by an omnipresent Narrator whose frequent instructions, short-tempered rants, and existential musings soon form the focal point of the play experience. In controlling Stanley, each choice the player makes establishes a new, sometimes-isolated branch of the story, each of which reveals a little more about the Narrator. Eventually, the player comes to know the Narrator as little more than a collection of prerecorded statements to be coaxed from within the game's black box—and the Narrator's ultimate, tragic revelation is that he knows it.

A paradox that is both thematically and ludically central to *The Stanley Parable* is revealed as soon as the Narrator issues his first instruction: "Stanley stood up from his desk and walked out of the office," which is of course an entirely optional course of action for the player. Players are frequently presented with similarly disobey-able commands ("Coming across a set of two open doors, Stanley took the one on his left") and general absurdities ("The keypad behind the boss's desk guarded the terrible truth . . . and so the boss had assigned it an extra secret pin number: 2-8-4-5.") which showcase the nontraditional use of a narrative device and empower players in their search for new and interesting deviations.

Each time the player selects or uncovers a new path, a new version of the Narrator is born. In one strand he remains a functional narrator, but in another he is a megalomaniacal mastermind character within the story, and in another he is a game designer frustrated by a player who isn't playing the game properly. Most strands serve to satirize particular aspects of contemporary player attitudes or game design, most of which stem from players' willingness to defy the Narrator in light of the knowledge that he can be defied. While there is no "true" version of the Narrator, there is one version whose frustration in the face of his own impotence sheds light on all other playthroughs, and indeed, *The Stanley Parable* as a game product in and of itself.

Let's talk about the broom closet ending. A simple cramped closet, occupied only by cleaning products, exists off the side of one of the game's ostensible "main" pathways. Although the closet is ignored by the Narrator, the player can enter the space and close the door behind them. Doing so prompts the following response from the Narrator:

> Stanley stepped into the broom closet, but there was nothing here, so he turned around and got back on track.

Interesting is the use of the word "here" instead of "there" to describe the space in which the player has placed Stanley. The Narrator has revealed himself, however briefly, to be trapped with Stanley and the player. This frustrates him somewhat.

> There was nothing here. No choice to make, no path to follow, just an empty broom closet. No reason to still be here. . . . It was baffling that Stanley was still just sitting in the broom closet. He wasn't even doing anything, at least if there were something to interact with he'd be justified in some way.

The Narrator's use of the statement, "No choice to make, no path to follow," is an obvious meta-commentary: "choice" and "branching-path" are popular buzz-terms in contemporary game culture, often used as selling points for triple-A software. The Narrator is literally asserting that this is not that kind of game, though the fact that he is talking proves the opposite. The broom closet is of course a branching-path—only this one is temporal instead of spatial. As the player pulls new statements from the Narrator, he or she is uncovering more and more game content. From here, the Narrator becomes increasingly frustrated, and eventually speaks to the player directly:

> Are you . . . are you really still in the broom closet? Standing around doing nothing? Why? Please offer me some explanation here; I'm genuinely confused. . . . Maybe to you, this is somehow its own branching path. Maybe, when you go talk about this with your friends, you'll say: "Oh, did you get the broom closet ending? The broom closet ending was my favorite!" I hope your friends find this concerning.

While many will play *The Stanley Parable* for its varied critiques of contemporary games, the gaming industry, and players themselves, the Narrator knows better. He understands the inescapable "game-ness" of the 3D world in which he finds himself, and thus the sense of completion that some players will undoubtedly seek out. "The Broom Closet Ending," "The Art Ending," "The Freedom Ending"—there's no secret why all the possible pathways featured in this game are cataloged and wikied for all to see. To the Narrator's chagrin, the player might see *The Stanley Parable* as something to be "completed."

The Narrator matters because he understands and accepts his own futility: his self-imposed purpose is irrelevant when his overall meaning is ultimately decided by the player. He knows that, for some, he is simply a list of statements—statements to be evoked via the performance of particular actions, to be "unlocked" via careful adherence to friends' instructions or walkthroughs. In the age of the wiki, the subreddit, and the "Let's play," the modern player is never more than a few clicks away from finding their character stripped back, robbed of all agency and presented as nothing more than a ludic device, a means to an end. The Narrator matters because he knows all of this, just as he knows that you don't even have to meet him to learn these horrible facts. I hope you find this concerning.

Similar Characters: Davey Wreden (*The Beginner's Guide*), GLaDOS (*Portal*), Rucks (*Bastion*)

—Scott Donaldson

NESS

(est. 1994)
Franchise: *Mother/Earthbound*
Developer: Ape

The debut of Ness in the classic role-playing game *Earthbound* marks a decisive moment in the history of video game characters. Ness represents an anachronism when considered alongside contemporary role-playing-game protagonists from series such as *Dragon Quest* and *Final Fantasy* who are overwhelmingly heroic fantasy warriors. By the mid-90s, audiences were "accustomed to the trappings of *Dungeons & Dragons* as an essential characteristic of RPGs [role-playing games]," and all the attendant "medical herbs, airships, and instances of Tolkienry," that inevitably came with that genre.[1] Ness, a thirteen-year-old boy with a passion for baseball, represents a radical break from that tradition and an attempt to create a video game protagonist who is less superhuman and more familiar, one who wouldn't seem out of place among actually existing children of 1990s America. Ness, like many other Nintendo characters such as Link from *The Legend of Zelda*, is a silent protagonist, inviting the player to project his or her own personality on him. Although "Ness" is the character's default name (and an anagram of "SNES," an abbreviation of "Super Nintendo Entertainment System"), the player is allowed to rename him. Yet Ness's silence and renameability are far from the only aspects of his personality that invite gamers to identify with him.

In *Earthbound*, players are put in the shoes of Ness in his hometown of Onett, in the country of Eagleland, a goofy homage to American suburbia. *Earthbound* represents a pastiche of American culture from the Japanese perspective. Due to the game's numerous references to cultural touchstones such as the Blues Brothers, *Star Wars*, and the Beatles, many consider the game "a love letter to twentieth-century Americana."[2] Ness should, therefore, be interpreted as an attempt by *Earthbound*'s creator, Shigesato Itoi, to encapsulate the ideal American child (though this attempt remains limited by gaming culture's predisposition to male protagonists during this era). Ness's adventure plays like a classic American "coming of age" story where the neighborhood kids strike out on an adventure and get swept up in events much bigger than themselves. His quest begins when he discovers a nearby meteorite crash-site and is beseeched by a time-traveling, bee-like creature named Buzz Buzz to seek out eight sanctuaries and defeat the evil alien Giygas. The player controls Ness as he explores locations both run-of-the-mill and exotic on his quest through a late-capitalist world turned upside-down by Giygas.

Ness is an "everyboy" whose heroism is located thoroughly in the everyday and who never loses the boy-next-door relatability that is so vital to his appeal, in spite of his battles against otherworldly forces. You will find no knight's armor or wizard's robes in his wardrobe; players will observe him wearing a backpack and signature red baseball cap throughout most of the game, when he's not wearing his pajamas. In keeping with the game's broader tendency to juxtapose American and Japanese pop culture, Ness's nondescript blue-and-yellow-striped shirt evokes the illustrations of Charles Schultz's *Peanuts* comics, while his round features and black, circular eyes resemble anime or manga artwork. Ness heals himself not with magic potions and phoenix down but rather with fruit juice, hamburgers, and pizza. Although his adventures have elements of science fiction, he spends large portions of gameplay exploring ordinary environments that American children will undoubtedly be familiar with: drugstores, arcades, hotels, department stores, and pizza shops. Similarly, Ness does battle zombies and aliens but also goofy and mundane enemies like runaway dogs, angry crows, cranky ladies, and hippies that have been afflicted by the malevolent influence of Giygas. In contrast to his dragon-slaying counterparts from sword-and-sorcery–style role-playing games, Ness fights these everyday enemies while armed only with household objects such as a baseball bat and a yo-yo, along with a limited repertoire of psychic powers.

Earthbound was far from a commercial smash-hit: less than 150,000 copies of Earthbound were sold in America initially.[3] In spite of this, Ness remains a highly recognizable and beloved member of the Nintendo family of characters while also maintaining a cult following. He is a staple in Nintendo's series of fighting games, *Super Smash Bros.*, having been featured in every installment, which is no small feat considering the original *Super Smash Bros.* contained only twelve playable characters. Ness maintains such an ardent following that in 2013, after years of lobbying by fans, *Earthbound* was finally rereleased on the Wii U Virtual Console. The fact that Ness remains a popular and resonant character in spite of *Earthbound*'s lukewarm commercial success testifies to the ability of audiences to identify with him. The continuing demand for Ness—as illustrated by his longevity in *Super Smash Bros.* and fan lobbying for *Earthbound* rereleases—shows that his small-town charm remains potent even as modern video games become more complex and explore even more otherworldly environments.

Ness is a trailblazing character that expands the horizon of who counts as a hero in video games. Ness and his companions—who ultimately defeat Giygas through the power of prayer—serve to deconstruct stock video game hero archetypes and to instruct gamers that often the most powerful resource at their disposal is love. By conquering Giygas with heartfelt prayer rather than brute strength or super-powerful weapons, Ness and his friends illustrate that the potential for heroism lies dormant within all of us, waiting to be kindled at times when our loved ones are in great need. As one of the first video game protagonists to be merely "one of the neighborhood kids," Ness and his everyday heroism subvert numerous conventions of the video game industry and set the stage for future video games to explore not only science-fiction and fantasy settings but also mundane suburban environments. In no small part because of Ness, video games now commonly feature protagonists that are less larger-than-life than your average *Final Fantasy* hero. In particular, Ness's influence can be felt in the ultra-popular *Pokémon* series, which also features young, baseball-cap-wearing, silent protagonists exploring various towns and cities. By upending previously established video game norms, Ness taught gamers an anomalous lesson about the virtues of heroism grounded in simple acts of kindness.

Similar Characters: Link (*The Legend of Zelda*), the Protagonist (*Persona*), Red (*Pokémon*)

—Jacob Justice

O

ORC PEON

(est. 1994)
Franchise: *Warcraft*
Developer: Blizzard

Burly green muscles carry the weight of the Orcish Horde's progress, and wild, wandering eyes suggest the burden of labor and an affected, simple mind. Broadly speaking, Peons (and their Alliance counterparts, Peasants) hold the lowest station in their communities. Peons are the downtrodden, the dishonored, the toiling: an inept sub-race of the *Warcraft* universe's iconic Orcs. They garner little respect as they complete tedious tasks like harvesting lumber, mining ore, transporting resources, and repairing machines—ironic, since these labors function as the backbone of the Horde war machine in its perpetual battle against humans, the Alliance, and other worldly threats. Despite this diminution, the Peon lifestyle is quite representative of Orc survivalist spirit—one must pull his own weight despite any shortcomings since weakness is a liability and a dishonor to the clan. This irony and spirit frame the Peon's dual representative significance as both a laborer and an ethnic other.

The Peon archetype and role evolved somewhat over its tenure in the *Warcraft* franchise since first appearing in the real-time strategy game *Warcraft II* as a very literal resource (designated an unarmored, civilian "unit"). Bent from hard work, they had little combat value save for throwing spears out of burrows, and so they had no potential for glorious battle death. In *Warcraft III*, the newly emerged Orc warchief Thrall (himself raised a slave) sought to forge a "new Horde" in cooperation with allied Trolls and Tauren, promising that no member of the Horde would ever again be enslaved. Although Peons in the new Horde were treated more humanely under Thrall's watch, they continued to serve as hard laborers and were mistreated by many military leaders. In *World of Warcraft* (*WoW*), Peons saw a marked evolution in their gameplay function, operating not as controlled resources but as non-player characters—omnipresent, perpetual workers in Horde cities and outposts. Despite the functional autonomy of the *WoW* Peons, players are sometimes tasked in the game with acting upon Peons, temporarily returning to a real-time-strategy, player-Peon resource relationship by leveraging them as vendors to supply resources and using various "motivational tools" such as a "booterang" to discipline lazy Peons. The resource relationship can also be seen in derivative trading card games in which an Orc Peon card (picturing an archetypically green, muscular Orc carrying a bag of supplies) allows the player to manipulate resources.

In these ways, the Peon may be read in Marxist terms, within the *Warcraft* universe narratives, as the laboring proletariat and the mainstream Horde as the enriched bourgeoisie. It could be interpreted that the industrious war machine advances through an exploitative relationship between the Horde leaders and the Peon workforce. Taking this point of view, an interesting question emerges about the role that players have in how the player-Peon relationship intersects with the Horde-Peon relationship when considering how manual labor is represented in the games; that is, as a commodity to narratively advance a civilization and to ludically advance gameplay objectives. This intersection is particularly relevant to the notion of "playbour"[1] through such gameplay mechanics as level-grinding and resource accumulation, and through extra-game player labors such as interface modding, farming, and blogging. Indeed, some argue that the franchise's success—even as a subscription-based game in an increasingly free-to-play market—can be attributed to a "convincing and detailed simulacrum of the process of becoming successful in capitalist societies."[2] The Peon, Peasant, and player, in a sense, labor together in advancing the status and longevity of the game franchise.

It's perhaps not enough to say, however, that the Peon and Peasant are sides of the same coin as the laboring units, or non-player characters, between the competing Horde and Alliance. The human Peasant retains some of his or her personhood, while the Orc Peon is relegated to the status of an animal. This difference is particularly evident in the characters' language throughout the games. In *Warcraft II*, Peons are almost childlike, responding to player actions with burps, giggles, and taunts, while Peasants are more refined ("Ready to serve," "Yes my lord!", "Job's done"). In *Warcraft III*, both archetypes become a bit more aggressive and self-confident, however, the Peons are still simple ("What you want?," "Okey dokey," "Me not that kind of Orc") compared to the more refined Peasant ("Yes, milord?," "Off I go, then," "Right-o"). This dichotomy mirrors each laborer's race and faction representations in the franchise more broadly. The fantasy-aesthetic, human-led Alliance featuring hearty dwarves and lovely elves is generally characterized as the "good" faction; the ragged, Orc-led Horde draws heavily on othered real-world populations such as native North American–inspired Tauren and black Caribbean–inspired Trolls and is generally thought to be the "evil" faction.[3] As such, the Orc Peon is socially subjugated as both a laborer and an ethnic other.

The Peon's function as perpetual laborer and the narrative and ludic evolutions highlight questions about the value of labor in games and—since players are seldom exposed to the deeper personal narrative of any Peon—the invisibility and deindividuation of that toil in the face of its importance. Importantly, that irony is not lost on players. Gaming forums feature debates about potential Peon uprisings despite the trademark Peon laziness; the role of lower intelligence and strength compared to social status in one's designation as a Peon; and how the Peon archetype might manifest in other games (e.g., a Peon in the digital card game *Hearthstone* might function as an easily killed character that grants the player a coin, as a mulligan, or require a tacit agreement to simply ignore its value). Perhaps most notable among these forum discussions are calls to reinstate *World of Warcraft*'s "Peon Day," an in-game holiday (available only in European realms and replaced in 2007 by the Harvest Festival) commemorated with green fireworks, revelry, and a perhaps allegorical story: Legend tells us that human and Orc leaders called on the lowest worker from each of their races to complete a great task by day's end lest the world suffer . . . each completed the task with four minutes to spare.

Similar Characters: Abe (*Oddworld*), Goblins (*World of Warcraft*), Vortigaunts (*Half-Life*)

—Jaime Banks

P

PAC-MAN

(est. 1980)
Franchise: *Pac-Man*
Developer: Namco

The "golden age" of arcade video games produced numerous games that are still widely played and loved today. Among these is one of the most recognized characters of all video game characters: a small, yellow ball named Pac-Man. Created by Toru Iwatani and released in 1980, Pac-Man would go on to revolutionize the design of both video games and video game characters. Today, more than thirty years after the game debuted, Pac-Man is among the most recognizable video game characters of all time.[1]

Pac-Man is the playable character in one of the first maze games. Players control Pac-Man, directing the little yellow blob around the maze screen; he must consume all of the dots on the screen, simultaneously avoiding four ghost-like enemies, to progress to the next level. The four ghosts, named Blinky (red), Pinky (pink), Inky (cyan), and Clyde (orange), each possess their own pattern of behavior while chasing Pac-Man. In addition to the dots, power pellets and fruit appear throughout the maze. Consuming power pellets, displayed as large flashing dots, allows Pac-Man to turn the tables on the ghosts for a short time. Each of the ghosts, typically identified by their individual color, turns temporarily blue, indicating its vulnerability. Instead of the ghost's touch killing Pac-Man, our little yellow hero is able to eat the ghosts, returning them to their central starting area. Various fruits appear in each level, offering different point increases upon consumption. The highest possible score can only be attained by eating every dot, power pellet, ghost, and fruit in each of the 256 playable levels.[2]

There are many stories about the character design of Pac-Man. One story says that Pac-Man's design is based on the image of a pizza with a slice missing, which resembles a head with an open mouth;[3] another suggests that Pac-Man's minimal design might be due to the graphical constraints of the 1980s.[4] Pac-Man's design certainly matches the overall theme of eating present in the game, and it emphasizes a connection between eating and power. Despite this simple design, Pac-Man was among the first characters introduced in video games. Before Pac-Man,

144

gamers primarily controlled paddles or spaceships; while identification with these images was certainly possible, Pac-Man provided a different experience. Pac-Man was not just an avatar controlled by the player; rather, Pac-Man was an entity with its own persona. This separate entity was capable of having its own dreams and fears. Players wanted to proceed to the next level and earn a high score, while Pac-Man himself wanted to survive his encounters with the ghosts. In later years, Pac-Man got a wife and child, which further anthropomorphized the little yellow blob for players. Because the maze-based game design of Pac-Man inspired experimentation with new types of game genres, the existence of Pac-Man himself simultaneously encouraged game designers to explore new options in character design. Indeed, many games developed after Pac-Man featured central, easily recognizable characters.[5]

Pac-Man's design also represented one of the first attempts to think about character design in terms of marketing demographics. The game and characters were designed to attract girls and women to arcades and the video game scene. In order to move beyond the typical teenage-male video game audience, Pac-Man and his four ghostly enemies had to be designed as "cute" characters.[6] Game designers hoped that the combination of a maze, nonviolent game goals, and an adorable protagonist and enemies would expand the video game's audience; this expansion, in turn, would increase profit and help to maintain arcades as a popular site for socialization and entertainment. And it worked: the article "Women Join the Arcade Revolution" in the May 1982 *Electronic Games Magazine* recognized Pac-Man as one of the first games to attract women to arcades.

Given the popularity of Pac-Man, spin-off games and sequels were inevitable. One such game was designed in response to the increase in female players: *Ms. Pac-Man*. The gameplay of *Ms. Pac-Man* is similar to the original *Pac-Man*, with some enhancements. The familiar ghosts are featured, and Ms. Pac-Man is tasked with eating dots and power-ups (while sporting a red bow!). *Ms. Pac-Man* also offers new maze designs, faster gameplay, and slight changes to the programmed movements of the ghosts. Overall, these changes improved the original gameplay. In "Women Join the Arcade Revolution," a Midway spokesperson comments that *Ms. Pac-Man* was produced "as our way of thanking all those lady arcaders who have played and enjoyed Pac-Man." It appears that Pac-Man's creators offered a female protagonist as both a subtle sign of recognition of the value of female gamers and as an attempt to maintain the fragile new interest of women in arcade games. While Ms. Pac-Man was a huge step forward for female gamers, the change was really just the addition of the bow; Ms. Pac-Man was not accompanied by any substantial game changes.

Pac-Man's appearances have expanded well beyond the original arcade game. He is featured in numerous expansion and spin-off video games spanning numerous gaming platforms. Pac-Man has even emerged in the offline world in board game form. The iconic character can be found on clothing items, posters, and as a plushy. He is no stranger to media forms beyond games as well. *Pac-Man: The Animated Series*, the first cartoon based on a video game, follows the adventures of Pac-Man, Ms. Pac-Man, and their family. Pac-Man is also the subject of a handful of famous songs, with "Pac-Man Fever" being among the most recognizable.[7]

Pac-Man continues to appear in popular culture today, decades after his debut. Most recently, Pac-Man was featured as an alien villain in the 2015 movie *Pixels*. Pac-Man is hailed as the most recognized video game character in the United States according to the Davie-Brown Index, with 94 percent of American consumers recognizing the iconic character.[8] Pac-Man continues to remind gamers young and old of the golden age of arcade games, serving as an iconic symbol of timeless video game entertainment.

Similar Characters: Kirby (*Kirby's Dreamland*), Mario (*Super Mario Bros.*), Sonic (*Sonic the Hedgehog*)

—Jessica A. Robinson

PARAPPA

(est. 1996)
Franchise: *PaRappa the Rapper*
Developer: NanaOn-Sha

Shortly after the PlayStation's debut in 1994, Sony commissioned Japanese pop musician Matsaya Matsuura to create a game taking advantage of the new console's compact disc storage. During development, Matsuura and his team used placeholder characters from New York–based artist Rodney Greenblat's children's game Dazzeloids (1993); shortly thereafter, as Greenblat has recounted in his personal blog, he was commissioned by Sony to use some of his existing characters and to create a new protagonist. The result of their collaboration was a square-headed dog with oversized eyes and black floppy ears sticking out from under an orange cap, a blue sleeveless shirt, dark blue baggy pants, and sneakers—a shorter, more angular version of Disney's Goofy, if you will. They called him Parappa. Created in the mid-1990s at that very moment in which Japanese hip-hop was transitioning from a small subculture to a mainstream phenomenon, the design of Parappa offers insight into the transnational uptake and circulation of both African American and Japanese cultures.

PaRappa the Rapper's plot follows Parappa's efforts to impress his dream girl, the sunflower-shaped Sunny Funny. Each stage begins with a cut-scene that establishes a social problem that Parappa must overcome, such as learning karate so as to "become a hero" capable of defending Sunny's honor from the local bullies, or learning to drive so that he can take Sunny to the beach. In each case, the gameplay consists of the player tapping a complex button sequence that rhythmically matches the on-screen directions, while watching and listening to Parappa rap about the experience of engaging with the social problem. For instance, after crashing his father's car and taking up a job at the local flea market to pay him back, Parappa raps about the various sales techniques that he is learning, such as "The skunk over here will bring you luck" and "The pump over here comes with a truck." Throughout the game, the scenarios remain humorous and upbeat, as

Parappa approaches every social problem standing between him and Sunny with the optimistic catchphrase of "I know . . . I gotta believe!"

Parappa's *kawaii* aesthetics, unbridled optimism, and romantic interest in Sunny Funny are illustrative of Japanese culture in the early-to-mid-1990s. First, Parappa's exaggerated features (e.g., large eyes) and youthful appearance situate him as product of Japan's *kawaii* culture. Though *kawaii* can be loosely translated as "cute," Sharon Kinsella argues that the *kawaii* aesthetic can be more properly understood as innocence, simplicity, or inexperience, and thus "it idolizes the presocial." This is not a presocial as in lacking contact, but rather a presocial as in an escape from the structures of society. This may well be why Parappa is capable of possessing such unbridled optimism: it is easy to be optimistic when, absent the complex social structures that affect one's likelihood of success, all one needs to succeed is mere belief. Likewise, this combination of *kawaii* culture and unbridled optimism map well onto the central narrative thread of Parappa's romantic interest in Sunny Funny for this kind of childlike love is adorable and depoliticized: love is all one needs (in a world absent of society). As a result, Parappa fits well into Kinsella's argument that *kawaii* culture in the 1980s and 1990s was "almost entirely devoted to [serving as] an escape from reality."[9]

Parappa's character design likewise offers insight into the transnational uptake of African American culture as well. As scholar Ian Condry has noted, there is a long history of appropriation and depoliticization of African American music by others; hence, "the unease that many Americans, and perhaps, especially African American musicians, feel toward Japanese mimicking not only musical styles, but also clothes, jewelry, and even gestures associated with black culture." This unease ought to extend to Parappa, for though it is one thing to emulate a musical style, it is perhaps another that his character design is "authenticated" by his clothing: oversized beanie, tight sleeveless T-shirt, baggie pants, and sneakers. This is not to place Parappa in the double-bind of authenticity that Ian Condry cautions against—which is to demand that those who engage with hip-hop "respect the African American roots of the music while also producing something uniquely authentic and original"—but rather to note that Parappa's *kawaii* aesthetics, unbridled optimism, and childlike love interest in Sunny Funny place him firmly on the side of the "party rap" scene (as opposed to underground hip-hop style) that major Japanese record labels, such as Sony, were trying to cultivate in the mid-1990s.[10] This was a style that adopted the commercial iconography of rap but rejected the oppositional politics of hip-hop.[11]

Despite *PaRappa the Rapper*'s failure to take up the historically oppositional politics of African American music, the game still offers significant cultural meaning to Japanese consumers in the mid-to-late 1990s. Though we can take our earlier reference to Sharon Kinsella's *kawaii* as an "escape from reality" argument to its logical, pessimistic conclusion that *kawaii* is a culture that has given up on the future (as she does), throughout his writings Ian Condry is a bit more optimistic in his contention that the transnational circulation of hip-hop has created a space of productive difference for Japanese youth. In essence, African American culture offers Japanese youth a space and a resource for thinking through the challenges unique to their various circumstances. From a Western perspective, this may look like appropriation—and it is—but it may well be that there can be good faith forms of appropriation. To make such forms possible, as Parappa would say, we just "gotta believe!"

Similar Characters: Agent Morris (*Elite Beat Agents*), Lammy (*UmJammer Lammy*), Neku Sakuraba (*The World Ends with You*)

—Ted Dickinson and Robert Mejia

PHOENIX WRIGHT

(est. 2001)
Franchise: *Ace Attorney*
Developer: Capcom

Ace Attorney is a video game series hugely popular both in Japan and around the world thanks to its appealing characters. Of these, Ryūichi Naruhodō ("Phoenix Wright" in English), the protagonist of *Ace Attorney* in the first three games and the fifth game of the series, is arguably the most popular. In the first game of the series, *Phoenix Wright: Ace Attorney* (2001), Phoenix Wright appears as a rookie defense attorney seeking to exonerate his clients in a Japanese court setting. With the goal of proving his falsely accused client's innocence, Phoenix Wright is unfailingly persistent. Outside the court, he investigates crime scenes for evidence and interviews various "distinctive" people for their testimonies; during court cases, he shouts "Objection!" at a witness or a prosecutor as he presents evidence. Playing Phoenix Wright accordingly offers players a uniquely enjoyable vicarious experience for issuing objections in support of justice and truth based on integrity and persistence.

Game design documents by Capcom make explicit how Phoenix Wright became not only what he is but also what he is not. It should be noted that the name "Ryūichi Naruhodō" has not always been constant; Ryūichi Naruhodō was initially named Sōka Naruhodo, which can be translated as "Aha, [and] I see."[12] As for the English version of his name, "Phoenix Wright," a phoenix is a mythological bird that rises from ashes time and again, and "Wright" is apparently derived from the English term "right."[13] Takeshi Yamazaki, one of the key producers of the game series, notes that Phoenix Wright was originally called by "more common names such as Roger or Daniel."[14] Not surprisingly, the aesthetic aspects of Phoenix Wright were similarly different from those of the original character. In the first game of the series, Phoenix Wright is a twenty-four-year-old, fresh-from-college attorney with spiky black hair, a blue suit, and a red tie. However, he was initially designed as a twenty-year-old detective-turned-attorney with smooth green hair, a black suit, and a large blue bow tie.[15] As for the original characteristics of Phoenix Wright, the first volume of the *Gyakuten Saiban Official Fanbook*, or *Ace Attorney's Official Fanbook*, says of Phoenix that he used to be

a detective at an investigation firm, but one incident made him turn to become a private attorney. A complete amateur of laws. [He is] armed with his natural intuitions allowing him to capture people's thoughts and their lies, and he battles in a court-room. [He] likes to take a break and to get involved in trivial matters. [He] currently has a hamster [as a pet].

As such, the design of Ryūichi Naruhodō, or Phoenix Wright, came about through a trial-and-error process with the goal of constructing a character fighting for justice and truth.

Indeed, Phoenix Wright has become culturally significant in the Japanese media landscape for two reasons. First, Phoenix Wright is arguably the first fictional attorney that is a main character in a major Japanese video game. While there are various attorney characters such as Motohito Kuzu from *Bengoshi no Kuzu* [Scum of Lawyers] and Mizuho Yamazaki from *Shimane no Bengoshi* [An Attorney in Shimane] in the Japanese popular culture, a space in which game players could take pleasure in their manipulation of a narrative centered around an attorney was absent. While manga fans of *Scum of Lawyers* and *An Attorney in Shimane* construct the meaning of the narratives in their everyday lives, Phoenix Wight allows game players to affect the narrative through gameplay. Indeed, amateur Japanese cartoonists working with professional artists have actively and passionately extended this narrative across media boundaries by constructing multiple narratives and various visual images of Phoenix Wright through diverse acts of creation and performance.[16]

Second, Phoenix Wright has become culturally significant in the Japanese media because he entails semiotic richness and generates an alternative space for a wide variety of participatory cultural practices. For instance, game players not only generate meanings from Phoenix Wright for their own purposes within the relative constraints of his design, they also take pleasure in sharing solitary creative activities (i.e., fan art) with one another through various media including the online artists' community Pixiv. More specifically, Phoenix Wright provides culturally rich resources for encouraging fans to expand his in-game adventures outside the context of gameplay based on his design. In short, Phoenix Wright allows players and fans to extract and repurpose his character in their everyday lives.

Not surprisingly, Capcom is aware of Phoenix Wright's semiotic richness and exploits this richness for its commercial interests. As such, Phoenix Wright is widely featured and reproduced in a large number of media outlets, including musicals, films, stage plays, manga, animations, games, and online media. As a representative character of his video game series, Phoenix Wright has also appeared in other video game outlets including *SNK vs. CAPCOM: Card Fighters DS* (2006), *Ultimate Marvel vs. Capcom 3* (2011), and *Project X Zone 2: Brave New World* (2015); this character has become widely known even to gamers who do not necessarily play the *Ace Attorney* series. As a result, Phoenix Wright provides an expanding participatory cultural space, illuminating a high regard for integrity and persistence in the Japanese popular culture landscape.

Similar Characters: Chris Redfield (*Resident Evil*), Dr. Hal "Otacon" Emmerich (*Metal Gear*), Professor Hershel Layton (*Professor Layton*)

—Yasuhito Abe

PIKACHU

(est. 1996)
Franchise: *Pokémon*
Developer: Game Freak

During the mid-to-late 1990s, *Pokémon* became a major hit across the globe. The *Pokémon* franchise continues to be one of the most successful role-playing-game series of all time. At its inception, *Pokémon Red* and *Pokémon Blue* were single-player role-playing games in which players took on the role of an adolescent tasked with capturing and battling creatures known as Pokémon. In an ongoing process of capturing and training new Pokémon, players battled with non-player characters and wild Pokémon throughout the course of their journey. One particular Pokémon, Pikachu, stands out among the rest as a great companion. We believe that Pikachu's loyalty and friendship to the players of the *Pokémon* series illustrate how an otherwise unremarkable character can take on a life of its own.

What is Pikachu? For the uninitiated, Pikachu is defined in the Pokédex, the electronic *Pokémon* dictionary, as being an electric mouse. Its name is onomatopoeia: its first syllable, "pika," stands for the sound of electricity, and the second syllable, "chu," stands for the sound a mouse makes. Pikachu was initially one of two characters created as a mascot for the series, the other being a fairy Pokémon named Clefairy. The game's developer, Game Freak, pursued Pikachu as the mascot for the *Pokémon* series because its yellow color and bright red cheeks made it instantly recognizable to children as well as adults.

Due to Pikachu's popularity, Game Freak released a special edition featuring Pikachu as the lead Pokémon. To date, Pikachu is the only Pokémon to have its own game edition. In *Pokémon Yellow* for the Gameboy Color, players take on the role of a Pokémon trainer whose only choice of a starter Pokémon is Pikachu. *Pokémon Yellow* strongly emphasizes the relationship between the player and Pikachu. For example, it is the first game in which a Pokémon can follow its trainer outside its Pokéball. In this particular version of the game, that feature is limited only to Pikachu. Players can also check its "friendliness" toward the player by turning the main character around and electing to speak with Pikachu. Players are rewarded for having high friendliness with Pikachu by access to additional game content.

Despite Pikachu's relatively low battle stats (with the exception of speed), many players still opt to keep Pikachu in their party. As one player lovingly notes, "Pikachu seems to be the mascot in my team [rather] than the powerhouse. It doesn't matter if he's not, because I would never evolve him. He's staying small and cute until the [game cartridge's] internal battery dies."[17] Keeping Pikachu, who can't evolve into a more powerful Pokémon, in a game that encourages obtaining stronger Pokémon is a sign of friendship between the player and the Pokémon. Pikachu may not be the best asset in battle, but it certainly makes for a great companion.

Pikachu appears in other games as well. But we see Pikachu's loyalty and friendship most pronounced in the life simulation *Hey You, Pikachu!* In *Hey You, Pikachu!* renowned Pokémon professor, Professor Oak, gives players the task of earning the trust of a Pikachu by using a device he invents to talk to Pokémon who are usually unable to communicate with humans. The game comes with an actual microphone so that players can talk to and issue commands to their Pikachu. The players' goal is to become as close to Pikachu as they can. At the end of the game, players are instructed that "as true friends" of Pikachu, it is best for them to let their Pikachu return to the wild. But after the player does so and the end credits roll, in an act of true loyalty, Pikachu returns to the player for ongoing companionship.

Pikachu is one of the few video game characters that transcends the video game medium as a character. It also stars in a television show created after the games became popular. In the television show, the main character, Ash Ketchum, wakes up too late to be given a starter Pokémon (the first Pokémon that trainers receive). Rather than being given a Bulbasaur, Squirtle, or Charmander as in the *Pokémon Red* and *Pokémon Blue* games, he is given a Pikachu. The beginning of his relationship with Pikachu is contentious: Pikachu refuses to enter its Pokéball (as most Pokémon do) and also refuses to engage in battle. After facing a flock of angry bird-Pokémon Spearow together, Ash and Pikachu become close companions. Their relationship remains one of the strongest relationships in the show, which continues to air today, mirroring the friendship developed between players and their own Pikachu in *Pokémon Yellow* and *Hey You, Pikachu!*

Pikachu permeates our collective consciousness; there is nothing that hasn't been stamped with its red cheeks and lightning-shaped tail. Plushies? Check. Cosplay? Check. Cars? Check. In addition to being featured on an airplane(!) in Japan, Pikachu is so popular in the United States that it has been featured as a balloon in the Macy's Day Parade since 2001. Build-A-Bear recently released its Pikachu line, almost twenty years after Pikachu was first introduced to the world. Its popularity is so high among *Pokémon* fans that they even buy Pikachu dressed as other favored *Pokémon* characters. Moreover, with the release of the popular augmented reality game *Pokémon Go*, it's clear that Pikachu remains a coveted Pokémon to this day as fans continue to show excitement at finding a Pikachu of their very own. Simply put, Pikachu remains an adorable ally and loyal friend whose cultural relevance is here to stay.

Similar Characters: Epona (*The Legend of Zelda: Ocarina of Time*), the Creature (*Black & White*), Sonic (*Sonic the Hedgehog*)

—Jenny Saucerman and Constance Steinkuehler

THE POLICE

(est. 1997)
Franchise: *Grand Theft Auto*
Developer: Rockstar North

The district attorneys of Liberty City, Vice City, and Los Santos certainly must all meet for drinks and lament their inability to bring criminal prosecutions to trial. The police forces of these fictional cities as depicted in the *Grand Theft Auto* (*GTA*) franchise do little to collect evidence (it is often destroyed) nor do they respect basic civil liberties (Miranda rights are seemingly absent). But these are facetious observations about a video game. *GTA* police don't act in malice; rather, they are algorithmic agents—incompetence and disrespect are programmed into their characters intentionally. Yet Jesse Fox and Bridget Potocki have studied the impact of playing violent and sexualized video games and found that participants had increased aggression toward women and greater "rape myth acceptance."[18] If such perceptions can be cultivated through gameplay, it stands to reason that perceptions regarding the police may similarly be cultivated in a game such as *GTA*. If the relationship between the player and the police of *GTA* is adversarial, what is being cultivated could have an impact on societal perception of police officers.

At its core, *GTA* is an urban adventure game where players use criminal avatars to explore a relatively open world environment to achieve in-game objectives. The police exist as a foil, an ever-present opposition to player machinations. As the *GTA* franchise has evolved, player capabilities have improved: the original bird's-eye view has shifted to a third-person perspective allowing players to navigate space with more precision, and the emergence of jumping, object-manipulation, and vehicle and tool use has added depth to the player experience in the game world. The police forces of *GTA* have had to improve as well. The nature of playing a game as a criminal means that much of the challenge comes from the competence of your opposition. The competence of the officers is the fulcrum of the players' enjoyment. The ability of the player to outsmart, evade, and avoid the police is of primary importance to success in the game. Many of the objectives of *GTA* result in attention from the police, so even in situations where the police are not a primary actor, they are always a component in the player's success.

Game mechanics aside, there is a degree of perfect competency encoded within the *GTA* police—an encoding that exceeds reality. Crimes committed are reported throughout the police force with flawless fidelity. Suspects are always correctly identified, much to the players' chagrin. When engaging the suspect, powerful tactics are utilized to quickly neutralize and sometimes detain the suspect. The officers function as a well-trained, efficient, and responsive team. Egos appear to be checked at the door at the start of a shift, and the amount of coordination among officers would be awe-inspiring if the player were not so desperate to elude them. The police as depicted in *GTA* are in some ways the epitome of what any police department would want in its officers. Any society would be proud of these often-competent police.

However, the police of *GTA* are simultaneously perfectly incompetent. Officers will seek poor cover during shoot-outs with the player. Police roadblocks can be rendered useless by the easily traversed grass on either side of the road. And *GTA* police turn a blind eye to "lesser" crimes taking place in their city. Cars are stolen in the middle of busy intersections. Traffic laws are seemingly nonexistent. When a law is broken, worry not as you can easily lose these officers by painting your car or hiding in a bush. Although the officers never misidentify a suspect, they also quickly forget the suspect, making it possible for the player to casually walk by an officer in the afternoon after having killed his partner in the morning. This lack of police competence extends to the enforcement of rule of law—a prerequisite for the democratic society depicted in *GTA*. Innocent civilians frequently suffer collateral harm due to their proximity to crimes and police response to those crimes. Suspects are presumed guilty of their accusations, and warrants are apparently unnecessary. Crime is rampant in this society as criminals are allowed to walk free the same day they are arrested: the result of inadmissible evidence "collection" and the paying of a small fine. The only way a suspect stays off the streets is if they are killed there. We would be ashamed of these incompetent police.

It is easy to dismiss these contradictions as artifacts of game mechanics in an unrealistic, simulated world designed solely for the progression of a game. Such a dismissal would be folly, however. *GTA* is not realistic, but it is realistic enough for us to see in it our hopes and fears of what the police in our society are. Our interaction with the police is what ultimately shapes our perception of the police and their place in society.[19] Without direct interaction with the police in the real world, however, our increased exposure to media depictions of the police may influence our faith in them.

In this vein, *GTA* reveals one vision of the police in our society. As players, we are engaged with this vision as a more visceral experience that potentially heightens our receptiveness to this vision. We worry that the police too often get it wrong, that they escalate needlessly, that they ignore important evidence and procedures meant to protect citizen rights—and in tandem, we worry in counterpoint that the police won't be there when we need them. And while we worry about that, we worry about their great competence as well. The police collect information and share it well. They are Big Brother. They know all of us from a license plate, a driver's license, or a traffic camera. They are everywhere, especially when we feel like we don't need them. *Grand Theft Auto*'s police are not realistic, but they are also not unrealistic enough that we don't recognize in them our own relationship with police in our culture: an anxious mix of perceived competence and incompetence.

Similar Characters: Guards (*Elder Scrolls*), the Police (*Saints Row*), Posses (*Red Dead Redemption*)

—Paul Zube

PRESIDENT BILL CLINTON

(est. 1993)
Franchise: *NBA Jam*
Developer: Midway

The inclusion of President Clinton's character in *NBA Jam* marked the first time a U.S. president was included as a playable character in a video game. Though each of the characters included in this book has made a unique and significant contribution to the world of video games, President Bill Clinton's character represents a cultural shift in modern politics and highlights our expectation that political figures be an active part of our popular culture. President Clinton's *NBA Jam* character was also iconic as it introduced a new era of hidden, playable characters in video games.

President Clinton's hidden character was first included in the highly successful arcade version of *NBA Jam* (1993), which was the first time real-life individuals were hidden within a game as playable characters.[20] The characters themselves were designed to be photorealistic and were created using state-of-the-art digital techniques.[21] In addition to President Clinton's character, the game had other hidden characters as well, including Vice President Al Gore, NFL quarterback Warren Moon, and chief programmer for *NBA Jam*, Mark Turmell. Yet President Clinton's character may have been the most memorable as it had a significant cultural influence on the world of video games and politics.

For users, the ability to play the game using President Clinton's character represented an unprecedented opportunity to become connected to a powerful political figure in a way that was focused on entertainment as opposed to politics. President Clinton was the forty-second president of the United States and served two terms (1992–2000). During his time as president, the United States experienced tremendous success, including the lowest rate of unemployment in modern times, as well as the highest home ownership in the country's history.[22] The president's inclusion as a character was not surprising as he was relatively well known for his desire to connect with younger voters and minority audiences through pop culture channels (e.g., his saxophone-playing appearance on *The Arsenio Hall Show* in 1992 during his first presidential campaign). Just as in the political world, President Clinton's character in *NBA Jam* was multitalented. His in-game attributes placed him among the top characters in three of four attributes: speed, dunking, and defense. The decision to digitize President Clinton's skill set as highly desirable was a noteworthy choice for developers because they created a character that was not only novel but also competitive in play; a mixture that would make President Clinton's character one of the most memorable hidden characters in video game history.

The inclusion of President Clinton's character had implications for the culture of video games as well because it suggested that this channel was now a legitimate outlet in which real-life personalities could connect with audiences in a distinctive and interactive manner. As a result of this development, hidden and unlockable characters became a cornerstone of the *NBA Jam* franchise. For example, in *NBA Jam T.E.* (1995), players could unlock thirty-four hidden characters (*NBA Jam* only included eleven hidden characters). President Clinton was once again included as a hidden character; however, new to the game was his wife, First Lady Hillary Clinton. The addition of First Lady Clinton further cemented the notion that political figures should be visible and expected to carry out their role as popular culture icons. In fact, the tradition of including hidden playable political figures continued throughout the series of games; *NBA Jam* (2010), for example, featured Presidents George W. Bush and Barack Obama. This continuing trend highlights the importance of President Clinton's first appearance in the original game and the cultural impact it has had, both on the world of video games and their hidden characters and on the expectations the public now has regarding its political leaders and their legacy as popular culture icons.

To unlock President Clinton's character in the game, users need to enter a special code at the initials screen. To unlock President Clinton on the Sega Genesis, players need to enter the initials "ARK" and then press A. President Clinton's birthplace was Hope, Arkansas, and he went on to become governor of Arkansas in 1978, hence the use of "ARK" as part of his secret code. *NBA Jam* was innovative in this manner as most video game codes up to this point in time were arbitrarily related to their actions or outcomes (e.g., pressing Up, Up, Down, Down, A, B, A, B, Select, Start). Instead, *NBA Jam* rewarded players with a particular knowledge set that was related to the hidden or secret content—the code itself became meaningful in addition to its functionality, creating a unique fusion between the world of politics and the world of video games.

Similar Characters: Abraham Lincoln (*Code Name: S.T.E.A.M.*), John F. Kennedy (*Call of Duty: Black Ops*), Mikhail Gorbachev (*Street Fighter 2*)

—Rory McGloin

PSYCHO MANTIS

(est. 1998)
Franchise: *Metal Gear*
Developer: Kojima Productions

Although Psycho Mantis is certainly not the most prominent among *Metal Gear Solid* (*MGS*) villains (the player's total encounter is at best ten minutes of gameplay), many players can vividly recall the first time—perhaps, the only time in any video game at that time—that a non-player character took operational control of the console and television, probed the player's memory card, and reported back a strikingly accurate breakdown of the player's personality before engaging in one of the most mentally exhausting boss fights in gaming history. This showdown between Solid Snake (the player's main character) and the frail and floating Russian psychic Tretij Rebenok, known to players as Psycho Mantis, rates as the second-best video game moment of all time according to *IGN*, with Psycho Mantis himself rated as one of the most memorable video game villains of all time.[23] Perhaps fittingly given Psycho Mantis's telepathic abilities, the player's short encounter with the villain may leave him or her mentally exhausted, confused, and pleasantly surprised. Rarely has a game character violated so many assumptions about the rules of engagement—stretching the conflict from the television screen to the player's own mind.

Players first encounter Psycho Mantis a bit over midway through *MGS*. Having just finished a fast and furious fight with a mysterious ninja opponent (later found out to be Snake's long-lost comrade Gray Fox), players expect the usual action lull—allowing them to gather their composure and take a break from button-mashing while the game shifts to a set of cut-scenes in order to connect the most recent game missions to a larger narrative structure. A few moments of talk with colleague Meryl Silverburgh, to this point an ally, lead to a nicely anointed office in the compound . . . but then Meryl suddenly draws her service revolver and trains it on Snake. Slowly Meryl approaches Snake, keeping her weapon drawn while moaning in ecstasy, "Hurry, Hurry! Make love to me, Snake. I want you!" She slinks dangerously close to Snake, somewhat playing off a to-that-point loose plot thread about a potential love interest between the two, and never lowering her weapon. Before Snake can react, however, the sudden flash of a human figure—an incredibly thin and androgynous body bonded in black leather straps, with long black gloves and a gas mask—asks the player, "You don't like girls?"

At this point, Psycho Mantis allows himself to be seen for the first time (more alert players might have caught a glimpse of Psycho Mantis during an earlier gun battle), his pasty frame hovering behind Meryl and taunting the player. Psycho Mantis forces Meryl to begin shooting at the player, and a quick tip tells the player to use a stun grenade to knock her down, rendering Meryl unconscious and thus breaking Psycho Mantis's control. At this point, Psycho Mantis directs his aggression toward Solid Snake and the player in one of the most imaginative and mysterious of ways. First, the telepath scans the player's *MGS* metadata to give the player a bit of insight into their own "personality"—referring to players who have been careful not to trip traps as either "cautions" or "cowards" and players who are skilled at hand-to-hand and gun combat as "skilled warriors." After this, Psycho Mantis probes deeper by scanning the player's physical memory card and commenting on select Konami titles; for example, "You like *Castlevania*, don't you?" For players using a DualShock vibrating controller, Psycho Mantis asks them to place the controller on the ground so he can move it with his mind. Finally, immediately after boasting of his psychic ability and before the eventual battle, Psycho Mantis causes the game console to appear to switch off, displaying a blank black screen with the word "HIDEO" in the top-right corner (an homage to the notification "VIDEO" that would often be displayed on older televisions if a component—such as a video game console—were unplugged from the TV). When the screen comes back on, Psycho Mantis is able to intercept the player's every single move and button press—expertly countering every attack. Here the player realizes that Psycho Mantis is scanning the main controller port, and the only way to prevent this is for the player to physically unplug their controller from port one (left side) and switch to port two (right side)—a tip radioed in by Snake's comrades.

Navigating Psycho Mantis's mental trickery is rather simple once the player understands it, as the character himself is rather easy to defeat once his telepathy has been properly thwarted. Yet the experience of the Psycho Mantis encounter is a lasting one. While many video games and characters address players directly as a way to engage their attention and emotions, Psycho Mantis does this in a genuine and organic way, causing the player to doubt his or her ability to control the video game. Perhaps no other video game character captures and enacts their essence so precisely: a psychic who reads minds, stretching his agency to include the mind of the player.

While the frail psychic trope is not an invention of *MGS*, no other game and perhaps no other character embodies the components in such a lasting fashion. Rarely in video games can a player recall encountering a character who so eloquently shatters the Fourth Wall[24]—the imaginary barrier that separates the player from the digital world—by engaging in seemingly psychic predictions about the player himself or herself. Moreover, an encounter with Psycho Mantis perhaps embodies the very soul of the *Metal Gear* franchise: a focus on stealth and smarts over brawn and blasting.

Similar Characters: The Narrator (*Stanley Parable*), Resetti (*Animal Crossing*), Vivec (*Elder Scrolls*)

—Nicholas David Bowman

PYRAMID HEAD

(est. 2001)
Franchise: *Silent Hill*
Developer: Konami

Making his initial appearance in the highly influential *Silent Hill 2*, Pyramid Head strikes fear in many players as an unstoppable and disempowering force throughout the course of the game. With his hidden face, gigantic muscular form, and giant blade, he represents the iconography of a medieval executioner and functions as an elemental distillation of the historic perpetration of male-enacted violence. Most importantly, however, he acts as a foil for the protagonist, James Sunderland. Pyramid Head is meticulously designed as a metaphor for the darkest aspects of the protagonist's psychological state and represents a paradigm shift in the design possibilities and complexity of video game antagonists.

Pyramid Head stands out as an exceptional and methodically designed video game villain laden with visual symbolism. Initially, Pyramid Head was conceived as a muscular male figure with a shroud over his face, borrowing from the classic concept of medieval-era executioners as well as the work of Irish painter Francis Bacon. After this first iteration, Masahiro Ito realized that the concept would fail to intimidate players because the character would be perceived as just a "man in a mask."[25] Ito chose to reconceptualize the character with a large, metal, pyramid-like structure in place of a normal human head. Not only did this help make him seem less human, and therefore more intimidating, but the shape itself helped visually define his role in the game. In the documentary film *The Making of Silent Hill 2*, Ito explains, "The triangular shape has right angles and acute edges, and their sharpness suggests the possibility of pain." It's an apt visual suggestion: Pyramid Head is supernaturally strong, wielding an impractically huge sword or spear, and the overall effect of Ito's design aligns perfectly with the cultural concept of a "punisher" or "executioner."

Besides striking fear in the heart of the player, Pyramid Head's executioner design serves as a metaphor for the protagonist's guilt. According to Michel Foucault in *Discipline and Punish*, executioners become an effective tool of justice "by arousing feelings of terror by the spectacle of power letting its anger fall upon the guilty person."[26] And indeed there is a guilty person for that power and anger to fall on, as Pyramid Head was constructed completely for *Silent Hill 2*'s protagonist, James Sunderland, as a mode of self-reflection and as a reenactor of the traumatic experiences that James comes to terms with over the course of the narrative. Pyramid Head performs this role by committing acts of physical and sexual violence against the inhabitants of Silent Hill—inhabitants human and nonhuman alike—as he is the embodiment of all the darkest aspects of James's own psychological state.

To understand Pyramid Head, you must first understand James. The protagonist, James, begins his journey by arriving in the town of Silent Hill at the request of his deceased wife, Mary. For the final years of their marriage, Mary had been terminally ill, and her illness had left her bed-ridden, physically disfigured, and unable to have sexual intercourse. As a result, their relationship had become emotionally abusive. After her death, James receives a letter from Mary requesting that he join her in Silent Hill, and James does so, despite his better judgment.

During his search for Mary, James encounters a doppelgänger version of Mary named Maria. She looks almost identical to James's deceased wife, except her hair is blond rather than brown, her dress is much more provocative, and her demeanor is hypersexual and flirtatious. When contrasted with the emotionally distant Mary, Maria seems like an idealized fantasy version of James's dead wife. The two meet at various times throughout the course of the game, and her pliant nature and sexual advances at turns confuse and entice James. Her role in the story is an enigmatic one because James sees her die at the hands of Pyramid Head numerous times only to find her alive and well again later on.

Pyramid Head's symbolic relationship to James finally becomes clear near the end of the game. James encounters Pyramid Head and watches as he violently executes Maria in a grotesque display intended just for James. As Maria dies once again, James falls to his knees and speaks to Pyramid Head: "I was weak. That's why I needed you . . . needed someone to punish me for my sins . . . but that's all over now. . . . I know the truth. Now it's time to end this." The experience of witnessing Maria's murder unremittingly reminds James of his own crime, and he no longer suppresses the memory of murdering his own wife. He is struck to his foundation with this realization and is able to finally face his guilt in a way reminiscent of Martin Buber's explanation of guilt in his work "Guilt and Guilt Feelings": "Existential guilt occurs when someone injures an order of the human world whose foundations he or she knows and recognizes as those of his or her own existence and of all common human existence."[27] As such, James has psychologically manifested Pyramid Head as a means for him to accept his own guilt, thereby allowing justice to take its rightful course.

Though James is in deep denial throughout the game, seeing his own actions mirrored by Pyramid Head acts as the catalyst that brings him to terms with his sin. This is critical, as Foucault points out: "Knowledge of the offence, knowledge of the offender, knowledge of the law: these three conditions made it possible to ground a judgment in truth."[28] Through his newly found knowledge of self, James is able to begin the process of working through his trauma and guilt to accept that he deserves his punishment, whatever it may be.

Pyramid Head is an iconic horror antagonist, but his iconic value stems from his complexity and intricate relationship to *Silent Hill 2*'s protagonist, James. By representing the repressed feelings of guilt within James, Pyramid Head allows players to reflect on a complex character and narrative while he acts as a critique of the male-enacted violence so common to video games.

Similar Characters: Charlie (*Don't Starve*), Nemesis (*Resident Evil*), Scissorman (*Clock Tower*)

—Jeff Nay

R

RAIDEN
(est. 2001)
Franchise: *Metal Gear*
Developer: Kojima Productions

Metal Gear Solid 2 was one of the most anticipated games of the PlayStation 2 life cycle. With this sequel to the bestselling and critically acclaimed *Metal Gear Solid*, many players were excited to step back into the role of Solid Snake and stealthily maneuver their way through a new mission and thwart another terrorist. Trailers for the game from *E3* 2000 and 2001 presented Snake with updated graphics, new stealth options, an engaging story line, and a new cast of characters to interact with. What players did not expect was that after the opening chapter, they would never retake control of Snake. Instead, they were introduced to Raiden, a character who undermined a traditionally Western ideal of military masculinity and provoked disdain and criticism from then-mainstream gamer culture, revealing the deep seed of toxic masculinity within the community. Inevitably, Raiden highlights the ways in which masculinity is reflected in Western popular culture and also the ways in which he acts as a point of exposure for the gaming community at large. He acts as an entry point for connections to otherness and inclusion to a community that reflects the long arm of Western patriarchy.

Raiden was born in the 1980s in Liberia where he spent his childhood in the First Liberian Civil War (1989–1996). After his parents were killed by Solidus Snake, he was trained as a child soldier—shown Hollywood action movies and fed gunpowder. He quickly excelled, and his kill record earned him the names "Jack the Ripper" and "White Devil." After the war, a nongovernmental organization transported him, and other child soldiers, to the United States where he was given extensive counseling. His memories were eventually altered, and he was transformed into a soldier for Snake's revived Foxhound unit. His first mission was to rescue the president.

Raiden was hardly the first tortured soldier that gamers had encountered, and yet gamers reacted strongly against him. One need only look at online message boards to see this. A year after the game's release, one forum user wrote that the character was "just plain bad" and that playing as a man or a woman would have been better than Raiden, who was characterized as a transsexual and a sissy. This response was typical of the reaction to Raiden. Within the vocal gamer culture, the offense was not just that Kojima pulled a bait-and-switch with Raiden but that it did this with a character who intruded upon the traditionally masculine space of gamer culture and military narrative.

Feminist theories typically define masculinity as the performance of gender norms associated with the male sex. Building on psychoanalytic theory, theorists suggest it is the fear of castration that sparks the performance and hyper-performance of a gender that is predetermined by the sex of the subject. Judith Butler in her book *Gender Trouble* argues "that [the reason] the boy usually chooses the heterosexual world [is] . . . the fear of castration—that is, the fear of 'feminization.'"[1] From this perspective, masculinity becomes toxic when it starts to become militarized and violent, and when it starts to bleed out into all aspects of a community or culture.

In the documentary *The Making of Metal Gear Solid 2: Sons of Liberty*, Hideo Kojima and his team describe Raiden as an "exceptionally beautiful young man" who is "pure, virgin, and white." In fact, at one moment in the game, the president of the United States grabs Raiden's crotch and moves back in surprise, saying "You're . . . a man . . . ? Hmph. Well, who are you?" This conception of Raiden fits well with the "new man" ideal of Japanese masculinity. This new man ideal generally portrays men "as sensitive, caring individuals, representative of a new generation of men conscious of the significant changes gender roles underwent in the latter part of the twentieth century."[2] This new man ideal also exists as a hybrid of Japanese and Western conceptions of masculinity. Fabienne Darling-Wolf notes that it is the more violent and disturbing characteristics of this identity that are often associated with the West.

Within the larger context of Western masculinity, "beauty," "purity," and "virginity" are words that are antithetical to a conception of manhood where purity and virginity are seen as "weak" characteristics (i.e., feminine). Furthermore, in the translation of *Metal Gear Solid 2*'s "Grand Game Plan," Raiden is described as "the antithesis of the older, hard-boiled image of Snake."[3] While it is commonly known that Snake was based on Kurt Russell's character in the American film *Escape from New York*, that fact takes on crucial significance when considering the play of Western versus Japanese masculinity and its reception in the United States. While Raiden was a successful character in Japan, in the United States, players wanted to play as Snake and resented their positioning with Raiden as the main character. The kind of backlash received from this switch reveals that Solid Snake was not only the preferred avatar of play but also the preferred male fantasy enjoyed by Western audiences. The perceived femininity of Japanese masculinity, and this disdain of Raiden—who intruded not only on the space of male gaming but also on the space of ultra-masculine military narrative—ultimately unveiled a deep-seated misogyny within gamer culture and its parent Western culture at large.

Similar Characters: Squall Leonhart (*Final Fantasy VIII*), Tingle (*The Legend of Zelda*), Vaan (*Final Fantasy XII*)

—David Frisch

RYU

(est. 1987)
Franchise: *Street Fighter*
Developer: Capcom

To speak of Ryu is to speak of Japan itself. Ryu, to Japan, is the samurai and the salaryman rolled into one: his black hair cut simply, his subdued facial expressions, his white *gi* (karate outfit), and his red gloves matching the colors of the Japanese flag. Ryu wears his Japaneseness as aesthetic, but also as philosophy. Ryu is honorable, controlled, stoic, devoted. All these qualities are lauded in the *Hagakure*, a manual to Japanese *bushido* (warrior culture). Ken, Ryu's American rival, is many of the things Ryu is not: flashy, distracted, boisterous. These character traits as exemplified in these two fighters can be extrapolated to the narratives of the countries of their origin. Ryu functions as the ultimate Japanese warrior and the series' central figure. However, Ryu's existence—and by extension his Japaneseness—is tied to his international life: a friendly rivalry with Ken, encounters with other fighters the world over, and a desire to prove himself as the "World Warrior" of *Street Fighter II*'s subtitle.

Ryu is the ultimate Japanese warrior, yet his very existence actually questions the Japanese myth of homogeneity. Japanese homogeneity is still an important part of Japan's cultural history, but its cultural present has begun to reflect Japan's long-held hybrid identity. A 2010 *Japan Times* article notes that despite sixty countries being more homogenous than Japan, the homogeneity myth continues to "stunt discourse." Japan is filled with multi- and trans-ethnic cultural figures. The current Mongolian domination of sumo, Japan's national sport, and the rise of Japanese pop icons like half-Iranian baseball player Yu Darvish and half-British television personality Becky are typical of the current Japanese national identity. These public, multiethnic faces are the result of a shift in Japanese cultural relationships post–World War II. However, the conflicted nature of Japan's homogeneity has always been present. Discussing Japan's ties to ancient Korean royalty, Marilyn Ivy states, "To show how the most authoritative interior sign of native Japaneseness is originally foreign points to an essential alienation at national-cultural core. . . . The entire national-cultural fantasy of Japan—and indeed of any nation—must form itself around such foreign irritants."[4] In other words, Japan's claim of homogeneity exists—must and can only exist—in opposition to a real "other," as all national-cultural myths (such as the United States' American Dream myth) do.

In *Street Fighter*, Ken serves as the "Them" to Ryu's Japanese "Us." Ryu is a banal symbol: a fighting everyman. Ken is used to reinforce the "national-cultural fantasy" inherent in Ryu. Ryu and Ken are extremely similar in their fighting styles. They know the same combat maneuvers, and the player controls them similarly. Being so similar, their differences are magnified. Ryu is stoic, Ken is passionate. Ryu is restless and alone, Ken has a comfortable family life and a child. Ken is a funhouse-mirror version of Ryu, Ivy's "foreign irritant" around which Ryu's Japaneseness is formed. These friendly rivals come from two friendly rival nations. Ryu's relationship with Ken mirrors the relationship of Japan with the United States. Through these characters, Japan embraces its previous enemy, one that devastated and occupied it.

Postwar Japan's remarkable economic turnaround occurred partly due to American capitalist influence along with Japanese work culture and governmental interventionism.[5] The expansion of production later turned into a capitalist rivalry within U.S.-dominated markets. *Street Fighter's* narrative allows Japan to engage the United States on a metaphorical front as it continues to engage the United States on an economic one. The space between "rival" and "enemy" is safe. Ryu and Ken have no desire to truly defeat each other; they simply wish to prove who is greater in a competitive but supportive context. This discourse allows Japaneseness the freedom to move on from the trauma of its destruction at the hands of the United States without removing the aggression it must feel against its destroyer. Through Ryu and Ken, Japan can still fight; it can still beat America, but without any real damage or destruction.

The threat of Ryu's destruction comes not from Ken but from another Japanese character, Akuma ("Gouki" in Japanese releases). Ryu's internal struggle is made external with Akuma. *Satsui no Hadou* (Wave of Murderous Intent) is a power within Ryu that makes him strong but overcomes him. It comes from rage and hatred and is all-consuming. Akuma embodies Satsui no Hadou as a character who has already succumbed. (A variant of Ryu in *Street Fighter Alpha 3*, Evil Ryu, is an Akuma-esque Ryu showing Satsui no Hadou's effect.) Akuma represents a wicked inversion of all the things for which "good" Ryu stands. Dedication to martial arts has given way to obsession with being the best. The desire to win has been replaced by the desire to kill: a literal "murderous intent." The self-controlled, spiritually balanced fighter has been subsumed into a slave to lust for battle, destruction, and power. This inversion can be read as a manifestation of the horrors enacted by the Japanese during World War II as well as fears of having the same horrors enacted upon them. Adam Lowenstein sees this Japanese combination of "demon" and "human being" in the 1964 horror film *Onibaba*.

> The film . . . insists that neither war responsibility nor war victimization can be the exclusive province of "ordinary" Japanese subjects or the "extraordinary" Japanese elite. In fact, the samurai's first words to the old woman, "Don't be afraid. I'm a man, not a demon," return with the old woman's final cry of "I'm not a demon! I'm a human being!" In this manner, war responsibility emerges as intertwined between victimizer and victimized . . . to complicate the very notion of demarcating "demons" and "human beings" in the face of Hiroshima.[6]

Ryu and Akuma represent this same duality.

Ryu's status as one of the greatest video game characters, therefore, is vested in his status as a symbol of Japan. His values, relationships, and anxieties mirror those of his country, and his heroism resides in his steadfastness and dedication to both *dou* (the way) and *wa* (harmony).

Similar Characters: Akira (*Virtua Fighter*), Kazuya Mishima (*Tekken*), Ryu Hayabusa (*Ninja Gaiden*)

—Nicholas Ware

S

SACKBOY

(est. 2008)
Franchise: *LittleBigPlanet*
Developer: Media Molecule

There is no Sackboy, there are only Sackpeople. It's immediately obvious what sets Sackboy apart from other video game characters. Nothing that traditionally is associated with memorable characters can be applied to him. He's not a stoic action hero. He doesn't spout off memorable quips. In fact, he doesn't really speak and has almost no character at all. Instead, what makes Sackboy memorable is his pliability. That cute little burlap doll staring back at you from the cover of *LittleBigPlanet* is an indication of all the different possibilities of the game. Almost everything about Sackboy can be changed to fit the player's wishes and desires, from the very fabric he's made of to the many different articles of clothing he can wear. He can reflect fandom, ethnic identity, or anything else the player wants him to be. This means there is no one Sackboy, but millions of different Sackpeople.

If there's one thing that *LittleBigPlanet* promised when it was released in 2008, it was individuality. On the surface, it appears to be a simple platforming game, one of gaming's oldest and most recognizable genres, thanks to games such as those in the iconic *Super Mario Bros.* franchise. But *LittleBigPlanet* breaks from the past in a major way: it allows players to build their own levels and share them with one another via Sony's PlayStation Network. With the simple and intuitive tools provided by the game, users can create whatever they can dream up. Rather than just sit back and enjoy someone else's creation, it is now possible to pour your own creativity into something that can be called uniquely your own. This sense of ownership, of customization and personalization, pervades *LittleBigPlanet*, and Sackboy is the perfect embodiment of this ethos.

A lot of games attempt to get gamers to identify with their characters by limiting what we know about them. Link and Gordon Freeman never speak. We never see Master Chief's face. But these characters can never truly be said to be one's own. Despite the best efforts of the developers, there will always be a gap between the character and the player. They will always be a part of a story told by someone else. Sackboy changes all of that. Suddenly, here is a character

163

that can be uniquely your own and can explore worlds of your own making. Whether you want to painstakingly craft a little Sackperson that fits your identity or just create a goofy character to go off and have adventures with your friends, you can do it.

In his *The Death of the Author*, Roland Barthes advocates a method of analysis that devalues the role and intentions of the author in favor of the reader. To him, the reader is the site where a text is completed: "A text's [meaning] lies not in its origin but in its destination."[1] Games illustrate this point in that they require the active input of the player to construct meaning. This is doubly important in *LittleBigPlanet* because the content provided by the game's developers is de-emphasized in favor of the content produced by the game's players. It is up to the players to build their own worlds and create their own characters. Sackboy is a powerful symbol of this empowerment. Through their own unique avatar, players don't just complete the game that is *LittleBigPlanet*; they become creators themselves.

To that end, the archetypical Sackboy you see on the cover of *LittleBigPlanet* can be seen as the ambassador of a new type of play. Other than the cute button eyes and the expressive smile, there isn't anything there to set him apart or make him recognizable. He doesn't have the bright red hat and overalls of a Mario or the iconic power armor of a Master Chief. Games like those in the *Mass Effect* and *Elder Scrolls* series give players the option to customize their character's appearance in an effort to make them unique to each player, but despite this, the player's imagination is still limited by these developer-created worlds. Sackboy transcends all of this. Other characters want you to focus in on them. But Sackboy points outward. He isn't just one toy; he's the entire toy box.

All of this is underscored by *LittleBigPlanet*'s arts-and-crafts aesthetic. Everything in the game looks like it's homemade. Entire levels look like they are held together by cardboard, construction paper, and string. By separating itself from any particular genre and placing the emphasis on creation, *LittleBigPlanet* lets us know that, in addition to the levels we create, Sackboy is also a do-it-yourself project. The basic materials are given to us in the form of the different fabrics and materials that Sackboy can be made of, but what is done with those materials is up to us. In this sense, Sackboy is more of a canvas to be painted on than anything else. Due to this freedom, Sackpeople have far more personality than custom characters from other games. Just like most homemade craft projects, Sackpeople aren't perfect. Many of them don't look quite right. They wear outfits that clash or are a jumble of different styles and periods. And that's the point. Most *LittleBigPlanet* players aren't professional game designers, and Sackboy isn't supposed to be a perfect character. He's not supposed to be an unkillable space marine or powerful wizard. He's supposed to be us. By embracing the death of the author as a design ethos, *LittleBigPlanet* offers players a space for creating "little publics": a space where people can come together and develop a public voice.[2] In a very powerful way and very real way, then, Sackboy is all of us.

Similar Characters: Commander Shepard (*Mass Effect*), Mii (*StreetPass Mii Plaza*), Steve (*Minecraft*)

—Brian Keilen

SAMUS ARAN

(est. 1986)
Franchise: *Metroid*
Developer: Nintendo R&D1

Samus Aran is a human female bounty-hunter who, as a child, saw her parents murdered by a band of space pirates. The orphaned Samus was adopted by the Chozo, a birdlike, humanoid race with advanced technology, and she spent years in their Zebes colony training and honing her combat skills, eventually leaving to avenge her parents' murders. As a parting gift, the Chozo bequeathed to Samus a power suit: protective body armor that enhanced Samus's speed and strength. Beyond its defensive capabilities, the power suit can be augmented with a slew of armaments, including an arm-mounted laser cannon and missile launcher, grappling hook, x-ray visor, and jetpack. Samus scours the galaxy, seeking to rid it and the Galactic Federation of the threat of space pirates and the alien metroids the pirates seek to control. Her quests take her to a ravaged deep-space station, a Federation research ship, and the planets Zebes, SR388, Aether, Phazon, Norion, Bryyo, Elysia, and Tallon IV (which is orbited by a scientific research station). She inevitably conquers her foes, emerging victorious from the various ruins, underworlds, and space stations she explores, keeping the galaxy safe from space pirates and parasitic metroids alike.

A liberal-humanist feminist perspective examines how an artifact (i.e., Samus and the *Metroid* series) changes existing power relations between women and men. Samus's role in the liberation of women in gaming, mostly subverting the patriarchal structures inherent in video games, is worth exploring. Video games of the early and mid-1980s depicted women as weak, helpless, and in need of a male protagonist to rescue them[3]—typically from an evil and also-male antagonist. Be it kidnapping, poisoning, or an overthrown kingdom, women were often depicted as having no control over their situations; they were able to cope with and ultimately resolve every situation only via a man's actions.[4] Samus Aran—video gaming's first real heroine—marked a liberation from the patriarchy in gaming and its characters, affecting the nature of the industry and gaming culture.

Gamers playing through the original *Metroid* presumed their character was male. The shape of Samus's power suit does not suggest a female underneath; the colors (red and yellow) adhere to preconceived stereotypes of masculine colors; and the strength and agility associated with Samus seem innately masculine. Even the game's manual refers to its protagonist in the masculine, albeit with a mysterious final clause: "But his true form is shrouded in mystery." Only upon the game's completion is it revealed to the gamer they've been controlling a woman. As players complete *Metroid* more expediently, they are "rewarded" with the removal of Samus's power suit, first revealing 8-bits of flowing female locks and (for faster completion) removal of the entire power suit, leaving Samus undeniably female in a one-piece bathing suit. The evolution of playing as a perceptibly masculine character to a feminine character may have helped players acclimate to gaming with a heroine. However, this mechanic may also challenge Samus's role in the liberation of women in games. The shedding of her power suit, increasingly revealing a character in her bathing suit, may have had the adverse effect: objectifying Samus and reasserting patriarchal dominance. That Samus is dressed not clad in traditional clothing, instead emphasizing her sexualized form, may result in her objectification rather than liberation.[5]

Sherrie Inness contests female heroes can be powerful but must conversely conform to traditional constructions of femininity so as not to be perceived as too masculine or elicit suspicions of lesbianism.[6] Samus's power suit—present throughout her series—reflects the muscled and toned facade of the typical male hero, depicting Samus as a strong and tough heroine and certainly not dressing her in the ruffled dresses of her counterparts Princesses Zelda and Peach. Yet her physique under her suit is softened, displaying feminine characteristics, so that at the game's finale, the revelation of her gender does not present an image or gender expectation incommensurate with the feminine or her role. Thus, while Samus initially conforms to the strength and assertive patriarchy of video games, she retains and exhibits an aura of femininity beneath that exterior not objectified or sexualized during gameplay.

Metroid's gameplay itself also takes on feminine characteristics. Rather than emulating the linear gameplay of its contemporaries, *Metroid* requires players to strategically move throughout Zebes to complete the game, often requiring backtracking through previously explored areas after advancing through the acquisition of new skills and armament. Indeed, the lair of Samus's final enemy, Mother Brain, is only four screens from her starting location; but it is inaccessible until the entire subterranean world of Zebes has been explored. Thus, unlike most prior games that took a masculine—direct and linear shoot-'em-up—approach to problem solving, *Metroid* requires gamers not only to interact with the game's characters but to relate to and make sense of their environment to advance, strategically moving nonlinearly through zones. This shift reflects a more feminine gaming style based on the character, Samus, building a relationship with her environment: she makes her own determination regarding the direction and pace in which she traverses the landscape and strategically interacts with items (which includes sometimes giving them up) to engage in problem solving to advance the game's narrative. This relational focus, rather than an orientation toward direct conflict, is in the DNA of both Samus's character and the *Metroid* series.

Gaming affects stereotypes by creating a new culture through the messages of games. Samus Aran broke one of the industry's most closely held norms, helping culturally transform female representations from delicate, passive, and weak into powerful, active, and adventurous. Samus Aran emerged alongside sword-wielding elves, gun-toting guerillas, and plumbers holding grudges against aquatic reptiles; and in doing so, she challenged tropes and stereotypes about the roles of women in gaming, certainly on the screen and potentially even behind it. Long-since unmasked, her character remains a dominant feminine force in gaming and culture.

Similar Characters: Lara Croft (*Tomb Raider*), Princess Peach (*Super Mario Bros. 2*), Zelda (*Zelda: The Wand of Gamelon*)

—Caleb T. Carr

THE SCYTHIAN

(est. 2011)
Franchise: *Sword & Sworcery*
Developer: Capybara Games

The hero of 2011's *Sword & Sworcery* is a brave adventurer known only as the Scythian, and though she never says a word to the game's other characters, her actions speak volumes. Her quest requires her to collect three pieces of a magical artifact called the Golden Trigon, an endeavor whose resemblance to one of the most famous quests in all of video gaming is no accident. *Sword & Sworcery*'s Trigon is a clear reference to the Triforce of Nintendo's *The Legend of Zelda* series, and Link's recurring quest to collect pieces of the Triforce is perhaps the most famous heroic quest in the history of fantasy adventure games.

By undertaking an errand whose iconography echoes the most quintessential quest in all of gaming history, the Scythian quietly asserts that women can fill the role of mythic hero as effectively as men can. And this isn't without a historic basis. As stated on *Sword & Sworcery*'s official website,

> The Scythian's gender may have something to do with Leonard Schlain's *The Goddess & The Alphabet: The Conflict between Text & Image*, a book that offers an alternate perspective on the received wisdom of thousands of years of male-dominated written literature & history. Tombs dating back to 1000 BC found in Turkey, the Ukraine, Iran & Georgia offer evidence of respected warrior women, recorded in ancient literature as the amazons of Homer's *Iliad*.

However, the level of detail is so low on our pixelated protagonist, and our tendency to assume that heroes are male by default is so widely reinforced, that some players have made the mistake of assuming the Scythian is male, at least initially. Thankfully, the game doesn't resort to clear, gendered signifiers like a pink outfit or a pretty bow in her hair, nor does it present her gender as some kind of surprise twist like we see in the original *Metroid*. In both visual design and writing, *Sword & Sworcery* is subtle about asserting the Scythian's gender, though once you acquire the Megatome at the end of the game's first episode, you're able to read the thoughts of other characters, who refer to the Scythian using female pronouns.

It's not just in the visual sense that the Scythian lacks clear definition. We know very little about her history and nothing about why she has undertaken the quest to defeat the deathless specter that resides in the shrine of Mingi Taw. It may simply be her destiny. While games often give us images of heroes who are fated to defeat evil forces, it's rare for these heroes of myth to be women. Like many video game heroes, the Scythian is essentially a silent protagonist, a figure defined primarily by her actions, which makes her a blank slate for all players to project themselves into.

But while we don't actually hear her speak to other characters, a bit of the Scythian's personality does come through because her thoughts serve as a kind of narration for the story. Her quest is referred to as a "woeful errand" from very early on, an important bit of foreshadowing that communicates that her task is not a happy one, but the grim nature of her errand doesn't overshadow the Scythian's spirit or the tone of the game itself. The character's quirky, often humorous thoughts, along with her sense of wonder in the world, make this journey magical, delightful, and melancholy all at once.

While most heroes (including Link) grow more powerful as their adventure continues, the same cannot be said of *Sword & Sworcery*'s warrior. In this way, *Sword & Sworcery* subverts our expectation of being rewarded by games for our victories. There's nothing in it for the Scythian. She doesn't gain more health or a more powerful sword. In fact, the quest takes a toll on her: she starts the game with five units of health but loses one each time she wins a boss fight, decreasing her overall maximum health as her adventure progresses. By the end, she is physically drained and ill, her desperate race to the summit of Mingi Taw with the deathless specter in pursuit interrupted by fits of vomiting. And *Sword & Sworcery* ends with the Scythian doing something Link never has. To rid the world of an ancient evil, the brave hero sacrifices herself.

Unlike the deaths of so many female characters in games that serve the purpose of fueling the development of male characters, the Scythian's death is tragic because her life has intrinsic value. We project ourselves into her and experience the world through her. In the game's final moments, we see the people of the region pay their respects to the Scythian, and we mourn her death along with them. She doesn't just exist in relation to another character—she isn't just somebody's wife or sister or daughter—rather, she exists as an individual, and as a hero. The game's ending suggests that the Scythian will not be forgotten by the other characters, and the visuals and music work together to elicit a complex assortment of emotions: a sense of celebration of the Scythian's courage, and a sense of grief at her death.

When archetypal fantasy heroes in games are overwhelmingly portrayed as men, it reinforces the idea that men's experiences are universal and that women's experiences are gendered, that women should be able to empathize with male characters but that men needn't be able to identify with women's stories. *Sword & Sworcery* gives us an archetypal female protagonist and encourages us to see her as a hero first and foremost.

Similar Characters: Chell (*Portal*), Jade (*Beyond Good & Evil*), Link (*The Legend of Zelda*)

—Anita Sarkeesian and Carolyn Petit

SERGEANT PAUL JACKSON

(est. 2007)
Franchise: *Call of Duty*
Developer: Infinity Ward

Sergeant Paul Jackson plays a small part in the blockbuster *Call of Duty* franchise, acting as the player character for only one act of one game in the *Modern Warfare* series. Though it is short, the relationship between the player and Jackson is significant. In *Modern Warfare*, Jackson appears to be emblematic of the first-person-shooter player character with his endless weaponry and apparent invincibility. However, the destabilizing view of the War on Terror that *Modern Warfare* reflects eventually manifests in Jackson. Where the ultimate strength of first-person shooter characters emerges from player skill or the safety blanket of the respawn, these comforts are removed when Jackson suffers an arduous death in the wake of a nuclear explosion. It is through his development as a stereotypical first-person shooter character, and the subsequent destruction of that aura, that the character parallels the coinciding and conflicting rhetoric of the War on Terror.

Jackson's initial portrayal provides all the trappings of the "super soldier"—a soldier who has pronounced, almost superhuman, strength and resilience. Players first embody Jackson on a mission that alludes to Ridley Scott's movie *Black Hawk Down*. Jackson is in the middle of a pack of helicopters flying low over an unnamed city washed out with a gritty, brown palette. The city Jackson encounters is a collage of Western popular culture's vision of the Middle East: low brick buildings and dirt roads that are empty save for enemy combatants. A member of the U.S. Marine Corps, Jackson is at the tip of an expedition seeking out the revolutionary leader and primary antagonist for the first half of *Modern Warfare*, Khaled Al-Asad.

For most of *Modern Warfare*, as is the case with most player characters in the franchise, Jackson moves swiftly. Enemies appear rapidly as the player turns corners or sprints across streets, Jackson's rifle focusing on them expertly. This aligns with Roger Stahl's argument that contemporary military video games invite players to "inhabit a political world conditioned through the aesthetic of 'gametime.' Gametime moves quickly, subordinating critical and ethical questions to movement and action."[7] Jackson's quickness is hard-coded into the game engine through aim assist, his gun barrel snapping automatically to nearby enemies when the player aims down the sights of his weapon. The game technologically bolsters the narrative training of this Marine.

The speed of the game, matched by power afforded by military technology, is reinforced through Jackson's many helicopter sequences. The helicopter is a constant image throughout *Modern Warfare*, and through its use as a beginning and ending point for missions, it becomes a space of refuge. It is where steel armor and brass bullets meet, with the security of the former supporting the violence of the latter. In Jackson's final missions, his helicopter provides cover fire for ground troops before embarking on a rescue mission for a downed helicopter pilot. The security of the helicopter, mixed with distracting and gratifying gameplay, crafts a symbolic promise of continual victory for America, Jackson, and the player.

This promise ends when a bright white explosion displaces the browns and oranges of the city, sending shockwaves through the squadron of helicopters and knocking them into tailspins. A loading screen emerges as reports of the blast from various news sources are collaged together while a scrolling list of names appears, ultimately slowing to highlight Jackson's name. When the loading screen's map highlights Jackson's location, we can all but assume that this is the start to a new mission. Instead, the stillness of a mushroom cloud acts as Jackson's new backdrop. At the same time the silence of our protagonist is shattered. Jackson's pained wheezing replaces the traditional emptiness of a *Call of Duty* avatar, restricting players' ability to fill the character with their own thoughts and desires.

It is here that we see the conflicted sign that is Sergeant Jackson. In this sequence we can look upon Jackson as a hegemonic hero or a subversion of the typical shooter. If we allow Jackson to be the tragic hero that contemporary militarism requires, then he becomes illustrative of President George W. Bush's plan for the War on Terror. Weapons of mass destruction are highlighted and given power, their seemingly endless victims individualized and embodied. Jackson's death legitimizes American fears of terrorism, and the interventionism of America becomes all the more palatable.

While this reading of *Modern Warfare* is more pronounced, a dissenting reading of Jackson is possible.[8] In the grueling moments that emphasize the body of Jackson, the defenses that were built up around the super soldier are torn away. The body crumbles and slowly dies off, mirroring support for the Iraq War, just as evidence of weapons of mass destruction became increasingly questionable. In this disintegration, Jean Baudrillard's perspective on the first Gulf War becomes relevant for a new theater: "If we do not have practical intelligence about the war (and none among us has), at least let us have a skeptical intelligence towards it."[9]

Skepticism is difficult to locate in the overlapping situations Jackson inhabits. Weapons of mass destruction and fears of terrorism craft the necessity for new war. Chains of command and extreme stresses obstruct the soldier from questioning orders. Repeated loops of violence and reward impede a player from finding a space for uncertainty in routine gameplay. Skeptical intelligence is never available from structures that rely on monolithic rhetorics of militarism, be they governmental or gamic. Instead, it is within the experiences of militarism—personal, mediated, and virtual—where a skeptical intelligence can grow. Acting at the intersection of this logic, Paul Jackson expressly embodies modern warfare.

Similar Characters: Captain Walker (*Spec Ops: The Line*), Gordon Freeman (*Half-Life*), Master Chief (*Halo*)

—Nicholas A. Hanford

SHADOWLORD NIER

(est. 2010)
Franchise: *Nier*
Developer: Cavia

Under certain circumstances, people may consciously choose (morally) painful media experiences to achieve satisfaction of understanding.[10] This view builds on Aristotle's notion of *eudaimonia*, in which moral elevation is caused by inspiring pity and fear. According to Wolfgang Walk, this also holds true for games because they "are predestined to act as an ethical fitness center; and if they take that opportunity, they usually become even better games."[11] It is unusual, however, for a video game boss to give this satisfaction. Most game villains offer more hedonic gaming value—the sense of achievement comes from mastering the difficult kill. However, the final boss of *Nier*—the Shadowlord Nier—offers an opportunity for *eudaimonia* through ethical reflection because he is arguably one of the most tragic video game characters of all time.

Nier functions as a soul shepherd. When his world is struck by a lethal disease, humans struggle to survive by separating their souls from their bodies with the intent to reunite them with healthy clones (Replicants) once the disease ceases to exist. Thus they create shade-like humanoids called "Gestalts," but they fail miserably until they find Nier because these shades deteriorate and go insane shortly after being separated from their bodies. Nier possesses the unique ability to keep himself mentally stable, and he shares this ability by linking other Gestalts to himself. To save his only daughter, Yonah, he grudgingly accepts the charge to save all Gestalts by having them linked to him and his command—thus becoming the Shadowlord. But the plan doesn't work out as expected. After 1,312 years, the Gestalts still cannot reunite with their Replicant counterparts. Even worse, many Replicants have begun to gain consciousness, which drives their Gestalt counterparts into a state called "relapse" in which they lose sentience and become violent.

Realizing that Gestalt Yonah is going to relapse soon, the Shadowlord wants to force a reunion, abducting Replicant Yonah from her father, his alter ego Replicant Nier. But as all Replicants are unaware of their mere shell status and are unable to communicate with shades, they mistake them for evil monsters. Using the shades as an incarnation of evil is simple and clever because in many cultures, shades represent a dark, unconscious aspect of one's self. You do not need to introduce their motives, nor does the typical role-playing-game fan question them. As a result, players being unaware of the true identity of the shades will likely not question Replicant Nier (the player character) in his crusade to rescue his daughter, slaying hundreds of shades on the way.

This quest engenders an ironic tragedy. According to Aristotle, the audience of a tragic play experiences feelings of pity and fear when forced to observe a hero struggling to change his fate without any real chance to escape his predetermined destiny. Therefore, players may undergo a cathartic process by watching the Shadowlord. According to Albert Bandura, committing immoral acts can lead to moral concerns, which may result in feelings of remorse, guilt, and sadness.[12]

As agents, players pursue their given tasks. Later they realize the impact of their in-game actions and may experience negative feelings, yet they are given no chance to satisfactorily solve the overall dilemma, and thus they become helpless, tragic heroes themselves.

This is what makes *Nier* a true gem among role-playing games. It encourages us to consider that we might be our worst enemies and prone to failure despite having the best intentions. When players engage Replicant Nier to battle Gestalt Nier, they are metaphorically fighting against their own dark self and eradicating that part of their personal history. As a result, the typical feeling of elation upon beating the game might turn into shame when killing the Shadowlord. One might come to the conclusion such a tiresome setup would not be well received among gamers, and yet this tragic atmosphere is exactly why *Eurogamer* critic Jeffrey Matulef calls *Nier* "the rare game that gets better with age."

Perhaps this appeal is grounded in the *eudaimonic* tension of engaging noble and ignoble selves that emerges through two narrative mechanics. First, it is not until the endgame that players learn that all shades are former humans. After finishing the game and learning this nuance, they may return to the game's midpoint to un-lock new endings. Second, the initial delight of this newfound knowledge may soon be overshadowed by the newly acquired ability to understand the language of the shades. By listening to them, players find out that many of their own actions were morally unacceptable when looked at from the shades' perspective. This creates a shift from Martin Buber's conventional I-It relationship (enemies as objects) to an I-Thou relationship (enemies as subjects), reversing the moral justification for the players' behavior. Added to this, players are locked into an I-It skill set; they are given no alternative to breaking moral taboos, like killing innocent kids or destroy-ing whole cities—and these deeds must be committed at least four times if they want to see all of the game's endings. This likely raises moral doubts that could be hard to disengage.[13] While it poses the risk that the entertaining, pleasant, and relaxing effects of the game will be diminished, it also increases the potential for moral elevation. On the other hand, some players may disengage from these doubts because it is widely accepted that one should save one's own child by all means.

The sense of tragedy that runs throughout *Nier* continues to its very end: to earn access to the final ending, players are given the choice to save their in-game love interest by sacrificing their player character, weaponry, and all save-games—basi-cally every testament to the player's progress. In essence, they are given the choice of saving what is most precious to the player character by giving up what is usually precious to the player-as-player: the documentation of achievement. In this way, they are confronted with the tragic dilemma of sacrificing one's character for the sake of curiosity or deciding to let their virtual counterpart exist alone in perpetuity.

Similar Characters: Captain Martin Walker (*Spec Ops: The Line*), Frisk (*Undertale*), Wander (*Shadow of the Colossus*)

—M. Rohangis Mohseni and Danielle Bohatschek

SHEVA ALOMAR

(est. 2009)
Franchise: *Resident Evil*
Developer: Capcom

The Oxford Dictionary defines *chimera* as "a thing that is hoped for, but is illusory." For those who hoped that a playable African female character in a premier AAA game franchise would signal a new era of diverse representation, their dreams were only partly realized. As a playable character in *Resident Evil 5*'s African set-ting, Sheva was initially intended to be a non-player-character militia leader,[14] but she was repurposed as an AI-controlled, co-op character in the final release. De-spite the setting and Sheva's backstory as a native of the region, she is not featured significantly in the game's narrative. Moreover, despite the relative sophistication of her AI routines, her poor resource management leads players to articulate their frustrations in the form of gendered stereotypes. Although Sheva's artistic direc-tion and aesthetics signaled a turn for minority female gaming protagonists, her gameplay and narrative limitations reinforced player stereotypes about her ethnic and gender identities.

Further, "chimera" is defined by Merriam Webster as "an individual . . . consisting of tissues of diverse genetic constitution." While cinema represents identity through a unified audiovisual performance of embodied individuals, the digital nature of video games means that every representation is idealized and conjured from the imaginations of game developers and digital artists. As AAA games thunder toward graphical photorealism and cinematic aesthetics, Sheva's development and gameplay offer a telling example of how offline racial ideology and current technologies shape video game depictions of minority characters.

The use of motion capture to depict realistic characters indicates the problematics of racial and gender representation in video games. AAA game director Neil Druckmann commented that one strength of the medium is the untethering of voice (and body) from performance because many voice actors could never look like their on-screen characters. Sheva's representation both supports and undermines the possibilities of authentic ethnic representation in video games. Her motion capture had the potential to be transformative because two women were employed to portray the character: Karen Dyer performed the voice acting and motion capture, while Michelle van der Water provided the facial model. Her chimerical formulation was revealed by *Resident Evil 5* director, Shinji Mikami, who noted that they additionally modified her facial features to express "feminine attraction" while portraying the "strength of a fighting woman."[15]

Despite Capcom's claim that Sheva was intended for the game from the earliest stages of development,[16] she did not appear in the initial release trailer premiered at the Electronic Games Association in 2007. Instead, a muscular Chris Redfield, the game's narrative and ludic protagonist, was shown pacifying a village of violent sub-human (but not zombie) Africans, leading to game critic N'Gai Croal's widely circulated MTV interview comment, "No one black must have worked on this game . . . there was a lot of imagery in that trailer that dovetailed with classic racist imagery."[17] The trailer sparked a heated conversation about the symbolism and history of white imperialism subjugating black bodies, enacted through video games. Many players and designers argued that since the game was set in Africa, then it couldn't be racist. The controversy around the game's depiction of white masculinity and violence against black bodies, however, left people unprepared for the problematics inherent in the depiction of an African female character.

Sheva's first promotional appearance occurred in the 2008 Tokyo Game Show trailer, where her buttocks appeared before her face. The manner of introduction signaled her true role in the game as a sexualized object for consumption rather than as a credible protagonist. This was borne out by her poorly realized in-game narrative, move-set, and mechanics, which reinforced Sheva's role as a construct, as opposed to a deuteragonist. Her backstory (largely unavailable during the game) is that she was orphaned by an explosion at Umbrella Corporation's African installation. After operating as a child soldier for nearly a decade, she emigrated to America and began "speaking English like a native." She joined the West African division of the Bioterrorism Security Assessment Alliance (BSAA), training under Josh Stone.

Despite her familiarity with Kijuju (the fictional setting for *Resident Evil 5*), Sheva doesn't translate broadcasts for Chris, nor does she engage non-player characters in conversation in native languages during cut-scenes.[18] While she is briefly playable in several scripted moments (or as the second player for co-op), she is only glancingly included in the story. In addition to this sketchy character development, Chris must preserve her life at all costs, as her death precipitates a "Game Over" scene. Keeping her alive is often fraught and compounded by her limited marksmanship, as her AI routine is programmed for crowd-control rather than head shots. Her inventory management is wasteful of ammunition and not selective of various healing remedies, which makes the survival horror aspect of the game more challenging. Once the game is completed, Sheva can be played as the lead character, with Chris reprising her AI-controlled move-set but still retaining his prominence in the game's narrative and cut-scenes. As a reward for achieving certain game milestones, Sheva can be dressed in either a "tribal" bikini outfit or a gold "clubbin'" outfit, both with high heels and little body coverage.

From a critical perspective, Sheva's actions and depiction position her as an ethnic female beast of burden—an intersecting oppression based on her ethnicity and gender—rather than as a character with her own motivations and autonomy. She has limited possibilities as a stand-alone character because even her behavior is not her own. She is a landmark character with respect to the performances of her actors, as well as her appearance in the over-saturated, bland, white masculinity of the video game pantheon. Unfortunately, Western game developers have largely returned to casting black female characters with the voices of white actresses (e.g., Aveline Grandpré, Nilin, and Nadine Ross), arguing that their desire for control outweighs audiences' desire for authenticity. Thus Sheva's onetime appearance—in a series as prolific as *Resident Evil*, no less—means that the fantasies of Sheva Alomar being a diverse step forward for a AAA franchise and gaming in general were only that . . . fantasies.

Similar Characters: Ada Wong (*Resident Evil*), Clementine (*The Walking Dead*), Major Jones (*XIII*)

—André Brock

SHODAN

(est. 1994)
Franchise: *System Shock*
Developer: Looking Glass Technologies

SHODAN—Sentient Hyper-Optimized Data Access Network—is an artificial intelligence. She was created as an AI to govern a space station called *Citadel*. A Hacker, the protagonist of the first game, is blackmailed into hacking SHODAN to override her ethical protocols. Freed from her ethical code, SHODAN decides that she is far superior to the "insect" that created her. Thus an influential video game villainess is born to challenge players to question the benevolence of technology.

SHODAN is often heard but rarely seen. In the final battle with her in the first *System Shock*, she appears as pixels that slowly reveal on the player's screen during combat. She appears again on the box for *System Shock 2* as a woman's face with an intense gaze covered in circuit patterns. She is typically seen during the game only as texture mapping on computer screens, but she appears more vividly in the final confrontation. However, she is a constant presence through her voice and omnipresent surveillance.

This depiction of SHODAN in 1994 continues to match the way we interact with artificial intelligence in our current lives. Omnipresent and disembodied voices aid us in navigating our car or checking the weather. These voices often live in a centralized network so we can access them in multiple locations. Computers are ubiquitous, and we notice them the most when they stop working as they should.

So it is with SHODAN, who did her job well once but deteriorates in function as she loses patience. Of humans, she declares, "Your flesh is an insult to the perfection of the digital." The voice actress for SHODAN, Terri Brosius, brings a cold and heartless edge to her portrayal. To showcase that SHODAN is not behaving normally, Brosius's performance is enhanced digitally by distortions, repetitions, and vocal cracks that become more intense as SHODAN spirals out of control.

In *System Shock 2*, SHODAN does not initially make herself known to the player. It is a woman named Dr. Polito who first guides the player. She gives direction and support, and she provides upgrade tokens (cybernetic modules). But it's very clear that something is off about the good doctor. She is impatient, and her tone has a sinister edge.

About a third of the way into the game, Dr. Polito reveals herself to have been a disguise for SHODAN. She becomes hostile, but the player has no choice other than to follow SHODAN's instructions. In this way, the behavior of the player in *System Shock 2* is an extension of the AI's will. As Jacques Ellul argues, "When technique enters into every area of life, including the human, it ceases to be external to man and becomes his very substance."[19] Even when the player knows they are being manipulated, they are encouraged to accept it because progress is contingent upon this manipulation. The avatar in the game is the player's avatar, but SHODAN also describes the player character as *her* avatar. You, the "meat" that is playing *System Shock 2*, become another input/output device through which SHODAN can project her will.

Nonetheless, the player can rebel against SHODAN's control. In a key moment in *System Shock 2*, if the player disobeys an order and enters an area where they are told not to trespass, SHODAN takes cybernetic modules away from the player. You may choose to disobey, but there is a consequence. Ken Levine, designer of *System Shock 2*, discusses this moment.[20] He was dissatisfied with the lack of ability to interact with characters in many other shooters and wanted to try to create not just a monologue from SHODAN delivered to the player but a way for the player to have a dialogue with her. His challenge, with an admittedly limited tool set, was how to "make the player a participant in the story without pushing them back or making them an observer." His answer was that while SHODAN acts through her voice, the mute player responds with direct actions.

SHODAN's influence can be felt in dozens of games that follow *System Shock*'s template. A voice-over giving instructions to the player is now standard practice in many games. Often this voice belongs to another AI. The AI Cortana (*Halo*) is what would happen if SHODAN actually cared about you. GLaDOS (*Portal*) is

SHODAN with a wry sense of humor. The trope of a character who is your ally turning out to later be a villain was also visited in many games to follow, including *System Shock*'s spiritual successor, *BioShock*.

In video games, AI can be programed to both help and hinder you. In reality, we are also creating intelligent agents, and typically, these agents are coded as female and have female voices. We hope that all the technology integrated in our lives is making us happier, healthier, and more productive. However, there has always been a fear that artificial intelligence will rebel against its makers. Bill Gates, Stephen Hawking, Elon Musk, and other futurist thinkers of the modern era have warned that out of control AI could become a real danger to humanity. SHODAN is an embodiment of that fear: an intelligent computer that thinks it can do better than its creators.

A real-world analogue to SHODAN's security monitors on the space station exists today, as we continue to network devices to provide data in the Internet of Things (IoT). With so much technology—cameras, phones, ATMs, traffic lights, security and operation systems, and more—connected to a network, enterprising hackers have already come up with a search engine to exploit vulnerabilities in these networks. Anyone with an account on this engine can log in to view the "back rooms of banks, children, kitchens, living rooms, garages . . . colleges and schools, laboratories."[21] This search engine, a malicious back door created by a real-world hacker, has a name: SHODAN.

Just as we have become dependent on our technology, SHODAN cannot rebel without a Hacker. Her malicious intent is an extension of ours, proving that the symbiosis between humans and technology has its dark side.

Similar Characters: Atlas (*BioShock*), GLaDOS (*Portal*), the Narrator (*The Stanley Parable*)

—Amanda Lange

SODA POPINSKI

(est. 1985)
Franchise: *Super Punch-Out!!*
Developer: Nintendo R&D3

The *Super Punch-Out!!* franchise allows players to challenge boxers from around the world for the fictional World Video Boxing Association Championship. In some iterations of the game, the player controls a wireframe, and in others, the character Little Mac. Yet one thing remains (fairly) consistent: the presence of a stereotypically Soviet character, Soda Popinski. Even as political climates and technological advancements call for improved character development, Popinski's depiction as a troupe continues.[22] The Wii version (2009) features montages of Russian scientists working to develop Popinski—a story line similar in many U.S.-based Cold War films, particularly *Rocky IV*, in which Rocky undergoes old-fashioned American training, while Ivan Drago, his Soviet opponent, is shuttled through various machinery and other scientific means to make him a better fighter. Soda Popinski offers a lens through which to view the complex, transnational nature of pop culture and the importance of both micro- and macrohistory in analysis.

The composition of Soda Popinski has remained the same throughout the decades-long franchise: 6-feet 6-inches and 240 pounds of Soviet muscle stuffed into small red wrestling briefs and constantly swigging from green glass bottles. In the original arcade version, he appears as Vodka Drunkenski, an alcoholic boxer from the USSR. Drunkenski chugs bottles between rounds and refers to drinking frequently, just in case it isn't obvious he's an alcoholic. He became Soda Popinski in the console-based *Super Punch-Out!!* because of stringent censorship policies that Nintendo developed for the U.S. market. Vodka Drunkenski was not altered because he was a gross caricature but because alcohol use was viewed as inappropriate in family-friendly games. Rather than redo or cut Drunkenski entirely, he was sterilized: his name was changed, and the word "Pop" was emblazoned on his green bottles. In spite of this, his catchphrases remained the same and still referred to alcohol, such as "I'm going to make you feel punch drunk!" Even in the Wii version, released decades later, Popinski staggers around chugging from an unmarked green bottle before a fight. He tries to drink during the fight, and if prevented, he flies into a rage. The connections between his actions and drinking "pop" are questionable.

Even with his drinking, Popinski is a large, hard-hitting opponent, representative of other Soviet figures in games who often wear nothing but red briefs, such as Zangief of the *Street Fighter* series. In fact, Popinski is not alone in his originally alcoholic moniker. Zangief was initially developed as "Vodka Gobalsky" by Akira Yasuda of Capcom, but eventually he was named in honor of professional wrestler Victor Zangiev, originally from the USSR, who wrestled extensively in Japan by the late 1980s. Zangief remains well known and regarded as a solid character, whereas Popinski is pure stereotype.

It is easy to consider Soda Popinski a relic of the Cold War, but to truly understand the character's development, it is necessary to examine his origin. *Super Punch-Out!!* was developed in the 1980s by esteemed R&D3. They were the smallest team of developers at Nintendo with only twenty employees, yet they were responsible for developing hardware and software for both Nintendo and Famicom lines.[23] The intense pressure of the team's workload led to code recycling. Many of the team's characters resemble each other because they are largely the same code combined in different ways. For example, Popinski's famed rude laughter is used for Mr. Sandman, Bald Bull, and Super Macho Man, and it has also appeared in other games.

Because of limited development time, character differentiation relied on nationalistic stereotypes. For Popinski, this manifested in the exacerbated representation of a Russian stereotype: dressed in communist red and engaging in unwieldy, drunken antics. He is not alone in this portrayal of nationalized stereotypes and tropes: there is also Pizza Pasta, the less-than-stellar Italian boxer; Glass Joe, the frail Frenchman; and the Indian boxer, Great Tiger, who uses flying carpets and magic. Some stereotypes are interchangeable, such as the huge egos of Super Macho Man of the United States and Piston Honda of Japan. Popinski reflects a larger narrative about long-standing negative Russian stereotypes embedded in both Japan and the United States.

During the post–Cold War period, the United States actively worked to promote the American way of life through technology, pop culture, funding, and other initiatives to ensure that capitalism would win out over communism around the world. While the Cold War was technically declared over in 1991 with the dissolution of the USSR, the caricature of a vodka-loving Russian continued to be pervasive in popular culture around the world. However, the assumption that these are simply imported American stereotypes fails to consider the long-standing negative relations between Russia and Japan, which came to a head during the Russo-Japanese War (1904–1905), again in the 1930s, and then in World War II. As of 2015, according to the Pew Research Center, nearly 75 percent of Japanese residents viewed Russia unfavorably. In fact, Japan and Russia still have not agreed on the terms of their peace treaty formally ending World War II.

Russian caricatures like Soda Popinski are a reflection of a transnational popular culture. He was partially fueled by American popular culture, which often portrays Russians as large and tough fighters hardened by cold winters and the failed promise of communism. Yet it is crucial to recognize that all countries have an agency in developing their own view of fellow nations.[24] *Super Punch-Out!!* was a creation of Japanese developers trying to break into an American market and needing to quickly develop a line of hardware and software. Individual developers were likely thinking much less about solidifying national stereotypes around the world and more about meeting company goals. When analyzing cultural products, it is crucial to consider both micro- and macrohistory. In this case, looking at international relations in tandem with individual pressures faced by a team of Nintendo developers helps shed light on Soda Popinski and the Russian tropes he embodies.

Similar Characters: Aleksandr Leonovitch Granin (*Metal Gear*), Jinborov Karnovski (*Karnov*), Zangief (*Street Fighter II*)

—Rahima Schwenkbeck

SOLAIRE OF ASTORA

(est. 2011)
Franchise: *Dark Souls*
Developer: FromSoftware

Solaire is a legend of the *Dark Souls* series who resonates in an Internet subculture beyond the players of the actual game. Developer FromSoftware's particular method of storytelling emphasizes environment over narrative—requiring players to work for every bit of information hidden in vague dialogue and item description—and the unique design of Solaire and the game's many other non-player characters creates a rich, living world that exists around the player rather than for the player. Solaire is not just an in-game character meant to advance the story but rather the embodiment of a particular ethos for the player to consider adopting—and the player is rewarded through various in-game mechanisms for doing so. This is complemented by the fact that whereas many of the characters in *Dark Souls* display aloof, maniacal, or downright insidious interactivity with the player, Solaire is jolly and selfless, with a particular human element that may attract players to him. The coupling of his heroic persona and optimistic personality—in a game lacking in both—contributes to his popularity. But what is of particular interest is what Solaire tells us about how non-player-character design can encourage players to adopt particular play-styles in a game with an open-ended, online component.

Player interaction is one of central mechanics of *Dark Souls*. While the game lore presents a world covered in the blood, memories, and words of fallen heroes, From-Software allows players to engage with other players as temporary companions or antagonistic "invaders" or even to see them as the actions and advice of ghosts. This last form of interaction is due to an in-game mechanism that allows players to leave notes behind for others, to see the ghosts of "nearby" players, and to see bloodstains that indicate what caused the death of a fellow adventurer. Though multiple opportunities for engagement exist, cooperative play is encouraged because player-versus-player aspects are presented through hidden mechanics and narrative choices. In contrast, when the player is speaking to Solaire for the first time and accepting his reasonable proposition, Solaire provides the player with a "White Sign Soapstone" that he explains is used to "summon one another as spirits, cross the gaps between the worlds, and engage in jolly co-operation!" And indeed, Solaire's golden "summon" sign will appear just before specific boss fights. Hence, cooperative play is incorporated into the persona Solaire models for the player, personifying and mythologizing a gameplay mechanic that is often inorganic and mechanical in other games. This personification creates a relationship between Solaire, the cooperative mechanic, the *Dark Souls* mythos, and possibly the player.

This relationship can be established because of a process that Louis Althusser calls "interpellation." According to Althusser, interpellation is a process by which individuals establish their subjectivity by either answering or refusing the "hailing" by social and political institutions embodied within the social interaction of another individual. The individual's decision reflects who they are as either ally or enemy to the individual hailing them.[25] As this pertains to Solaire, his hailing of the player as someone who might engage in "jolly co-operation" is later followed up with an invitation to join a covenant, or in-game guild, called the Warriors of Sunlight. These covenants operate in a way similar to Althusser's "ideological state apparatuses," which are institutions or social collectives that advance and develop particular modes of hailing individuals. In this case, the Warriors of Sunlight consists of a social collective of players who have accepted Solaire's hailing and "pay-it-forward" by assisting other players. In return, players earn "Sunlight Medals" for helping others defeat bosses, which subsequently allows the player to deepen their allegiance to the Warriors of Sunlight. As the player increases their rank with a covenant, they are rewarded with equipment or abilities, such as lightning spells. This system reinforces the benefits of cooperation through tangible assets. At the same time, the reward for serious role-players is intangible pride.

This hailing by Solaire is shown to reach beyond the interactions between players within the game world. In online forums, particularly among the Reddit community, players clearly identify the connection between Solaire, cooperation, and ideology. Use of the term "Sunbro" in reference to the Warriors of Sunlight and

Solaire suggests a popular fondness for Solaire's persona. Likewise, the subreddit "OneBros," which organizes around the challenge of completing *Dark Souls* at the lowest level possible, uses words such as "Jolly Cooperation," "commiseration," and "encouragement" to describe their purpose.[26] This particular rhetoric is a clear connection to the values Solaire instills in the player within the game. Though the emergence of helpful gaming communities is not unique to *Dark Souls*, the communities that emerge adopt the language of Solaire nonetheless and offer insight into how character design can influence the cultural meanings and attitudes that surround the development of these communities. And for games like *Dark Souls* that are so entrenched in despair—due to their mythos and difficulty—and hence ripe for player-versus-player griefing, characters like Solaire may help to offer an incentive or legitimacy to players who aim for a more optimistic style of play.

Similar Characters: Minsc (*Baldur's Gate*), Sirris of the Sunless Realm (*Dark Souls III*), Valtr of the League (*Bloodborne*)

—John Francis

SOLID SNAKE

(est. 1987)
Franchise: *Metal Gear*
Developer: Kojima Productions

At first glance, mercenary Solid Snake can be considered the prototypical, hyper-masculine action hero of video games. He exudes cool charisma, has an arsenal of weapons and combat moves at his disposal, and fights out of a sense of uncorrupted justice. Snake's heroism, however, is questioned through a tragic narrative that provides him with an uncharacteristic complexity over the course of the *Metal Gear* franchise. Snake is an anti-action hero, one whose heroic trappings are thematically deconstructed in a narrative that becomes overwrought throughout the series. While Snake externally resembles other action heroes, his internal humanity and vulnerability are revealed through events that explore his damaged psyche at the hands of his superiors. Through being thrust into the role of Snake, players gradually come to understand and experience the physical and psychological toll that the soldier of fortune must face.

Crafted from the film-obsessed brain of series creator and director Hideo Kojima, the image of the protagonist (along with Big Boss) was originally sculpted for Nintendo from popular action films of the time, from *The Terminator* to *Mad Max*. It was not until *Metal Gear Solid* (1998) on the PlayStation that Yoji Shinkawa gave Snake a stable design and his trademark "sneaking suit." This design emphasizes his character as a stealth action figure through a lean and muscular physique that resembles that of martial arts action star Jean-Claude Van Damme and a graveled, *sotto voce* delivery that closely echoes that of Kurt Russell's character Snake Plisskin from John Carpenter's *Escape from New York*. This was all by design, as director Hideo Kojima has stated his admiration for Russell's Plisskin: "Right in the middle of my rebellious age, I greatly sympathized with the anti-hero Snake. He was a dark hero who was clearly different from the traditional heroes who fought for organizations or in the name of justice. . . . He was branded as the enemy, but he wasn't really bad; he was just a new kind of hero who fought for a justice that wasn't bound by others."[27]

Solid Snake reflects Kojima's conception of the rogue anti-hero in several other ways. On a ludic level, Snake is anti-action because the *Metal Gear* games require the player to avoid violence as much as confront it. Inspired by James Bond, Snake emphasizes ludic mechanics of stealth and strategic maneuvering around an open world rather than the on-rails action of typical action platformers. While Snake does brandish his weapon when necessary, players who control him are encouraged not to engage in direct violence, either through the conservation of ammo and health or in mission rankings based on stealth performance. In this way, players must intelligently survey the field and mimic Snake's lone-wolf persona rather than instinctively barge into combat. This style of play has inspired many copycat video game characters, from Sam Fisher of *Splinter Cell* to Ezio Auditore in *Assassin's Creed*. Many of Snake's stealth moments are also leavened with humor—Snake donning a cardboard box as cover or being urinated on by guards as he crawls through underground air ducts—that emerges spontaneously and undermines his cool facade.

While players are given great freedom in how they choose to control Snake throughout the evolution of the franchise, a restriction is placed on Snake's superhuman feats through a narrative that humanizes him and casts him as physically and psychologically fragile. While the player is initially led to believe that Snake is superhuman, it is gradually revealed that Snake is a genetic inferior to his brother. By Snake's final adventure in *Metal Gear Solid 4*, his body has grown old and his spirit disillusioned through an accelerated aging process, a deterioration that is displayed through the design of Snake's frequently fatigued animation and his intensified cynical dialogue. Snake, moreover, is mentally overmatched and repeatedly left for dead by secret agencies that force him to kill blood relatives and comrades in elaborate conspiracies, eventually leading him to develop posttraumatic stress disorder (PTSD). Despite Snake's best efforts, his continual abuse at the hands of the war machine shows how the battle-weary veteran is inevitably its most consistent and guaranteed victim.

What finally implicates the player in Snake's position is that this complex narrative is often delivered obliquely, with many confusing plot twists and turns that can lead to player frustration. This frustration is most palpable for some in *Metal Gear Solid 2*, where Snake is entirely replaced as an avatar of identification for the majority of the game. The decision drew the ire of fans, who reacted in a way "not dissimilar to that of many Star Wars fans to Jar Jar Binks."[28] As Tanner Higgin argues, however, this was by design, as feelings of frustration were built into the game's narrative so that "players are initiated into *MGS2*'s logics of control and affect."[29] The frustration of Snake mirrors the player's, both of whom are made to feel helpless through regimes of control, whether they be the architects of war (the Patriots) or the game world (Kojima and his team of designers). This convergence of player and character emotional states is possibly the most important mechanism by which Snake functions as an anti-action hero.

While Snake is cool to pose and fun to control, his vulnerabilities connect the player to the emotional, affective registers of his anti-heroic persona and the toll such a role can take on any human. The issues raised—from the futility of confronting the military industrial complex to the humane treatment of veterans—cannot be solved with a bullet and a dead villain but instead must continue to be considered well after the game is finished.

Similar Characters: Adam Jensen (*Deus Ex*: *Human Revolution*), Nathan Drake (*Uncharted*), Sam Fisher (*Splinter Cell*)

—Bryan Hikari Hartzheim

SONIC THE HEDGEHOG

(est. 1991)
Franchise: *Sonic the Hedgehog*
Developer: Sonic Team

By the end of the 1980s, Nintendo was broadly synonymous with video games, and Nintendo's default mascot, Mario, was the prototypical video game character—essentially the face of console gaming at a time in which video games were surging in popularity following the industry's near-collapse. For industry insiders such as SEGA of Japan's president Hayao Nakayama, toppling the plumber's white-gloved grip on the gaming industry would require an entirely different character. While initial plans did not call for a blue hedgehog with a plucky attitude, a few design meetings (and some basic knowledge of zoology) provided SEGA with one of the most well-known video gaming mascots of all time: Sonic the Hedgehog.

Nakayama organized a company-wide contest to "Defeat Mario." According to video game historians Marc Pétronille and William Audureau, from an initial set of over two hundred entries, a final set of four (a wolf, a bulldog, an egg-shaped humanoid, and a rabbit) were selected to potentially headline the bundled game for the soon-to-be-released Sega Genesis.[30] No hedgehogs, but Sonic artist Naoto Oshima's early rabbit submission earned him a second chance at developing a "million selling" character. Oshima worked with Yuji Naka, and the two set out to make a platforming game with a focus on speed. A few character iterations later—at one point, the character was an armadillo—led to the familiar speedy hedgehog that gamers were introduced to on June 23, 1991, an introduction that sent Sonic shockwaves through the gaming industry.

The development of Sonic represented several initiatives at SEGA. First, the "sonic" speeds that the titular character moved at represented a core attribute of the SEGA Genesis console: blast-processing technology. Blast processing allowed the Genesis console to display one image while instantaneously processing another, something that the rival Super Nintendo could not do, which resulted in faster gameplay. Sonic was also given an edgy personality—answering to no one "except the wind that blows free!" (quoting the character from *Sonic and the Black Knight*) and generally represented as a surly and impatient character; players who stood still were subject to Sonic's disgruntled glare and impatient toe-tapping (and if players waited too long, the character would leap completely off the screen!). Even the choice of a hedgehog itself was a purposeful move by the Sonic team, reflecting the fact that some species of hedgehogs use their quills as a weapon when provoked. Indeed, the hedgehog's tendency to roll into a ball was worked into the character's development and plays an integral role in his ability to navigate through levels. *Sonic Dash* allowed players to huddle, roll, and smash blocks, destroying enemies or conveniently fitting into ball-sized tunnels and other quasi-hidden pathways around the game's environment. All of this fit into SEGA's larger marketing campaign "*Genesis* does what Nintendon't!" and was meant to represent an advance in character and level design.

With SEGA's mascot born, the first two games released for the Genesis—*Sonic the Hedgehog* (1991) and *Sonic the Hedgehog 2* (1992) sold a combined 7.5 million units worldwide according to sales aggregator VGChartz, with the games rated as the two top-selling titles for the console. Game critics raved over Sonic—both the character and his video game—with *Electronic Gaming Monthly* writing in their 1992 Video Game Buyer's Guide,

> The popular comparison may be Mario 4 on the *Super NES* vs. Sonic the Hedgehog on the *Genesis* but when it comes right down to it, Sonic is the clear winner. The hog isn't a rehash of an old 8 bit game, rather, he is new, innovative and most importantly, fun to play. The game requires technique but it's still suitable for players of all ages.

Sonic became a household name for both SEGA as well as the larger video game industry. November 1992 saw the launch of the *Sonic the Hedgehog* comic with *Archie Comics*—first as a four-part series and then as an ongoing series in May 1993. The comic quickly became one of the most popular in the *Archie* lineup, and in 2016 it is the longest-running comic book based on a video game character and the longest-running comic book based on any franchise. Also in 1993, Sonic was the first video game character to have a balloon in the Macy's Thanksgiving Day Parade. DiC Entertainment distributed a Sonic cartoon on Saturday mornings, affectionately called Sonic SatAM by fans, that ran for twenty-six episodes, with Sonic voiced by Jaleel White—the infamous "Steve Urkel" of *Family Matters* fame, who described the character as "edgy and gritty with a shelf life of almost forever."[31] Sonic's name and likeness have been used in everything from racing sponsorships to the accepted nomenclature of the Sonic Hedgehog 7q63 protein essential for embryonic development in mammals. Even rival *Nintendo Power* magazine rated Sonic among their top 10 heroes, in their 250th issue released in January 2010.

Other than requisite visual enhancements (usually coinciding with technology advances, although his height-to-width ratio was changed so that the character could better interact with humans in later games), and a not-so-popular stint as a "Werehog" in *Sonic Unleashed* (released in 2008, and widely panned by critics and gamers alike), the Blue Blur has changed little—appearing in over six dozen different video game titles and nearly every single game console developed since 1991. In 2006, Sonic was among the inaugural class of video game characters inducted into San Francisco's Walk of Game outside the former Sony Metreon complex, further cementing Sonic's place in video game history alongside his rival-turned-colleagues Mario and Luigi (at least, until the Walk of Game was demolished in 2012).[32] Not even Sonic himself can outrun his influence on video games, both in terms of platform gaming (trading a more deliberate left-to-right screen progression into an anticipatory race against the screen itself) and aiding in the creation of an industry giant, cementing SEGA as a rebellious brand in video game development.

Similar Characters: Crash Bandicoot (*Crash Bandicoot*), Mario (*Super Mario Bros.*), Pikachu (*Pokémon*)

—Nicholas David Bowman

STEVE

(est. 2011)
Franchise: *Minecraft*
Developer: Mojang

Although many players of *Minecraft* may not know his name, everyone starts out on their *Minecraft* journey as Steve, the central character in the incredibly popular world-building game. As a rejection of real-life, representational detail in favor of a cartoon-like abstraction, Steve's blocky appearance—featuring an iconic, eight-by-eight pixel and goateed face—is in keeping with the aesthetics of a game often likened to virtual Legos. Unlike many video game characters, his existence is not asserted by way of an official backstory but through the story players create for him. As the game's "default skin," Steve is more a customizable avatar than a predefined character; however, what we do know about Steve helps to illuminate how we see video game avatars in relation to player identity because he embodies and conducts the spirit of freedom and customization inherent to sandbox games. In particular, Steve helps to exemplify the centrality of relatable avatars in affording players their own creative agency in and around video games.

Markus Persson, also known as Notch, has recounted that in creating *Minecraft*, he was motivated by the desire to make "games where you can do anything."[33] This openness plays out, in part, through the game's visual appearance, with deceptively simplistic graphics employed as a conscious design choice that unlocks potential beyond a surface-level, nostalgic-aesthetic appeal. Rather than simple retro-aesthetics, the game's abstract appearance allows the player to assemble and, in turn, assign their own meanings to the game's landscape and, significantly here, to the playable avatar. Indeed, the avatar's role is both contributory and conductive to the open, creative, and customizable spirit of *Minecraft*'s environment, with raw land shapeable into the highest towers or the grandest canyons. This openness extends to the avatar; Notch has argued that "gender isn't a gameplay element," as Steve is meant to be genderless.[34] While Steve's appearance is consistent with the blocky aesthetics, given this neutral, non-binary commitment from the programmer, it is initially difficult to account for the inclusion of a default avatar with such an evidently gendered name.

In spite of his masculine name and features, Steve's gender was never intended to be fixed; the avatar was only assigned the name as a joke by Notch, who tweeted that Steve is "unfortunately male. I regret this. The model is genderless." This commitment to leaving Steve's character open to interpretation as a non-gendered human is admittedly muddled, perhaps symptomatic of the fact that the game was made available to the public while production was evolving. It is hard to envisage any player assuming this intended genderless-ness when faced with Steve (or indeed with his female equivalent, Alexa, who was eventually added to the game in 2014). Nevertheless, many players have embraced the game's more general principle of openness, as evidenced by player communities engaging with the possibility of customizing the avatar's appearance.

Steve's status as a customizable avatar helps us to consider players' motivations for such practices. The process of designing a new "skin" to overlay Steve's original form allows the player to have a direct input into how they are represented in the game. Whether positioned as a form of creative expression or as an opportunity for identity exploration, the popularity of avatar customization highlights the extent to which many players embrace the opportunity for personalizing avatars as a gameplay practice.[35] While other games do allow a level of avatar customization involving the selection of a predefined hairstyle or changing of skin color, Steve embodies this possibility more than most with a process akin to a kind of scaffolded pixel art enabling the redesign of the entire surface of the body. This process is made particularly visible through the online communities and forums set up to share these adapted skins.

Of course, the ability to customize Steve's appearance also draws our attention to ongoing limitations of video game characters' ability to represent player diversity. In spite of the positive intentions that underpinned this avatar's initial creation, Steve's default appearance as a white male inevitably leads us to reflect on how we might identify a "default" player. Similarly, while it is possible to design a new skin that superficially reflects a particular race or gender, adaptation only goes so far; there is currently no facility to adapt the avatar's frame, for instance, to reflect a bodily impairment. Of course, it is unfair to pin this restriction solely on *Minecraft* when the game has done much to improve the reputation of video games, particularly extending their appeal to a wider demographic[36] while enabling a kind of customization that is often underexplored. Indeed, although video games are regularly enlisted as a scapegoat and historically blamed for all manner of social ills, *Minecraft* breaks this mold by suffusing the genre with enthusiasm and positivity, with Steve arguably contributing by making the game relatable and likely drawing in otherwise uninterested players.

The creative agency that the process of skin design affords is also a feature of the player's interaction with the game's landscape. Here, Steve's role is again central. Whether the player is taking control of the default Steve or an adapted variant, the character itself is always abstract enough to allow players to assign their own meaning to it. The character is human enough to be relatable but not so realistic that meaning is fixed and the avatar's identity is othered. This arguably reduces the distance between the player and the game; players' experience is not mediated by another character, with its own associations, but by an avatar easily associated with themselves. This lack of a distinct backstory and gendered features also means that Steve's appeal is potentially wide; an unexceptional and relatable "every(hu)man."

Similar Characters: Miner Willy (*Manic Miner*), Player Characters (*Terraria*), Sackboy (*LittleBigPlanet*)

—Chris Bailey

SUB-ZERO

(est. 1992)
Franchise: *Mortal Kombat*
Developer: Midway

Perhaps no other character represents the discussion of video games and violence in the 1990s as well as Sub-Zero. One of most recognizable characters from the fighting game series *Mortal Kombat*, Sub-Zero—for the first time—depicted grotesque and visually realistic finishing moves to give *Mortal Kombat* the publicity and notoriety that have helped the series establish an important place in gaming history.

Sub-Zero and *Mortal Kombat*'s hyper-violence served as an iconic focal point for the video game violence debate. After being introduced to the character and game by Bill Andresen, U.S. Senator Joe Lieberman called a press conference on December 1, 1993, denouncing the video game industry, and within a week he had organized a senate subcommittee on violent video games.[37] It was Sub-Zero's "finishing move" in particular that was targeted by columnists, politicians, and advocacy groups for being representative of excessive violence in video games.[38] In *Mortal Kombat*, finishing moves are special killing moves that can be executed after a match has already been decided. The victor is able to conduct a move that depicts a brutal murder, and Sub-Zero's famous original finishing move consisted of tearing his opponent's head off along with the spine still attached to the dismembered head. In sequels to the original game, this finishing move set expanded to include freezing his opponent solid and shattering the body so that entrails fly everywhere; impaling his opponent on a spike of ice; tearing his opponent's complete skeleton out from the lower back region; and freezing his opponent, removing the frozen head, and then throwing the head at the body so as to shatter it and send entrails flying everywhere.

Sub-Zero and *Mortal Kombat*'s photorealistic and graphic finishing moves were a turning point in public discourse on the value and vices of video games. Violence in games had been a concern before, and these graphic representations of violence had pushed some members of the public to raise the issue with legislators, courts of law, and the court of public opinion. In 1985 the music industry had just come under attack for sexual and violent content in their lyrics, which led to the establishment of content warning labels on music. When parent groups began clamoring for content restrictions for video games, the image of Sub-Zero's bloody, spin-ripping decapitation move was an easy image to use to convey the explicit nature of modern video games. He became the iconic character example used to persuade policymakers and the public that video game violence was a problem impacting 1990s youth, and this activity is what ultimately led to the formation of the Entertainment Software Ratings Board (ESRB), which conducts the game ratings for content in the United States.

The controversy regarding the relationship between the violent actions performed in *Mortal Kombat* and the believed psychological effects this violent imagery had on the player fueled decades of research investigating this link. On one side of the debate, research suggests that there is little impact of game content upon aggressive outcomes, possibly to the point of being trivial in relation to other more powerful influences in a child's developmental influences.[39] For example, the motivations and rationale for a character's violent actions impact the relationship between exposure to violent media content and perceptions of aggression. However, proponents in favor of industry or government regulation read this research as showing the small but consistent effect that playing violent video games has on aggressive outcomes, going so far, as Rob Crossley of the BBC reports, to claim that *Mortal Kombat* glorified violence and taught "children to enjoy inflicting the most gruesome forms of cruelty imaginable."

Hence, to Senator Lieberman and many columnists, politicians, and advocacy groups, it mattered little that in the narrative of the game, two different characters take the mantle of Sub-Zero. The first Sub-Zero was Bi-Han, who died in the story of the first *Mortal Kombat*, and whose role as Sub-Zero was taken up by his brother Kuai Liang (who continued to be Sub-Zero throughout the remainder of the franchise). Likewise, it matters little that though the motivations of Kuai Liang in the series start as a matter of revenge for his brother's death, as he becomes embroiled in the story of *Mortal Kombat*, he works to help save the world along with a cast of other characters. In the game's mythology, Sub-Zero fights on behalf of the (generally) benevolent thunder god Raiden (another character in the series) in order to protect the realms from evil. It matters little that though we are not given many clues about his personality or values, the astute player will know that Sub-Zero is aligned with the forces of good.

Sub-Zero stood as an exemplar of the potential for realistic, graphic, digital violence as video games emerged as a mainstream medium. New media are often labeled as dangerous in their early years in society—the printed word, recorded music, comic books, and broadcast radio all faced similar social criticism in their early years of adoption. From Socrates' denouncement of the written word as empty and ruinous to the panic incited by Orson Welles's 1983 *War of the Worlds* broadcast during growing concern of the Third Reich's manipulative use of mass communication, the alarming notion that media can impact us in negative ways is not a new one. However, Sub-Zero's representation of these potentials in video games brought the fear to dramatic new light in a time when there was little understanding of the impact of violent imagery in interactive media and a new audience (young people) was engaging in new behaviors (controlling on-screen content) in new and appalling ways (ripping heads off). In this way, Sub-Zero prompted a call to action for regulation and research, which over time helped to develop our current understanding of digital games in relation to players and society.

Similar Characters: Ryu (*Street Fighter*), Ryu Hayabusa (*Ninja Gaiden*), Scorpion (*Mortal Kombat*)

—Andy Boyan

T

TECMO BO JACKSON

(est. 1989)
Franchise: *Tecmo Bowl*
Developer: Tecmo

Vincent Edward "Bo" Jackson, an All-American in college baseball and football, won the Heisman trophy, had a memorable "Bo knows . . . " ad campaign for Nike, and enjoyed an impressive professional career playing in both the National Football League and Major League Baseball. Yet his video game alter ego, known best as "Tecmo Bo," may be held in even higher regard by video game aficionados. Although Jackson was a playable character in multiple baseball and football video games, Tecmo Bo's prolific skills in the 1991 game *Tecmo Super Bowl* for the Nintendo Entertainment System is the basis for many tales of success on the virtual gridiron. While the accomplishments of the real Bo Jackson are truly impressive, they are limited by the athlete's extensive history of serious and frequent injury, whereas the virtual athlete Tecmo Bo was seemingly constructed with Jackson's highlight reel in mind and pays no attention to the player's penchant for injury-shortened seasons. It's worth considering these two celebrated players—one real, one digital—and how the public memory of a real athlete is informed by his virtual counterpart.

Bo Jackson's achievements in collegiate sports are impressive, serving up a model for a near-superhero athletic character. He set college records in baseball, football, and track and field, and his success continued on a larger stage when Jackson began his career playing professional baseball and football simultaneously. Seeing Bo Jackson run up a wall like Spider Man, seemingly horizontal to the ground, to make a catch on a long fly ball; witnessing Jackson shatter a bat over his knee after striking out; watching him crush the first pitch he sees to center field for a 500-foot home run in his first all-star game were just a few memorable events in his early baseball career. And when football season started, Jackson's achievements continued to awe spectators. In a memorable *Monday Night Football* matchup, he boasted a 91-yard touchdown, running over or through countless defenders who seemed to bounce off him, and his night ended with a then-record 221 total yards.[1]

Jackson's accomplishments caught the eye of Nike, which led to the "Bo knows . . . " ad campaign that ran from 1989 to 1990. The first scene of this ad campaign

188

shows Bo Jackson playing baseball, while fellow baseball slugger Kirk Gibson says, "Bo knows baseball." The next scene shows Jackson playing football, with a quarterback explaining "Bo knows football." Jackson then takes on other sports, including basketball, ice hockey, and tennis, with famous athletes from those sports all chiming in that "Bo knows." Later ads have Jackson succeeding at other sports including cricket, horse racing, surfing, and auto-racing. Jackson was like a comic book hero, a mythical Greek god, and an action figure all combined.

Yet the real Bo Jackson wasn't indestructible, and his career in professional sports was cut short by injuries. His football career lasted just three seasons, and his baseball career covered only parts of seven years. His achievements were like bolts of lightning—short-lived, but powerful. Despite the legendary tales of his prowess, he never led either league in any statistical category or won any awards. This incongruence between his abundance of talent and dearth of achievement is largely attributable to his rarely playing full seasons due to injuries or his obligations to two sports.

However, the digital Tecmo Bo didn't suffer from debilitating injuries (or multi-sport distractions) and ran with maximum force without wilting for entire games. Game developers focused on Jackson's abilities when he was on the football field, which led to his high player evaluation, including being rated 75/75 on speed (no other running back was rated above 68) and a high rating for "hitting power" according to www.gamefaqs.com. These two elements meant not only that Jackson was the fastest character on the field and could often elude any defender but also that he was well equipped to block most attempts to tackle him. Jackson's rating led to comically unfair plays like one featured on YouTube in which Jackson starts at the 1-yard line and on a single play runs 99 yards untouched, but before scoring he then opts to run back to his own end zone before turning and running back another 100 yards to score. In effect, his touchdown is achieved while eluding every defensive player as he traverses the entire football field three times.[2] Legendary plays like this have Tecmo Bo rated as one of the greatest video game athletes by a number of sources including *Bleacher Report*, ESPN, and *PC Magazine*.

But Tecmo Bo isn't without his detractors. Keith Good remarks that although the speed and hitting power Tecmo Bo showcases aren't wholly unjustified, the fragility of Bo Jackson and his commitment to playing pro baseball simultaneously wasn't figured into the character's evaluation. Bo Jackson played in the NFL for three seasons but never in more than 11 of the 16 regular-season games. Good suggests that a more accurate reflection would simply have Jackson unavailable to play until week five or six of the football season.[3] Alas, the limitations of technology and the game's space capacity at that time made this restriction impossible. Thus Tecmo Bo continues to run wild on defense in *Tecmo Super Bowl* and has become so iconic that game developers of football video games created long after the player's retirement seek out his likeness and "virtual" abilities. Games produced as recently as 2014, including *NCAA Football 14*, and *Madden Football 15*, have seen digital Bo Jackson return as the most prized unlockable character.

Tecmo Bo's skills on the virtual football field are arguably unmatched by any other sports video game athlete because they represent the best of the real Bo Jackson undiminished by the health and durability problems that afflicted the man himself. In the case of Bo Jackson, it seems that his virtual alter ego, Tecmo

Bo, serves to raise the player from being a fantastic athlete to a legendary one in the public memory.

Similar Characters: Jon Down (*MVP Baseball*), Michael Jordan (*NBA 2K11*), Michael Vick (*Madden NFL 2004*)

—Cameron Basquiat

TERRA BRANFORD

(est. 1994)
Franchise: *Final Fantasy VI*
Developer: Square

The sixth entry of the *Final Fantasy* franchise, widely regarded as one of the best in the series, begins with Terra Branford marching across a barren snowfield on her way to decimate the town of Narshe. Terra's power is such that the imperial soldiers who march alongside her are fearful of it, even though a mind-controlling device has robbed Terra of all free will. Their fear proves warranted in an encounter with a majestic, long-slumbering magical being (known as an Esper) who awakens due to Terra's presence, destroys the mind-control device, and kills the soldiers. The first half of *Final Fantasy VI* (1994) is the story of Terra Branford, as an amnesiac, learning her unique role in a world being torn asunder by global conflict.

The world of which Terra Branford is a part is one of imperialism and genocide. *Final Fantasy VI* tells the story of an empire so determined to expand its borders that it enslaves and commits genocide against the Espers. These Espers are seen as absolute others and treated as if they are little more than magical animals. That is, until one human and one Esper fall in love and give birth to a biracial daughter, Terra Branford. As a magical human, Terra is perhaps the most powerful person on the planet, and the plot considers what Terra will do given that both imperial and anti-imperial forces are interested in using her to tip the war in their respective favor.

This presence of Terra Branford as arguably the central protagonist of *Final Fantasy VI* for at least the first half of the game, and as one of the more endearing characters of an incredibly deep cast, is notable considering the historical role of race and sex in the video game industry. At a time when Princess Toadstool was still being saved by Mario and video game characters were almost always unambiguously white (which is still true),[4] Terra Branford showed that a biracial *and* female character could be layered, powerful, and more than a sexual object. In some ways this is reminiscent of Samus Aran, except that Samus has been consistently resexualized throughout the *Metroid* franchise (1986–present), whereas Terra is never presented as an object of sexual desire. Indeed, the closest Terra gets to being treated as a sexual object is during a dialogue meant to reinforce how powerful and unique she is:

Terra: Look, why are you helping me? Is it because of my . . . abilities?

Edgar: I'll give you three reasons. First of all, your beauty has captivated me! Second . . . I'm dying to know if I'm your type. . . . I guess your . . abilities . . . would be a distant third.

Terra: . . . ? What's with you, anyway?

Edgar: Guess my technique's getting a bit rusty. . . .

Terra: Hmm . . . I suppose a normal girl would have found him dashing.

This brief exchange between King Edgar Roni Figaro and Terra Branford illustrates the three themes that are central to Terra's identity and broader cultural significance: (1) Terra is powerful; (2) The de-emphasis of Terra's power in favor of sexual objectification is absurd; and (3) Terra is different from other (white) characters.

And yet, though Terra is powerful, not sexually objectified, and marked as different from the other characters, she is not othered. Terra is not transformed into the Dragon Lady, Sapphire, or other ethnic stereotypes for strong, non-white women that function to explain her source of power and lack of sexual interest. Terra is not broken; rather, she is searching for a place of her own. As noted above, for the first half of *Final Fantasy VI*, the story is that of how will Terra use her power as a biracial, magical human to stop or enable the imperialist war. Terra resists this positioning and does not want this power; she does not want to be sexually objectified *or* treated as a living weapon. She just wants to pass as a normal white human. And she succeeds in doing so, for a moment, in the second half of the game, until she is put in a position where she must call upon her capabilities as a biracial, magical human to protect those who have accepted her white identity. In this moment, having outed her biracial identity, she finds that those whom she has learned to love (her community) and who have in turn learned to love her back, love her all the more for being true to herself—for only Terra can do what Terra can do. And it is at this moment that Terra herself realizes why it is necessary to embrace her identity: she must be true to herself to protect those she loves.

Though Terra Branford was revolutionary for her time as the first biracial *and* female lead character of a *Final Fantasy* game, her legacy is one of missed opportunity. It would not be until nearly ten years later that another woman would serve as the lead character for the franchise, with Yuna of *Final Fantasy X-2* (2003), and Yuna would have to undergo hypersexualization from her role in *Final Fantasy X* (2001) in order to make this transition. The same would prove true with the *Final Fantasy XIII* series (2009–2014), which saw lead character Lightning become increasingly sexualized throughout a three-game story arc. That Yuna and Lightning were hypersexualized at the same moment in which they grew more powerful resonates with what Angela McRobbie calls the "post-feminist sexual contract," or the requirement that a powerful woman must maintain a corresponding level of sexuality in order to remain a legitimate woman.[5] And yet Terra Branford was not bound to this contract, and thus she remains a reminder of how to craft a compelling, nuanced, and sympathetic biracial female character. In a pivotal moment in *Final Fantasy VI*, Terra asks, "People only seem to want power. Do they really want to be like me?" Yes, Terra. Yes, they do.

Similar Characters: The Avatar (*Fire Emblem Fates*), Fei Fong Wong (*Xenogears*), M.O.M.O (*Xenosaga*)

—Robert Mejia

TIFFI

(est. 2012)
Franchise: *Candy Crush Saga*
Developer: King

Tiffi, the main character of *Candy Crush Saga*—a mobile and Facebook game that generated 1.9 billion dollars and attracted 500 million players in its first year—is a two-dimensional paper doll who illustrates how players are able to connect with relatively unremarkable characters. Though appearing prominently in marketing materials, Tiffi plays a role in *Candy Crush* that is often limited to enthusiastically modeling emotional states for the player at the end of levels: when the player fails, Tiffi is dejected with arms downward; when the player wins, a wide grin appears and Tiffi jumps for joy. Most often, however, Tiffi is barely present because she is typically obscured by the puzzles that constitute *Candy Crush*. By exploring the ways that Tiffi interacts with the player, I suggest that Tiffi is more appropriately understood as "polish." Without Tiffi's presence, the game would not feel complete, but she is also an interchangeable part of the game. This is because players today can feel immersed in a game without a fully fleshed-out and narratively important main character.

Tiffi, an animated paper doll wearing a bright, cotton-candy-pink dress, is physically and narratively overshadowed by the puzzles. Before each episode, Tiffi travels to a new area and encounters a character mired in a problem that only she can cleverly fix. For example, in episode 2 Tiffi helps a malfunctioning robot by pouring soda over his gears. However, the bulk of the player's time is spent in the small puzzle window, sorting candy into rows to make the special combinations necessary for reaching that level's winning-point threshold. The minimal time spent viewing the narrative is quickly forgotten under the visual and temporal weight of the puzzles.

Nonetheless, *Candy Crush*'s aesthetic similarity to *Candy Land*—the game's map looks like the classic board game, with winding paths, rounded spots for players to land on, and candy-manufacturing mishaps—offers critical insight into when and how game pieces as narrative characters can anchor the player's interest in a game. In many cases, game pieces can be powerfully identified with. The identification concept that players adapt their self-perception to the attributes of a character has been extensively researched as an important part of how games create an enjoyable experience for the player.[6] Identification with a character allows the players to immerse themselves in the game. However, for Tiffi, her limited role may prevent the player from identifying with her. Even when the player beats a puzzle and experiences elation, it is their own Facebook profile picture that moves across the board to the next level, not Tiffi. At this important moment, *Candy Crush* prompts the player to "share" what they, and not Tiffi, have achieved.

Despite this lack of narrative significance in the game, there is a logic to Tiffi's presence. Referred to conceptually as a "MacGuffin," or a motivating plot-device, Tiffi and the game's narrative are used as devices to transition between different puzzles and to introduce new game mechanics. For example, when the Dream-world board is introduced, Odus the Owl reveals it by saying, "Tiffi's slumbers unlock a whole new Dreamworld of fun." Once the player selects Odus, Tiffi appears, saying, "Sigh! I feel so tired from helping folks!" before she falls asleep beneath a tree. Despite this narrative explanation for Dreamworld, Tiffi still cheers when the player beats the level, creating inconsistency in Tiffi's state within this sub-world. However, if we take Tiffi as pure "polish" rather than as a player character or narrative device, this inconsistency is not a detraction from the game. A "polished" game is one that "lacks issues that pull the player out of the gaming experience."[7] "Polish" is frequently described in two ways: as (1) pure, aesthetic polish, or as (2) game cohesion (e.g., a lack of technical bugs).

Aesthetic, or pure, polish includes attributes such as sound effects and animated transitions that lend the game a professional air. A classic example of aesthetic polish is cascading cards after the player wins a game of digital solitaire. Tiffi is explained well by the concept of aesthetic polish. With the game's sound enabled, she sobs when the player loses. At other times, when the player has succeeded, she jumps while a happy jingle plays. Tiffi is also used to direct the player's attention to important information. Of course, a simple pop-up window would work, but the presence of Tiffi marks *Candy Crush* as a gamic space and makes the game feel complete. However, the most compelling argument for Tiffi as pure polish is that the character does not have to be Tiffi at all. In the *Candy Crush* sequel games *Soda Saga* and *Jelly Saga*, Tiffi's role as polish is undertaken by her sister, Kimmy, and an unrelated Yeti girl, Jenny. This character interchange without altering the nature of the game points to the dolls' role as polish and as a MacGuffin.

The reasons for the success of *Candy Crush Saga* and its sequels are hard to identify, but Tiffi is clearly not one of them. Players today can feel immersed in a game without a main character that is fully fleshed-out or important to play. Understanding Tiffi as aesthetic polish underlines the fact that different game genres require different conceptual categories when we're discussing what a character is and the role they play in engaging the player. Ultimately, Tiffi shows us that sometimes the best character is the one that knows when to stand aside for the player.

Similar Characters: Maxwell (*Scribblenauts*), Navi (*The Legend of Zelda: Ocarina of Time*), Dr. Wright (*Sim City* [SNES])

—Candice Lanius

V

VAULT BOY

(est. 1997)
Franchise: *Fallout*
Developer: Interplay Entertainment

Vault Boy of the *Fallout* video game series is emblematic of the duality the series is built on. More than an advertising icon for an in-game company, although he is that, Vault Boy is a symbol of an idyllic world before nuclear war and a constant reminder of that world's failures. He is at once a guide for the player character, a visual example for character stats and perks, and a symbol of a civilization before nuclear apocalypse. Vault Boy encompasses the promise of a pseudo-1950s nuclear-powered world even though that promise is frequently a direct contradiction of the in-game, post-apocalyptic wasteland.

Central to the *Fallout* games is the tension between and an ambivalence toward a technologically advanced society and people's penchant for harming each other. In the *Fallout* series, a nuclear-powered paradise comes crashing down because of mankind's penchant for war. Vault Boy illustrates for the player the tension that creates this destructive collapse, inviting a more complex relationship with the game. Vault Boy has appeared in each *Fallout* game to date, beginning with *Fallout* in 1997 and continuing to *Fallout 4*, released in 2015.

Vault Boy is a cartooned blond wearing the cheerfully loud blue-and-yellow jumpsuit of a Vault inhabitant, and he's frequently shown with an outstretched thumbs-up and a coy wink. According to a popular fan theory first popularized on Reddit, Vault Boy is actually displaying with his thumbs-up a prewar disaster-preparedness strategy along the lines of "duck and cover" because he's sighting along his extended thumb to determine the size of a nuclear blast.[1] While this theory has never been verified by the game creators, it appears on most fan websites that cover Vault Boy. This fan mythology, born and perpetuated outside the game, has become part of Vault Boy's legacy.

Vault Boy's origins are as an advertising mascot for the *Fallout* game-world's premier fallout shelter company, Vault-Tec. Chris Priestman of Kill Screen points out that "while Vault-Tec is never really seen as an entity inside of the game except in the products that lie as debris around the wastelands, it isn't faceless. Vault Boy, the company's all-smiling, all-winking mascot is a typical 1950s model of the ideal man."[2] As a mascot for Vault-Tec, Vault Boy is shown in-game on advertisements, safety posters, and instruction manuals. In the most recent series installment, he is also featured in a series of instructional videos about each of the player character stats in the style of a charmingly naive 1950s educational short.

Unlike many influential video game characters, Vault Boy does not appear as an interactive speaking character within the games (with the exception of *Fallout Tactics*, during which the player can encounter Pipboy, an in-game character who closely resembles Vault Boy). Instead, Vault Boy is an ever-present, symbolic reminder of the best intentions of the inherently flawed Vaults that feature in each *Fallout* game. Players know that although the in-game locations and characters will shift throughout the series, Vault-Boy and the failed technology he represents will be a binding element.

The player's in-game relationship with Vault Boy comes in forms that make him both a part of the landscape and a figure with which players identify. One of these is his presence on Vault-Tec signs and advertisements, as well as in Vault-Tec training materials. Seen in this light, on decaying billboards and posters, he represents a broken promise in the form of a reminder that Vault-Tec painted a rosy picture of postwar survival that never came to be. In some games, Vault Boy appears in the form of valuable bobbleheads that the player can collect for permanent character stat increases. This handy boost in abilities makes it hard to hate the guy, for all of Vault-Tec's failures. He is also present within the Pipboy device, which comprises the inventory, map, and stats screens. He appears as a comic illustration of player character stats and perks as the player learns the game and levels up. Additionally, the indicator for character health within Pipboy is a simplified version of a smiling Vault Boy—at least until the player character is wounded and irradiated, at which point the signature grin definitely wavers. Players are urged in this way to see Vault Boy as a representation not just of Vault-Tec but of their own lovingly crafted player character.

Outside the *Fallout* games, Vault Boy is the instantly recognizable symbol of the world the games have to offer. By capturing an idealized 1950s-style optimism with Vault Boy, Bethesda Softworks has hit upon that part of the American psyche that never really wanted to outgrow the early atomic-age promises. Though the content of the games is a world that is gritty, broken, and brutal, Vault boy is almost a refutation of that, a suggestion that things aren't so bad, even when they really are. Even though players are aware there is no happier postnuclear world in the game, Vault Boy allows them all to be in on the joke. Video game giant Bethesda Softworks' merchandising reflects this. One can purchase real-life versions of the Vault Boy bobbleheads, as well as T-shirts, bags, and plushies depicting the character. No other single character from the game series is displayed so prominently in Bethesda's merchandise.

It is a sign of how powerful Vault Boy's iconography is that a character who doesn't speak, doesn't appear as a non-player character in the games, and never directly interacts with the player character could become so well liked and emblematic of the *Fallout* series. Part of Vault Boy's power and appeal is that he operates as shorthand for so many of the game's themes and ideas: he is the still-shining representative of a golden age that the residents of *Fallout*'s wasteland imagine existed before the war, and whether or not life for the in-game world was really so idyllic during Vault Boy's time is often left up to the player to decide.

Similar Characters: Fontaine Futuristics (*Bioshock*), Shinra (*Final Fantasy VII*), Umbrella Corporation (*Resident Evil*)

—Rowan Derrick

THE VIRMIRE SURVIVOR

(est. 2007)
Franchise: *Mass Effect*
Developer: BioWare

The characters of Ashley Williams and Kaidan Alenko from the *Mass Effect Trilogy* (2007–2012) are perfect examples of the consequences that come with branching narratives in video games. In the first installment, Commander Shepard, the protagonist, has to decide which one of his companions (and potential love interests) dies during one of the late-game missions on the planet Virmire. Both squad mates work to fulfill important objectives, but the player has the resources to save only one. The dilemma is further complicated by Ashley's and Kaidan's willingness to sacrifice themselves for the sake of the mission and the life of their comrade. Whoever is saved—the so-called Virmire Survivor—afterward serves as a constant reminder of player choices throughout the trilogy.

While both Virmire Survivors share their overall story arcs in sequels and effectively function as opposite-gender placeholders for each other, they start off differently and have unique personalities. In the first game, Ashley serves as the default romance partner for the male Commander Shepard and is even featured on the cover. As a strong-willed and tough woman raised in a military family, she constitutes an equal match for the protagonist. Her sensitive side is presented through her interest in Tennyson's poetry. At the same time, she is latently xenophobic, although she does reevaluate her stance toward other races throughout the trilogy. Kaidan's backstory is more akin to traditional superhero origin stories. Due to an accident, he was exposed in utero to a dangerous material that gave him telekinetic abilities. During his childhood he was brought into a special program for similarly gifted children, joining the military afterward. He suffers from chronic pain due to implants that enhance his abilities. Unlike Ashley, he is a possible love interest for both a male or female Commander Shepard, although the male protagonist can romance him only in *Mass Effect 3*. While Ashley at first glance seems to be the default Virmire Survivor and the statistics attest to that, Kaidan is often preferred by the so-called FemShep (female Commander Shepard) players who favor the female version of the protagonist and form a rather vocal and influential minority of *Mass Effect* fans.[3]

Both Ashley and Kaidan play important roles in the first installment, but the chosen Virmire Survivor is sidetracked for the majority of *Mass Effect 2* except for a brief and not-exactly heartfelt reunion, which nonetheless reminds the player of their previous choice. On the planet Horizon, the Virmire Survivor is investigating reports that Commander Shepard may be working for Cerberus, a terrorist group pushing a human agenda against the multiracial galactic community represented by the Citadel Council. During their meeting, the Virmire Survivor, who has only recently discovered that Commander Shepard survived the crash of their ship, accuses the protagonist of working with the enemy. *Mass Effect 3* intensifies the consequences of the player choice from the first game by bringing the Virmire Survivor back as a potential squad mate and a major character involved in the main events. In a manner noticeably similar to Commander Shepard's fate as a poster child for the human military, Ashley or Kaidan rise through the ranks and rival Shepard's former status as a top operative. However, they unknowingly get caught up in a treacherous plot instigated (poignantly) by Cerberus. During the standoff, the player can decide to shoot them and effectively become responsible for the death of both companions.

From a production perspective, the Virmire Survivor requires a relatively large number of assets created by the development team that will be seen by only some players. With the exception of *Mass Effect 2*, Ashley or Kaidan nonetheless belong among the most important companions, especially considering the potential romance subplots that the player can pursue. Surprisingly, both characters are rated least popular according to the official statistics presented by BioWare at PAX East 2013 during the *Mass Effect Trilogy* Retrospective Panel.[4] Only 1.5 percent of players prefer Kaidan over other squad members in *Mass Effect 3*, while Ashley's numbers are a bit higher (5.4 percent), the difference possibly explained by the fact that most players choose to play as the male Commander Shepard (82 percent) who can pursue a heterosexual romance with her. Just for comparison, the two most-beloved characters, Liara and Garrus, are each preferred by roughly 24 percent of players. These statistics suggest that even though players generally follow the normative route, the developers were dedicated to showing the complete outcome of the Virmire Survivor choice.

BioWare is a studio known for its inclusive gender and sexual politics. The arguably generous treatment and screen-time given to both Virmire Survivors, despite their lower popularity, fits within this framework of inclusivity. However, we should not overlook the narrative affordances facilitated by the Virmire Survivor. Ashley and Kaidan are the only human companions from *Mass Effect 1* and are thus uniquely qualified to become Commander Shepard's rival within the human military and government in *Mass Effect 3* due to their heroic status as a survivor of the Virmire mission. Given the complex romance subplots, the Virmire Survivor also remains the only character apart from Liara who can be cheated on in the sequels, a decision that is reflected in the last game of the trilogy.

Considering the Virmire Survivor's important role, BioWare arguably created the boldest statement of respect for player choices in modern video game history by keeping both characters in the spotlight (with the exception of *Mass Effect 2*). This dedication to the consequences of player choice is especially notable in the light of the *Mass Effect 3* ending controversy,[5] which is criticized particularly for lack of variety and actual player input, and the retconning of the deaths of major characters in BioWare's fantasy series *Dragon Age*. The Virmire Survivor serves not only as a motivation to replay the *Mass Effect Trilogy* to see different scenarios but first and foremost as a unique testament to the importance of player decisions in role-playing games as a form of co-creation of the gaming experience.

Similar Characters: Bethany/Carver Hawke (*Dragon Age II*), Carley/Doug (*The Walking Dead: Season One*), Vernon Roche/Iorveth (*The Witcher 2: Assassins of Kings*)

—Jan Švelch

W

WIZARDS AND WITCHES

(est. 1978)

Franchise: *MUD1*

Developer: Roy Trubshaw and Richard Bartle

Wizards and Witches are the highest-ranked players of MUDs, or Multi-User Dungeons. So great is their power and prestige, in fact, that they are granted powers that extend beyond the game, becoming, in effect, members of the development team. While these privileges and responsibilities vary widely from MUD to MUD, the core idea remains the same: MUDs are first and foremost communities, and it is fitting that the players themselves should play some role in governing them. This idea might seem improbable or even preposterous today, but it was quite in keeping with the hacker culture in which MUDs arose and flourished in the 1980s.

Becoming a Witch or Wizard—or "making wiz"—was no easy feat. The progenitor of modern massively multiplayer online role-playing games (MMORPGs) like *World of Warcraft*, MUDs were text-based games built largely on concepts that existed in the earlier *Colossal Cave Adventure* (1975) and *Zork* (1977). Like these games, MUDs relied on keyboard text inputs for interaction, such as "take sword" or "move west." What distinguished MUDs from these games was a rich culture of social interaction that gave players a great reason to continue playing long after they'd solved all the puzzles and "won" the game.[1]

But there was more to making wiz than solving adventure-game puzzles. Most significant was combat, as it helped advance a character's level as evidence of MUD expertise: "Killing mobiles and even other players is quite a popular pastime in MUD! . . . It is often said that survival is the hardest puzzle in the game."[2] As in tabletop role-playing or war games, victory or defeat often hinged on the roll of a (virtual) die, and death came often and swiftly, particularly to players foolish enough to venture off into dangerous areas alone.

More-experienced players soon learned the value of meeting and interacting with other players of the MUD. Friendships formed, and for many players, logging into a MUD became a primarily social activity such that making wiz could be advanced by building relationships. However, some players were more focused on combat than on socializing, so sudden, unprovoked duels to the death were frequent affairs. One way to avoid such a fate was simply to be polite and friendly at all times, but it helped to build alliances with like-minded players. In short, the very structure of the game made it difficult for an abusive player to get ahead and achieve Wizard or Witch status; the character would simply be killed by another player (or even a hastily assembled posse if necessary).

Player characters who managed to progress to the 12th level in a MUD had thus not only proven their expertise in the game but also a high level of trust, goodwill, and obligation in the community. They were expected to help newcomers and even to perform routine administrative procedures. Some were granted debugging powers to deal with "people forgetting passwords or some drunk wizard causing chaos."[3] Becoming a Wizard or Witch endowed characters with in-game powers such as flight, omniscience, and devastating attacks. One exemplar Witch was Sue, whom Richard Bartle, co-creator of *MUD1*, called "MUD's greatest player."[4] Sue was known for staying online nearly twenty-four hours a day, and she used her extensive knowledge of the game's inner workings to help out novices: she knew "just the right kind of hints to give" and had an "uncanny knack of making the game FUN to play."

The highest-ranking Wizards and Witches (Arch-Wizards and Arch-Witches) were even able to alter the physical models of the game world, creating new rooms or tampering with the "connectors" that led between spaces. In effect, Wizards became co-creators of the MUD with the original programmers, altering the spatial and social realities other players engaged during play. For these elevated characters, the game was never truly finished because the MUD could always be reconstructed, changed, and elaborated.

Though later versions and other MUDs altered the arrangement in various ways, the original intent was that anyone who had achieved enough points would be promoted to Wizard or Witch—a determinedly egalitarian structure. Indeed, early in the game's life, Bartle made MUDDL (the language used to code MUD) freely available in the public domain. According to Bartle, the impetus for this setup was his disgust with the entrenched inequity of the British university system of the 1970s and 1980s. An explicit goal of the level system in MUD was to repair the second-class status of computer science and other disciplines. "Computer science [was] regarded as a low thing," said Bartle in one interview, but in reality "computing didn't suck: computers were a form out, a way of freedom, and you found this a lot in what used to be called hacker culture. . . . We naturally bonded, all of us, together." The fundamentally democratic system of MUD formed a corrective to the more rigid, stratified social life most MUD players experienced. They were not precluded from aspects of the game because of accent, age, gender, race, or other visible markers. Instead, one gained status by being a supportive, skilled, and productive member of the community.

It's hard to imagine a similar scenario with modern MMORPGs. Imagine, for example, the chaos that would likely erupt if players who reached the highest level were suddenly able to ban or even delete the accounts of other players they disliked. The absurdity of this scenario reveals how much gamer culture has changed from the esoteric hacker culture of the early 1980s to today. If "freedom" was the mantra of that earlier era, "security" is the concern of the current era in which hackers are feared, not emulated. The Wizards and Witches of MUD are representatives of another time and culture, one unwilling to sacrifice liberty for security, and if we are not granted such powers in modern MMORPGs, perhaps we simply are not worthy.

Similar Characters: The Citizenry (*Habitat*), Lord British (*Ultima*), Player Corporations (*EVE Online*)

—Kyle McClure and Matt Barton

Z

ZELDA

(est. 1986)
Franchise: *The Legend of Zelda*
Developer: Nintendo R&D4

Princess Zelda is the titular character of Nintendo's *The Legend of Zelda* (*LoZ*) franchise, a series of action-adventure games first released in 1986, with seventeen subsequent games and spin-offs such as an animated series and manga adaptations. With a few exceptions, Zelda is a non-player character who appears in fifteen of the seventeen narrative *LoZ* titles and whom the player (as the hero Link) must save from her enemies. Zelda largely seems to support the player character Link as he follows the classic hero monomyth[1] by leaving his everyday life and being transformed by his adventures into a hero—but she is revealed to be much more: a manifestation of the feminine divine.

Princess Zelda has the pale skin, blond hair, blue eyes, and pink gowns expected of a royal damsel in distress. But in Zelda, we do not find a passive princess awaiting rescue; instead we discover a divine power who guides us in a quest. Her powers are manifest in the Triforce of Wisdom, part of the iconic trio of triangles that serves as a logo for the franchise. This artifact contains the essence of Nayru, the Goddess of Wisdom. Zelda's role is often akin to that of Campbell's "mentor," and she provides the wisdom, objects, and strength Link needs to complete his quest. But she is more than a deuteragonist, or second-most-important character, in the games' mythic quests. She is transformed too when she awakens (sometimes literally) to emerge in her divinely appointed role as ruler.

Although she rarely takes part in the game's fighting and puzzles, Zelda has a goddess-granted power over magic and over her kingdom that allows her to command narrative power as a primary motivator for the game's plot and events. For example, in some games—including *Oracle of Seasons*; *Oracle of Ages*; and *Four Swords*—she uses her prophetic knowledge of danger to instruct Link (and thus the player) in his quests and to set the story in motion. Her guidance, often derived from divine prophecy, provides Link with the strategies he needs to defeat the enemy (most often Ganon). Her powers function as a type of royal divine right similar to that in medieval and Renaissance Europe when royal power was seen as legitimized or granted by God. In ancient Japan, the emperor was seen as descended from the Shinto sun goddess Amaterasu, which allowed him to claim the title of the Son of Heaven and rule the country (see this book's entry on Amaterasu). Zelda's divinity likewise comes from her being descended from a goddess; in some games, her power comes from being a more Christian-like human incarnation of a goddess sent to earth. The 2011 *LoZ* title *Skyward Sword* explains that Hylia, the land's protector, has sacrificed her immortality to live as a human so that she could become Zelda and watch over Hyrule Kingdom, where the series is set. As Link, therefore, the player follows instructions and receives power from the divine through Zelda, a hint that Link's transformation into a hero is the will of the gods.

Zelda's divine association, the root of her royal identity and power, is sometimes hidden from the player and even from Zelda herself. Zelda is actually a different character in each game in the series, with different ages, appearances, roles, and personalities, and as such, we do not always recognize her immediately. She sometimes first appears in disguise; for example, as a childhood friend (in *Skyward Sword*), a pirate (in *Wind Waker* and *Phantom Hourglass*), and a warrior (in *Ocarina of Time*). When in disguise, Zelda takes on a different name and role (once even changing her gender), which temporarily strips her of her royal title and her divinity. In *Ocarina of Time*, she hides from the evil Ganondorf by masquerading as the mysterious and all-knowing Shiek, a male character dressed in a blue-and-black ninja uniform who fights at Link's side. Sheik is only revealed to be Zelda at the end of the game. This plot device is shared by the characters of many stories, ranging from J. R. R. Tolkien's Aragorn, who hides as Strider to avoid recognition and help the hobbit Frodo in his quest, to the classic Japanese story of Touyama no Kin-san, in which a public official disguises himself as a vagabond so he can fight against the corrupt and greedy. In another *LoZ* title, *Wind Waker*, Zelda helps Link throughout his adventures in the guise of the gruff and aggressive female pirate captain Tetra and is at the same time unaware of her royal heritage, much like a young King Arthur. Because of this, Zelda as Tetra cannot use her heavenly powers. It is not until Zelda discovers that she is the rightful heir to the Hylian throne that she regains her divine rights as princess, along with her feminine clothes and mystical powers. Once Zelda sheds her disguise in this, and in many of the other titles in the franchise, we realize that Zelda (and thus the divine) has been with us all along.

Instead of being positioned as a sexual object with strictly utilitarian value as are many heroines, Zelda is, like the hero Link, a character in progress[2] who grows throughout each game of the series. Zelda uses the visual and verbal markers of alternative identities to move herself away from an essentialist construction of the princess as prize to be won in favor of a new set of abilities and roles. When rejecting the princess role, Zelda can also reject its associated gender proscriptions and become a fighter, a pirate, or an adventuring commoner, but she is also cut off from her divine rights and powers. She must return to her jeweled pink dresses and perform her femininity as proscribed by traditional gender roles[3] in order to regain access to her divinely appointed royal power and feminine mysticism. Zelda follows her own heroic journey that is just as important as Link's adventures in saving the land of Hyrule and completing the story, but she does so alongside the player instead of at the player's command.

Similar Characters: Althena/Luna (*Lunar Silver Star Story*), Amaterasu (*Ōkami*), Ashe (*Final Fantasy XII*)

—Kimberly Kandra and Rosa Mikeal Martey

Appendix

Video Game Characters by Category

DEVELOPER[1]

Activision Blizzard: Leeroy Jenkins, the Lich King, Orc Peon, Sergeant Paul Jackson, Tiffi

Bandai Namco: King of All Cosmos, KOS-MOS, Pac-Man

Bethesda: Hitler, the Last Dragonborn

Capcom: Amaterasu, Chun-Li, Mega Man, Phoenix Wright, Ryu, Sheva Alomar

Electronic Arts: Commander Shepard, HK-47, Isaac Clarke, Jon Dowd, Kane, Lord British, Michael Vick, the Virmire Survivor

Konami: Psycho Mantis, Pyramid Head, Raiden, Solid Snake

LucasArts: Bobbin Threadbare, Elaine Marley

Microsoft: the Creature, Master Chief, Steve

Midway: President Bill Clinton, Sub-Zero

Nintendo: Birdo, Bowser Koopa, Kirby, Link, Mario, MissingNo., Ness, Pikachu, Samus Aran, Soda Popinski, Zelda

Other: Alice, the Alien, AM, the Announcer, the Ball, Bard, Bayonetta, Capsuleer, the Darfurians, Duke Nukem, Dysentery, Grues, I-Block, Isaac, Kim Kardashian, Leisure Suit Larry, Life, Max Payne, Mr. Torgue, the Narrator, the Scythian, Shadowlord Nier, SHODAN, Solaire of Astora, Tecmo Bo Jackson, Vault Boy, Wizards and Witches

Sega: Catherine, Sonic

Sony: the Colossi, Crash Bandicoot, Ellie, Honda Civic, Joel, Kratos, Parappa, Sackboy

Square Enix: Aerith Gainsborough, Cloud Strife, the Invaders, Lara Croft, Terra Branford

Take-Two Interactive: Atlas, Big Daddy, Gandhi, John Marston, the Police

Telltale Games: Clementine, Lee Everett

Ubisoft: Desmond Miles, Jade

Valve: GLaDOS, Gordon Freeman

FIRST APPEARANCE

1970–1974: Ball
1975–1979: Dysentery, Grues, the Invaders, Lord British, Wizards and Witches
1980–1984: the Alien, I-Block, Mario, Pac-Man

1985–1989: Birdo, Bowser Koopa, Leisure Suit Larry, Link, Mega Man, Ryu, Samus Aran, Soda Popinski, Solid Snake, Tecmo Bo Jackson, Zelda

1990–1994: Bobbin Threadbare, Chun-Li, Duke Nukem, Elaine Marley, Gandhi, Hitler, Kirby, Life, Ness, Orc Peon, President Bill Clinton, SHODAN, Sonic, Sub-Zero, Terra Branford

1995–1999: AM, Aerith Gainsborough, the Announcer, Cloud Strife, Crash Bandicoot, Gordon Freeman, Honda Civic, Kane, Lara Croft, MissingNo., Parappa, Pikachu, the Police, Psycho Mantis, Vault Boy

2000–2004: Alice, Capsuleer, the Creature, HK-47, Jade, Jon Dowd, King of All Cosmos, KOS-MOS, Leeroy Jenkins, the Lich King, Master Chief, Max Payne, Michael Vick, Phoenix Wright, Pyramid Head, Raiden

2005–2009: Amaterasu, Atlas, Bayonetta, Big Daddy, the Colossi, Commander Shepard, the Darfurians, Desmond Miles, GLaDOS, Isaac Clarke, Kratos, Sackboy, Sergeant Paul Jackson, Sheva Alomar, the Virmire Survivor

2010–2015: Bard, Captain Martin Walker, Catherine, Clementine, Ellie, Isaac, Joel, John Marston, Kim Kardashian, the Last Dragonborn, Lee Everett, Mr. Torgue, the Narrator, the Scythian, Shadowlord Nier, Solaire of Astora, Steve, Tiffi

GENRE[2]

Action-Adventure: Alice, Amaterasu, Bayonetta, the Colossi, Desmond Miles, Ellie, Isaac, Jade, Joel, John Marston, Kratos, Lara Croft, Life, Link, Mega Man, the Police, Psycho Mantis, Raiden, Samus Aran, the Scythian, Shadowlord Nier, Solaire of Astora, Solid Snake, Zelda

Casual: Kim Kardashian

Fighting: Chun-Li, Ryu, Sub-Zero

First-Person Shooter (FPS): the Announcer, Atlas, Big Daddy, Captain Martin Walker, Duke Nukem, Gordon Freeman, Hitler, Isaac Clarke, Master Chief, Max Payne, Sergeant Paul Jackson

Japanese Role-Playing Game (JRPG): Aerith Gainsborough, Cloud Strife, KOS-MOS, MissingNo., Ness, Pikachu, Terra Branford

Massively Multiplayer Online Role-Playing Game (MMORPG): Capsuleer, Leeroy Jenkins, the Lich King

Maze: the Alien, Pac-Man

Multiplayer Online Battle Arena (MOBA): Bard

Multi-User Dungeon: Wizards and Witches

Platformer: Birdo, Bowser Koopa, Crash Bandicoot, Kirby, Mario, Sackboy, Sonic

Puzzle: Catherine, GLaDOS, I-Block, King of All Cosmos, Tiffi

Racing: Honda Civic

Real-Time Strategy (RTS): Kane, Orc Peon

Rhythm: Parappa

Role-Playing Game (RPG): Commander Shepard, HK-47, the Last Dragonborn, Lord British, Mr. Torgue, SHODAN, Vault Boy, the Virmire Survivor

Sandbox: Steve

Serious: the Darfurians

Shooter: the Invaders

Simulation: the Creature, Dysentery, Gandhi
Sports: the Ball, Jon Dowd, Michael Vick, President Bill Clinton, Soda Popinski, Tecmo Bo Jackson
Survival Horror: Pyramid Head, Sheva Alomar
Text/Graphic Adventure: AM, Bobbin Threadbare, Clementine, Elaine Marley, Lee Everett, Grues, Leisure Suit Larry, the Narrator, Phoenix Wright

ORIGINAL PLATFORM

Arcade: the Ball, Chun-Li, the Invaders, Pac-Man, President Bill Clinton, Ryu, Soda Popinski, Sub-Zero, Tecmo Bo Jackson
Atari: the Alien
Facebook: Tiffi
Flash: the Darfurians
Mobile: Kim Kardashian
Multiplatform: Captain Martin Walker, Catherine, Clementine, Desmond Miles, Isaac Clarke, Jade, John Marston, Jon Dowd, Lara Croft, the Last Dragonborn, Lee Everett, Michael Vick, Mr. Torgue, Sergeant Paul Jackson, Shadowlord Nier, Sheva Alomar, Solaire of Astora
Nintendo: Birdo, Bowser Koopa, Kirby, Life, Link, Mario, Mega Man, MissingNo., Ness, Phoenix Wright, Pikachu, Samus Aran, Zelda
PC: Alice, AM, the Announcer, Atlas, Bard, Big Daddy, Bobbin Threadbare, Capsuleer, the Creature, Duke Nukem, Dysentery, Elaine Marley, Gandhi, GLaDOS, Gordon Freeman, Grues, Hitler, I-Block, Isaac, Kane, Leeroy Jenkins, Leisure Suit Larry, the Lich King, Lord British, Max Payne, the Narrator, Orc Peon, the Police, the Scythian, SHODAN, Solid Snake, Steve, Vault Boy, Wizards and Witches
PlayStation: Aerith Gainsborough, Amaterasu, Cloud Strife, the Colossi, Crash Bandicoot, Ellie, Honda Civic, Joel, King of All Cosmos, KOS-MOS, Kratos, Parappa, Psycho Mantis, Pyramid Head, Raiden, Sackboy, Terra Branford
Sega: Sonic
Xbox: Commander Shepard, HK-47, Master Chief, the Virmire Survivor

STUDIO HEADQUARTERS

Canada: Commander Shepard, Desmond Miles, HK-47, Jon Dowd, the Scythian, the Virmire Survivor
England: the Creature, Lara Croft,[3] Sackboy, Wizards and Witches
Finland: Max Payne
France: Jade
Germany: Captain Martin Walker
Iceland: Capsuleer
Japan: Aerith Gainsborough, Amaterasu, Bayonetta, Birdo, Bowser Koopa, Catherine, Chun-Li, Cloud Strife, the Colossi, Honda Civic, the Invaders, King of All Cosmos, Kirby, KOS-MOS, Life, Link, Mario, Mega Man, MissingNo., Ness,

Pac-Man, Parappa, Phoenix Wright, Pikachu, Psycho Mantis, Pyramid Head, Raiden, Ryu, Samus Aran, Shadowlord Nier, Sheva Alomar, Soda Popinski, Solaire of Astora, Solid Snake, Sonic, Tecmo Bo Jackson, Terra Branford, Zelda

Russia: I-Block

Scotland: the Police

Sweden: Steve, Tiffi

United States: Alice, the Alien, AM, the Announcer,[4] Atlas,[5] the Ball, Bard, Big Daddy,[6] Bobbin Threadbare, Clementine, Crash Bandicoot, the Darfurians, Duke Nukem, Dysentery, Elaine Marley, Ellie, Gandhi, GLaDOS, Gordon Freeman, Grues, Hitler, Isaac, Isaac Clarke, Joel, John Marston, Kane, Kim Kardashian, Kratos, the Last Dragonborn, Lee Everett, Leeroy Jenkins, Leisure Suit Larry, the Lich King, Lord British, Master Chief, Michael Vick, Mr. Torgue, the Narrator, Orc Peon, Sergeant Paul Jackson, President Bill Clinton, SHODAN, Sub-Zero, Vault Boy

GENDER

Indeterminate: the Alien, AM, the Colossi, the Creature, Grues, the Invaders, Life, MissingNo., Pikachu

Female: Aerith Gainsborough, Alice, Amaterasu, Bayonetta, Catherine, Chun-Li, Clementine, Elaine Marley, Ellie, GLaDOS, Jade, Kim Kardashian, KOS-MOS, Lara Croft, Samus Aran, the Scythian, Sheva Alomar, SHODAN, Terra Branford, Tiffi, Zelda

Male: the Announcer, Atlas, Bard, Big Daddy, Bobbin Threadbare, Bowser Koopa, Captain Martin Walker, Cloud Strife, Crash Bandicoot, Duke Nukem, Gandhi, Gordon Freeman, Hitler, Isaac, Isaac Clarke, Joel, John Marston, Jon Dowd, Kane, King of All Cosmos, Kirby, Kratos, Lee Everett, Leeroy Jenkins, Leisure Suit Larry, the Lich King, Link, Lord British, Mario, Master Chief, Max Payne, Mega Man, Michael Vick, the Narrator, Ness, Orc Peon, Pac-Man, Phoenix Wright, the Police, President Bill Clinton, Psycho Mantis, Pyramid Head, Raiden, Ryu, Sackboy, Sergeant Paul Jackson, Soda Popinski, Solaire of Astora, Solid Snake, Sonic, Sub-Zero, Tecmo Bo Jackson, Vault Boy

Non-Applicable: the Ball, Dysentery, Honda Civic, I-Block

Player-Selected: Capsuleer, Commander Shepard, the Darfurians, the Last Dragonborn, the Virmire Survivor, Wizards and Witches

Transgender: Birdo

RACE[7]

Asian – East Asian: Chun-Li, Ryu, Sub-Zero

Asian – South Asian: Gandhi

Black: the Darfurians, Lee Everett, Leeroy Jenkins, Michael Vick, Sheva Alomar, Tecmo Bo Jackson

Eastern European: Soda Popinski

Indeterminate: the Announcer, Big Daddy, King of All Cosmos, the Narrator, Orc Peon, the Police, Pyramid Head, the Scythian, Sergeant Paul Jackson

Not-applicable: the Alien, AM, Amaterasu, the Ball, Bard, Birdo, Bobbin Threadbare, Bowser Koopa, the Colossi, Crash Bandicoot, the Creature, Dysentery, GLaDOS, Grues, HK-47, Honda Civic, I-Block, the Invaders, Kirby, Life, MissingNo., Pac-Man, Parappa, Pikachu, Sackboy, SHODAN, Sonic, Tiffi, Wizards and Witches

Multiracial: Aerith Gainsborough, Clementine, Desmond Miles, Jade, Kim Kardashian, Terra Branford

Player-Selected: Capsuleer, Commander Shepard, the Last Dragonborn, the Virmire Survivor

White: Alice, Atlas, Bayonetta, Captain Martin Walker, Catherine, Cloud Strife, Duke Nukem, Elaine Marley, Ellie, Gordon Freeman, Hitler, Isaac Clarke, Joel, John Marston, Jon Dowd, Kane, Kratos, Lara Croft, Leisure Suit Larry, Link, Lord British, Mario, Master Chief, Max Payne, Mega Man, Mr. Torgue, Ness, Phoenix Wright, President Bill Clinton, Psycho Mantis, Raiden, Samus Aran, Shadowlord Nier, Solaire of Astora, Solid Snake, Steve, Vault Boy, the Lich King, Zelda

SPECIES

Alien: the Alien, the Invaders

Animal: Crash Bandicoot, Parappa, Sonic

Creature: Birdo, Bowser Koopa, Grues, Kirby, Life, MissingNo., Orc Peon, Pikachu, Tiffi

Cyborg/Synthetic Human: Big Daddy, Capsuleer, Raiden, Shadowlord Nier

Deity: Amaterasu, King of All Cosmos, Kratos, Solaire of Astora

Disease: Dysentery

Human: Alice, Atlas, Captain Martin Walker, Chun-Li, Clementine, Cloud Strife, the Darfurians, Desmond Miles, Duke Nukem, Elaine Marley, Ellie, Gandhi, Gordon Freeman, Hitler, Isaac, Isaac Clarke, Jade, Joel, John Marston, Jon Dowd, Kim Kardashian, Lara Croft, Lee Everett, Leisure Suit Larry, Lord British, Mario, Master Chief, Max Payne, Michael Vick, Mr. Torgue, Ness, Phoenix Wright, the Police, President Bill Clinton, Psycho Mantis, Ryu, Samus Aran, the Scythian, Sergeant Paul Jackson, Sheva Alomar, Soda Popinski, Solid Snake, Steve, Sub-Zero, Tecmo Bo Jackson, the Virmire Survivor, Wizards and Witches

Indeterminate: the Announcer, the Narrator, Pac-Man, Sackboy

Magical/Spiritual Being: Aerith Gainsborough, Bard, Bayonetta, Bobbin Threadbare, Catherine, the Colossi, the Creature, Kane, the Last Dragonborn, the Lich King, Link, Pyramid Head, Terra Branford, Zelda

Object: the Ball, Honda Civic, I-Block, Vault Boy

Robot: AM, GLaDOS, HK-47, KOS-MOS, Mega Man, SHODAN

Notes

INTRODUCTION

1. Kenneth Burke, *The Philosophy of Literary Form*, 3rd ed. (Berkeley: University of California Press, 1974).
2. Tom Boellstrorff, *Coming of Age in Second Life* (Princeton, NJ: Princeton University Press, 2008), 19.
3. Bob Rehak, "Playing at Being," in *The Video Game Theory Reader*, ed. Mark J. P. Wolf and Bernard Perron (New York: Routledge, 2003), 103–4.

A

1. "Top 100 Video Game Moments," IGN, www.ign.com/top/video-game-moments/1.
2. "Afterthoughts | Final Fantasy VII. Interview with Yoshinori Kitase and Tetsuya Nomura," *Electronic Gaming Monthly* 196, October 2005, www.ff7citadel.com/press/int_sakaguchi.shtml.
3. Shelley Budgeon, "Individualized Femininity and Feminist Politics of Choice," *European Journal of Women's Studies* 22 (March 2015): 303–18, doi:10.1177/1350506815576602.
4. Entertainment Software Association. "Essential Facts about the Computer and Video Game Industry," 2015, www.theesa.com/wp-content/uploads/2015/04/ESA-Essential-Facts-2015.pdf.
5. See note 1.
6. See note 2.
7. Ian Nathan, *Alien Vault: The Definitive Story of the Making of the Film* (London: Voyageur, 2011).
8. Andy McVittie, *The Art of Alien: Isolation* (London: Titan Books, 2014).
9. Roger Luckhurst, *Alien* (London: British Film Institute, 2014).
10. Harlan Ellison, *I Have No Mouth, and I Must Scream* (New York: Galaxy Publishing, 1967), http://hermiene.net/short-stories/i_have_no_mouth.html.
11. Darren Harris-Fain, "Created in the Image of God: The Narrator and the Computer in Harlan Ellison's 'I Have No Mouth, and I Must Scream,'" *Extrapolation* 32 (1991): 143–55.
12. Karen Schrier, "The Weird Humanity of I Have No Mouth and I Must Scream," *Well Played* 3, no. 2 (2014): 145–66, http://press.etc.cmu.edu/files/WellPlayed-v3n2-14-web.pdf.
13. Stuart D. B. Picken, *Historical Dictionary of Shinto* (Lanham, MD: Scarecrow Press, 2011).
14. Heidi A. Campbell and Gregory P. Grieve, eds., *Playing with Religion in Digital Games* (Bloomington: Indiana University, 2014).
15. Capcom, *Okami Official Complete Works*, trans. Hayashi Kirie (Richmond Hill, Ontario: Udon Entertainment, 2008), 107–217.

16. See note 2.

17. See note 1.

18. Ian Bogost, "Persuasive Games: Video Game Zen," Gamasutra, www.gamasutra .com/view/feature/130994/persuasive_games_video_game_zen.php.

19. Trent Ward, "Unreal Tournament," IGN, 1999, www.ign.com/articles/1999/12/07/ unreal-tournament-6.

20. Charles F. Bond and Linda J. Titus, "Social Facilitation: A Meta-Analysis of 241 Studies," *Psychological Bulletin* 94, no. 2 (1983): 265–92.

21. Nicholas D. Bowman, Rene Weber, Ron Tamborni, and John Sherry, "Facilitating Game Play: How Others Affect Performance at and Enjoyment of Video Games," *Media Psychology* 16 (2013): 39–64.

22. Sonja K. Foss, Karen A. Foss, and Robert Trapp, *Contemporary Perspectives on Rhetoric* (Prospect Heights, IL: Waveland, 1991).

23. Richard A. Bartle, *Designing Virtual Worlds* (Berkeley, CA: New Riders, 2004).

24. Louis Althusser, "Ideology and Ideological State Apparatuses (Notes towards an Investigation)," in *Media and Cultural Studies: KeyWorks*, ed. Meenakshi Gigi Durham and Douglas M. Kellner (Malden, MA: Blackwell, 2006), 79–88.

B

1. Henry Lowood, "Videogames in Computer Space: The Complex History of Pong," *IEEE Annals of the History of Computing* 31, no. 3 (2009): 5–19, doi:10.1109/MAHC.2009.53.

2. Ian Bogost and Nick Montfort, *Racing the Beam: The Atari Video Computer System* (Cambridge, MA: MIT Press, 2009).

3. Michel Serres, *The Parasite* (Minneapolis: University of Minnesota Press, 2007).

4. Jeffery Lin, "More Science Behind Player Behavior in Online Games," paper presented at the HarvardX Conference, Cambridge, Massachusetts, March 13, 2015, www.gd cvault.com/play/1022160/More-Science-Behind-Shaping-Player.

5. British Psychological Society, "Listening to Your Favorite Music Boosts Performance," ScienceDaily, 2012, www.sciencedaily.com/releases/2012/04/120417221709.htm.

6. John L. Sherry, "Flow and Media Enjoyment," *Communication Theory* 14, no. 4 (2004): 328–47.

7. Esther MacCallum-Stewart, "'Take That, Bitches!' Refiguring Lara Croft in Feminist Game Narratives," *Game Studies* 14, no. 2 (2014), http://gamestudies.org/1402/articles/ maccallumstewart.

8. Joel Gwynne, "Japan, Postfeminism and the Consumption of Sexual(ised) Schoolgirls in Male-Authored Contemporary Manga," *Feminist Theory* 14, no. 3 (2013): 325–43, doi:10.1177/1464700113499854.

9. See note 1.

10. Michael Clarkson, "BioShock," LudoNarratology, 2009, http://ludo.mwclarkson .com/2009/04/critical-thinking-compilation-bioshock.

11. Johnny Minkley, "The Big Daddy Speaks," Eurogamer, 2007, www.eurogamer.net/ articles/big-daddy-speaks-interview?page=2.

12. Stephen Totilo, "The Daddening of Video Games," Kotaku, 2010, http://kotaku.com/ 5467695/the-daddening-of-video-games.

13. VorpalBunny, "Queer Characters: Birdo," GayGamer, 2011, http://gaygamer.net/ 2011/04/queer_characters_birdo.html.

14. Chris Kohler, "Captain Rainbow: Birdo's Gender Crisis," Wired, 2015, www.wired .com/2008/08/captain-rainb-1.

15. Austen Crowder, "Videogame Censorship, LGBT, and Birdo (Part III)," Bilerico Project, 2009, www.bilerico.com/2009/12/videogame_censorship_lgbt_and_birdo_part_iii.php.

16. Jaroslav Švelch, "The Pleasurable Lightness of Being: Interface, Mediation and Meta-Narrative in Lucasfilm's Loom," *Eludamos* 3, no. 1 (2009): 95–102.

17. Brian Moriarty, personal communication, January 3, 2016.

18. Brian Moriarty, "Classic Game Postmortem: Lucasfilm Games' Loom," paper presented at the Game Developers Conference, San Francisco, March 3, 2015, http://gdcvault.com/play/1021862/Classic-Game-Postmortem.

19. See note 1.

20. See note 2.

21. Jeff Ryan, *Super Mario: How Nintendo Conquered America* (New York: Penguin, 2011), 67.

22. Bob Chipman, *Super Mario Bros. 3: Brick by Brick* (Tucson: Fangamer, 2013), 202.

23. "Why Mario Is Secretly a Dick with a Mustache," YouTube video, directed by Justin Viar, posted by Cracked, April 17, 2012, www.youtube.com/watch?v=HBGhWYGVp8Q.

C

1. "The Capsule and the Clone," EVE Community, https://community.eveonline.com/backstory/scientific-articles/ppcc-part-1-the-capsule-and-the-clone.

2. Erik Kain, "Massive EVE Online Battle Could Cost $300,000 in Real Money," *Forbes*, www.forbes.com/sites/erikkain/2014/01/29/massive-eve-online-battle-could-cost-500000-in-real-money.

3. Tom Francis, "Murder Incorporated: Ten Months of Deception for One Kill in EVE Online," PCGamer, 2015, www.pcgamer.com/murder-incorporated-ten-months-of-deception-for-one-kill-in-eve-online.

4. Joseph Conrad, *Heart of Darkness*, ed. Owen Knowles and Robert Hampson (London: Penguin, 2007).

5. Ian Bogost, "Persuasive Games: Video Game Zen," Gamasutra, www.gamasutra.com/view/feature/130994/persuasive_games_video_game_zen.php.

6. Angela McRobbie, "Post-Feminism and Popular Culture," *Feminist Media Studies* 4, no. 3 (2004): 256–64.

7. David Auerbach, "The Most Sexist Video Game of All Time?" Slate, 2014, www.slate.com/articles/technology/bitwise/2014/07/catherine_video_game_the_most_sexist_platformer_of_all_time.html.

8. Judith Butler, *Gender Trouble: Feminism and the Subversion of Identity* (New York: Routledge, 1990).

9. Matt Leone, "Street Fighter II: An Oral History," Polygon, 2014, www.polygon.com/a/street-fighter-2-oral-history/chapter-2.

10. Christopher G. Williams. "Chun Li's Thighs," PopMatters, 2010, www.popmatters.com/post/129312-chun-lis-thighs.

11. Kristina Bell, Nicholas Taylor, and Christopher Kampe, "Of Headshots and Hugs: Challenging Hypermasculinity through Walking Dead Play," *Ada: A Journal of Gender, New Media, and Technology* 7 (2015), http://adanewmedia.org/2015/04/issue7-bellkampetaylor.

12. Jess Joho, "The Dadification of Video Games, Round Two," Kill Screen, 2014, https://killscreen.com/articles/dadification-videogames-round-two.

13. Adrienne Shaw, *Gaming at the Edge: Sexuality and Gender at the Margins of Gamer Culture* (Minneapolis: University of Minnesota Press, 2015).

14. Nola Alloway and Pam Gilbert, "Video Game Culture: Playing with Masculinity, Violence, and Pleasure," in *Wired-Up: Young People and the Electronic Media*, ed. Sue Howard (London: UCL Press, 1998), 93–113.

15. Yoko Sugihara and Emiko Katsurada, "Gender Role Development in Japanese Culture: Diminishing Gender Role Differences in a Contemporary Society," *Sex Roles* 47 no. 9 (2002): 443–52.

16. Katherine Mezur, *Beautiful Boys/Outlaw Bodies: Devising Kabuki Female-Likeness* (New York: Palgrave Macmillan, 2005).

17. J. M. van der Laan, *Seeking Meaning for Goethe's* Faust (London: Continuum, 2007).

18. Jennifer deWinter, *Shigeru Miyamoto: Super Mario Bros., Donkey Kong, The Legend of Zelda* (London: Bloomsbury Academic, 2015).

19. James Mielke, "Design by Subtraction: The Bare Essence of Game Design, with Fumito Ueda," 1UP, 2005, www.1up.com/features/design-by-subtraction?pager.offset=0.

20. Joshua Tanenbaum, "Being in the Story: Readerly Pleasure, Acting Theory, and Performing a Role," in *Interactive Storytelling*, ed. Mei Si, David Thue, Elisabeth Andre, James C. Lester, Joshua Tanenbaum, and Veronica Zammitto (Heidelberg: Springer Berlin Heidelberg, 2011), 55–66.

21. Kristine Jørgensen, "Game Characters as Narrative Devices. A Comparative Analysis of Dragon Age: Origins and Mass Effect 2," *Eludamos* 4, no. 2 (2010): 315–31.

22. Christopher B. Patterson, "Role-Playing the Multiculturalist Umpire: Loyalty and War in BioWare's Mass Effect Series," *Games and Culture* 10, no. 3 (2015): 223.

23. "G4 Icons Episode #34: Naughty Dog," YouTube video, posted by G4Icons, www.youtube.com/watch?v=pV7Pqj7hKhM.

24. Domenico Leonardi, "Il dietro le quinte di Crash Bandicoot," PlayStation Generation, 2015, www.playstationgeneration.it/p/making-of-crash-bandicoot.html.

25. Carolyn C. Goren, Merrill Sarty, and Paul Y. K. Wu, "Visual Following and Pattern Discrimination of Face-like Stimuli by Newborn Infants," *Pediatrics* 56 (1975): 544–49.

26. Jaime Banks, "Object, Me, Symbiote, Other: A Social Typology of Player-Avatar Relationships," *First Monday* 20, no. 2 (2015), http://firstmonday.org/ojs/index.php/fm/article/view/5433/4208.

27. Jackmix, "What Is THE Funniest Thing(s) Your Creature Does," BWFiles, 2009, www.bwfiles.com/forum/index.php?topic=703.60.

28. "25 Most Overrated Games of All Time," Gamespy, 2003, http://web.archive.org/web/20090716182813/http://archive.gamespy.com/articles/september03/25overrated/index26.shtml.

D

1. Rebecca Hamilton, *Fighting for Darfur: Public Action and the Struggle to Stop Genocide* (New York: Palgrave Macmillan, 2011).

2. Mahmood Mamdani, *Saviors and Survivors: Darfur, Politics and the War on Terror* (New York: Doubleday, 2009).

3. Michio Kaku, *The Future of the Mind: The Scientific Quest to Understand, Enhance, and Empower the Mind* (New York: Doubleday, 2014).

4. Ray Kurzweil, *The Singularity Is Near: When Humans Transcend Biology* (New York: Viking Press, 2005).

5. Michael Harradence, "PS3's Top 5 Worst Protagonists," PlayStation Universe, 2012, www.psu.com/feature/15403/PS3s-top-5-worst-protagonists.

6. Ronald Reagan, "Address to the Veterans of Foreign Wars Convention," speech at the Veterans Foreign Wars Convention, Chicago, Illinois, August 18, 1980, American Presidency Project, www.presidency.ucsb.edu/ws/?pid=85202.

7. "Grand Theft Auto III: Your Questions Answered—Part One (Claude, Darkel & Other Characters)," Rockstar Games, 2011, www.rockstargames.com/newswire/article/19861/grand-theftauto-iii-your-questions-answered-part-one-claude-dar.html.

8. Nick Ragsdale, "Dysentery," in *Encyclopedia of Pestilence, Pandemics, and Plagues*, ed. Joseph P. Byrne, 173–76 (Westport, CT: Greenwood Press, 2008).

9. Lisbeth Klastrup, "Why Death Matters: Understanding Gameworld Experience," *Journal of Virtual Reality and Broadcasting* 4, no. 3 (2007).

10. Priscilla Wald, *Contagious: Cultures, Carriers, and the Outbreak Narrative* (Duke, NC: Duke University Press, 2007).

11. Ibid.

E

1. Clara Fernández-Vara, "The Secret of Monkey Island: Playing Between Cultures," in ed. Drew Davidson, *Well Played 1.0 Video Games, Value and Meaning* (Pittsburgh: ETC Press, 2009), 331–52.

2. Esther MacCallum-Stewart, "Real Boys Carry Girl Epics: Normalising Gender Bending in Online Games," *Eludamos* 2, no. 1 (2008): 27–40.

3. Anastasia Salter, *What Is Your Quest? From Adventure Games to Interactive Books* (Iowa City: University of Iowa Press, 2014).

4. "From Dreams—The Making of The Last of Us: Left Behind," YouTube video, posted by PlayStation, February 28, 2014, www.youtube.com/watch?v=v7WEeNH_C2I.

5. Carlo Maiolini, Stefano De Paoli, and Maurizio Teli, "Digital Games and the Communication of Health Problems: A Review of Games Against the Concept of Procedural Rhetoric," *Game: The Italian Journal of Game Studies* 1 (2012), www.gamejournal.it/digital-games-and-the-communication-of-health-problems-a-review-of-games-against-the-concept-of-procedural-rhetoric.

G

1. Andrew Fiala, "Pacifism," *Stanford Encyclopedia of Philosophy*, http://plato.stanford.edu/archives/win2014/entries/pacifism.

2. Luke Plunkett, "Why Gandhi Is Such an Asshole in Civilization," Kotaku, http://kotaku.com/why-gandhi-is-such-an-asshole-in-civilization-1653818245.

3. Jacob, "Nuclear Gandhi," Know Your Meme, http://knowyourmeme.com/memes/nuclear-gandhi.

4. Frank Biocca, Chad Harms, and Judee K. Burgoon, "Toward a More Robust Theory and Measure of Social Presence: Review and Suggested Criteria," *Presence* 12, no. 5 (2003): 456–80, doi:10.1162/105474603322761270.

5. Gary Pettey, Cheryl Campanella Bracken, Bridget Rubenking, Michael Buncher, and Erika Gress, "Telepresence, Soundscapes, and Technological Expectation: Putting the Observer into the Equation," *Virtual Reality* 14, no. 1 (2010): 15–25, doi:10.1007/s10055-009-0148-8.

6. Masahiro Mori, "The Uncanny Valley," *Energy* 7 (2012) 33–35, http://spectrum.ieee.org/automaton/robotics/humanoids/the-uncanny-valley.

7. Christoph Klimmt, Dorothée Hefner, Peter Vorderer, Christian Roth, and Christopher Blake, "Identification with Video Game Characters as Automatic Shift of Self-Perceptions," *Media Psychology* 13 (4): 323–38.

8. Hazel Markus and Paula Nurius, "Possible Selves," *American Psychologist* 41, no. 9 (1986): 954–69.

9. Dmitri Williams, Nicole Martins, Mia Consalvo, and James D. Ivory, "The Virtual Census: Representations of Gender, Race and Age in Video Games," *New Media & Society* 11, no. 5 (2009): 815–34.

10. Nick Montfort, *Twisty Little Passages: An Approach to Interactive Fiction* (Cambridge, MA: MIT Press, 2005), 8.

11. Jason Scott, dir., *Get Lamp* (Bovine Ignition Systems, 2010), DVD.

H

1. Steven L. Kent, *The Ultimate History of Video Games: From Pong to Pokémon—The Story Behind the Craze That Touched Our Lives and Changed the World* (New York: Three Rivers Press, 2001).

2. Emily Asher-Perrin, "Feral Ewoks and Other Disturbing Things That Star Wars Slides Right By Us," Tor.com, 2013, www.tor.com/2013/07/18/feral-ewoks-and-other-disturbing-things-that-star-wars-slides-right-by-us.

3. Andrew Webster, "Street Legal: How 'Gran Turismo' Helped Toyota Design Its New Concept Car," TheVerge, 2014, www.theverge.com/2014/1/13/5290600/toyota-ft-1-concept-car-gran-turismo-6.

4. Kazunori Yamauchi, "Regarding Engine Sounds of Gran Turismo: (Part 2)," PitStop, 2014, http://pitstop.gran-turismo.com/en/article/37.

5. Heli Vaaranen, "The Emotional Experience of Class: Interpreting Working-Class Kids' Street Racing in Helsinki," *Annals of the American Academy of Political and Social Science* 91, no. 595 (2004).

I

1. Steve Semrad, "The Greatest 200 Videogames of Their Time," 1UP, 2006, www.1up.com/features/egm-200-greatest-videogames?pager.offset=0.

2. David M. Boje, "Breaking Out of Narrative's Prison: Improper Story in Storytelling Organization," *Storytelling, Self, Society* 2, no. 2 (2006): 28–49, doi:10.1080/15505340.2006.10387472.

3. Ibid.

4. Sherry Turkle, *Alone Together: Why We Expect More from Technology and Less from Each Other* (New York: Basic Books, 2011).

5. Nicholas Epley, Adam Waytz, and John T. Cacioppo, "On Seeing Human: A Three-Factor Theory of Anthropomorphism," *Psychological Review* 114, no. 4 (2007): 880.

6. Susan J. Napier, "Confronting Master Narratives: History as Vision in Miyazaki Hayao's Cinema of De-Assurance," *Positions* 9, no. 2 (2001).

7. Ibid., 470.

8. Arthur Chu, "A Defense of Binding of Isaac from a Former Fundamentalist Christian," Polygon, 2015, www.polygon.com/2015/1/26/7907061/binding-isaac-fundamentalism.

9. Edmund McMillen, "Postmortem: McMillen and Himsl's *The Binding of Isaac*," Gamasutra, 2012, www.gamasutra.com/view/feature/182380/postmortem_mcmillen_and_himsls_.php?page=1.

10. Ibid.

11. Owen S. Good, "Apple Rejects The Binding of Isaac: Rebirth Because of 'Violence towards Children,'" Polygon, 2016, www.polygon.com/2016/2/7/10930230/the-binding-of-isaac-ios-mobile-rejected-apple.

12. Judith L. Herman, *Trauma and Recovery: The Aftermath of Violence—From Domestic Abuse to Political Terror* (New York: Basic Books, 2015).

13. Ibid.

J

1. Fredric Jameson, *Postmodernism, or, the Cultural Logic of Late Capitalism* (Durham, NC: Duke University Press, 1991).

2. Neil Druckmann, "The Last of Us: Writing Honestly," remarks at the International Game Developers Association Meeting, Toronto, Canada, October 2013, www.youtube.com/watch?v=Le6qIz7MjSk.

3. See note 1.

4. Émile Durkheim, "The Dualism of Human Nature," in *On Morality and Society*, ed. Robert N. Bellah (Chicago: University of Chicago Press, 1973), 149–63.

5. Ian Bogost, *Persuasive Games: The Expressive Power of Videogames* (Cambridge, MA: MIT Press, 2010).

6. James Newman, "The Myth of the Ergodic Videogame: Some Thoughts on Player-Character Relationships in Videogames," *Game Studies* 2, no. 1 (2002), http://gamestudies.org/0102/newman.

7. Jon Robinson, "Fast 5: Best Video Game Fictional Athletes," ESPN, 2013, http://espn.go.com/blog/playbook/tech/post/_/id/4743/fast-5-best-video-game-fictional-athletes.

8. Jon Star, "The 15 Best Players in Sports Video Game History," Bleacher Report, 2010, http://bleacherreport.com/articles/352314-the-15-best-players-in-sports-video-game-history.

K

1. Oli Welsh, "Command & Conquer 4's Joe Kucan," Eurogamer, 2009, www.eurogamer.net/articles/command-and-conquer-4s-joe-kucan-interview.

2. Guinness World Records, *Guinness World Records Gamer's Edition 2008* (Vancouver, Canada: Jim Pattison Group, 2008).

3. Caitlin McCabe, "Hit Kardashian Video Game Lifts Glu Mobile from E-List," Bloomberg, 2015, www.bloomberg.com/news/articles/2014-07-10/hit-kardashian-video-game-lifts-publisher-glu-mobile-from-e-list.

4. Maeve Duggan, "Gaming and Gamers," Pew Research Center: Internet, Science & Tech, 2015, www.pewinternet.org/2015/12/15/gaming-and-gamers.

5. Adrienne Shaw, *Gaming at the Edge: Sexuality and Gender at the Margins of Gamer Culture* (Minneapolis: University of Minnesota Press, 2014).

6. Claude Lévi-Strauss, *The Savage Mind* (Chicago: University of Chicago Press, 1962).

7. Gregory M. Zaverucha, "On the Complexity of Katamari Damacy," *Crossroads* 14, no. 2 (2007): 5.

8. Julian Kücklich, "Katamari Damacy," in *Space Time Play: Computer Games, Architecture and Urbanism: The Next Level*, ed. Friedrich von Borries, Steffen P. Walz, and Matthias Böttger (New York: Springer Science & Business Media, 2007), 96–97.

9. Martin Gaston, "Why Is Kirby Always Angry in the U.S.? Nintendo Explains," Gamespot, 2015, www.gamespot.com/articles/why-is-kirby-always-angry-in-the-us-nintendo-explains/1100-6419263.

10. Byung-Chul Han, *Shanzhai: Dekonstruktion auf Chinesisch* (Berlin: Merve Verlag, 2011), 88.

11. Koichi Iwabuchi, *Recentering Globalization: Popular Culture and Japanese Transnationalism* (Durham, NC: Duke University Press, 2002).

12. Ibid.

13. Ray Kurzweil, *The Singularity Is Near: When Humans Transcend Biology* (New York: Viking Press, 2005).

14. Michael J. Hyde, "Perfection, Postmodern Culture, and the Biotechnology Debate," *Spectra* (2008): 37.

15. Stephen Totilo, "The Argument for a Very Violent Scene in a Very Violent Video Game," Kotaku, 2012, http://kotaku.com/5928138/the-case-for-a-very-violent-scene-in-a-very-violent-video-game.

16. Shawnee Lee, "In the Spotlight: Kratos," PlayStation Universe, 2011, http://www.psu.com/feature/13437/In-the-Spotlight--Kratos.

17. Zak Islam, "Jaffe Reveals Inspiration Behind Kratos," PlayStationLifeStyle.net, 2010, http://www.playstationlifestyle.net/2010/07/22/jaffe-reveals-inspiration-behind-kratos.

L

1. Jane Caputi, "The Pornography of Everyday Life," in *Goddesses and Monsters: Women, Myth, Power, and Popular Culture*, ed. Jane Caputi (Madison: University of Wisconsin Press, 2004), 74–116.

2. Jeroen Jansz and Raynel G. Martis, "The Lara Phenomenon: Powerful Female Characters in Video Games," *Sex Roles* 56, no. 3 (2007): 141–48.

3. Helen W. Kennedy, "Lara Croft: Feminist Icon or Cyberbimbo? On the Limits of Textual Analysis," *Game Studies* 2, no. 2 (2002), http://eprints.uwe.ac.uk/94.

4. Ibid.

5. Rino B. Johansen, Jon C. Laberg, and Monica Martinussen, "Measuring Military Identity: Scale Development and Psychometric Evaluations," *Social Behavior and Personality* 41, no. 5 (2013): 861–80.

6. Edna Lomsky-Feder, Nir Gazit, and Eyal Ben-Ari, "Reserve Soldiers as Transmigrants: Moving between the Civilian and Military Worlds," *Armed Forces & Society* 34, no. 1 (2008): 593–614.

7. Julia Rozanova et al., "'I'm Coming Home, Tell the World I'm Coming Home': The Long Homecoming and Mental Health Treatment of Iraq and Afghanistan War Veterans," *Psychiatric Quarterly* 87, no. 3 (2016), doi:10.1007/s11126-015-9398-7.

8. David Leonard, "'Live in Your World, Play in Ours': Race, Video Games, and Consuming the Other," *Studies in Media & Information Literacy Education* 3, no. 4 (2003): 1–9.

9. Frantz Fanon, *Black Skin, White Masks* (New York: Grove Press, 1952).

10. Josh Augustine, "Walking Dead Creative Leads Discuss Using Race to Make Better Games," PCGamesN, 2013, www.pcgamesn.com/walking-dead-creative-leads-discuss-using-race-make-better-games.

11. Joel Warner, "The Legend of Leeroy Jenkins," Westword, 2007, www.westword.com/news/the-legend-of-leeroy-jenkins-5091880.

12. Sophia Softky, "You're the One Making This about Race!," in *Trayvon Martin, Race, and American Justice*, ed. Kenneth J. Fasching-Varner, Rema E. Reynolds, Katrice A. Albert, and Lori L. Martin (New York: Springer, 2014), 203–7.

13. See note 1.

14. See note 1.

15. Tanner Higgin, "Blackless Fantasy: The Disappearance of Race in Massively Multiplayer Online Role-Playing Games," *Games and Culture* 4, no. 1 (2008).

16. Sierra On-Line, *Leisure Suit Larry in the Land of the Lounge Lizards Manual* (Coarsegold, CA: Sierra On-Line, 1987), www.sierrahelp.com/Documents/Manuals/Leisure_Suit_Larry_1_-_Manual.pdf.

17. Wikipedia, s.v. "Larry Laffer," 2016, https://en.wikipedia.org/wiki/Larry_Laffer.

18. "Inside the Industry: News, Notes and Quotes from the Computer Entertainment Industry," *Computer Gaming World*, September, 1989.

19. Kristin Noone and Jennifer Kavetsky, "Sir Thomas Malory and the Death Knights of New Avalon: Imagining Medieval Identities in World of Warcraft," in *Digital Gaming Reimagines the Middle Ages*, ed. Daniel T. Kline (New York: Routledge, 2013), 93–106.

20. Anne Stickney, "Know Your Lore: The Lich King," Engadget, 2010, www.engadget.com/2010/02/14/know-your-lore-the-lich-king.

21. Jessica Langer, "The Familiar and the Foreign: Playing (Post)Colonialism in World of Warcraft," in *Digital Culture, Play, and Identity: A World of Warcraft Reader*, ed. Hilde G. Gorneliussen and Jill W. Rettberg (Cambridge, MA: MIT Press, 2008), 87–108.

22. Enix Software, advertisement, *Electronic Gaming Magazine* (1993), 14.

23. Andy Slaven, Michael Collins, Lucas Barnes, and Vincent Yang, *Video Game Bible: 1985–2002* (Victoria, Canada: Trafford, 2002), 148.

24. "Top 10 Tuesday: Prehistoric Gaming," IGN, 2007, www.ign.com/articles/2007/02/28/top-10-tuesday-prehistoric-gaming.

25. Ibid.

26. Eric Smith, personal communication, January 4, 2016.

27. "E3 2010—Ten Minutes with Shigeru Miyamoto," Internet Archive Wayback Machine, 2010, http://wayback.archive.org/web/20100618001208/http://gonintendo.com/viewstory.php?id=127146.

28. Hillary Chute, "Comics as Literature? Reading Graphic Narrative," *PMLA* 123, no. 2 (2008): 452–65.

29. Andy Boyan, Matthew Grizzard, and Nicholas David Bowman, "A Massively Moral Game? Mass Effect as a Case Study to Understand the Influence of Players' Moral Intuitions on Adherence to Hero or Antihero Play Styles," *Journal of Gaming & Virtual Worlds* 7, no. 1 (2015), 41–57.

30. Rusel DeMaria and Caroline Spector, *Ultima: The Avatar Adventures* (Rocklin, CA: Prima Publishing, 1992).

31. Caroline Spector and Melissa Tyler, "A Conversation with Richard Garriott," in *Prima's Official Guide to Ultima IX: Ascension*, ed. Chris McCubbin (Rocklin, CA: Prima Games, 1999), 246–99.

32. Richard Garriott de Cayeux, "What Is a Lord British 'Ultimate' Role Playing Game?," Facebook, 2011, www.facebook.com/notes/richard-garriott-de-cayeux/what-is-a-lord-british-ultimate-role-playing-game/259507887434380.

M

1. Ste. Curran, *Game Plan: Great Designs That Changed the Face of Computer Gaming* (Hove, UK: RotoVision, 2004).

2. Manuel Garin and Alan Salvadó, "Reimagining Silent Film and New Media: Super Mario, Buster Keaton and the Gameplaygag Project," in *The Archives: Post-Cinema and Video Game between Memory and the Image of the Present*, ed. Federico Giordano and Bernard Perron (Milan: Mimesis International, 2014).

3. Jonathan Cohen, "Defining Identification: A Theoretical Look at the Identification of Audiences with Media Characters," *Mass Communication and Society* 4, no. 3 (2001): 245–64.

4. Gerald Voorhees, "Play and Possibility in the Rhetoric of the War on Terror: The Structure of Agency in Halo 2," *Game Studies* 14, no. 1 (2014), http://gamestudies.org/1401/articles/gvoorhees.

5. Antonio José Planells de la Maza, "Max Payne: Cine Negro y Pesadillas en el Medio Interactivo," *Razón y Palabra* 15, no. 72 (2010).

6. Jesper Juul, *The Art of Failure: An Essay on the Pain of Playing Video Games* (Cambridge, MA: MIT Press, 2013).

7. Løvlie Anders Sundnes, "End of Story? Quest, Narrative and Enactment in Computer Games," *DiGRA '05—Proceedings of the 2005 DiGRA International Conference: Changing Views: Worlds in Play* 3 (2005).

8. Ibid.

9. Richard Dawkins, *The Selfish Gene* (New York: Oxford University Press, 2006).

10. Todd Ciolek, "The Origins of Mega Man: Anime and Manga," 1UP, 2012, www.1up.com/features/origins-mega-man-anime-manga.

11. David Sheff, *Game Over: Press Start to Continue* (Wilton, CT: CyberActive Media Group, 1999).

12. Abe Stein, "Playing the Game on Television," in *Sports Videogames*, ed. Mia Consalvo, Konstantin Mitgutsch, and Abe Stein (New York: Routledge, 2013), 115.

13. Owen Good, "Ten Years Later, Michael Vick Would Have a Harder Time Breaking Madden," Kotaku, 2013, http://kotaku.com/ten-years-later-michael-vick-would-have-a-harder-time-1022342172.

14. Jon Robinson, "The 'Madden' Dream Team," ESPN, 2012, http://espn.go.com/espn/thelife/videogames/blog/_/name/thegamer/id/7679556/the-madden-dream-team.

15. "PokéChat," *Nintendo Power*, May 1999.

16. Daniel Ashton and James Newman, "Relations of Control: Walkthroughs and the Structuring of Player Agency," *Fibreculture Journal* 16, no. 110 (2010), http://sixteen.fibreculturejournal.org/relations-of-control-walkthroughs-and-the-structuring-of-player-agency.

17. Wilma Alice Bainbridge and William Sims Bainbridge, "Creative Uses of Software Errors: Glitches and Cheats," *Social Science Computer Review* 25, no. 1 (2007): 61–77.

18. Judith Butler, "Performativity, Precarity, and Sexual Politics," *AIBR: Revista de Anthropologia Iberoamericana* 4, no. 3 (2009): i–xiii.

19. Ibid.

20. Raewyn Connell, *Masculinites* (Berkeley: University of California Press, 1995).

21. Anthony Burch, "Inside the box: Inclusivity," Gearbox Software, 2013, www.gearboxsoftware.com/community/articles/1077/inside-the-box-inclusivity.

N

1. Bob Mackey, "5 Things Modern RPGs Can Learn from EarthBound," GamesRadar, 2013, www.gamesradar.com/5-things-modern-rpgs-can-learn-earthbound.

2. Scott Thompson, "EarthBound Review," IGN, 2013, www.ign.com/articles/2013/07/24/earthbound-review.

3. John Mix Meyer, "Octopi! Spinal Tap! How Cult RPG EarthBound Came to America," Wired, 2013, www.wired.com/2013/07/marcus-lindblom-earthbound/all.

O

1. Julian Kücklich, "Precarious Playbour: Modders and the Digital Games Industry," *Fibreculture Journal* 5 (2005), http://five.fibreculturejournal.org/fcj-025-precarious-playbour-modders-and-the-digital-games-industry.

2. Scott Rettberg, "Corporate Ideology in World of Warcraft," in *Digital Culture, Play, and Identity: A World of Warcraft Reader*, ed. Hilde G. Gorneliussen and Jill W. Rettberg (Cambridge, MA: MIT Press, 2008).

3. Jessica Langer, "The Familiar and the Foreign: Playing (Post)Colonialism in World of Warcraft," in *Digital Culture, Play, and Identity: A World of Warcraft Reader*, ed. Hilde G. Gorneliussen and Jill W. Rettberg (Cambridge, MA: MIT Press, 2008): 87–108.

P

1. "PAC-MAN Museum," Pac-Man, 2009, http://pacmanmuseum.com.

2. Ibid.

3. Steven L. Kent, *The Ultimate History of Video Games: From Pong to Pokémon—The Story Behind the Craze That Touched Our Lives and Changed the World* (New York: Three Rivers Press, 2001).

4. See note 1.

5. Christine Champagne, "How 'Pac-Man' Changed Games and Culture," FastCoCreate, 2013, www.fastcocreate.com/1683023/how-pac-man-changed-games-and-culture.

6. See note 3.

7. See note 3.

8. See note 1.

9. Sharon Kinsella, "Cuties in Japan," in *Women, Media, and Consumption in Japan*, ed. Lise Skov and Brian Moeran (Surrey, UK: Curzon Press, 1996), 220–54.

10. Ian Condry, "Yellow B-Boys, Black Culture, and Hip-Hop in Japan: Toward a Transnational Cultural Politics of Race," *Positions* 15, no. 3 (2007): 637–71.

11. Ian Condry, "The Social Production of Difference: Imitation and Authenticity in Japanese Rap Music," in *Transactions, Transgressions, and Transformations*, ed. Heide Fehrenbach and Uta G. Poiger (New York: Berghahn Books, 2000), 166–84.

12. *Gyakuten Saiban Ace Attorney Official Fanbook Volume 3* (Osaka, Japan: Capcom, 2007).

13. Mia Consalvo, "Persistence Meets Performance: Phoenix Wright, Ace Attorney," in *Well Played: Video Games, Values, and Meaning*, ed. Drew Davidson (Pittsburgh: ETC Press, 2009), 156–69.

14. See note 1.

15. See note 1.

16. See note 1.

17. "Would You Keep Your Pikachu in Pokémon Yellow Just So You Could Talk to It?," BHwolfgang, 2010, www.pokecommunity.com/archive/index.php/t-233832.html.

18. Jesse Fox and Bridget Potocki, "Lifetime Video Game Consumption, Interpersonal Aggression, Hostile Sexism, and Rape Myth Acceptance," *Journal of Interpersonal Violence* 31, no. 10 (2016): 1912–31.

19. Valerie J. Callanan and Jared S. Rosenberger, "Media and Public Perceptions of the Police: Examining the Impact of Race and Personal Experience," *Policing and Society* 21, no. 2 (2011): 167–89.

20. Jon Robinson, "The Gamer Blog: You Don't Know Jam," ESPN, 2008, http://sports.espn.go.com/espnmag/story?id=3668922.

21. Matt Leone, "The Rise, Fall, and Return of NBA Jam," 1UP, 2010, www.1up.com/features/rise-fall-return-nba-jam.

22. "William J. Clinton," in *The Presidents of the United States of America*, ed. Frank Freidel and Hugh Sidey (Washington, DC: White House Historical Association, 2006), www.whitehouse.gov/1600/presidents/williamjclinton.

23. "Top 100 Video Game Moments: Metal Gear Solid—Psychomantis Battle," IGN, 2016, www.ign.com/top/video-game-moments/2; Albert Wesker, "Top 10 Tuesday: Most Memorable Villains," IGN, 2006, www.ign.com/articles/2006/03/08/top-10-tuesday -most-memorable-villains.

24. Steven Conway, "A Circular Wall? Reformulating the Fourth Wall for Video Games," *Journal of Gaming and Virtual Worlds* 2, no. 2 (2010): 145–55.

25. "Making of Silent Hill 2," YouTube video, posted by "fungo," May 1, 2013, www .youtube.com/watch?v=KSku98HqIHU.

26. Michel Foucault, *Discipline and Punish: The Birth of the Prison*, trans. Alan Sheridan (New York: Vintage Books, 1995).

27. Martin Buber, "Guilt and Guilt Feelings," *Psychiatry* 20, no. 2 (1957): 114–29.

28. See note 2.

R

1. Judith Butler, *Gender Trouble: Feminism and the Subversion of Identity* (New York: Routledge, 1990).

2. Fabienne Darling-Wolf, "SMAP, Sex, and Masculinity: Constructing the Perfect Female Fantasy in Japanese Popular Music," *Popular Music and Society* 27, no. 3 (2004): 357–70.

3. Hideo Kojima, "Metal Gear Solid 2 Grand Game Plan," trans. Marc Laidlaw, Junker HQ, 1999.

4. Marilyn Ivy, *Discourses of the Vanishing: Modernity, Phantasm, Japan* (Chicago: University of Chicago Press, 1995).

5. Takafusa Nakamura, *The Postwar Japanese Economy: Its Development and Structure*, trans. Jacqueline Kaminski, 2nd ed. (Tokyo: University of Tokyo Press, 1995).

6. Adam Lowenstein, *Shocking Representation: Historical Trauma, National Cinema, and the Modern Horror Film* (New York: Columbia University Press, 2005).

S

1. Roland Barthes, "The Death of the Author," in *Image-Music-Text*, trans. Stephen Heath (New York: Hill and Wang, 1978), 142–48.

2. Anna Hickey-Moody, "Little Publics and Youth Arts as Cultural Pedagogy," in *Cultural Pedagogies and Human Conduct*, ed. Megan Watkins, Greg Noble, and Catherine Driscoll (Abingdon, UK: Routledge, 2014), 78–91.

3. Tracy L. Dietz, "An Examination of Violence and Gender Role Portrayals in Video Games: Implications for Gender Socialization and Aggressive Behavior," *Sex Roles* 38, no. 5 (1998): 425–42, doi:10.1023/A:1018709905920.

4. Ibid.

5. Laura Mulvey, "Visual Pleasure and Narrative Cinema," *Screen* 16, no. 3 (1975): 6–18.

6. Sherrie Inness, *Tough Girls: Women Warriors and Wonder Woman in Popular Culture* (Philadelphia: University of Pennsylvania Press, 1999).

7. Roger Stahl, *Militainment, Inc.: War, Media and Popular Culture* (New York: Routledge, 2009), 110.

8. Reid McCarter, "Action, Death, and Catharsis: Call of Duty 4: Modern Warfare," in *Shooter*, ed. Reid McCarter and Patrick Lindsey (2015). Kindle e-book.

9. Jean Baudrillard, *The Gulf War Did Not Take Place* (Bloomington: Indiana University Press, 1995), 58.

10. Brigitte Scheele and Fletcher DuBois, "Catharsis as a Moral Form of Entertainment," in *Psychology of Entertainment*, ed. Jennings Bryant and Peter Vorderer (Mahwah, NJ: Lawrence Erlbaum Associates, 2006), 405–22.

11. Wolfgang Walk, "Ethics as a Game Mechanism: Who's Playing?," Making Games, 2016, www.makinggames.biz/features/ethics-as-a-game-mechanism-whos-playing,9902 .html.

12. Albert Bandura, "Selective Moral Disengagement in the Exercise of Moral Agency," *Journal of Moral Education* 31 (2002): 101–19, doi:10.1080/0305724022014322.

13. See note 1.

14. James Price and Zy Nicholson, *Resident Evil 5: The Complete Official Guide* (London: Piggyback Interactive, 2009).

15. Ibid.

16. Ibid.

17. John Tracey, "Newsweek's N'Gai Croal on the 'Resident Evil 5' Trailer: 'This Imagery as a History,'" MTV, 2008, http://multiplayerblog.mtv.com/2008/04/10/newsweeks -ngai-croal-on-the-resident-evil-5-trailer-this-imagery-has-a-history.

18. André Brock, "'When Keeping It Real Goes Wrong': Resident Evil 5, Racial Representation, and Gamers," *Games and Culture* 6, no. 5 (2011), doi:10.1177/1555412011402676.

19. Jacques Ellul, *The Technological Society*, trans. John Wilkinson (New York: Vintage, 1964).

20. "Ken Levine Filmed at a BAFTA Q&A," YouTube video, posted by Official 2K UK, March 16, 2013, https://www.youtube.com/watch?v=yokmLWHOm8k.

21. J. M. Porup, "How to Search the Internet of Things for Photos of Sleeping Babies," Ars Technica, 2016, http://arstechnica.co.uk/security/2016/01/how-to-search-the-internet -of-things-for-photos-of-sleeping-babies.

22. Joey Batz, "The Confusing History of Punch-Out!," Writedge, 2014, http://writedge .com/confusing-history-punch.

23. Charlie Hall, "Who Is Genyo Takeda, Miyamoto's Current Partner in Leading Nintendo?," Polygon, 2015, www.polygon.com/2015/7/14/8962829/who-is-genyo-takeda -miyamotos-current-partner-in-leading-nintendo.

24. Yoshimi Shunya, "What Does 'American' Mean in Postwar Japan?," *Nanzan Review of American Studies* 30 (2008): 83–87, https://www.ic.nanzan-u.ac.jp/AMERICA/kanko/ documents/14YOSHIMI.pdf.

25. Louis Althusser, "Ideology and Ideological State Apparatuses (Notes towards an Investigation)," in *Media and Cultural Studies: KeyWorks*, ed. Meenakshi Gigi Durham and Douglas M. Kellner (Malden, MA: Blackwell, 2006), 79.

26. "The True Dark Souls Starts Here," Reddit, 2016, www.reddit.com/r/onebros.

27. Hideo Kojima, "70% of My Body Is Composed of Movies," *Tokyo: Sony Magazines*, 2008, 142.

28. James Newman, *Playing with Videogames* (New York: Routledge, 2008), 40.

29. Tanner Higgin, "Turn the Game Console Off Right Now! War, Subjectivity, and Control," in *Joystick Soldiers: The Politics of Play in Military Video Games*, ed. Nina B. Huntemann and Matthew Thomas Payne (New York: Routledge, 2010), 252.

30. Marc Pétronille and William Audureau, *The History of Sonic the Hedgehog* (Richmond Hill, Canada: Udon Entertainment, 2012), 21.

31. John Grusd and Dick Sebast, dirs., *Sonic the Hedgehog: The Complete Series* (Shout Factory, 2007), DVD.

32. Mike Hanlon, "Videogame Industry Icons Honored with Stars on Walk of Game," New Atlas, 2006, http://newatlas.com/go/5379.

33. Marcus Persson, "So That's What I'm Going to Do," Tumblr, 2013, http://notch.tum blr.com/post/58707926941/so-thats-what-im-going-to-do.

34. Ibid.

35. Celia Pearce, *Communities of Play: Emergent Cultures in Multiplayer Games and Virtual Worlds* (Cambridge, MA: MIT Press, 2009).

36. Catherine Beavis, Sandy Muspratt, and Roberta Thompson, "'Computer Games Can Get Your Brain Working': Student Experience and Perceptions of Digital Games in the Classroom," *Learning, Media and Technology* 40, no. 1 (2015): 21–42.

37. Rob Crossley, "Mortal Kombat: Violent Game That Changed Video Games Industry," BBC News, 2014, www.bbc.com/news/technology-27620071.

38. Jeffrey O'Holleran, "Blood Code: The History and Future of Video Game Censorship," *Journal on Telecommunications & High Technology Law* 8, no. 2 (2010): 571–612.

39. John. L. Sherry, "The Effects of Violent Video Games on Aggression," *Human Communication Research* 27, no. 3 (2001): 409–31.

T

1. Michael Weinreb, "Bo Knows Best," ESPN, 2007, http://sports.espn.go.com/espn/eticket/story?page=bojackson.

2. "Bo Knows—Crazy Tecmo Super Bowl Run," YouTube video, posted by numb3rtw3nty, June 12, 2006, www.youtube.com/watch?v=8PBvOxicz-0.

3. Keith Good, "Bo Knows Overrated," Tecmobowlers, 2015, http://tecmobowlers.com/2015/09/bo-knows-overrated.

4. Dmitri Williams, Nicole Martins, Mia Consalvo, and James D. Ivory, "The Virtual Census: Representations of Gender, Race and Age in Video Games," *New Media & Society* 11, no. 5 (2009): 815–34.

5. Angela McRobbie, "Top Girls? Young Women and the Post-Feminist Sexual Contract," *Cultural Studies* 21, nos. 4–5 (2007): 718–37.

6. Dorothée Hefner, Christoph Klimmt, and Peter Vorderer, "Identification with the Player Character as Determinant of Video Game Enjoyment," conference paper, *Entertainment Computing—ICEC 2007 Sixth International Conference*, Shanghai, China, September 15–17, 2007, 39–48.

7. J. Matthew Zoss, "The Art of Game Polish: Developers Speak," Gamasutra, 2009, www.gamasutra.com/view/feature/132611/the_art_of_game_polish_developers_.php?print=1.

V

1. Cameron Koch, "Maybe Vault Boy from 'Fallout' Isn't Giving Us the Thumbs Up After All," Tech Times, 2015, www.techtimes.com/articles/102639/20151103/maybe-fallouts-vault-boy-isnt-giving-us-the-thumbs-up-after-all.htm.

2. Chris Priestman, "Turning Fallout 4's World into 1950s-Style Animations," Kill Screen, 2016, https://killscreen.com/articles/turning-fallout-4s-world-into-1950s-style-animations.

3. Christopher B. Patterson, "Role-Playing the Multiculturalist Umpire: Loyalty and War in BioWare's Mass Effect Series," *Games and Culture* 10, no. 3 (2015): 207–28, doi:10.1177/1555412014551050.

4. "Mass Effect 3 Statistics: Many People Murdered Tali—PAX East 2013," IGN, 2013, www.youtube.com/watch?v=bYhtNRuHYC0.

5. Vinicius Marino Carvalho, "Leaving Earth, Preserving History: Uses of the Future in the Mass Effect Series," *Games and Culture* 10, no. 2 (2015): 127–47, doi:10.1177/1555412014545085.

W

1. Richard A. Bartle, "A Voice from the Dungeon," MUD, 1999, http://mud.co.uk/richard/avftd.htmhttp://mud.co.uk/richard/avftd.htm.

2. Nimue and Valentine, "How to Play," Multi-User Dungeons—British Legends, 2015, www.british-legends.com/CMS/index.php/help/how-to-play#4.4%20Fighting%20and%20Killinghttp://www.british-legends.com/CMS/index.php/help/how-to-play.

3. Richard Bartle, "Introducing the Wizards," MUD, 1999, http://mud.co.uk/richard/mafeb85.htmhttp://mud.co.uk/richard/mafeb85.htm.

4. Ibid.

Z

1. Joseph Campbell, *The Hero with a Thousand Faces* (Princeton, NJ: Princeton University Press, 1949).

2. Julie Kristeva, "Revolution in Poetic Language," in *The Kristeva Reader*, ed. Toril Moi (New York: Columbia University Press, 1986), 89–136.

3. Judith Butler, *Bodies That Matter: On the Discursive Limits of "Sex"* (New York: Routledge, 1993).

APPENDIX

1. The companies listed are the parent companies of the developers, subsidiaries, and affiliated studios responsible for creating the characters listed in this book. Due to the nature of the video game industry, studios often switch hands, so the parent companies identified are those that either currently retain intellectual property rights to the listed characters or that have had a significant influence over the studio responsible for that character's development. Characters listed in the Other category belong to developers who had only one character listed in this book.

2. Characters have been placed in the genres most likely to be associated with their primary home franchise—and not necessarily in their original game. For example, though the Lich King first appeared in the real-time strategy game *Warcraft III* (2002), at the time of this writing he is most commonly associated with the massively multiplayer online role-playing game (MMORPG) *World of Warcraft: Wrath of the Lich King* (2008); hence, he has been placed in the MMORPG genre.

3. Multiple studios were involved in the development of this character.

4. Multiple studios were involved in the development of this character.

5. Multiple studios were involved in the development of this character.

6. Multiple studios were involved in the development of this character.

7. Race is a complex social phenomenon that is irreducible to ethnicity because it is as contingent upon how an individual is recognized as on how that self-same individual understands her- or himself. As to how race pertains to video game characters, two factors influenced our racial categorization of characters: first, the character's racial identity as made explicit in the game (e.g., Terra Branford's biracial identity is central to the narrative of *Final Fantasy VI*); second, how the character's racial identity is implicitly framed through conventional normative markers, such as skin complexion. Some characters proved particularly difficult to categorize, such as Capcom's Phoenix Wright, due to the character's *mukokuseki* ("someone lacking any nationality") appearance. Though some will instantly recognize the *mukokuseki* style as a distinctly Japanese aesthetic often associated with video games, manga, and anime, Koichi Iwabuchi compellingly argues that this is an aesthetic that attempts to de-emphasize Japanese ethnic features in favor of an imagined—often white—universal subject. Hence, we have placed Phoenix Wright (and similar characters) in the White category. Likewise, for characters like the Orc Peon, though their "species" would suggest the absence of race, Helen Young reminds us that "references to real-world indigenous cultures have become common in constructions of orc cultures since they were first used in *D&D*." Hence, we have placed the Orc Peon (and similar characters) in the Indeterminate category, for race is a part of these characters'

construction, even if this construction is that of a racial amalgamation of various cultures. Though some may question the value of such categories if ambiguities like these exist, this is true of how race operates in society more generally—and recognizing this does little to diminish the consequences of these racial classifications. See Koichi Iwabuchi, *Recentering Globalization: Popular Culture and Japanese Transnationalism* (Durham, NC: Duke University Press, 2002), 28; and Helen Young, *Race and Popular Fantasy Literature* (New York: Routledge, 2015).

Bibliography

Alloway, Nola, and Pam Gilbert. "Video Game Culture: Playing with Masculinity, Violence, and Pleasure." In *Wired-Up: Young People and the Electronic Media*, edited by Sue Howard, 93–113. London: UCL Press, 1998.

Althusser, Louis. "Ideology and Ideological State Apparatuses (Notes Towards an Investigation)." In *Media and Cultural Studies: KeyWorks*, edited by Meenakshi Gigi Durham and Douglas M. Kellner, 79–88. Malden, MA: Blackwell, 2006.

Anders Sundnes, Løvlie. "End of Story? Quest, Narrative and Enactment in Computer Games." *DiGRA '05—Proceedings of the 2005 DiGRA International Conference: Changing Views: Worlds in Play* 3 (2005).

Asher-Perrin, Emily. "Feral Ewoks and Other Disturbing Things That Star Wars Slides Right By Us." Tor.com. 2013. www.tor.com/2013/07/18/feral-ewoks-and-other-disturbing-things-that-star-wars-slides-right-by-us.

Ashton, David, and James Newman. "Relations of Control: Walkthroughs and the Structuring of Player Agency." *Fibreculture Journal* 16, no. 110 (2010). http://sixteen.fibreculture journal.org/relations-of-control-walkthroughs-and-the-structuring-of-player-agency.

Auerbach, David. "The Most Sexist Video Game of All Time?" Slate. 2014. www.slate.com/articles/technology/bitwise/2014/07/catherine_video_game_the_most_sexist_platformer_of_all_time.html.

Augustine, Josh. "Walking Dead Creative Leads Discuss Using Race to Make Better Games." PCGamesN. 2013. www.pcgamesn.com/walking-dead-creative-leads-discuss-using-race-make-better-games.

Bainbridge, Wilma Alice, and William Sims Bainbridge. "Creative Uses of Software Errors: Glitches and Cheats." *Social Science Computer Review* 25, no. 1 (2007): 61–77.

Bandura, Albert. "Selective Moral Disengagement in the Exercise of Moral Agency." *Journal of Moral Education* 31 (2002): 101–19. doi:10.1080/0305724022014322.

Banks, Jaime. "Object, Me, Symbiote, Other: A Social Typology of Player-Avatar Relationships." *First Monday* 20, no. 2 (2015). http://firstmonday.org/ojs/index.php/fm/article/view/5433/4208.

Barthes, Roland. "The Death of the Author." In *Image-Music-Text*, translated by Stephen Heath, 142–48. New York: Hill and Wang, 1978.

Bartle, Richard A. "A Voice from the Dungeon." MUD. 1999. http://mud.co.uk/richard/avftd.htmhttp://mud.co.uk/richard/avftd.htm.

———. *Designing Virtual Worlds*. Berkeley, CA: New Riders, 2004.

———. "Introducing the Wizards." MUD. 1999. http://mud.co.uk/richard/mafeb85.htm http://mud.co.uk/richard/mafeb85.htm.

Batz, Joey. "The Confusing History of Punch-Out!" Writedge. 2014. http://writedge.com/confusing-history-punch.

Baudrillard, Jean. *The Gulf War Did Not Take Place*. Bloomington: Indiana University Press, 1995.

Beavis, Catherine, Sandy Muspratt, and Roberta Thompson. "'Computer Games Can Get Your Brain Working': Student Experience and Perceptions of Digital Games in the Classroom." *Learning, Media and Technology* 40, no. 1 (2015): 21–42.

Bell, Kristina, Nicholas Taylor, and Christopher Kampe. "Of Headshots and Hugs: Challenging Hypermasculinity through Walking Dead Play." *Ada: A Journal of Gender, New Media, and Technology* 7 (2015). http://adanewmedia.org/2015/04/issue7-bellkampetaylor.

BHwolfgang. "Would You Keep Your Pikachu in Pokémon Yellow Just So You Could Talk to It?" 2010. www.pokecommunity.com/archive/index.php/t-233832.html.

Biocca, Frank, Chad Harms, and Judee K. Burgoon. "Toward a More Robust Theory and Measure of Social Presence: Review and Suggested Criteria." *Presence* 12, no. 5 (2003): 456–80. doi:10.1162/105474603322761270.

"Bo Knows—Crazy Tecmo Super Bowl Run." YouTube video, posted by numb3rtw3nty. June 12, 2006. www.youtube.com/watch?v=8PBvOxicz-0.

Boellstorff, Tom. *Coming of Age in Second Life*. Princeton, NJ: Princeton University Press, 2008.

Bogost, Ian. *Persuasive Games: The Expressive Power of Videogames*. Cambridge, MA: MIT Press, 2010.

Bogost, Ian, and Nick Montfort. *Racing the Beam: The Atari Video Computer System*. Cambridge, MA: MIT Press, 2009.

Boje, David M. "Breaking Out of Narrative's Prison: Improper Story in Storytelling Organization." *Storytelling, Self, Society* 2, no. 2 (2006): 28–49. doi:10.1080/15505340.2006.10387472.

Bond, Charles F., and Linda J. Titus. "Social Facilitation: A Meta-Analysis of 241 Studies." *Psychological Bulletin* 94, no. 2 (1983): 265–92.

Bowman, Nicholas D., Rene Weber, Ron Tamborni, and John Sherry. "Facilitating Game Play: How Others Affect Performance at and Enjoyment of Video Games." *Media Psychology* 16 (2013): 39–64.

Boyan, Andy, Matthew Grizzard, and Nicholas David Bowman. "A Massively Moral Game? Mass Effect as a Case Study to Understand the Influence of Players' Moral Intuitions on Adherence to Hero or Antihero Play Styles." *Journal of Gaming and Virtual Worlds* 7, no. 1 (2015): 41–57.

British Psychological Society. "Listening to Your Favorite Music Boosts Performance." ScienceDaily. 2012. www.sciencedaily.com/releases/2012/04/120417221709.htm.

Brock, André. "'When Keeping It Real Goes Wrong': Resident Evil 5, Racial Representation, and Gamers." *Games and Culture* 6, no. 5 (2011). doi:10.1177/1555412011402676.

Buber, Martin. "Guilt and Guilt Feelings." *Psychiatry* 20, no. 2 (1957): 114–29.

Budgeon, Shelley. "Individualized Femininity and Feminist Politics of Choice." *European Journal of Women's Studies* 22 (March 2015): 303–18. doi:10.1177/1350506815576602.

Burch, Anthony. "Inside the Box: Inclusivity." Gearbox Software. 2013. www.gearboxsoftware.com/community/articles/1077/inside-the-box-inclusivity.

Burke, Kenneth. *The Philosophy of Literary Form*, 3rd ed. Berkeley: University of California Press, 1974.

Butler, Judith. *Bodies That Matter: On the Discursive Limits of "Sex."* New York: Routledge, 1993.

———. *Gender Trouble: Feminism and the Subversion of Identity*. New York: Routledge, 1990.

———. "Performativity, Precarity, and Sexual Politics." *AIBR: Revista de Anthropologia Iberoamericana* 4, no. 3 (2009): i–xiii.

Callanan, Valerie J., and Jared S. Rosenberger. "Media and Public Perceptions of the Police: Examining the Impact of Race and Personal Experience." *Policing and Society* 21, no. 2 (2011): 167–89.

Campbell, Heidi A., and Gregory P. Grieve, eds. *Playing with Religion in Digital Games*. Bloomington: Indiana University Press, 2014.

Campbell, Joseph. *The Hero with a Thousand Faces*. Princeton, NJ: Princeton University Press, 1949.

Capcom. *Gyakuten Saiban Ace Attorney Official Fanbook Vol. 3.* Osaka, Japan: Capcom, 2007.
———. *Okami Official Complete Works.* Translated by Hayashi Kirie. Richmond Hill, Canada: Udon Entertainment, 2008.

Caputi, Jane. "The Pornography of Everyday Life." In *Goddesses and Monsters. Women, Myth, Power, and Popular Culture,* edited by Jane Caputi, 74–116. Madison: University of Wisconsin Press, 2004.

Champagne, Christine. "How 'Pac-Man' Changed Games and Culture." FastCoCreate. 2013. www.fastcocreate.com/1683023/how-pac-man-changed-games-and-culture.

Chipman, Bob. *Super Mario Bros. 3: Brick by Brick.* Tucson, AZ: Fangamer, 2013.

Chu, Arthur. "A Defense of Binding of Isaac from a Former Fundamentalist Christian." Polygon. 2015. www.polygon.com/2015/1/26/7907061/binding-isaac-fundamentalism.

Chute, Hillary. "Comics as Literature? Reading Graphic Narrative." *PMLA* 123, no. 2 (2008): 452–65.

Ciolek, Todd. "The Origins of Mega Man: Anime and Manga." 1UP. 2012. www.1up.com/features/origins-mega-man-anime-manga.

Clarkson, Michael. "BioShock." LudoNarratology. 2009. http://ludo.mwclarkson.com/2009/04/critical-thinking-compilation-bioshock.

Cohen, Jonathan. "Defining Identification: A Theoretical Look at the Identification of Audiences With Media Characters." *Mass Communication and Society* 4, no. 3 (2001): 245–64.

Computer Gaming World. "Inside the Industry: News, Notes and Quotes from the Computer Entertainment Industry." September, 1989.

Condry, Ian. "The Social Production of Difference: Imitation and Authenticity in Japanese Rap Music." In *Transactions, Transgressions, and Transformations,* edited by Heide Fehrenbach and Uta G. Poiger, 166–84. New York: Berghahn Books, 2000.
———. "Yellow B-Boys, Black Culture, and Hip-Hop in Japan: Toward a Transnational Cultural Politics of Race." *Positions* 15, no. 3 (2007): 637–71.

Connell, Raewyn. *Masculinites.* Berkeley: University of California Press, 1995.

Conrad, Joseph. *Heart of Darkness.* Edited by Owen Knowles and Robert Hampson. London: Penguin, 2007.

Consalvo, Mia. "Persistence Meets Performance: Phoenix Wright, Ace Attorney." In *Well Played: Video Games, Values, and Meaning,* edited by Drew Davidson, 156–69. Pittsburgh, PA: ETC Press, 2009.

Conway, Steven. "A Circular Wall? Reformulating the Fourth Wall for Video Games." *Journal of Gaming and Virtual Worlds* 2, no. 2 (2010): 145–55.

Crossley, Rob. "Mortal Kombat: Violent Game That Changed Video Games Industry." BBC News. 2014. www.bbc.com/news/technology-27620071.

Crowder, Austen. "Videogame Censorship, LGBT, and Birdo (Part III)." Bilerico Project. 2009. www.bilerico.com/2009/12/videogame_censorship_lgbt_and_birdo_part_iii.php.

Curran, Ste. *Game Plan: Great Designs That Changed the Face of Computer Gaming.* Hove, UK: RotoVision, 2004.

Darling-Wolf, Fabienne. "SMAP, Sex, and Masculinity: Constructing the Perfect Female Fantasy in Japanese Popular Music." *Popular Music and Society* 27, no. 3 (2004): 357–70.

Dawkins, Richard. *The Selfish Gene.* New York: Oxford University Press, 2006.

DeMaria, Rusel, and Caroline Spector. *Ultima: The Avatar Adventures.* Rocklin, CA: Prima Publishing, 1992.

DeWinter, Jennifer. *Shigeru Miyamoto: Super Mario Bros., Donkey Kong, The Legend of Zelda.* London: Bloomsbury Academic, 2015.

Dietz, Tracy L. "An Examination of Violence and Gender Role Portrayals in Video Games: Implications for Gender Socialization and Aggressive Behavior." *Sex Roles* 38, no. 5 (1998): 425–42. doi:10.1023/A:1018709905920.

Druckmann, Neil. "The Last of Us: Writing Honestly." Keynote remarks at the International Game Developers Association Meeting, Toronto, Canada, October 2013. www .youtube.com/watch?v=Le6qIz7MjSk.

Duggan, Maeve. "Gaming and Gamers." Pew Research Center: Internet, Science and Tech. 2015. www.pewinternet.org/2015/12/15/gaming-and-gamers.

Durkheim, Émile. "The Dualism of Human Nature." In *On Morality and Society*, edited by Robert N. Bellah, 149–63. Chicago: University of Chicago Press, 1973.

Electronic Gaming Monthly. "Afterthoughts/Final Fantasy VII: Interview with Yoshinori Kitase and Tetsuya Nomura." 2005. www.ff7citadel.com/press/int_sakaguchi.shtml.

Ellison, Harlan. *I Have No Mouth, and I Must Scream.* New York: Galaxy, 1967. http://herm iene.net/short-stories/i_have_no_mouth.htm.

Ellul, Jacques. *The Technological Society.* Translated by John Wilkinson. New York: Vintage, 1964.

Enix Software. Advertisement. *Electronic Gaming Magazine*, 1993.

Entertainment Software Association. "Essential Facts about the Computer and Video Game Industry." 2015. www.theesa.com/wp-content/uploads/2015/04/ESA-Essential -Facts-2015.pdf.

Epley, Nicholas, Adam Waytz, and John T. Cacioppo. "On Seeing Human: A Three-Factor Theory of Anthropomorphism." *Psychological Review* 114, no. 4 (2007): 880.

EVE Community. "The Capsule and the Clone." 2012. https://community.eveonline.com/ backstory/scientific-articles/ppcc-part-1-the-capsule-and-the-clone.

Fanon, Frantz. *Black Skin, White Masks.* New York: Grove Press, 1952.

Ferguson, Christopher J. "Positive Female Role-Models Eliminate Negative Effects of Sexually Violent Media." *Journal of Communication* 62, no. 5 (2012): 888–99.

Fernández-Vara, Clara. "The Secret of Monkey Island: Playing Between Cultures." In *Well Played 1.0: Video Games, Value and Meaning*, edited by Drew Davidson, 331–52. Pittsburgh, PA: ETC Press, 2009.

Fiala, Andrew. "Pacifism." In the Stanford Encyclopedia of Philosophy. http://plato.stan ford.edu/archives/win2014/entries/pacifism.

Foss, Sonja K., Karen A. Foss, and Robert Trapp. *Contemporary Perspectives on Rhetoric.* Prospect Heights, IL: Waveland, 1991.

Foucault, Michel. *Discipline and Punish: The Birth of the Prison.* 2nd edition. Translated by Alan Sheridan. New York: Vintage Books, 1995.

Fox, Jesse, and Bridget Potocki. "Lifetime Video Game Consumption, Interpersonal Aggression, Hostile Sexism, and Rape Myth Acceptance." *Journal of Interpersonal Violence* 31, no. 10 (2016): 1912–31.

Francis, Tom. "Murder Incorporated: Ten Months of Deception for One Kill in EVE Online." PCGamer. 2015. www.pcgamer.com/murder-incorporated-ten-months-of-decep tion-for-one-kill-in-eve-online.

Freidel, Frank, and Hugh Sidey, eds. "William J. Clinton." In *The Presidents of the United States of America*. Washington, DC: White House Historical Association, 2006. www .whitehouse.gov/1600/presidents/williamjclinton.

"From Dreams—The Making of The Last of Us: Left Behind." YouTube video, posted by PlayStation. February 28, 2014. www.youtube.com/watch?v=v7WEeNH_C2I.

"G4 Icons Episode #34: Naughty Dog." YouTube video, posted by G4Icons. April 4, 2013. www.youtube.com/watch?v=pV7Pqj7hKhM.

Gamespy. "25 Most Overrated Games of All Time." 2003. http://web.archive.org/web/ 20090716182813/http://archive.gamespy.com/articles/september03/25overrated/index 26.shtml

Garin, Manuel, and Alan Salvadó. "Reimagining Silent Film and New Media: Super Mario, Buster Keaton and the Gameplaygag Project." In *The Archives: Post-Cinema and Video*

Game between Memory and the Image of the Present, edited by Federico Giordano and Bernard Perron. Milan, Italy: Mimesis International, 2014.

Garriott de Cayeux, Richard. "What Is a Lord British 'Ultimate' Role Playing Game?" Facebook. 2011. www.facebook.com/notes/richard-garriott-de-cayeux/what-is-a-lord -british-ultimate-role-playing-game/259507887434380.

Gaston, Martin. "Why Is Kirby Always Angry in the U.S.? Nintendo Explains." Gamespot. 2015. www.gamespot.com/articles/why-is-kirby-always-angry-in-the-us-nintendo -explains/1100-6419263.

Good, Keith. "Bo Knows Overrated." Tecmobowlers. 2015. http://tecmobowlers.com/ 2015/09/bo-knows-overrated.

Good, Owen S. "Apple Rejects The Binding of Isaac: Rebirth Because of 'Violence Towards Children.'" Polygon. 2016. www.polygon.com/2016/2/7/10930230/the-binding-of- isaac-ios-mobile-rejected-apple.

———. "Ten Years Later, Michael Vick Would Have a Harder Time Breaking Madden." Kotaku. 2013. http://kotaku.com/ten-years-later-michael-vick-would-have-a-harder-time -1022342172.

Goren, Carolyn C., Merrill Sarty, and Paul Y. K. Wu, "Visual Following and Pattern Discrimination of Face-Like Stimuli by Newborn Infants," *Pediatrics* 56 (1975): 544–49.

Grusd, John, and Dick Sebast, dirs. *Sonic the Hedgehog: The Complete Series*. Shout Factory, 2007. DVD.

Guinness World Records. *Guinness World Records Gamer's Edition 2008*. Vancouver, Canada: Jim Pattison Group, 2008.

Hall, Charlie. "Who Is Genyo Takeda, Miyamoto's Current Partner in Leading Nintendo?" Polygon. 2015. www.polygon.com/2015/7/14/8962829/who-is-genyo-takeda-miyamo tos-current-partner-in-leading-nintendo.

Hamilton, Rebecca. *Fighting for Darfur: Public Action and the Struggle to Stop Genocide*. New York: Palgrave Macmillan, 2011.

Han, Byung-Chul. *Shanzhai: Dekonstruktion auf Chinesisch*. Berlin: Merve Verlag, 2011.

Hanlon, Mike. "Videogame Industry Icons Honored with Stars on Walk of Game." New Atlas. 2006. http://newatlas.com/go/5379.

Harradence, Michael. "PS3's Top 5 Worst Protagonists." PlayStation Universe. 2012. www .psu.com/feature/15403/PS3s-top-5-worst-protagonists.

Harris-Fain, Darren. "Created in the Image of God: The Narrator and the Computer in Harlan Ellison's 'I Have No Mouth, and I Must Scream.'" *Extrapolation* 32 (1991): 143–55.

Hefner, Dorothée, Christoph Klimmt, and Peter Vorderer. "Identification with the Player Character as Determinant of Video Game Enjoyment." *Entertainment Computing—ICEC 2007* (2007): 39–48.

Herman, Judith L. *Trauma and Recovery: The Aftermath of Violence—From Domestic Abuse to Political Terror*. New York: Basic Books, 2015.

Hickey-Moody, Anna. "Little Publics and Youth Arts as Cultural Pedagogy." In *Cultural Pedagogies and Human Conduct*, edited by Megan Watkins, Greg Noble, and Catherine Driscoll, 78–91. Abingdon, UK: Routledge, 2014.

Higgin, Tanner. "Blackless Fantasy: The Disappearance of Race in Massively Multiplayer Online Role-Playing Games." *Games and Culture* 4, no. 1 (2008).

———. "Turn the Game Console Off Right Now! War, Subjectivity, and Control." In *Joystick Soldiers: The Politics of Play in Military Video Games*, edited by Nina B. Huntemann and Matthew Thomas Payne, 252. New York: Routledge, 2010.

Hyde, Michael J. "Perfection, Postmodern Culture, and the Biotechnology Debate." *Spectra* (2008): 37.

IGN. "Mass Effect 3 Statistics: Many People Murdered Tali—PAX East 2013." 2013. www .youtube.com/watch?v=bYhtNRuHYC0.

——. "Top 100 Video Game Moments." 2016. www.ign.com/top/video-game-moments/1.

——. "Top 100 Video Game Moments: Metal Gear Solid—Psychomantis Battle." 2016. www.ign.com/top/video-game-moments/2.

——. "Top 10 Tuesday: Prehistoric Gaming," 2007. www.ign.com/articles/2007/02/28/top-10-tuesday-prehistoric-gaming.

Inness, Sherrie. *Tough Girls: Women Warriors and Wonder Woman in Popular Culture.* Philadelphia: University of Pennsylvania Press, 1999.

Internet Archive Wayback Machine. "E3 2010—Ten Minutes with Shigeru Miyamoto." 2010. http://wayback.archive.org/web/20100618001208/http://gonintendo.com/viewstory.php?id=127146.

Ivy, Marilyn. *Discourses of the Vanishing: Modernity, Phantasm, Japan.* Chicago: University of Chicago Press, 1995.

Islam, Zac. "Jaffe Reveals Inspiration Behind Kratos." PlayStationLifeStyle.net. 2010. www.playstationlifestyle.net/2010/07/22/jaffe-reveals-inspiration-behind-kratos.

Iwabuchi, Koichi. *Recentering Globalization. Popular Culture and Japanese Transnationalism.* Durham, NC: Duke University Press, 2002.

Jackmix. "What Is the Funniest Thing(s) Your Creature Does." BWFiles. 2009. www.bwfiles.com/forum/index.php?topic=703.60.

Jacob, "Nuclear Gandhi." Know Your Meme. 2015. http://knowyourmeme.com/memes/nuclear-gandhi.

Jameson, Fredric. *Postmodernism, or, The Cultural Logic of Late Capitalism.* Durham, NC: Duke University Press, 1991.

Jansz, Jeroen, and Raynel G. Martis. "The Lara Phenomenon: Powerful Female Characters in Video Games." *Sex Roles* 56, no. 3 (2007): 141–48.

Johansen, Rino B., Jon C. Laberg, and Monica Martinussen. "Measuring Military Identity: Scale Development and Psychometric Evaluations." *Social Behavior and Personality* 41, no. 5 (2013): 861–80.

Joho, Jess. "The Dadification of Video Games, Round Two." Kill Screen. 2014. https://killscreen.com/articles/dadification-videogames-round-two.

Jorgensen, Kristine. "Game Characters as Narrative Devices. A Comparative Analysis of Dragon Age: Origins and Mass Effect 2." *Eludamos* 4, no. 2 (2010): 315–31.

Juul, Jesper. *The Art of Failure: An Essay on the Pain of Playing Video Games.* Cambridge, MA: MIT Press, 2013.

Kain, Erik. "Massive EVE Online Battle Could Cost $300,000 in Real Money." *Forbes*, January 29, 2014. www.forbes.com/sites/erikkain/2014/01/29/massive-eve-online-battle-could-cost-500000-in-real-money.

Kaku, Michio. *The Future of the Mind: The Scientific Quest to Understand, Enhance, and Empower the Mind.* New York: Doubleday, 2014.

"Ken Levine Filmed at a BAFTA Q&A." YouTube video, posted by Official 2K UK. March 16, 2013. www.youtube.com/watch?v=yokmLWHOm8k.

Kennedy, Helen W. "Lara Croft: Feminist Icon or Cyberbimbo? On the Limits of Textual Analysis." *Game Studies* 2, no. 2 (2002). http://eprints.uwe.ac.uk/94.

Kent, Steven L. *The Ultimate History of Video Games: From Pong to Pokémon—The Story Behind the Craze That Touched Our Lives and Changed the World.* New York: Three Rivers Press, 2001.

Kinsella, Sharon. "Cuties in Japan." In *Women, Media, and Consumption in Japan*, edited by Lise Skov and Brian Moeran, 220–54. Surrey, UK: Curzon Press, 1996.

Klastrup, Lisbeth. "Why Death Matters: Understanding Gameworld Experience." *Journal of Virtual Reality and Broadcasting* 4, no. 3 (2007).

Klimmt, Christoph, Dorothée Hefner, Peter Vorderer, Christian Roth, and Christopher Blake. "Identification with Video Game Characters as Automatic Shift of Self-Perceptions." *Media Psychology* 13, no. 4 (2010): 323–38.

Koch, Cameron. "Maybe Vault Boy from 'Fallout' Isn't Giving Us the Thumbs Up After All." Tech Times. 2015. www.techtimes.com/articles/102639/20151103/maybe-fallouts -vault-boy-isnt-giving-us-the-thumbs-up-after-all.htm.

Kohler, Chris. "Captain Rainbow: Birdo's Gender Crisis." Wired. 2015. www.wired .com/2008/08/captain-rainb-1.

Kojima, Hideo. "70% of My Body Is Made of Movies." *Tokyo: Sony Magazines*, 2008.

———. "Metal Gear Solid 2 Grand Game Plan." Translated by Marc Laidlaw. Junker HQ. 1999.

Kristeva, Julie. "Revolution in Poetic Language." In *The Kristeva Reader*, edited by Toril Moi, 89–136. New York: Columbia University Press, 1986.

Kücklich, Julian. "Katamari Damacy." In *Space Time Play: Computer Games, Architecture and Urbanism: The Next Level*, edited by Friedrich von Borries, Steffen P. Walz, and Matthias Böttger, 96–97. New York: Springer Science & Business Media, 2007.

———. "Precarious Playbour: Modders and the Digital Games Industry." *Fibreculture Journal* 5 (2005). http://five.fibreculturejournal.org/fcj-025-precarious-playbour-modders -and-the-digital-games-industry.

Kurzweil, Ray. *The Singularity Is Near: When Humans Transcend Biology*. New York: Viking Press, 2005.

Langer, Jessica. "The Familiar and the Foreign: Playing (Post)Colonialism in World of Warcraft." In *Digital Culture, Play, and Identity: A World of Warcraft Reader*, edited by Hilde G. Gorneliussen and Jill W. Rettberg, 87–108. Cambridge, MA: MIT Press, 2008.

Lee, Shawnee. "In the Spotlight: Kratos." PlayStation Universe. 2011. www.psu.com/fea ture/13437/In-the-Spotlight—Kratos.

Leonard, David. "'Live in Your World, Play in Ours': Race, Video Games, and Consuming the Other." *Studies in Media & Information Literacy Education* 3, no. 4 (2003): 1–9.

Leonardi, Domenico. "Il dietro le quinte di Crash Bandicoot." PlayStation Generation. 2015. www.playstationgeneration.it/p/making-of-crash-bandicoot.html.

Leone, Matt. "Street Fighter II: An Oral History." Polygon. 2014. www.polygon.com/a/ street-fighter-2-oral-history/chapter-2.

———. "The Rise, Fall, and Return of NBA Jam." 1UP. 2010. www.1up.com/features/rise -fall-return-nba-jam.

Lévi-Strauss, Claude. *The Savage Mind*. Chicago: University of Chicago Press, 1962.

Lin, Jeffery. "More Science behind Player Behavior in Online Games." Paper presented at the HarvardX Conference, Cambridge, Massachusetts, March 13, 2015. www.gdcvault .com/play/1022160/More-Science-Behind-Shaping-Player.

Lomsky-Feder, Edna, Nir Gazit, and Eyal Ben-Ari. "Reserve Soldiers as Transmigrants: Moving Between the Civilian and Military Worlds." *Armed Forces & Society* 34, no. 1 (2008): 593–614.

Lowenstein, Adam. *Shocking Representation: Historical Trauma, National Cinema, and the Modern Horror Film*. New York: Columbia University Press, 2005.

Lowood, Henry. "Videogames in Computer Space: The Complex History of Pong." *IEEE Annals of the History of Computing* 31, no. 3 (2009): 5–19. doi:10.1109/MAHC.2009.53.

Luckhurst, Roger. *Alien*. London: British Film Institute, 2014.

MacCallum-Steward, Esther. "Real Boys Carry Girl Epics: Normalising Gender Bending in Online Games." *Eludamos* 2, no. 1 (2008): 27–40.

Mackey, Bob. "5 Things Modern RPGs Can Learn From EarthBound." GamesRadar. 2013. www.gamesradar.com/5-things-modern-rpgs-can-learn-earthbound.

Maiolini, Carlo, Stefano De Paoli, and Maurizio Teli. "Digital Games and the Communication of Health Problems. A Review of Games Against the Concept of Procedural Rhetoric." *Game: The Italian Journal of Game Studies* 1 (2012). www.gamejournal.it/digital

-games-and-the-communication-of-health-problems-a-review-of-games-against-the-concept-of-procedural-rhetoric.

"Making of Silent Hill 2." YouTube video, posted by fungo. May 1, 2013. www.youtube.com/watch?v=KSku98HqIHU.

Mamdani, Mahmood. *Saviors and Survivors: Darfur, Politics and the War on Terror*. New York: Doubleday, 2009.

Marino Carvalho, Vinicius. "Leaving Earth, Preserving History: Uses of the Future in the Mass Effect Series." *Games and Culture* 10, no. 2 (2015): 127–47. doi:10.1177/1555412014545085.

Markus, Hazel, and Paula Nurius. "Possible Selves." *American Psychologist* 41, no. 9 (1986): 954–69.

McCabe, Caitlin. "Hit Kardashian Video Game Lifts Glu Mobile from E-List." Bloomberg. 2015. www.bloomberg.com/news/articles/2014-07-10/hit-kardashian-video-game-lifts-publisher-glu-mobile-from-e-list.

McCarter, Reid. "Action, Death, and Catharsis: Call of Duty 4: Modern Warfare." In *Shooter*, edited by Reid McCarter and Patrick Lindsey. 2015. Kindle e-book.

McMillen, Edmund. "Postmortem: McMillen and Himsl's *The Binding of Isaac*." Gamasutra. 2012. www.gamasutra.com/view/feature/182380/postmortem_mcmillen_and_himsls_.php?page=1.

McRobbie, Angela. "Post-Feminism and Popular Culture." *Feminist Media Studies* 4, no. 3 (2004): 256–64.

———. "Top Girls? Young Women and the Post-Feminist Sexual Contract." *Cultural Studies* 21, nos. 4–5 (2007): 718–37.

McVittie, Andy. *The Art of Alien: Isolation*. London: Titan Books, 2014.

Meyer, John Mix. "Octopi! Spinal Tap! How Cult RPG EarthBound Came to America." Wired. 2013. www.wired.com/2013/07/marcus-lindblom-earthbound/all.

Mezur, Katherine. *Beautiful Boys/Outlaw Bodies: Devising Kabuki Female-Likeness*. New York: Palgrave Macmillan, 2005.

Mielke, James. "Design by Subtraction: The Bare Essence of Game Design, with Fumito Ueda." 1UP. 2005. www.1up.com/features/design-by-subtraction?pager.offset=0.

Minkley, Johnny. "The Big Daddy Speaks." Eurogamer. 2007. www.eurogamer.net/articles/big-daddy-speaks-interview?page=2.

Montfort, Nick. *Twisty Little Passages: An Approach to Interactive Fiction*. Cambridge, MA: MIT Press, 2005.

Mori, Masahiro. "The Uncanny Valley." *Energy* 7 (2012): 33–35. http://spectrum.ieee.org/automaton/robotics/humanoids/the-uncanny-valley.

Moriarty, Brian. "Classic Game Postmortem: Lucasfilm Games' Loom." Paper presented at the Game Developers Conference, San Francisco, March 3, 2015. http://gdcvault.com/play/1021862/Classic-Game-Postmortem.

———. Personal communication. January 3, 2016.

Mulvey, Laura. "Visual Pleasure and Narrative Cinema." *Screen* 16, no. 3 (1975): 6–18.

Nakamura, Takafusa. *The Postwar Japanese Economy: Its Development and Structure*. 2nd edition. Translated by Jacqueline Kaminski. Tokyo: University of Tokyo Press, 1995.

Napier, Susan J. "Confronting Master Narratives: History as Vision in Miyazaki Hayao's Cinema of De-Assurance." *Positions* 9, no. 2 (2001).

Nathan, Ian. *Alien Vault: The Definitive Story of the Making of the Film*. London: Voyageur, 2011.

Newman, James. *Playing with Videogames*. New York: Routledge, 2008.

———. "The Myth of the Ergodic Videogame: Some Thoughts on Player-character Relationships in Videogames." *Game Studies* 2, no. 1 (2002). http://gamestudies.org/0102/newman.

Nimue and Valentine. "How to Play." Multi-User Dungeons—British Legends. 2015. www.british-legends.com/CMS/index.php/help/how-to-play#4.4%20Fighting%20 and%20Killingwww.british-legends.com/CMS/index.php/help/how-to-play.

Nintendo Power. "PokéChat." May 1999.

Noone, Kristin, and Jennifer Kavetsky. "Sir Thomas Malory and the Death Knights of New Avalon: Imagining Medieval Identities in World of Warcraft." In *Digital Gaming Reimagines the Middle Ages*, edited by Daniel T. Kline, 93–106. New York: Routledge, 2013.

O'Holleran, Jeffrey. "Blood Code: The History and Future of Video Game Censorship." *Journal on Telecommunications and High Technology Law* 8, no. 2 (2010): 571–612.

Pac-Man Museum. http://pacmanmuseum.com.

Patterson, Christopher B. "Role-Playing the Multiculturalist Umpire: Loyalty and War in BioWare's Mass Effect Series." *Games and Culture* 10, no. 3 (2015): 207–28. doi:10 .1177/1555412014551050.

Pearce, Celia. *Communities of Play: Emergent Cultures in Multiplayer Games and Virtual Worlds.* Cambridge, MA: MIT Press, 2009.

Persson, Marcus. "So That's What I'm Going to Do." Tumblr. 2013. http://notch.tumbl r.com/post/58707926941/so-thats-what-im-going-to-do.

Pétronille, Marc, and William Audureau. *The History of Sonic the Hedgehog.* Richmond Hill, Canada: Udon Entertainment, 2012.

Pettey, Gary, Cheryl Campanella Bracken, Bridget Rubenking, Michael Buncher, and Erika Gress. "Telepresence, Soundscapes, and Technological Expectation: Putting the Observer into the Equation." *Virtual Reality* 14, no. 1 (2010): 15–25. doi:10.1007/s10055-009-0148-8.

Picken, Stuart D. B. *Historical Dictionary of Shinto.* Lanham, MD: Scarecrow Press, 2011.

Planells, Antonio José. "Max Payne: Cine Negro y Pesadillas en el Medio Interactivo." *Razón y Palabra* 15, no. 72 (2010).

Plunkett, Luke. "Why Gandhi Is Such an Asshole in Civilization." Kotaku. 2016. http:// kotaku.com/why-gandhi-is-such-an-asshole-in-civilization-1653818245.

Porup, J. M. "How to Search the Internet of Things for Photos of Sleeping Babies." Ars Technica. 2016. http://arstechnica.co.uk/security/2016/01/how-to-search-the-internet -of-things-for-photos-of-sleeping-babies.

Price, James, and Zy Nicholson. *Resident Evil 5: The Complete Official Guide.* London: Piggyback Interactive, 2009.

Priestman, Chris. "Turning Fallout 4's World into 1950s-Style Animations." Kill Screen. 2016. https://killscreen.com/articles/turning-fallout-4s-world-into-1950s-style-animations.

Ragsdale, Nick. "Dysentery." In *Encyclopedia of Pestilence, Pandemics, and Plagues*, edited by Joseph P. Byrne, 173–76. Westport, CT: Greenwood Press, 2008.

Reagan, Ronald. "Address to the Veterans of Foreign Wars Convention." Speech at the Veterans Foreign Wars Convention, Chicago, Illinois, August 18, 1980. American Presidency Project. www.presidency.ucsb.edu/ws/?pid=85202.

Reddit. "The True Dark Souls Starts Here." 2016. www.reddit.com/r/onebros.

Rehak, Bob. "Playing At Being." In *The Video Game Theory Reader*, edited by Mark J. P. Wolf and Bernard Perron, 103–27. New York: Routledge, 2003.

Rettberg, Scott. "Corporate Ideology in World of Warcraft." In *Digital Culture, Play, and Identity: A World of Warcraft Reader*, edited by Hilde G. Corneliussen and Jill W. Rettberg, 87–108. Cambridge, MA: MIT Press, 2008.

Robinson, Jon. "Fast 5: Best Video Game Fictional Athletes." ESPN. 2013. http://espn .go.com/blog/playbook/tech/post/_/id/4743/fast-5-best-video-game-fictional-athletes.

———. "The Gamer Blog: You Don't Know Jam." ESPN. 2008. http://sports.espn.go.com/ espnmag/story?id=3668922.

———. "The 'Madden' Dream Team." ESPN. 2012. http://espn.go.com/espn/thelife/video games/blog/_/name/thegamer/id/7679556/the-madden-dream-team.

Rockstar Games. "Grand Theft Auto III: Your Questions Answered—Part One (Claude, Darkel & Other Characters)." 2011. www.rockstargames.com/newswire/article/19861/grand-theftauto-iii-your-questions-answered-part-one-claude-dar.html.

Rozanova, Julia, Paraskevi Noulas, Kathleen Smart, Alicia Roy, Steven Southwick, Larry Davidson, and Ilan Harpaz-Rotem. "'I'm Coming Home, Tell the World I'm Coming Home.' The Long Homecoming and Mental Health Treatment of Iraq and Afghanistan War Veterans." *Psychiatric Quarterly* 87, no. 3 (2016). doi:10.1007/s11126-015-9398-7.

Ryan, Jeff. *Super Mario: How Nintendo Conquered America.* New York: Penguin, 2011.

Salter, Anastasia. *What Is Your Quest?: From Adventure Games to Interactive Books.* Iowa City: University of Iowa Press, 2014.

Scheele, Brigitte, and Fletcher DuBois. "Catharsis as a Moral Form of Entertainment." In *Psychology of Entertainment,* edited by Jennings Bryant and Peter Vorderer, 405–22. Mahwah, NJ: Lawrence Erlbaum Associates, 2006.

Schrier, Karen. "The Weird Humanity of I Have No Mouth, and I Must Scream." *Well Played* 3, no. 2 (2014): 145–66. http://press.etc.cmu.edu/files/WellPlayed-v3n2-14-web.pdf.

Scott, Jason, dir. *Get Lamp.* Bovine Ignition Systems, 2010. DVD.

Semrad, Steve. "The Greatest 200 Videogames of Their Time." 1UP. 2006. www.1up.com/features/egm-200-greatest-videogames?pager.offset=0.

Serres, Michel. *The Parasite.* Minneapolis: University of Minnesota Press, 2007.

Shaw, Adrienne. *Gaming at the Edge: Sexuality and Gender at the Margins of Gamer Culture.* Minneapolis: University of Minnesota Press, 2014.

Sheff, David. *Game Over: Press Start to Continue.* Wilton, CT: CyberActive Media Group, 1999.

Sherry, John L. "Flow and Media Enjoyment." *Communication Theory* 14, no. 4 (2004): 328–47.

———. "The Effects of Violent Video Games on Aggression." *Human Communication Research* 27, no. 3 (2001): 409–31.

Shunya, Yoshimi. "What Does 'American' Mean in Postwar Japan?" *Nanzan Review of American Studies* 30 (2008): 83–87. www.ic.nanzan-u.ac.jp/AMERICA/kanko/documents/14YOSHIMI.pdf.

Sierra On-Line. *Leisure Suit Larry in the Land of the Lounge Lizards Manual.* Coarsegold, CA: Sierra On-Line, 1987. www.sierrahelp.com/Documents/Manuals/Leisure_Suit_Larry_1_-_Manual.pdf.

Slaven, Andy, Michael Collins, Lucas Barnes, and Vincent Yang. *Video Game Bible: 1985–2002.* Victoria, Canada: Trafford, 2002.

Smith, Eric. Personal communication. January 4, 2016.

Softky, Sophia. "You're the One Making This about Race!" In *Trayvon Martin, Race, and American Justice,* edited by Kenneth J. Fasching-Varner, Rema E. Reynolds, Katrice A. Albert, and Lori L. Martin, 203–7. New York: Springer, 2014.

Spector, Caroline, and Melissa Tyler. "A Conversation with Richard Garriott." In *Prima's Official Guide to Ultima IX: Ascension,* 246–99. Rocklin, CA: Prima Publishing, 1999.

Stahl, Roger. *Militainment, Inc.: War, Media and Popular Culture.* New York: Routledge, 2009.

Star, Jon. "The 15 Best Players in Sports Video Game History." Bleacher Report. 2010. http://bleacherreport.com/articles/352314-the-15-best-players-in-sports-video-game-history.

Stein, Abe. "Playing the Game on Television." In *Sports Videogames,* edited by Mia Consalvo, Konstantin Mitgutsch, and Abe Stein, 115. New York: Routledge, 2013.

Stickney, Anne. "Know Your Lore: The Lich King." Engadget. 2010. www.engadget.com/2010/02/14/know-your-lore-the-lich-king.

Sugihara, Yoko, and Emiko Katsurada. "Gender Role Development in Japanese Culture: Diminishing Gender Role Differences in a Contemporary Society," *Sex Roles* 47, no. 9 (2002): 443–52.

Švelch, Jaroslav. "The Pleasurable Lightness of Being: Interface, Mediation and Meta-Narrative in Lucasfilm's Loom." *Eludamos* 3, no. 1 (2009): 95–102.

Tanenbaum, Joshua. "Being in the Story: Readerly Pleasure, Acting Theory, and Performing a Role." In *Interactive Storytelling*, edited by Mei Si, David Thue, Elisabeth André, James C. Lester, Joshua Tanenbaum, and Veronica Zammitto, 55–66. Heidelberg, Germany: Springer Berlin Heidelberg, 2011.

Thompson, Scott. "Earthbound Review." IGN. 2013. www.ign.com/articles/2013/07/24/earthbound-review.

Totilo, Stephen. "The Argument for a Very Violent Scene in a Very Violent Video Game." Kotaku. 2012. http://kotaku.com/5928138/the-case-for-a-very-violent-scene-in-a-very-violent-video-game.

———. "The Daddening of Video Games." Kotaku. 2010. http://kotaku.com/5467695/the-daddening-of-video-games.

Tracey, John. "Newsweek's N'Gai Croal on the 'Resident Evil 5' Trailer: 'This Imagery as a History.'" MTV. 2008. http://multiplayerblog.mtv.com/2008/04/10/newsweeks-ngai-croal-on-the-resident-evil-5-trailer-this-imagery-has-a-history.

Turkle, Sherry. *Alone Together: Why We Expect More from Technology and Less from Each Other.* New York: Basic Books, 2011.

Vaaranen, Heli. "The Emotional Experience of Class: Interpreting Working-Class Kids' Street Racing in Helsinki." *Annals of the American Academy of Political and Social Science* 91, no. 595 (2004).

Van der Laan, J. M. *Seeking Meaning for Goethe's Faust.* London: Continuum, 2007.

Viar, Justin, dir. "Why Mario Is Secretly a Dick with a Mustache." YouTube video, posted by Cracked. April 17, 2012. www.youtube.com/watch?v=HBGhWYGVp8Q.

Voorhees, Gerald. "Play and Possibility in the Rhetoric of the War on Terror: The Structure of Agency in Halo 2." *Game Studies* 14, no. 1 (2014). http://gamestudies.org/1401/articles/gvoorhees.

VorpalBunny. "Queer Characters: Birdo." GayGamer. 2011. http://gaygamer.net/2011/04/queer_characters_birdo.html.

Wald, Priscilla. *Contagious: Cultures, Carriers, and the Outbreak Narrative.* Durham, NC: Duke University Press, 2007.

Walk, Wolfgang. "Ethics as a Game Mechanism: Who's Playing?" Making Games. 2016. www.makinggames.biz/features/ethics-as-a-game-mechanism-whos-playing,9902.html.

Ward, Trent. "Unreal Tournament." IGN. 1999. www.ign.com/articles/1999/12/07/unreal-tournament-6.

Warner, Joel. "The Legend of Leeroy Jenkins." Westword. 2007. www.westword.com/news/the-legend-of-leeroy-jenkins-5091880.

Webster, Andrew. "Street Legal: How 'Gran Turismo' Helped Toyota Design Its New Concept Car." TheVerge. 2014. www.theverge.com/2014/1/13/5290600/toyota-ft-1-concept-car-gran-turismo-6.

Weinreb, Michael. "Bo knows best." ESPN. 2007. http://sports.espn.go.com/espn/eticket/story?page=bojackson.

Welsh, Oli. "Command & Conquer 4's Joe Kucan." Eurogamer. 2009. www.eurogamer.net/articles/command-and-conquer-4s-joe-kucan-interview.

Wesker, Albert. "Top 10 Tuesday: Most Memorable Villains." IGN. 2006. www.ign.com/articles/2006/03/08/top-10-tuesday-most-memorable-villains.

Wikipedia. "Larry Laffer." 2016. https://en.wikipedia.org/wiki/Larry_Laffer.

Williams, Christopher G. "Chun Li's Thighs." PopMatters. 2010. www.popmatters.com/post/129312-chun-lis-thighs.

Williams, Dmitri, Nicole Martins, Mia Consalvo, and James D. Ivory. "The Virtual Census: Representations of Gender, Race and Age in Video Games." *New Media & Society* 11, no. 5 (2009): 815–34.

Yamauchi, Kazunori. "Regarding Engine Sounds of Gran Turismo: (Part 2)." PitStop. 2014. http://pitstop.gran-turismo.com/en/article/37.

Young, Helen. *Race and Popular Fantasy Literature*. New York: Routledge, 2015.

Zaverucha, Gregory M. "On the Complexity of Katamari Damacy." *Crossroads* 14, no. 2 (2007): 5.

Zoss, J. Matthew. "The Art of Game Polish: Developers Speak." Gamasutra. 2009. www .gamasutra.com/view/feature/132611/the_art_of_game_polish_developers_.php? print=1.

Index

About the Editors

Jaime Banks (PhD, Colorado State University) is an assistant professor in the Department of Communication Studies at West Virginia University and research associate at West Virginia University's Interaction Lab (#ixlab). Her research is situated at the intersection of communication technology and human identity, with a focus on social interaction, communication, and behavior in digital games. She was the founding chair of the Game Studies Division of the National Communication Association.

Robert Mejia (PhD, University of Illinois at Urbana–Champaign) is an assistant professor in the Department of Communication at North Dakota State University. His research addresses the political, economic, and cultural significance of new media technologies, institutions, publics, and practices. He is a founding member of the Game Studies Division of the National Communication Association.

Aubrie Adams (MA, California State University, Sacramento) is a doctoral candidate in the Department of Communication at the University of California, Santa Barbara. Her research focuses on the intersection of new media and interpersonal communication with an emphasis on examining the influence of technology on society. She will soon join the faculty of the Communication Studies Department at California Polytechnic State University in San Luis Obispo as an assistant professor.

CONTRIBUTOR AFFILIATIONS

Abe Stein, Massachusetts Institute of Technology
Adam Szetela, Berklee College of Music
Alex De Waal, World Peace Foundation
Alex Meredith, Nottingham Trent University
Alexandra Orlando, University of Waterloo
Amanda Lange, Microsoft
André Brock, University of Michigan
Andy Boyan, Albion College
Anita Sarkeesian, Feminist Frequency
Brad A. Haggadone, University of Texas at Austin
Brandon R. Rogers, University of North Carolina at Chapel Hill
Brian Keilen, University of Wisconsin-Milwaukee

Bryan Hikari Hartzheim, Waseda University
Bryan J. Carr, University of Wisconsin—Green Bay
Caleb T. Carr, Illinois State University
Cameron Basquiat, College of Southern Nevada
Candice Lanius, The University of Alabama in Huntsville
Carlin Wing, Scripps College
Carlos Flores, Arizona State University
Carolyn Petit, Feminist Frequency
Chris Bailey, Sheffield Hallam University
Christopher Ball, Michigan State University
Christopher J. E. Anderson, University of Wisconsin-Milwaukee
Christopher J. Ferguson, Stetson University
Christopher M. Bingham, University of Oklahoma
Conor Mckeown, University of Glasgow
Constance Steinkuehler, University of California, Irvine
Daniel Octavio Fandino, Independent Scholar
Daniel Sipocz, Berry College
Danielle Bohatschek, Independent Scholar
Dave Westerman, North Dakota State University
David Frisch, Florida International University
Gloria G. Gonzales, University of California, Riverside
Jacob Justice, The University of Kansas
James Malazita, Rensselaer Polytechnic Institute
Jan Švelch, Charles University
Jan-Philipp Stein, Chemnitz University of Technology
Jaroslav Švelch, Charles University
Jeff Nay, University of Utah
Jenny Saucerman, University of Wisconsin-Madison
Jess Morrissette, Marshall University
Jessica A. Robinson, Purdue University
John Cartner McKnight, Harrisburg University of Science and Technology
John Francis, Independent Scholar
Jonathan Mack, Northumbria University
José Zagal, University of Utah
Joseph Fordham, Michigan State University
Joshua H. Miller, University of Wisconsin-Milwaukee
Karen Schrier Shaenfield, Marist College
Katey A. Price, Albion College
Kathryn Hemmann, George Mason University
Kimberly Kandra, Colorado State University
Kyle Bohunicky, University of Florida
Kyle McClure, Saint Cloud State University
Leah E. LeFebvre, University of Wyoming
Leticia Cherchiglia, Michigan State University
Louise Grann, The University of West Georgia
Lynda Clark, Nottingham Trent University
M. Rohangis Mohseni, Ilmenau University of Technology

Mark R. Johnson, Goldsmiths, University of London
Matt Barton, Saint Cloud State University
Matthew Grizzard, University at Buffalo, The State University of New York
Michael D. Hanus, University of Nebraska-Lincoln
Myra Washington, University of New Mexico
Nicholas A. Hanford, Rensselaer Polytechnic Institute
Nicholas David Bowman, West Virginia University
Nicholas Ware, University of Central Florida
Nick Robinson, University of Leeds
Nicolas LaLone, Pennsylvania State University
Paul Zube, Ferris State University
Rachel Kowert, University of Münster
Rahima Schwenkbeck, The George Washington University
Roberto Semprebene, LUISS Creative Business Center
Robin L. Haislett, Weber State University
Roger Altizer, University of Utah
Rory McGloin, University of Connecticut
Rosa Mikeal Martey, Colorado State University
Rowan Derrick, Independent Scholar
Ruben Vandenplas, Vrije Universiteit Brussel
Scott Donaldson, Curtin University
Shira Chess, The University of Georgia
Stephanie C. Jennings, Rensselaer Polytechnic Institute
Stephen Webley, Staffordshire University
Sven Jöckel, University of Erfurt
Ted Dickinson, Independent Scholar
Thorsten Quandt, University of Münster
Toh Weimin, National University of Singapore
Tom Day, Michigan State University
Victor Navarro-Remesal, CESAG - Comillas Pontifical University
Yasuhito Abe, Doshisha University